The Negro and the American Labor Movement

JULIUS JACOBSON, an active socialist for many years, was managing editor of the Marxist journal *The New International*. He was the founding editor of the Socialist student journal *Anvil*, and at present is the editor of the Socialist quarterly *New Politics*. He earns his livelihood as a machinist.

The Negro and the American Labor Movement

EDITED BY JULIUS JACOBSON

ANCHOR BOOKS
DOUBLEDAY & COMPANY, INC.
GARDEN CITY, NEW YORK
1968

The Anchor Books edition is the first publication of
The Negro and the American Labor Movement

Anchor Books Edition: 1968

Library of Congress Catalog Card Number 68–12042

CONTENTS

Introduction: Union Conservatism: A Barrier to
Racial Equality, JULIUS JACOBSON   1

I: Attitudes of Negro Leaders Toward the
American Labor Movement from the
Civil War to World War I,
AUGUST MEIER and ELLIOTT RUDWICK   27

II: The Negro and the United Mine Workers
of America, HERBERT G. GUTMAN   49

III: The Negro in Southern Unions,
RAY MARSHALL   128

IV: The American Federation of Labor and
the Negro Worker, 1894–1949,
MARC KARSON and RONALD RADOSH   155

V: The CIO Era, 1935–55, SUMNER M. ROSEN   188

VI: The Economic Situation of Negro Labor,
SIDNEY M. PECK   209

VII: The Negro Worker in the Chicago Labor
Market, HAROLD M. BARON and
BENNETT HYMER   232

VIII: Two Views on Racial Attitudes and
Practices of the Contemporary Labor
Movement

(A) The Racial Practices of Organized Labor:
The Contemporary Record
HERBERT HILL   286

(B) Contemporary Labor's Attitude
Toward the Negro, GUS TYLER   358

Contents

IX: Trade Union Racial Practices and the Law,
   ROBERT L. CARTER and MARIA L. MARCUS   380

Notes   401

List of Contributors   427

The Negro and the American Labor Movement

Introduction

UNION CONSERVATISM:
A BARRIER TO RACIAL EQUALITY

JULIUS JACOBSON

Some may attempt to define our system in terms of private investment in corporate enterprise, where goods are produced for sale at profit.

But, as I see it, the distinguishing feature of this American system is its emphasis on people, on freedom, on free institutions, and on the opportunity for betterment. The Bill of Rights, the Constitution, and our educational system are all integral parts of our economic order and more essential to it than the stock exchange or any corporate board.

The above quotation from a speech provides a clue to understanding why the Negro masses today, on the whole, have an attitude that covers the narrow range from indifference to pronounced hostility toward the American trade union movement. For this speech, with its dubious proposition that the Bill of Rights is more fundamental to the American economic system than the stock exchange and corporate boards, and its Fourth of July tribute to our system's alleged emphasis on "the opportunity for betterment," is from the formal address of an American labor leader of some note, not a banker. And it is not from an address by Samuel Gompers at the turn of the century to a convocation of the National Civic Federation (an early alliance of bankers, AFL leaders, and public figures) but from one delivered by George Meany, President of the American Federation of Labor-Congress of Industrial Organizations, to the Fiftieth Anniversary World Convocation of the National Industrial Conference Board in New York City in September 1966.

While Meany's thoughts on the American system are crudely put, they are not his alone. They are shared, among others, by a whole school of American sociology which has been saying essentially the same thing for many years, though, of course, with far greater sophistication and artfulness. According to this school, America is not dominated by an economic class; there are, so the theory goes, no real hard and fast economic classes in America—this is the land of "social mobility" (or, as Meany would put it, there is "opportunity for betterment"). Since there are no economic classes, there can be no class struggle. Since there is no class struggle, there is no room for "ideologies" which reflect the special social and political needs and aspirations to power of an economic class. This rather euphoric view of America does not deny that there are antagonisms in American life, such as sectional differences or ethnic conflicts. But given the positive "distinguishing features" of the American system, these differences can be amicably settled through a give-and-take process of compromise and the judicious intervention of enlightened government. Militancy or "extremist" programs and actions are decried as being injurious to all.

One difficulty with the "end of ideology" theory of a classless America, especially as popularized, consciously or not, by George Meany, is that it does not correspond to the real world. Here, we can only note the credibility gap between the theory and the reality of life for the vast majority of twenty million Negro Americans. A detailed account is not needed; we need only remember that the lot of the Negroes, after all the promises and good resolutions, remains one of economic, social, political, and personal discrimination and humiliation. They have an unemployment rate double that of whites (one out of every three Negro youths is unemployed) and the disproportion continues to grow. In the ten-year period following the merger of the AFL and CIO there has been a decline in

Negro family income relative to whites (from 56 per cent to 53 per cent). Approximately one half of Negro families have an annual income of less than $4500 a year. Nearly one fourth of the Negroes in Los Angeles are poverty-stricken, and this appalling figure is lower than in many other urban areas. (This is based on federal government definitions of poverty, which are understated.) By any meaningful, relative definition of poverty, there are, in absolute numbers, more poor Negroes today than during the Great Depression. Also, while integration is the law of the land, segregation remains the reality, North and South, and the ghetto continues to grow while homes continue to deteriorate. But the measure of oppression can never be gauged by statistics. The frustration, anger, and sorrow produced by bigotry and racism do not lend themselves to statistical surveys. One thing is certain: the victims of racism can hardly be placated by such assurances as "our educational system" is an "integral part of our economic order"; nor, we suspect, would Meany's assurances that this is not a profit-motivated corporate economy carry the ring of truth if told to a Negro worker taking home less than fifty dollars a week in a New York City sweatshop, with poverty wages protected by an AFL-CIO contract.

Fortunately, oppression not only breeds misery, it also inspires resistance. We need only point to the multifaceted Negro revolution which began nearly fifteen years ago. Unfortunately, this resistance does not always receive the support it should from its "natural allies." The union movement is a prime case in point.

Actually, the union movement in this country has never fully met its responsibility to the Negro people in general, or to the Negro worker in particular. The early history of the American Federation of Labor reveals little more than contempt for the Negro worker, motivated in large measure by racial prejudice among AFL affiliates (the United Mine Workers is an important exception) and in the Gompers leadership.

However, even if the AFL were not guilty of racist policies, it probably could not have had a major impact on the conditions of life of Negro workers, especially in the earliest years of the century. The AFL was primarily a federation of craftsmen organized on the basis of their various skills. This narrow form of organization gave it the strength to survive anti-union pressure from employers in a period when industrial unionism was simply not the order of the day. The large corporations, particularly in steel, had enormous financial resources and allies in all levels and branches of government; they could buy armies of Pinkerton men, judges, politicians, and strikebreakers. They were simply too powerful for the nascent industrial unions to take permanent hold. This was made tragically clear in the Great Steel Strike of 1919 and in the events of the next decade, which witnessed not only the collapse of industrial unionism and near-demise of the once powerful United Mine Workers, but also the decline of long-established craft unions. By 1933 the unions could claim only a membership of two and a quarter million, and even that figure was arrived at by inflating numbers and crediting membership to unions that existed only on paper. The bulk of AFL affiliates which survived the massive open-shop drives of the twenties were the most racially oriented craft unions, such as those in the building trades. On the other hand, the AFL unions that were the first to succumb to the anti-labor offensive were the weak all-Negro "federal" locals directly affiliated with the AFL Executive Council. Thus by 1930 a generous estimate of total Negro membership in the AFL was around fifty thousand.

To say that the AFL could not have successfully transformed itself into an industrial union in this period, organizing the millions of white and Negro laborers in mass-production industries, is not to rationalize its racial policies, which had deleterious effects on Negro workers, white workers, and the trade union movement. There *were* thousands of Negro craftsmen ignored by the AFL; others were kept in segregated locals. And no less damaging was the fact that in strikebound plants employers found it easier to recruit strikebreakers among Negroes who never developed a trade union consciousness and could see no reason why they should forsake a much needed day's pay for the sake of a white man's union.

The American Dream crumbled in the crash of '29. Despair and hunger supplanted the self-confidence of the twenties. The large corporations remained powerful, but less so. The union-busting drives of the twenties, euphemistically called the American Plan, could no longer rally public opinion as before, nor could the corporations depend to the same extent on the assistance of congenial Presidents, Attorney Generals, and judges. The unskilled, culturally divided immigrant workers of earlier decades were now largely replaced by a more culturally integrated work force—it was "Americanized." New economic circumstances interacting with a heightened political and social consciousness forged in the Depression created, at last, the proper soil to nourish the cause of industrial unionism. Relentless pressure was exerted within the AFL to focus its efforts on the organization of steel, packing house, rubber, etc. The effort was naturally resisted by the most powerful AFL leaders, who clung desperately to their principles of craft organization.

Those trade unionists determined to plant the union flag in mass-production industries realized that they could not succeed without winning the support of Negro workers, who constituted a significant and cohesive percentage of the work force. This the industrially oriented unionists proceeded to do. But it was not only necessity that promoted their efforts to win Negro support and build democratic, interracial unions. Much of the personnel for the Committee for Industrial Organization was provided by John L. Lewis' United Mine Workers with its relatively equalitarian traditions on the race issue (although, in practice, many UMW locals were not free of segregationist practices). In addition to UMW organizers, the ranks of early CIO activists were swelled by a colorful phalanx of equalitarian, socially con-

5

scious militants—Socialists, Trotskyists, Lovestoneites, independent radicals, ex-Wobblies, ex-members of the Detroit-based Proletarian Party*—all of whom worked to overcome Negro resistance to unionization and, at least, to neutralize white workers' resistance to Negroes. (Some of these radicals had been members of the UMW, but opposed to Lewis. Lewis, who ruled the UMW with an iron fist, drove the opposition leaders out of the union and out of the industry. But they were among the most talented and courageous men in the union movement and he felt obliged to call upon them to take leading posts in the CIO drive. Frank Brophy, for example, accepted Lewis' invitation to act as Secretary for the top Committee of Five.) By 1937, when the Committee was expelled by the AFL and became the Congress of Industrial Organizations, it had thirty-two incipient internationals.

Given the special political problems posed by the campaign to organize the mass-production industries, the greater political bent of those who led the CIO drive and the need for welfare legislation to protect the interests of mass-production workers, the CIO was soon committed to social programs and political campaigns. These, in turn, acted as further incentives to seek the support of Negro workers in the unions, directly involving them in the unions' internal and political affairs, and, in addition, to seek out and solidify an alliance of the CIO and a host of Negro organizations. In the legislative program of the early CIO a high priority was given to civil rights causes.

If only out of self-interest, competitively motivated, the AFL loosened some of its racial barriers, made new overtures to Negro organizations, paid lip service to civil rights programs and some legislation, and generally tried to project

* The Communist Party was opposed to the formation of the CIO and did not bring the Party-led unions into the organization until the spring of 1937. However, many individual Communists, in advance of their more cautious Party, were swept along by the rising tide of industrial unionism and played a prominent role in 1935–36.

the image of a movement that abhorred bigotry and racist practices.

The CIO-Negro alliance managed to hold together throughout the war. However, some friction was created by the actions of Communists, who had become an extremely powerful force in the CIO. The Communists, out of allegiance to the Russo-American alliance, emerged as the extreme right wing of the labor movement. They advocated the speed-up, proposed incentive pay, denounced strikes, defended the proposal for a labor draft, and announced that it was the duty of workers "to force better profits on unwilling employers." They also made it quite explicit that they were prepared to sacrifice the rights of Negroes in the interests of the war. Thus, Negro leaders, who could see no contradiction between the fight against Hitlerism and the continued struggle for civil rights and fair employment practices at home, were roundly denounced by Communist leaders. Most notably, the March on Washington Movement, which, under the leadership of A. Philip Randolph, threatened to assemble in Washington in a mass demonstration to protest job discrimination, was subjected to Communist vilification. Randolph was described as "a Fascist helping defeatism." The attitude of the Communists provoked Willard S. Townsend, the Negro President of the CIO-affiliated United Transport Service Employees, to note that "the present line of the Communist carpetbaggers on the Negro question . . . is indistinguishable from that of many of our southern poll taxers and carpetbaggers." Had the Communist line been adopted by the CIO during the war, the alliance with the Negro organizations might have ended then and there.

While the record of the CIO was a marked improvement over what had been, it was not without blemish. There were instances of segregationist acts, particularly in Southern locals, and it did not aggressively pursue in action the equalitarian policies it advocated during the war years (e.g. it failed to support the March on Washington Movement). In the immediate postwar period when the AFL tried to counter the CIO "Operation Dixie" with its own organizing drive in the South, it tried to project an equalitarian image before Negro workers with attacks on the racial practices of CIO unions. The criticism was hypocritical, but not all of it was fanciful. Most serious is that the efforts of the CIO leadership to raise the rank and file to its own level of equalitarian consciousness were inadequate.

The alliance of Negro and labor organizations, particularly the CIO, continued in the postwar period. A tribute to its effectiveness was Truman's surprise victory in the 1948 presidential election. But the extent to which organized labor went all-out for Truman's victory was symptomatic of a creeping inner malaise in the trade union movement that eventually deepened the gulf between organized labor and the Negro working class. This malaise was the increasing political conservatism and bureaucratization of the CIO. The reasons for this devolution cannot be detailed here. But the fact must be recognized. Postwar evidence of this retrograde change is the support given to Truman in 1948, the manner in which the CIO purged its ranks of Communist-led unions, its response to the McCarthyite madness, and the fact that its alliance with traditional Negro organizations took place within the framework of the Democratic Party, involving further alliances and deals with corrupt city machines.

In the enthusiasm generated by its successful campaign for Truman, the CIO compromised its political autonomy and conveniently overlooked the anti-labor record of its candidate. From a lesser evil, Truman emerged as a positive good. Yet, to give but one instance of his record, it was Truman who responded to a series of massive strikes in the spring of 1946 (one year after VE Day, and six months after Japan surrendered) with strikebreaking proposals that might have given pause even to a Coolidge or a Harding. He proposed that in strikebound plants taken over by the federal government, authority be granted to induct strikers into the Army and imprison strike leaders. Though the labor draft provision was removed from the bill (not by Truman) and the bill never enacted into law, it reveals the conservative temper of the man supported by the CIO two years later as a hard-hitting champion of the oppressed.

Nor did the CIO take full and honest public cognizance of the fact that it was the Truman Administration that provided the prelude to McCarthyism. As for the Wisconsin Senator himself, one would be hard put to find a CIO document clearly exposing McCarthy as a dangerous demagogue and decrying the alarming erosion of democratic liberties in the early fifties. Indeed, the CIO seemed to take a lesson from McCarthy when it came to dealing with the Communist threat inside the CIO. Of course, Communists presented a real menace to the CIO while the threat of the American Communist Party to the American "way of life" was largely the diabolical product of McCarthy's morbid fancy. Nevertheless, the CIO leadership, operating under the pressures of the cold war and having grown cynical and conservative where democracy was concerned, removed its Communist threat in the most expeditious, bureaucratic fashion—it simply expelled the Communist-led unions. That was in 1950. It was a far cry from the manner in which several CIO unions had earlier handled the Communist issue. The most notable contrast was provided by Walter Reuther, who led a militant faction in the UAW to victory over a powerfully entrenched Communist and fellow-traveling machine. Reuther's faction defeated the Communists not with organizational edicts or the crude epithets of "red-baiting" but with an attack from the left, exposing the basically reactionary nature of the Communist movement and its readiness to sacrifice democratic principles and basic trade union objectives in order to further Party-dictated Stalinist political objectives. The difference between Reuther's methods and those used by the CIO as a whole was far greater than the mere two-year difference in time implies.

Despite the endless bill of grievances that could be drawn against the AFL and the CIO by those concerned with political and trade union democracy, hope and enthusiasm were revived by their merger in 1955. A unified labor movement of fifteen million including one and a half million Negroes could provide a dynamic new force in America. This seemed justified by the initial efforts of the AFL-CIO to rid itself of utterly corrupt and gangster-ridden affiliates. The movement would continue to reform itself at the same time that it engaged in dramatic campaigns to organize the South, concerned itself with the serious problem of attracting white-collar workers, became again a pole of attraction for the idealistic young, and, in general, would emerge as a viable instrument for political and economic democratization.

The fusion itself might not precipitate the sought-after change in the labor movement. But there was the upheaval in the Negro and civil rights movements that was already a year in ferment. It was clear that Negro consciousness and militancy would grow; new forces would develop in the civil rights movement; and in the struggle even traditional, conservative Negro organizations would develop a more active, militant character. Surely, the unified labor movement would feel obliged to move along with the changing times if only to keep in step and maintain its alliance with the Negro organizations. At the very least, along with eliminating racketeering unions from the house of labor, it would conduct an uncompromising campaign to cleanse itself of discriminatory racial practices—particularly in the old-line AFL craft organizations.

These were not unreasonable expectations. But they proved too high. Instead, after thirteen years the unified labor movement is encased by a bureaucratic encrustation as impenetrable to change as high-tensile armor plating to buckshot. Even Walter Reuther is obliged to recognize this publicly. Speaking before a special convention of the United Automobile Workers held in April 1967, Reuther delivered a blistering attack on the AFL-CIO leadership in which he summed up his view that "in the eleven years of the merger we believe that the AFL-CIO has become stagnant and is vegetating. I say, to put it simply and understandably, it has an acute case of hardening of the arteries."

However, every bureaucratic institution has its intellectual apologists. The union movement is no exception. Thus books and articles in great profusion have recently appeared to counter the charge that the union movement is dying spiritually. In answer to the critics of organized labor, one finds the usual litany of statistics, quotations from resolutions about civil rights, financial reports, accounts of labor contributions to welfare legislation in the past and commitment to carry on in the same spirit in the future—only better. The real issues are thereby skirted, or obscured. A major symptom of the AFL-CIO's malaise is its inability to attract the young and idealistic. Yet one of the saving graces of this decade is that in the younger generation today there are thousands of young people prepared to lay their bodies on the line for idealistic causes. Few of them have found their way into the labor movement. There are exceptions, such as the involvement of hundreds of youngsters in the struggle to organize the California agricultural workers. Even here, what is instructive is that the youngsters who assisted in the organization and strike responded to the appeal of the Mexican workers with greater zeal than did the upper echelons of the AFL-CIO.

The truth that must be confronted is that the young see nothing idealistic in the labor movement as a whole. There was little to inspire enthusiasm in the AFL-CIO support of the Bay of Pigs adventure or in Meany's dash from his television set to the telephone on October 22, 1962 to wire President Kennedy "the support of the entire labor movement" for his action in the missile crisis that threatened the world with nuclear annihilation. Young people could not be expected to appreciate the heartiness of the labor movement's applause for Johnson's invasion of the Dominican Republic and they are not likely to be moved by reports that at its 1967 Executive Council gathering in Bal Harbour organized labor is again on record with a hawklike position on Vietnam. What is more, young people will hardly be impressed by the Executive Council's assessment hailing social progress under Johnson as "a record unsurpassed in any period of democratic government."

On domestic issues, the AFL-CIO stance is that of moderate liberalism; on foreign policy issues, it is that of right-wing reaction. But what of its internal life and organization? A fair and objective characterization of its internal structure is—authoritarian and corrupted. There are exceptions, of course—in both directions: some unions permit a degree of democracy while others veer in a totalitarian direction. It is interesting to note that in the various charts and statistics found in the literature on the labor movement today there is nothing on salaries and expenses of officers. This is not a trifling question, since the extent to which a union officer will enrich himself is a fair index of the quality of his organization. Perhaps this is why it is seldom mentioned that in recent years wages in AFL-CIO affiliates for union notables run to over $100,000 a year (plus expenses). Most damning, though, is that few unions will tolerate opposition. This is true not only of the old-line craft unions but of industrial unions as well, where to organize opposition—even to voice it—entails the risk of the loss of one's job or physical assault or both. These hard facts of life usually go unnoticed in much of the current apologias on the labor movement.

In the civil rights revolution, the trade union movement has not been able to move beyond the limits of its bureaucratic, socially conservative mentality. It has been unable to meet the special needs and problems of the Negro working class because it cannot truly recognize its existence. Left to its own resources, it cannot eliminate discriminatory practices within the house of labor since it refuses to acknowledge how widespread they are. Given its conservative temper and intolerance, it cannot accept constructive criticism from within or outside its ranks. It is insensitive to changing moods because it doesn't really care enough.

(This bureaucratic inertia is harmful not only to the civil

rights cause but for the organizational needs of the AFL-CIO itself. For example, the AFL-CIO's ability to conduct a major organizational drive in the South is limited since a massive drive there requires more than money; it calls for a missionary spirit in the ranks which is possible only if the leadership encourages membership participation in union affairs. A frightening prospect for labor autocrats!)

On paper and in resolutions the AFL-CIO is committed to racial equality in a most general way. One test of its sincerity is how it responds to various calls to action from the civil rights movement. Take the March on Washington of 1963, designed to further the cause of civil rights legislation. It won the support and sponsorship of an extraordinarily wide section of civil rights organizations, liberal groups, churches, and a few unions with large Negro memberships. Notorious for its absence from the list of sponsors or supporters was the AFL-CIO. This was not an oversight. The AFL-CIO Executive Council discussed the March and refused to endorse it. More than that, it refused to recommend that affiliated unions give their endorsement, leaving it instead to "individual union determination."

On the issue of "preferential hiring" of Negro workers the AFL-CIO position is as undistinguished as on other civil rights demands. The call for "preferential" treatment for weak or oppressed or disadvantaged minorities is in principle thoroughly democratic, though the term "preferential" lends itself to demagogic abuse, of which the Meany leadership has taken full advantage. It is, in fact, widely applied in the United States. The graduated income tax, for example, is a form of preferential treatment for low-income groups. With the exception of a few crackpots, no one has recently denounced the tax system for discriminating in favor of those with lower incomes.

To illustrate the point by another analogy: if in the thirties the demand had been raised that immigration quotas be revised so that German Jews be given preference over other nationalities because of their uniquely disadvantaged position, would anyone with an ounce of humanity have raised the cry that such "preferential" treatment was unfair because it would have discriminated against or inconvenienced Englishmen or Swedes also seeking to emigrate to the United States?

What, then, is either extreme or unfair in the demand that Negro workers who have so long been oppressed be partially compensated for crimes against them (including crimes by racist unions which deprived them of a livelihood) by giving them preferential consideration in hiring practices?

One might argue that the slogan of preferential hiring is a poor one to raise, from a tactical point of view, but this is not the sole objection of the AFL-CIO, which has made it a matter of principle. As Meany expressed it in testimony to the House Judiciary Committee in 1963, preferential hiring is a "pitfall" since it "would merely replace one kind of discrimination with another." What upsets labor leaders about a perfectly moderate, democratic demand is that it is too radical for their tastes (just as the moderate March on Washington was too radical to endorse) and, no less important, if preferential hiring were practiced on a wide scale it might tend to correct the racial imbalance of racist unions, thereby threatening the power of entrenched leaderships. (There are a number of unions with little to fear on this score since they already have written into their constitutions provisions that prohibit members from running for national office unless they have held office for a specific number of years previously!)

If the AFL-CIO Executive Council could not find room in its heart to endorse the Washington March with its moderate demands, one can hardly expect Meany or his fellows to have kind words for the advocates of Black Power. Nonetheless, the level and style of their repudiation of Black Power shed light on their lack of compassion and understanding.

In a letter to A. Philip Randolph, written in October 1966, praising the Negro labor leader for repudiating Black Power concepts, Meany had the following to say:

Your restatement of commitment to the attainment of racial justice by the democratic process, your repudiation of the strategies of violence, reprisals or vigilantism, your reaffirmation of the goals of integration commends itself to every thinking American.

You and I agree that extremism is the antithesis of democracy and extremism by advocates of justice for America's minority population cannot be countenanced any more than extremism by advocates of white supremacy.

To dispute the legitimacy of Black Power is one thing. To equate, however, the extremism of the victims with the extremism of their oppressors is bewildering. But if Meany's letter ignores the difference between the two, it at least has the virtue of being restrained. It was, after all, a letter to Randolph.

However, a month before Meany sent his letter, another union leader discussed Black Power at greater length in the union press. Excerpts follow:

Somehow or other I can't accept the proposition that a bunch of hoodlums who hurl rocks at bypassers, throw gasoline torches into buildings, and upturn and set fire to parked cars are freedom fighters and not just plain bums out for a spree of violence. . . .

In support of this weighted balance of favor toward Negroes I offer the testimony of Cicero, Illinois, where a whole community of stupid whites massed to commit racist violence against a cluster of do-and-dare Negro Yahoos. The latter were mobilized under the auspices of the Student Nonviolent Coordinating Committee, a group composed of violent nonstudents at present dominated by a character named Stokely Carmichael, who, I understand, passed a course in surliness *cum laude*, and was accorded the honorary title of B.P. for "Black Power." . . .

However, I've got news for Mr. Carmichael, the reputed author of the Black Power slogan. The Negro goons who go on racist rampages know exactly what Black Power means. To them it means the chance to go on a spree of violence with a testimonial as a "freedom fighter" for a cover; a chance to do pillaging and looting with little likelihood of punishment. . . .

How is it possible for a trade unionist to describe with such malice Negroes who raise the slogan of Black Power because they despair of ever being accepted as equals by whites?

It is true, of course, that many Black Power advocates have fallen victim to an inverted kind of racism. But even here, how can anyone confuse the pain and anguish of black people treated as less than human with the cruelty and howls of their white tormentors?

What adds to the significance of these coarse descriptions of Negro protest is that they did not appear in the press of some old, conservative, hard-bitten craft union but were printed in *The Hat Worker*, written by its editor, Jack Rich, and published by the old-time socialistic Millinery Workers International.

That the AFL-CIO leadership has grown calloused and is becoming irrelevant to the lives of the Negro masses was demonstrated by its response to the urban racial upheavals in the summer of 1967. It could not grasp that these were more than "riots" (though less than revolutions). The best that George Meany could do in his 1967 Labor Day message was to call for legislative programs and anti-poverty moneys that would "strike at the evils which breed riots." At the same time, Meany—who so well reflects the temper and consciousness of the trade union leadership as a whole—associated the "riots" with "The criminal madness of a few . . ." as he inveighed against "The mindless riots of this unhappy summer [which] cannot be condoned. Arson, looting, and murder have no relations to civil rights; they are criminal wrongs and an affront to the very ideals which motivate the quest for a better society."

In his plea for law and order President Meany is somewhat confused about who was murdering whom in these "mindless riots"; eighty dead black bodies—men, women, children—in Detroit and Newark suggest that Meany's accusing finger is pointing in the wrong direction. Such false accusations, along with shallowness and conservatism, typified the reaction among trade union leaders. These are postures which can only retard the cause of racial justice, hinder the cause of trade unionism, and widen the breach between organized labor and the Negro people.

Much has been written in criticism and defense of the internal racial practices of the AFL-CIO. One thing to which all agree: racial discrimination exists inside major international unions affiliated with the Federation. In dispute are how deep and extensive it is and how to combat it.

In discussing the problem several years ago, President Meany maintained that:

> We have never at any time tried to gloss over the shortcomings of unionism on the subject of equal opportunity. Yes, some of our members take a wrongheaded view. . . . But we in the labor movement publicly deplore these few holdouts against justice. We do our utmost to bring them around to the right side. And at the same time, the employers—who actually do the hiring—escape in many instances with no criticism whatever.

It is a disingenuous performance. It is a matter of record that the AFL-CIO tried to minimize, or gloss over, these shortcomings and union leaders were loath to discuss, much less deplore, them in public. Of special interest is Meany's passing the blame on to employers. No one doubts that employers discriminate. Nevertheless, it is no less true that in innumerable cases it is the unions that, in effect, do the hiring and the discriminating while individual employers are often prepared to employ Negroes. That is the way it works in many of the building craft unions. One of the more widely publicized union-versus-Negro worker battles recently waged is illustrative.

In New Rochelle, a suburb of New York City, a new shopping center was being built recently until work was stopped as a result of a dispute between civil rights organizations and the discriminatory building trades unions. At issue was the fact that these unions have no Negro

17

members, nor do they accept Negro apprentices for training. New Rochelle has a large Negro population with many unemployed Negro workers. The R. H. Macy Company, whose building is the largest in the center, publicly offered to pay some of the cost involved in training Negro apprentices since the dispute caused the entire building project to come to a full halt. To be sure, Macy's management was not altruistic—just realistic. But it is an employer in this case, as in many others, who was willing to break the race barrier. The unions, however, remain obdurate in their racial policies. Charges of discriminatory practices against Negroes by Local 501 of the International Brotherhood of Electrical Workers, Local 38 of the Sheet Metal Workers and Local 86 of the Plumbers Union were brought before the New York State Commission for Human Rights by the New Rochelle Human Rights Commission. On November 15, 1967, the State Commission found the electrical and sheet metal locals guilty of discriminatory practices against Negroes.

According to the Commission, the business agent for Local 501 of the IBEW admitted that in his thirty-nine years of union membership he had never known of a Negro apprentice or journeyman in the local.

Meany maintains that the AFL-CIO is doing its utmost to eliminate discriminatory practices. This claim is somewhat weakened when, a few minutes later, he notes that "we are the only one, among civil rights forces, which has openly called for legislation for the correction of shortcomings in its own ranks."

It is never made clear which are the other civil rights forces requiring correction of shortcomings. More important here, why should the AFL-CIO have to rely so heavily on legislation to eliminate discrimination in its own house? If the CIO could expel unions for being Communist-controlled and the merged union movement found it possible to expel affiliates for corruption, why can't the AFL-CIO establish its own forceful legislation and discipline to overcome discriminatory practices in its own organization?

Moreover, the problem of union discrimination is much broader than Meany suggests. The mounting evidence is that not "some" members take a wrongheaded view but that the bulk of the union movement, on one level or another, follows discriminatory policies, and has successfully resisted the minimal internal union pressures and heavier external effort to bring full equality into the labor movement. A detailed account is not possible here, but at the very least we can point to the recent findings of the New York City Commission on Human Rights.

After conducting a series of hearings on allegations of racial discrimination in the building trade unions in 1963, the Commission reported:

> A pattern of exclusion exists in a substantial portion of the building construction industry, effectively barring nonwhites from participating in this area of the city's economic life.

In March 1967 the Commission ended another series of hearings on the construction industry, and its sixty-four-page report reveals only minimal variations from the 1963 pattern. There are two major exceptions to this pattern of exclusion—the electricians' and carpenters' unions.

Bolstering these conclusions is a study recently completed by the department of economics at the University of Texas for the Office of Manpower Policy, Evaluation and Research of the U. S. Labor Department. Entitled "Negro Participation in Apprenticeship Programs," the report is a survey of union practices in eleven major cities across the country, including New York.

Between March 1963 and March 1966, the report reveals, the Elevator Constructors Union in New York City admitted only two nonwhites to its apprenticeship training program. Local 2, Plumbers Union (Manhattan) admitted only nine. (This is the local of which President Meany is still a member.) It admitted no nonwhite apprentices at all during 1965–66. Local 1, Plumbers Union (Brooklyn and Queens) admitted twenty-two nonwhites to its apprenticeship program between 1963 and 1966, but in the 1965–66 period only six nonwhites were admitted to the program.

The report shows that considerable progress has been made by the Carpenters District Council and the International Brotherhood of Electrical Workers, Local 3. Between March 1963 and March 1966, 630 nonwhites were admitted to the carpenters' apprenticeship program and, during the same period, the IBEW admitted 275 nonwhites. The number of nonwhites admitted to apprenticeship by the electricians is particularly important, the Texas report says, because of "the fact that the U. S. Census of 1960 reported only 79 Negro electrical apprentices in the entire nation."

Sheet Metal Workers Local 28 admitted no nonwhites until 1966. It is a glaring example of the bitterness with which some craft unions resist democratic racial practices. It took the courts to order Local 28 to hold apprenticeship training tests. Those passing the tests would then have to be taken into the union's apprenticeship training program. Before the court decision the sheet metal workers' apprenticeship training program had worked on a father-son basis, which, in effect, excluded Negroes.

Under court order, the tests were given at the New York University testing center. A number of Negro youths applied for the tests and, in preparation for the difficult examinations, were tutored in a special program set up by the Workers Defense League. When the test results were revealed, nine of the ten top scorers were Negroes, and twenty-six out of the top sixty were Negroes. Local 28 was legally obliged to take them into the union as apprentices-trainees. Embittered by the prospect of Negro apprentices, the local refused to take them in, suggesting that Negroes who scored so high could have done so only if they cheated. At this point the State Commission on Human Rights went to court and successfully enjoined Local 28 from denying the Negro youths their rights. Apparently the discriminatory craft unions want to have it both ways: on the one hand, they argue that one reason Negroes are not found in the craft unions is that they do not have the skills; on the other hand, when Negroes prove that they do have the skills, it is argued that they must have cheated. At the time of this writing it is not certain whether Local 28 will continue its efforts in the courts to bar Negro trainees from its apprenticeship program.

One final point on the question of union attitudes toward the Negro worker in particular and the Negro in general. What is so damaging to the union posture is the evident racist attitudes of its rank and file. There is little room to doubt that a high percentage of the American working class—above all, the industrial proletariat, many of them union members—is violently racist. To arrive at this conclusion, we need not turn to interviews or questionnaires. We need only refer to newspapers and television to see that it is in working-class districts—in Chicago, Cicero, Cleveland, etc.—that Negro demonstrators have encountered the most hysterical and violent opposition from whites.

The racist attitudes of American workers are a social problem, with roots that are deep and complex. The unions are certainly not responsible for this state of affairs. The AFL-CIO does not preach discrimination. On the contrary, its formal educational material invariably advances the ideas of racial equality and nothing said here is intended to detract from what the labor movement has contributed to civil rights legislation. The point is that the good that the union movement does is primarily on an elitist level, i.e. it is done from above. There has been no corresponding effort to bring the principles of racial equality home to the rank and file. For this reason, the union movement, bureaucratized and elitist, must assume its share of responsibility for the racial savagery and ignorance exhibited by so many rank-and-file workers.

If principle and logic prevailed, there would be no conflict between the Negro working class and the trade union movement since they share basic interests and needs that eliminate all rational reasons for serious friction between them. The most obvious common denominator is the fundamental economic objective of unions to improve the economic position of the working class, an objective that should benefit both Negro and white workers. But more than that, the welfare of the unions, Negro workers, and the Negro people as a whole is dependent on the viability of political and social democracy. The unions' right to organize, to bargain collectively, to improve the welfare of their members must be fortified constantly by progressive, democratic social and economic legislation. Similarly, the position of the Negro worker in American society, not merely as a worker but as a Negro with unique needs and interests, cannot be improved without a continual growth and application in life of democratic principles.

It is this fundamental identity of interests which, more than any other factor, accounts for the development within the civil rights movement of the school of "coalitionism," which stresses the immediate importance and relevance of an alliance of the existing civil rights groups, trade unions, and liberal forces. The concept has been detailed most effectively in articles by Bayard Rustin and Tom Kahn, Executive Director of the League for Industrial Democracy.

In the best-known of these articles ("From Protest to Politics," *Commentary*, February 1965), Rustin wrote:

> The future of the Negro struggle depends on whether the contradictions of this society can be resolved by a coalition of progressive forces which becomes the *effective* political majority in the United States. I speak of the coalition which staged the March on Washington, passed the Civil Rights Act, and laid the basis for the Johnson landslide—Negroes, trade unionists, liberals, and religious groups. [Emphasis in original]

Actually, these are more or less traditional views held by the more conservative Negro organizations that have in the past maintained some sort of working relationship with important sections of the labor movement and worked in coalition with labor organizations and liberals within the Democratic Party. What is new about the Rustin thesis is threefold: first, it is more sharply formulated in a clear ideological manner by men who learned to polemize and generalize in the radical movement, even if they have abandoned radical politics; second, and more important, the current appeal for coalition politics takes place at a time when the elements of this coalition have undergone significant alterations. In earlier years the trade union movement had a degree of vigor and appeal that it no longer possesses; on the other hand, the civil rights movement today has broken the monopoly of traditional Negro organizations to take on a new militancy which has affected even the older, more conservative groups.

The third difference is that where traditional conservative Negro coalitionists have a mass base in their organizations, the new style theorists of coalition politics have no mass base at all. Thus, while such leaders as Roy Wilkins believe in coalitionism, they owe their first allegiance to their members and organizations. This means that in the event of conflict between the NAACP, for example, and one of its presumed allies in the White House or in the AFL-CIO, Wilkins cannot be taken for granted. For instance, in the dispute between Negroes and unions which have flared into the open, Wilkins has said things about unions that one ally usually does not say about the other. On the other hand, when we come to the theorists of coalition, such as Rustin and Kahn, who have no mass base in a Negro (or any) organization, we are dealing with ideologists who are not similarly influenced and pressured by conflicts between the needs of the Negroes and the actions of their alleged allies. Unhampered by a mass base, the theoreticians of coalitionism dogmatically pursue their objectives even at the expense of the welfare of the Negro people.

But what happens to the Negro-labor alliance when, in the course of the struggle for jobs and economic betterment, it is brought home to the Negro masses that major obstacles to their acquiring skills and entering the job market have been set up and defended by powerfully entrenched sections of the same union movement that is the presumable ally of Negro organizations and an advocate of civil rights legislation? And what happens when it becomes equally clear that a liberal Democratic administration in Washington, to which the labor movement is heavily committed, is not truly responsive to their demands or needs? Clearly, the powerful Negro upsurge from below, which even radicalizes some of the most staid Negro leaders, places an enormous strain on the Negro-labor alliance operating within the confines of the Democratic Party.

The alliance can be protected in one of two contradictory ways: either pressure can be put on the labor movement to clean its house, to break down its discriminatory policies, and, generally, to make itself worthy of a continuing alliance; or, moving in the opposite direction, one can exert pressure on civil rights militants to cool it for the sake of preserving allies in the labor movement and maintaining friendly ties to the Johnson Administration.

The coalition school, with Rustin as its major ideologue and strategist, has opted for the latter course: to limit the militancy of the civil rights movement for the sake of placating liberals and the White House and maintaining the alliance with labor. This means to substitute for "Freedom Now" the policy of "Coalition Now—Freedom Later." Thus, in 1964, for the sake of Johnson's electoral chances, the Coalition Now advocates succeeded in persuading some —but not all—civil rights leaders to declare a moratorium on demonstrations: "to observe a broad curtailment, if not total moratorium on all mass marches, mass picketing, and mass demonstrations until after Election Day, November 3."

This statement, signed by Randolph among others, and endorsed and promoted by Rustin, was a strange reversal for both men. In 1944 it was Randolph who organized the March on Washington Movement that was prepared to demonstrate in Washington during World War II to advance the cause of civil rights. At that time the Communists argued that men like Randolph and Rustin were endangering the long-range interests of Negroes and that such militant action as the March on Washington had to be postponed in the interests of the "war against Fascism." Their conservative arguments fell on deaf ears then. Yet those ready to March on Washington during the war are just as ready, today, to call off demonstrations for the sake of furthering an LBJ victory.

The conservative nature of the Coalition Now strategy is also found in the opposition of Rustin, Kahn, and others to the demand for preferential hiring of Negroes. No less important is that in a concrete sense it means abandoning or curtailing pressure on specific craft unions to open their doors to Negro workers and apprentices. Just one example of how Coalition Now works out in real life is provided by the instance we have already mentioned of the young Negroes who, after passing the apprentice training tests, were then denied admittance to an apprentice training program by Sheet Metal Local 28. To get them into the union, as earlier noted, Local 28 had to be taken into court. But it was taken into court not by the A. Philip Randolph institute headed by Rustin, which had helped to train the young men, but by the State Commission on Human Rights with an *amicus* brief filed by the NAACP. Rustin's organization would not handle the case legally or send a formal representative to the hearings! It wanted the youths taken into Local 28 *but not if it meant a fight with the union*— particularly as the case received widespread coverage in the press. The apostles of Coalition Now were prepared to abandon their own efforts to break down the racial barriers in one of the most hard-bitten exclusionist craft organizations. This is but a recent case. There are others, all instances of a logical extension of a conservative theory that reduces the concept of a Negro-labor alliance to a fetishism. (It is relevant to note that the conservative manifestations of Coalition Now transcend civil rights issues. Its intellectual exponents have almost to a man shifted from the politics of opposition to that of accommodation to the

Establishment, from pacifist and Socialist opposition to war to defenders—in some cases, just noncritics—of Johnson's war in Vietnam.)

There is no reason to doubt the enormous contribution that could be made to society as a whole by an alliance of the Negro masses and the labor movement. For reasons already summarized, that alliance is, in theory, a natural one. But a theory or an abstraction mechanically applied can be dangerous and self-defeating. If the alliance of Negroes and labor is to emerge as a significant instrument for democratic change, then the labor movement must prove itself equal to the task by breaking down its own internal barriers to the equal treatment of the Negro working class.

Chapter I

ATTITUDES OF NEGRO LEADERS TOWARD THE AMERICAN LABOR MOVEMENT FROM THE CIVIL WAR TO WORLD WAR I

AUGUST MEIER AND ELLIOTT RUDWICK

The belief that interracial cooperation between white and black workers would be a significant factor in solving the problems of the Negro masses can be traced back for at least a century. But the practices of white labor unions and the middle-class orientation of most Negro leaders both tended to minimize the acceptance of such a philosophy. In the post-Civil War era many prominent Negro leaders briefly took an interest in fostering trade unionism among Negro workers, though most of them took the very middle-class point of view that unionism would help Negro working-men to become capitalists. During the 1880s the Knights of Labor elicited favorable notices in many quarters, and a handful of intellectuals espoused a truly radical economic philosophy. Subsequently, paralleling the rise of the discriminatory American Federation of Labor, Negro leaders exhibited extreme disillusionment with the policies of the trade unions. The anti-labor views of Booker T. Washington epitomized the attitudes of Negro leaders at the turn of the century. Nevertheless a few Negro "radicals," who opposed Washington's accommodating ideology, also endorsed the idea of the solidarity of the Negro and white working classes and the socialization of the American economy. Most notable among this group was W. E. B. Du Bois. But even they practically gave up in discouragement as a result of the AFL's firm policy of discrimination, culminating in labor's role in the tragic East St. Louis race riot of 1917.

Negroes had displayed incipient interest in the organized labor movement during the ante-bellum period, and had also formed benevolent labor societies of their own. But both before and after the Civil War considerable enmity toward Negroes existed among white workers and unionists, and though colored workers were admitted to some craft unions, often in segregated locals, prejudice was strong and exclusion common. The National Labor Union, formed in 1866, was more idealistic in its orientation, and Negro participation was in fact invited. But in view of the attitudes and practices of the constituent craft unions, the issue was too controversial to enable its leadership to insist upon integration of Negroes into the unions themselves. Consequently, Negro skilled workers, longshoremen, hod carriers, and waiters had organized their own protective and benevolent associations in the major Northeastern and border cities.[1] Discouraged by the temporizing of the National Labor Union, the Baltimore Negro trade unionists, under the leadership of the ship caulker Isaac Myers, took the initiative in calling a Colored National Labor Convention, which met in Washington in December 1869.[2]

Myers, one of nine Negro labor representatives at the 1869 convention of the National Labor Union, was one of the leading colored citizens of Baltimore. Negroes had been an important part of the ante-bellum labor force in the Baltimore shipyards. Myers, a free Negro, was but sixteen years of age when, in 1851, he was apprenticed to a prominent local Negro to learn the ship-caulking trade. Four years later he was superintending the caulking of large clipper ships. In 1865 a strike of white workers against the presence of colored mechanics and longshoremen resulted in the dismissal of over a hundred Negroes from their jobs in the Baltimore shipyards. In this crisis Myers organized the Chesapeake Marine Railway and Dry Dock Company. Within four months he raised $10,000 cash in shares sold at $5 each, and purchased a yard and railway worth $40,000. This cooperative venture, owned entirely by Negroes, was an instantaneous success. It secured a lucrative government contract, employed a number of white mechanics, and paid off its debt within five years. Even though it later lost its government contract to competing firms which employed white workers at lower rates, the company remained in business for another six years, paying dividends of between 4 and 10 per cent. The shift to steel ships spelled the doom of this company after roughly a decade of activity. But its mission had been accomplished, for the white caulkers' union had meanwhile been compelled to admit Negroes.[3]

Myers' experience with this combination of labor organization and business enterprise was to have an enormous impact on the vision of Negro leaders in the following years as they grappled with the problems facing Negro urban workers. Such producers' cooperatives, organized by workingmen, fitted the middle-class outlook of these leaders, who, in accordance with the American dream, hoped to make Negroes independent farmers and capitalists.

The Colored National Labor Convention held in 1869 and a similar meeting that followed in 1871 were part of a historical tradition of Negro conventions that began in 1830 and extended until nearly the close of the nineteenth century. For over a generation Negro leaders had met irregularly in national and state conventions to formulate plans for the solution of the problems facing the race. The significance of these meetings derived from the fact that they were attended and managed by the most distinguished leaders—important editors, clerics, businessmen, and, after passage of the Fourteenth Amendment, officeholders. The 1869 convention called by Myers was no exception. While many representatives from labor organizations attended, a disproportionate number of the delegates were independent entrepreneurs, government clerks, ministers, and politicians. Except for Myers, in fact, the actual leaders were the bishops, politicians, and perennial conventioneers; the presiding officer was a leading North Carolina political figure, James H. Harris.

As in the case of other conventions held during the Reconstruction period, the delegates in their resolutions stressed the value of education and the importance of political rights, but the labor conventions were unique because they focused mainly on economic problems. The resolutions of the 1869 conclave insisted upon the right of labor to organize, but constantly harped upon the theme that there was no real conflict between capital and labor, and that indeed it should be the aim of every man to become a capitalist. In pursuit of this goal the delegates held that the masses should be encouraged to learn trades and professions, and that workingmen should be taught that all labor was honorable and a sure road to wealth; that habits of economy and temperance, combined with industry and education, would elevate the race. Workers therefore should organize cooperative trade unions to establish enterprises that would provide jobs for unemployed Negroes. Special attention was given to the problems of the Southern tenant farmers. The convention intimated that they would be justified in organizing to compel the planters to respect their claims for adequate pay; but it also appealed to Congress for relief from economic and political oppression by the plantation owners, and for the distribution of public lands in forty-acre lots. The convention also protested against the exclusion of Negroes from apprenticeships and workshops by trade unions as "an insult to God and injury to us, and disgrace to humanity." It therefore created a Colored National Labor Union—stressing, however, that it would make no discrimination as to nationality or color. For a labor movement based upon such discrimination would be "suicidal," arraying against each other laboring men of the two races who actually should be closely allied.[4]

Both this convention and the one held in January 1871, which expressed a similar outlook, revealed not only that Negro leaders were concerned with the problems of the working classes, but that, like the officials of the white labor unions of that time, they had a characteristic middle-class ideology. Isaac Myers' opening address to the 1871 convention epitomized this attitude. "There is not a natural antagonism between capital and labor," he declared. "Their relationship and interest are mutual. One cannot exist without the other." To expect the millennium in economic relationships would be futile, but unless labor learned to be more frugal and to invest its savings judiciously, gross inequality would exist forever, "and no combination that can be formed by the wisdom and cunning of man can control it." But Myers did not mince words in his criticism of capitalists. He recognized that even the honest, industrious, and frugal worker often received less than a living wage. In the cotton states thousands of laborers were robbed of their wages. Accordingly it was natural that labor should seek protection by forming unions to advance its interests. However, Myers declared that the unwise counsel of "brainless leaders" provoked numerous disastrous strikes. He held that very few strikes, if any, led to any permanent good for the workers. But Myers insisted that labor did have a right to organize, and he thought that cooperative labor organizations were the most effective mode of organization. He urged that workers pool a portion of their weekly earnings "for the purpose of forming a capital with which to establish a business in the event capital will not concede living wages to the laborer." He pointed to the existence of several prosperous worker cooperatives, and added that such associations also were good schools for laborers who wanted to become capitalists, for they forced habits of frugality, temperance, and economy.[5]

As already suggested, the views of the Colored Labor Conventions were similar to those of the National Labor Union. The chief differences were that the latter leaned toward the Democrats or a third party in politics, while the Negroes, for historical reasons, believed in the Republican Party as the source of all reforms. Attempts at cooperation between the two groups foundered on this issue.[6] It is likely, however, that the discriminatory policies of the white unions would have prevented any long-range effective collaboration.

At least one leader in the labor convention movement espoused a more genuinely radical point of view. This was Peter H. Clark, principal of the Colored High School in Cincinnati. As a representative of the Colored Teachers Cooperative Association of Cincinnati, he had attended the National Labor Union Convention when it met there in 1870.[7] Originally, like Myers and others, he called for workers' cooperatives. By the middle seventies, however, he was moving to the left and had become highly critical of the selfishness of capital. In 1877 he joined the Workingmen's Party, perhaps becoming the first Negro Socialist in the United States. He supported the strikers in the dramatic railroad strikes that hit Cincinnati and other cities in the summer of that year; and in the fall he ran for state superintendent of schools on the Workingmen's Party ticket. In contrast to Myers, Clark did not believe that capital and labor were useful and necessary to each other. Rather he saw the situation as one of class conflict and, unlike Myers, he endorsed strikes.[8] Though Clark subsequently turned Democrat, his espousal of socialism and strikes was evidence of the type of solution to which alienated intellectuals like T. Thomas Fortune and W. E. B. Du Bois would later turn.

During the post-Reconstruction years Negro leaders increasingly subscribed to a philosophy that emphasized thrift and industry and Negro support of Negro business—a philosophy that envisioned the elevation of Negroes to an independent entrepreneurial status. In the face of the loss of the Negro's constitutional rights in the South, growing indifference in the North, and a rising crescendo of mob violence, many leaders were coming to believe that by securing economic independence Negroes would gain the respect of whites and thereby obtain from them the recognition of the race's constitutional rights.

For a brief period in the 1880s and early 1890s, however, there was a significant group of leaders who expressed economic doctrines of a more radical tinge, and who were more inclined toward economic solidarity among the laboring classes than toward economic solidarity within the race. The

Colored Farmers' Alliance claimed a membership of a million, and Negroes participated significantly in the Populist movement, especially in Georgia and North Carolina. About sixty thousand Negroes were members of the Knights of Labor at the height of the organization's strength in 1886. Not only did large numbers of Negro farmers and workers and their local leaders thus apparently view cooperation with members of the white working classes as a solution to their economic problems, but at least a few men of national prominence expressed sympathy with trade unionism and radical economic ideologies.

For example, Frederick Douglass, who had earlier been an active participant in the Colored Labor Conventions and for a time editor of the Colored Labor Union's newspaper, the *New National Era*, during the 1880s generally endorsed an economic program of business activity and self-help. But occasionally he revealed glimpses of a different insight. Thus in 1883 he held that "Experience demonstrates that there may be a slavery of wages only a little less galling and crushing . . . than chattel slavery, and that this slavery of wages must go down with the other." He maintained further that the cause of the Southern farm laborers was one with that of the working class all over the world, and he urged that "the labor unions of this country should not throw away this colored element of strength."[9] Similarly, John R. Lynch, Reconstruction Congressman and former Speaker of the Mississippi House of Representatives, felt that while Negroes should not identify themselves with violence, socialism, or anarchism, they ought to join trade unions. He believed that

> The colored people cannot peaceably live . . . as a separate and distinct class or race, representing . . . separate and antagonistic [to the whites'] interests. The true solution of the race question . . . is political and industrial . . . assimilation. It would be just as unwise to have labor organizations composed exclusively of colored people to antagonize the laboring whites, as to have political organizations composed exclusively of colored people.[10]

As a matter of fact, the Knights of Labor received some favorable comments in the Negro press. The Cleveland *Gazette*, for instance, urged Negroes to join the Knights: "No one disputes the fact that the organization referred to has worked and is working a wonderful good for the Northern Laborer of all nationalities, and there is no intelligent colored or white man who is not aware . . . of the grand possibilities of the organization of colored laborers of the South as 'Knights of Labor.'" The Washington *Bee* called the Knights one of the most worthy and liberty-loving organizations in the country, doing more for labor than Congress and state legislatures combined. At the 1886 convention of the National Colored Press Association, Negroes were urged to join unions, and the Knights were specifically endorsed.[11]

Other influential journals, however, were either equivocal or hostile toward unions. The *Christian Recorder*, organ of the African Methodist Episcopal Church, recognized that the Knights aimed to protect Negro workers against discrimination by white labor, not only in the North but in the South as well. However, it appeared to recommend that Negro workers should remain neutral in the labor struggles in which the Knights were engaged; and it asserted that the really important thing for Negro labor was to increase its skillfulness and exhibit neatness, thrift, and industry. The influential Indianapolis *Freeman* opposed the Knights, and identified them with the Haymarket anarchists.[12]

A small group of intellectuals, influenced by the Farmers' Alliance, the Knights of Labor, and the thinking of Henry George, revealed close affinities with native American radical ideologies. D. A. Straker, a Detroit lawyer and jurist who had taught briefly at the University of South Carolina during Reconstruction, thought that the true relationship of the Negro to all labor organizations should be one of perfect harmony between the two races. He protested against exploitation by industrialists, discrimination by labor unions, and the activities of the oppressive land power of the South, which condoned lynching, was responsible for segregation, and kept both the Southern poor white man and the Negro in a state of servitude. Though he did not favor the single tax, he agreed with Henry George in attacking land concentration in the South—a state of affairs he regarded as particularly vicious because Southern landowners placed barriers in the way of Negroes buying land. He denounced the disproportion in wealth between capital and labor. Though the two forces should not, theoretically, be in conflict, in actuality capital oppressed labor by paying low wages and enforcing long hours. The true remedy for this condition, he continued, lay in labor organization. It was well known that white labor discriminated against the Negro; yet the Negro's relation to labor should be that of a close friend. Trade unions, he insisted, ought to be reforming agencies, and therefore should not exclude Negroes, because if labor required protection against capitalist exploitation it could not afford to be divided against itself.[13]

T. McCants Stewart, a prominent lawyer and member of the Brooklyn, New York Board of Education, speaking in 1891, maintained that the great problem of the day was the elimination of the extremes of wealth and poverty. True, capital was an invaluable stimulant of labor, but capital was artificial, being the creation of labor. Therefore he favored heavy taxes on unused land and a fairer distribution of profits.[14]

It was T. Thomas Fortune of New York, the leading Negro editor in the last years of the century, who made the most thoroughgoing application of native reformist thought to the problems of the Negro during the 1880s. The laboring classes, he declared, systematically victimized by politicians and businessmen, in the last analysis paid all the taxes. The prime cause of economic inequalities lay in land monopoly. In this the South was no different from other places, and the future conflict in that section would not be racial or political in character, but a struggle between capital and labor. The land system had, ironically, turned the "roses of freedom into thorns to prick the hands of the black man of the South"; had "created that arrogant class who have exhausted the catalogue of violence to obtain power and the lexicon of sophistry for arguments to extenuate the exceeding heinousness of a crime. . . . To tell a man he is free when he has neither money nor opportunity to make it is simply to mock him. To tell him he has no master when he cannot live except by permission of the man who . . . monopolizes all the land is to deal in the most tantalizing contradiction of terms." When the government failed to distribute plantation lands among the freed slaves, it simply added four million to the laboring classes to work for the enrichment of vast soulless corporations and a privileged class of individuals whom the government had permitted to usurp the soil from which the laboring masses obtained subsistence.[15]

Society should control its resources and industry for the people's welfare, rather than permit wealth and power to become concentrated in the hands of a few. Fortune was opposed to privileged classes and aristocracies, because they "make inequalities, out of which grow all the miseries of society, because there is no limit to their avarice, parsimony, and cruelty." All over the world labor was defrauded in order to maintain the great capitalists in idleness and luxury. "What are millionaires, anyway, but the most dangerous enemies of society, always eating away its entrails, like the vultures that preyed upon the chained Prometheus?"[16]

Conditions were alike for white and black workers in the South, and so, said Fortune, they should unite under one banner and work upon the same platform for the more equal distribution of the product of labor and capital. The land that had given birth to chattel slavery, in the hands of unrepentant rebels, was giving birth to industrial slavery: "a slavery more excruciating in its exactions, more irresponsible in its machinations than any other slavery. . . . The hour is approaching when the labor classes of our country . . . will recognize that they have a *common cause*, a *common humanity* and a *common enemy*; and that, therefore, if they would triumph over wrong . . . they must be united!"[17]

In praising the Knights of Labor for including all workers, Fortune saw an imminent conflict of labor against the "odious and unjust tyranny" of capital. "The revolution is upon us, and since we are largely of the laboring population it is very natural that we should take sides with the labor forces in their fight for a juster distribution of the results of labor. We cannot afford to stand off from or to antagonize the army under whose banner we labor in the common lot of toil. . . . All we can do is to fall into line on the right or left, and which side it will be will depend entirely upon whether we are a capitalist or a laborer."[18]

Not until W. E. B. Du Bois was converted to Socialism some twenty years later did another distinguished Negro leader and intellectual state with such vigor the thesis of class conflict, the identity of the interests between black and white workers, and the importance of their working together in trade unions. Meanwhile, by the end of the decade Fortune was veering away from his early radicalism and had come to criticize the Farmers' Alliance.[19] And though as late as 1892 he welcomed the strikes of cotton pickers in Arkansas and of stevedores in Savannah as evidence of the growth of trade unionism among Negroes, he usually expressed a program more in consonance with the American middle-class tradition. As he wrote in 1907, "the determination of trade unions arbitrarily to dominate capital" was a "robbery of consumers and employers."[20]

Fortune's shift of view heralded Negro disillusionment with the labor and agrarian movements. The leadership of the AFL, which had first discouraged color discrimination, by the end of the century had come to terms with the exclusionist and racist policies of many of its constituent unions.[21] Meanwhile hopes entertained in connection with Populism had also miscarried. All in all, the eighties marked the high point of Negro interest in the labor movement. A few intellectuals had expressed genuinely radical ideologies. But the passing of the Knights of Labor, the failure of Southern agrarians to wipe out the color line, and a parallel decline of radical leanings among the few outstanding men who had subscribed to them combined to give

Negro thought even more of a petit-bourgeois tone than it otherwise would have had. The *Christian Recorder* summed up the usual attitude well enough when its editor declared in the course of discussing some recent labor disturbances: "The duty of the colored worker under the circumstances is sufficiently clear. . . . He must acquire competency as a workman and skillfulness as a laborer." As a skilled and reliable workman, his labor would be in greater demand than ever. The editorial concluded by urging race leaders to instruct the masses to be patient and eschew "the folly and danger of cooperating with labor malcontents in their fight against capital."[22]

Both the rise of disfranchisement in the South and the failure to achieve any effective collaboration with the white working classes forced Negroes to turn their greatest efforts toward achieving wealth and middle-class respectability by their own efforts. Ordinarily, labor unions were mentioned only to criticize them. The Afro-American Council, an organization comparable to the Negro convention movement of earlier years, passed a resolution at its 1899 convention, criticizing organized labor for its "shortsighted and cruel" attitude. It recommended that a committee be appointed "to wait upon the labor leaders" and seek by every effort to secure cooperation between Negroes and the trade unions.[23] More typical was the frank acceptance of the idea that white capital, rather than white labor, was the Negro's ally, expressed by the Washington *Colored American* in an editorial toward the end of the century:

There is seldom a time when a strike is justifiable. . . . To attempt to break up another man's business because he employs labor unsatisfactory to you, or because he grants equal privileges to all respectable citizens, is revolutionary and anarchistic. The use of force to keep another man from working wherever he can secure employment is a crime against society. The driving of those colored miners out of Pana, Illinois, and Washington, Indiana, by union strikers was a cowardly and criminal act.[24]

Others were more explicit in their endorsement of the use of Negroes as strikebreakers. For example, several years later students of race relations in Chicago found Negro leaders there seriously thinking of organizing unions of colored artisans who would act as strikebreakers whenever possible, as long as the AFL excluded them.[25]

But the man who best represented the anti-labor point of view was the conservative accommodator Booker T. Washington, who achieved national prominence and leadership in the Negro community as a result of his noted address at the opening ceremonies of the Atlanta Exposition in 1895. Washington urged Negroes to accept segregation and disfranchisement, and to secure their constitutional rights through the gradual and indirect process of first becoming successful businessmen. Washington felt a deep sympathy with the wealthy; he wanted nothing more than to see Negroes work hard, save their money, and become "captains of industry." His closest white friend was William H. Baldwin, president of the Long Island Railroad and a leading figure in the Southern and Pennsylvania systems. He felt most at home with industrialists like Andrew Carnegie, John D. Rockefeller, and other "Christ-like" philanthropists. He praised Robert C. Ogden, philanthropist and merchant prince, as one who thought of uplifting the Negro partly as a humanitarian endeavor and partly as a means of developing "one of the neglected resources of the South." He also thought most highly of H. H. Rogers, the Standard Oil and railroad magnate, in whose sight Negroes "were part of the resources of the country which he wanted to develop."[26]

Part and parcel of this bourgeois ideology was Washington's outlook on labor unions—a point of view reinforced by the growing racism of organized labor. Though he claimed he had been a member of the Knights of Labor for several years while a coal miner during his youth in West Virginia,[27] Washington later recalled a strike that the workers had lost and commented: "Before the days of strikes in that section . . . I knew miners who had considerable money in the bank, but as soon as the professional labor agitators got control, the savings of even the more thrifty ones began disappearing."[28] To some extent he thought that the loss of the Negroes' hold in skilled trades in the South was due to the unions.[29] But he underestimated the role of white unions in this development, because it was his basic position that the decline in the number of Negro artisans was the race's own fault, for it had sought higher education and ignored training in the trades. As the leading spokesman for the ideologies of industrial education and self-help, Washington failed to perceive the degree to which labor unions were responsible for the Negro's economic plight. His criticism of unions therefore is to be attributed chiefly to his general petit-bourgeois outlook and mentality, and his close relationships with white capitalist-philanthropists. He even gloried in the assertion that Negro workers were "the best free labor in the world," unequaled if treated fairly, "not given to strikes and lockouts."[30]

In an article written toward the end of his career, Washington appeared on the surface somewhat more open-minded toward labor unions; but basically his hostility had not been dissipated, and his tactful approach only cloaked a not-too-veiled intimation that if labor did not change its policies, it would be justifiable for Negroes to serve as strikebreakers. In this essay, published in the *Atlantic Monthly*, Washington stated that the average Negro did not understand the advantages of a labor organization "which stands between him and his employer and aims apparently to make a monopoly of the opportunities for labor." Negro attitudes were also conditioned, he said, by discriminatory practices, Negroes therefore becoming "very willing strikebreakers." On the other hand, Washington admitted that "many instances have been called to my attention, in which labor unions have used their influence in behalf of Negroes," even in the South; and he took note that the AFL national council in 1910 urged Negroes to enter Jim Crow unions. Answers to questionnaires that he had sent union leaders revealed that even the officials of discriminatory unions said they desired to see Negroes organized. He himself knew of instances in which Negroes had proven enthusiastic and active members of predominantly white unions. Nevertheless, Washington felt that, on the whole, labor organizations discriminated and that Negro strikebreakers would have the "advantage, [in that] they are engaged in a struggle to maintain their right to labor as free men." He concluded that unions would continue to discriminate as long as it paid them to do so, but that their leaders have recognized "that race prejudice is a two-edged sword, and that it is not to the advantage of organized labor to produce among the Negroes a prejudice and fear of union labor such as to create in this country a race of strikebreakers."[31]

Because of his control over philanthropy and political appointments under Presidents Theodore Roosevelt and William Howard Taft, Washington was the dominant figure among American Negroes for nearly two decades after his famous speech at Atlanta in 1895. But there were always a few who openly criticized his accommodating approach, and the number grew after the turn of the century. In 1905, under the leadership of W. E. B. Du Bois, then a professor of sociology at Atlanta University, the "radicals" or "anti-Bookerites" established the Niagara Movement. This tiny protest organization agitated against American race discrimination and criticized Washington and his philosophy. In 1909 most of the members of the Niagara Movement joined with a small group of prominent white liberals and Socialists to establish the National Association for the Advancement of Colored People. By the time Washington died in 1915, this protest organization was coming to represent the dominant view among articulate Negroes.

The majority of Negro "radicals" were radical only on the race question, and retained the typical middle-class outlook that characterized the period. But among these racial radicals was a minority who expressed a deeper criticism of the American social order, and advocated an alliance with white labor rather than white capital. A few of them expressed socialistic views. Du Bois was most prominent among the members of this group.

In Du Bois' first major sociological monograph, *The Philadelphia Negro* (1899), he had condemned both labor unions and employers for excluding Negroes from economic opportunities. Although he advised Negro laborers to form their own unions, his allegiance to a middle-class ideology was evident when he told the Philadelphia Negro "aristocracy" to acquire wealth and become "captains of industry over their people." Only as the black bourgeoisie gained economic independence would they feel secure enough to elevate the Negro masses. Three years later in his Atlanta University monograph, *The Negro Artisan*, Du Bois vividly portrayed discrimination in the AFL and the independent trade unions. Though carefully noting the varying degrees of discrimination existing in the different unions (the United Mine Workers being clearly the most equalitarian), Du Bois concluded that white laborers were the Negroes' "bitterest opponents."[32]

In the following months Du Bois' whole ideological outlook underwent a shift from a conservative to a "radical" orientation on the race question. In the spring of 1903 his noted *Souls of Black Folk* appeared with its critical essay on Booker T. Washington. By 1904 he was contending that the Negro problem was related to the "unjust and dangerous economic conditions" in the country and he considered himself a well-wisher of the Socialist movement, though "scarcely a Socialist." Three years later he was "a Socialist-of-the-Path," believing that most business should be nationalized by the government. Agreeing that "the socialistic trend" was the "one great hope" of the Negro race, he nonetheless maintained reservations about the Socialists because they had not succeeded in freeing themselves of racial discrimination. Clearly, an identification with Socialism made him more certain in 1907 that the Negro and white working classes would unite "against the aggressions of exploiting capitalists." At the same time, he had become deeply suspicious about the black bourgeoisie, with their "old trodden ways of grasping individualistic competition, where the shrewd, cunning, skilled and rich among them will prey upon the ignorance and simplicity of the mass of the race and get wealth at the expense of the general well being."[33] Du Bois joined the Socialist Party briefly in 1911–12; but during the period under discussion he remained essentially an independent who was very sympathetic to Socialism.

Earlier, in 1905, when Du Bois founded the Niagara Movement, one of the demands that the new organization made was equal employment opportunities from both labor unions and industry. The first address made by the Niagara Movement to the country, which Du Bois wrote, declared: "We hold up for public execration the conduct of two opposite classes of men: the practice among employers of importing ignorant Negro-American laborers in emergencies, and then neither affording them protection nor permanent employment; and the practice of labor unions of proscribing and boycotting and oppressing thousands of their fellow-toilers, simply because they are black. These methods have accentuated and will accentuate the war of labor and capital, and they are disgraceful to both sides."[34]

The Niagara Movement, however, was composed mostly of college-educated Negroes who (aside from a Socialist-oriented handful like Du Bois, and the ministers J. Milton Waldron and Reverdy Ransom) showed little interest either in attracting the Negro masses or in demonstrating how much they had in common with white laborers. Shortly before the 1908 Niagara Conference, Mary White Ovington, a white social worker who a few months later became one of the leading founders of the NAACP, told Du Bois that she planned to address the Niagaraites on the subject "The Relation of the Negro to Labor Problems," because "I should like to hammer that side of things into some of the aristocrats who are in the membership." Men like Du Bois and Waldron were pleased because they had not given up their hope that the Niagara Movement could find means to cooperate with the working-class whites and the Socialists. Du Bois' own vision of cooperation was even worldwide, and in the last annual address issued by the Niagara Movement (1909), he wrote that Negroes should unite with the other "oppressed" workers of the United States, Mexico, India, Russia, and the rest of the world.[35]

Despite Du Bois' Socialist-labor orientation, the Niagara Movement continued to give only limited attention to the economic salvation of the race, and persisted in placing paramount importance upon securing the ballot as a panacea for many of the Negroes' problems. Nevertheless, several of Du Bois' editorials in *Horizon* magazine, an unofficial organ of the Niagara Movement, clearly showed his devotion to a hoped-for alliance with organized labor. In the presidential election of 1908, his views paralleled those of the AFL. He supported William Jennings Bryan for President because he thought that the Democratic Party advocated control of corporations and improved working conditions for American wage earners. He contended that the Democrats comprised an "impossible alliance" between the "radical socialistic" wing of the North and the "aristocratic caste party of the South"—a coalition that was, accordingly, doomed to disintegration. However, Du Bois warned that if Negro voters continued to oppose Northern liberal Democrats, the latter would be reluctant to break with the South.[36]

A few months after Bryan lost the election, Du Bois and many of the Niagara members attended the National Negro Committee Conference in New York, the conclave from which the NAACP developed. Among the other founders of the new organization were such white Socialists as William English Walling, Mary White Ovington, and Charles Edward Russell. Despite the vital role played by these Socialists, the NAACP's major concern was fighting for the Negroes' constitutional rights rather than attacking the economic problems of the masses. The lack of emphasis upon economic problems of the black worker was at least partly due to the fact that the Negro members of the NAACP in the early years were drawn from the upper class. Moreover, NAACP leaders also believed that American Negroes could not progress very far economically without the power of the franchise. Du Bois himself expressed this position very forcefully at the 1909 conference when he declared that the economic position of a nonvoting Negro working class could be destroyed by a white working class which had the ballot.[37]

As director of publicity and editor of *Crisis*, Du Bois was the NAACP's leading propagandist. In a 1912 editorial he proclaimed his faith in organized labor; and so that no one could possibly misunderstand, he noted that "we carry on our front cover the printers union label to signify that the printing and binding of this magazine is done under conditions and with wages satisfactory to the printers unions." Yet, despite his loyalty to labor unions, he declared that union exclusion policies forbade Negroes "under ordinary circumstances" from working as printers, bakers, blacksmiths, carpenters, hatters, butchers, tailors, street or railway employees, as well as in many other occupations. He observed that "some unions, like the printers and carpenters, admit a lone colored man here and there so as to enable them the more easily to turn down the rest." In another *Crisis* editorial written in 1918, he declared: "I am among the few colored men who have tried conscientiously to bring about understanding and cooperation between American Negroes and the Labor Unions. . . . I carry on the title page, for instance, of this magazine the Union label, and yet I know, and every one of my Negro readers knows, that the very fact that this label is there is an advertisement that no Negro's hand is engaged in the printing of this magazine, since the International Typographical Union systematically and deliberately excludes every Negro that it dares from membership, no matter what his qualifications."[38]

During the years between these two editorials, Du Bois recorded numerous illustrations of union racism and discrimination, culminating in the 1917 East St. Louis race riot, the most serious example of racial violence in the twentieth century. He moved from pain to anger to almost complete hopelessness, declaring that the AFL and many other independent unions treated the Negro as "half a man," with the result that members of the race had little choice other than "scabbing" and strikebreaking.[39]

Though it stressed other matters, the NAACP did give

some attention to fighting union discrimination. It demonstrated concern about the Ohio "full crew" law which the all-white Brotherhood of Railway Trainmen lobbied through the legislature. The law, providing that each train crew contain a certain number of brakemen, resulted in the firing of approximately thirty veteran Negro porters who had performed these duties but were refused admission to the union as "brakemen." In 1913, when similar bills were introduced in Illinois and Kansas, the Chicago and Kansas City NAACP branches successfully fought against their passage.[40]

When World War I opened up many jobs in Northern industry, Du Bois encouraged Southern Negroes to leave their region "as a means of self-defense and as the most effective protest against Southern lynching, lawlessness, and general deviltry." However, AFL leaders considered the Negro migration from the South a source of "anxiety" and "danger," charging that industrialists were importing the Negroes "for the purpose of filling the places of union men demanding better conditions." At its Thirty-sixth Annual Convention the AFL passed a resolution "to inaugurate a movement looking toward the organization of these men in the Southern states, to the end that they may be instructed and educated along the lines of the trade union movement, and thereby eliminate this menace to the workers of the Northern states."[41]

Despite the resolution, the traditional AFL policy remained basically unaltered. In various cities such as East St. Louis, labor leaders showed little interest in organizing Negroes and, in the spring of 1917, charged that the influx of migrants "has reached the point where drastic action must be taken . . . to get rid of a certain portion of those who are already here." Within a week after this call for drastic action in East St. Louis, a race riot erupted, the prelude to the holocaust that occurred on July 2. When Du Bois learned about the first outbreak he wrote, "It is this attitude of many labor unions and Northern working men who make the mobs of East St. Louis, that keeps many Negroes living among Memphis lynchers. But it cannot keep them all. The stream of migration is large. It is going to be larger. The hand of the government can be depended on in East St. Louis to put down mobs; it cannot be depended on in Memphis. . . . It is lynching, forced labor, and discrimination that is sending the Negro North. When he comes North he may find jobs and hostile labor unions, but he will also find the law and the law will be enforced."[42]

But on July 2 the "hand of the government" in East St. Louis could not be counted upon because of its corruptness, bigotry, and cowardice, and the police force as well as units of the Illinois militia surrendered the community to white mobs, resulting in the deaths of at least thirty-nine Negroes. The NAACP sent Du Bois to the scene to determine the causes of the outbreak. Declaring that employers had imported Negroes from the South to break a strike and undercut organized labor, Du Bois charged "This program [was] engineered by Gompers and his Trade Unions." Despite his ideological commitment to the principles of trade unionism, he concluded that the massacre "brought the most unwilling of us to acknowledge that in the present Union movement, as represented by the AFL, there is absolutely no hope of justice for an American of Negro descent."[43]

This mood of depression was characteristic of other articulate Negroes and was even stronger after the spring of 1918, when the two leading racial advancement organizations, the NAACP and the National Urban League, attempted to negotiate "a square deal" with the AFL leadership. The AFL officials simply went through the motions of negotiating and blandly asserted that the Federation practiced no discrimination.[44]

Thus, in dealing with organized labor, Negro leaders in the five decades after the Civil War had employed a variety of approaches. These ranged from enthusiastic endorsement of a close alliance between Negro and white labor to veiled endorsements of the use of Negro strikebreakers. But despite the diversity of ideologies expressed and tactics employed, the relationship between Negroes and most trade unions had not changed in any fundamental way. After half a century of varied efforts, Negro leaders were still faced with the seemingly insoluble problem of securing the acceptance of Negro workers into the American labor movement.[45]

Chapter II

THE NEGRO AND THE
UNITED MINE WORKERS OF AMERICA
*The Career and Letters of Richard L. Davis and
Something of Their Meaning: 1890–1900*

HERBERT G. GUTMAN

I

In April 1877, fifteen hundred Braidwood, Illinois, coal
miners struck against the Chicago, Wilmington & Vermillion
Coal Company to protest a third wage cut in less than a year
and a resulting 33 per cent drop in wages.* Two months
later the company imported Kentucky and West Virginia
Negroes to replace the stubborn strikers, and its superintendent contentedly reported the Negroes as saying they
had "found the Land of Promise." But in July the strikers
chased four hundred Negroes and their families from Braidwood, and only a couple of Illinois militia regiments
brought them back. When winter approached, the defeated
strikers returned to work. The violence accompanying the

* The author is indebted to the State University of New York at
Buffalo for making available research funds to gather the materials
for this essay. Critical comments by Professor C. Vann Woodward
of Yale University resulted in significant changes in the tone of
the concluding section of this essay. I remain indebted to him for
the frankness of his comments—and his wisdom. The Center for
Advanced Study in the Behavioral Sciences, Stanford, California,
made it possible for me to read portions of this essay at the annual
meetings of the Association for the Study of Negro Life and History in Baltimore, Maryland, in October 1966.

great 1877 railroad strikes drew national attention away from Braidwood, but in that small town only the coming of the Negroes mattered, not the faraway riots in Pittsburgh and other railroad centers. John Mitchell, then a seven-year-old orphan, lived in Braidwood and witnessed these events.[1] No record exists of young Mitchell's feelings at that time, but twenty-two years later an older Mitchell, now the newly elected President of the nine-year-old United Mine Workers of America, gave testimony before the Industrial Commission (set up by Congress in 1898) that might suggest to the innocent only that history repeats itself. Relations between Negroes and whites in the coal-mining industry troubled Mitchell and other UMW leaders. In 1898 and 1899 violence and death had followed the coming of Negro strikebreakers and armed white police to the Illinois towns of Pana, Virden, and Carterville. "I might say, gentlemen," Mitchell advised the Commission in 1899, "that the colored laborers have probably been used more to decrease the earnings in the mines . . . than in any other industry." To this fact Mitchell attributed much unrest. "I know of no element," he continued, "that is doing more to create disturbances than is the system of importing colored labor to take white men's places and to take colored men's places."[2]

Mitchell and the other UMW witnesses before the Commission did not draw the conclusion that such Negro strikebreaking justified the exclusion of Negroes from trade unions. They said the opposite and took pride in their interracial union. Although Mitchell personally believed that the Negro "standard of morality" was "not as high as that of white people," he nevertheless berated only those operators who used Negroes against the union and, insisting that the UMW constitution did not bar Negroes from membership, told the Commission: "Our obligation provides that we must not discriminate against any man on account of creed, color, or nationality."[3] Even more explicit than Mitchell, UMW Secretary-Treasurer W. C. Pearce insisted before the Commission:

As far as we are concerned as miners, the colored men are with us in the mines. They work side by side with us. They are members of our organization; [and] can receive as much consideration from the officials of the organization as any other members, no matter what color. We treat them that way. They are in the mines, many of them good men.

Pearce objected to Negroes only when they became strike-breakers, but he blamed this condition on "their ignorance of the labor movement and the labor world" and on the frequent deceptions practiced against Negroes by operators. "When they get to a certain place," he said of these Negroes, "why, they are there, and some of them, I know, many times are sorry for it."[4]

These pages consider certain aspects of the early contact between the United Mine Workers and Negro miners. Too little is yet known for that story to be told fully, much less clearly understood. By 1900, when the UMW was only ten years old, Mitchell and Pearce estimated that between 10 and 15 per cent of the nation's four hundred thousand coal miners were Negroes.[5] They almost all worked as bituminous miners, and their number varied between regions. Few labored in western Pennsylvania, and many concentrated in the Border South (West Virginia, Kentucky, and Tennessee) and Alabama. The older bituminous areas of the Middle West all had smaller numbers of Negro miners than the South—and Negro miners spread through other states, too.[6] Some first came as strikebreakers, but most Negroes became miners in a more normal fashion—seeking work as unskilled or semiskilled laborers in a rapidly expanding industry. At the same time as the mining population increased in the 1890s, its ethnic composition changed radically. Traditional dominance of native whites and British and Irish immigrants began to decline as East and South European Catholic immigrants and American Negroes settled into the industry. So heterogeneous a population posed vexatious problems for early UMW leaders. "With all of these differences," existing in industries like the mining industry, the Industrial Commission concluded in 1901, "it is an easy matter for employers and foremen to play race, religion, and faction one against the other." Even where employers made no such efforts, nationality and ethnic differences separated men in a common predicament. But although early UMW bituminous locals were based on nationalities, by 1900 they had given way to mostly "mixed" locals. In many mining districts the union "mixed" recent immigrants with "old" immigrants and native miners—and Negroes with whites.[7] Negro support explained part of the union's early successes among bituminous miners. By 1900, Negroes had contributed significantly to the building of that union, and twenty thousand Negroes belonged to it. Here we give attention mainly to the role and the ideas of one early UMW Negro leader.

II

The most important of these Negro miners, Richard L. Davis, twice won election to the National Executive Board of the United Mine Workers, in 1896 and 1897, but it is the way his entire career challenges traditional explanations of the relationships between Negro workers and organized labor in the 1890s and not alone his high office that forces attention on him. Biographical material so essential to fully knowing Davis and other Negro UMW officers is scant, and in Davis' case comes mainly from his printed letters and scattered references to him in the *United Mine Workers' Journal.* Such limited information allows only the piecing together of the barest outlines of his life. Much must be inferred and much is unknown, even his status at birth. Davis was born in Roanoke, Virginia, in 1864, the day before Christmas and only a few months before the Civil War ended, but there is not even a hint that he came of either slave or free Negro parents. The *Journal* called him "a full-blooded colored man" but said nothing else about his forebears. For several years Davis attended the Roanoke schools during the winter months. At eight, he took employment at a local tobacco factory and remained with that job for nine years when, "disgusted with the very low wage rate and other unfavorable conditions of a Southern tobacco factory," he started work as a coal miner in West Virginia's Kanawha and New River regions. In 1882 Davis moved to Rendville, Ohio, a mining village in the Hocking Valley region and southeast of Columbus. He married, supported a family of unknown size, and lived and labored there the rest of his brief life. Apparently only union duties took him away from Rendville and then but for brief periods. Davis died there in 1900. Of his life other than his work as a miner and his union career, nothing else is known.[8]

Life as a miner allowed Davis few amenities. Unsteady work made him, like other miners, complain frequently of recurrent unemployment. The depression in the mid-1890s hit Ohio miners hard. "Times in our little village remain the same . . . —no work and much destitution with no visible signs of anything better," Davis reported in February 1895.[9] More than a year later he wrote again: "Work here is a thing of the past. I don't know what we are going to do. We can't earn a living, and if we steal it we will be prosecuted."[10] The year 1897 proved little better. One week Davis' mine worked only half a day.[11]

His commitment to trade unionism added difficulties ordinary miners did not face. In August 1896, after certain Negro miners blamed Davis and another miner for organizing a strike to restore a wage scale, Davis went without work. "Just how they could stoop so low I am unable to tell," an angered Davis wrote of these Negroes, "and some of them, if not all, call themselves Christians or children of the most High God, but in reality they are children of his satanic majesty." Some Negro coworkers he called "as true as can be found anywhere" but his betrayers were "as mean men as ever breathed."[12] The *Journal* defended Davis and reminded Ohio readers he deserved their "respect and moral support" because of "his devotion to the cause of unionism."[13] But nearly four months later Davis, still without work, feelingly complained: "Others can get all the work they want; but I, who have never harmed anyone to my knowledge, must take chances with winter and its chilly blasts without the privilege of a job so as to earn a morsel of bread for my wife and little ones."[14] Two years afterward, in 1898, and for reasons unknown, Davis lived in a pitiful condition—this time, black-listed. A letter dated May 16, 1898 poured forth a pained despair:

> I have as yet never boasted of what I have done in the interest of organized labor, but will venture to say that I have done all I could and am proud that I am alive to-day, for I think I have had the unpleasant privilege of going into the most dangerous places in this country to organize, or in other words, to do the almost impossible. I have been threatened; I have been sandbagged; I have been stoned, and last of all, deprived of the right to earn a livelihood for myself and family.

> I do not care so much for myself, but it is my innocent children that I care for most, and heaven knows that it makes me almost crazy to think of it. I have spent time and money in the labor movement during the past six-teen years, and to-day I am worse off than ever, for I have no money, nor no work. I will not beg, and I am not inclined to steal, nor will I unless compelled through dire necessity, which I hope the good God of the universe will spare me. . . . I can not think of my present circumstances and write [more], for I fear I might say too much. Wishing success to the miners of this country, I remain, as ever, a lover of labor's cause.[15],*

* "Old Dog," a Congo, Ohio, Negro miner, took up Davis' complaint. "He can't get work in the mines, and he says he can't get work to do as an organizer." Old Dog called Davis "a staunch union man" and reminded *Journal* readers that Davis had "done more" than any single person to bring Ohio Negroes into the union. "I think he should be provided for in some way," he went on. "You do not often meet up with colored men like Dick. . . . He has a family to keep and I think we owe him something. He nor [sic] his children can not live on wind, and further, if he was a white man he would not be where he is—mark that—but being a negro he does not get the recognition he should have . . . such

In December of that year Davis still sought work. "I am still a miner," he remarked, "but cannot secure work as a miner. Yet I love the old principles I have always advocated. Even though a negro, I feel that which is good for the white man is good for me, provided, however, it is administered in the right way. I want to see the negro have an equal show with the white man, and especially when he deserves it. I want it in the local, in the district, and in the national."[17] Little time remained for the fulfillment of Davis' wishes. Thirteen months later, one month after his thirty-fifth birthday and while the UMW met in convention in another city, Davis died of "lung fever."[18]

Learning of his death, the UMW convention delegates paused to pay special tribute to their deceased Negro brother.

---

treatment will not tend to advance the interest of our union, but will retard its progress and cause colored men to look with suspicion upon it. . . . Give us an equal show. Dick deserves better usage. . . . He feels sorely disappointed. . . . For my part, I think if we would do right he could either go in mines to work or we should see to it that he was started up in a small business or given field work. I want President [Michael] Ratchford to show all colored men that he values a man irrespective of his color and he can best do this by giving Dick a helping hand. I hope you will excuse my bad writing and language and also method of speaking, but I believe in calling a spade a spade. I am sure we are not being treated just as we should."[16] In 1909, William Scaife, British-born, an Illinois miner and then retired editor of the *United Mine Workers' Journal*, remembered the troubled last years of Davis. Scaife gave no details but noted: "R. L. Davis, by his devotion to the miners' union, deserved better treatment than that accorded him in the last few years of his life." He scorned those who criticized Davis as a "has been" and "a barnacle," calling them "some of the mushroom growth of latter-day leaders" who were "unmanly and unremindful of the past." Davis had worked for the union when it "took sand, pluck, and grit to do it." Scaife lamented: "I sometimes think the poet of nature was hitting the right head with a ten-pound hammer when he said, 'Man's inhumanity to man makes countless thousand mourn.' . . . Our ignorance has often led us to injure, abuse and crucify our best friends." (Old Timer [William Scaife], "Forty Years a Miner and Men I Have Known," *United Mine Workers' Journal*, Nov. 19, 1909.)

Davis deserved their attention. Enduring many difficulties, he had been one of the founders and pioneer organizers of the United Mine Workers during the 1890s, its first and perhaps most difficult decade. The delegates called attention to the "many years of his life . . . devoted to advancing the interests of his craft" and lamented that the union had "lost a staunch advocate of the rights of those who toil, and his race a loyal friend and advocate."[19] The particular experiences that drew Davis toward organized labor are unknown, and only scant evidence links him to the Ohio miners' unions that preceded the UMW in the 1880s and to the Knights of Labor. But there is no doubt of his importance to the UMW after 1890. The evidence is overwhelming. Many of his letters appeared in the weekly *Journal* and related quite fully his role in the Ohio unions, his career as a local and national organizer, and his feelings and ideas about the Negro, organized labor, and the changing structure of American industrial society.

Davis' formal role in the UMW can be described simply. In 1890 he attended its founding convention as delegate and also won election to Ohio's District 6 Executive Board. Another year he spurned efforts to nominate him for the vice-presidency of District 6. But until 1895, when he ran for the National Executive Board and lost by only a small vote, Davis won annual re-election to the District 6 office. His close defeat for national office in 1895 proved* "very clearly" to him that the "question of color in our miners' organization will soon be a thing of the past," and he predicted that "the next time some good man of my race will be successful."[20] The year 1896 found Davis right. He and fourteen others stood for the National Executive Board at the annual UMW convention and Davis got the highest vote, 166. The next largest vote, 149, went to a white Illinois miner, James O'Connor.[21] A year later, Davis won re-election and ranked second among those vying for that

* Twenty-eight men stood for the office; six were elected; Davis ran seventh and got 173 votes.

high office.* The *Journal* celebrated Davis' first election in its customary fashion by printing brief biographical sketches of all new officers. It called Davis ("Dick") a man of "very fair" education, "a good reader," and the author of a "very good letter." It boasted that he gained election because UMW members found him "a good representative of his race and because the miners believe the colored men of the country should be recognized and given a representative on the [the executive] board." The *Journal* made much of the fact that he was Negro:

> He will in a special way be able to appear before our colored miners and preach the gospel of trade unions and at the same time will be able to prove to our white craftsmen how much progress may be made with very limited opportunities. . . . If it be a good principle to recognize races or nationalities on the board in preference to individuals, per se, the convention has done well to elect Dick, for he has certainly merited this recognition. In fact, he has merited it from either standpoint, for as a man, and more especially as a union man, he has deserved well of the miners of the country.[23]

The weekly wished Davis "success," and Davis took his charge with great seriousness, enthused over "this manifestation of kindness in recognizing my people." He felt his election to be of great importance to all Negro miners:

> Not only am I proud but my people also. I know that a great deal has not been said publicly, but I do know that our people are very sensitive, and upon many occasions I have heard them make vigorous kicks against taxation without representation. Now, then, they cannot kick this year, for although the representative himself may be a poor one, it is representation just the same.

He promised to "try to so act that those who elected me shall not be made to feel ashamed."[24]

---

* Although renominated in 1898, he failed to win a third term. For unknown reasons, his popularity among convention delegates fell dramatically, and he got only ninety-four votes.[22]

III

The particular language and mode of expression found in so many of Davis' letters strongly suggests the influence of evangelical Protestantism on his thoughts and feelings. This strain of postmillennial Christianity was common among many self-educated late-nineteenth-century American reformers and radicals bred in a rural or semirural world. Davis, then, was not different from them. Religious images recurred often in his writings. Urging compact organization, he commanded: "Let us resolve to do better. We are taught by the teachings of the Holy Writ that in unity there is strength."[25] The acquittal of a Pennsylvania sheriff involved in the shooting of several Polish anthracite miners in 1898 caused the lament: "It is as we expected. . . . The miner has no rights that the coal barons are bound to respect. Surely, oh Heaven, this condition of things will not last forever."[26] Davis found in the United Mine Workers a secular church that promised redemption from an evil social order, and he gave his work all the zeal and devotion expected of a dedicated missionary. When Massillon, Ohio, miners threatened to quit the UMW, he reminded them of Paul's words in the New Testament: "Except those abide in the ship, ye cannot be saved." Preachers designated the "ship as a church," but Davis saw matters differently. He called the UMW "the ship" and explained: "I now exhort you that except ye abide in the ship ye can not be saved. . . . If her crew will only remain at their posts and not mutiny, I think she will make the harbor safely."[27] Thus did Davis war against factionalism by drawing from and reinterpreting a common religious language. Another time, addressing nonunion Negroes, he dismissed their frequent complaint that the UMW was "a white man's organization."

Now, my dear people, I, as a colored man, would ask of you to dispel all such ideas as they are not only false but foolish and unwise. Think a moment and see if you cannot come to the conclusion that you yourselves are men, and that you have the same interest at stake as your white brother, because I believe that to be the proper phrase; inasmuch as I believe in the principle of the fatherhood of God and the brotherhood of all mankind no matter what the color of his skin may be.

Davis castigated those who saw religious salvation only in other-worldly terms. He reminded nonunion Negroes that "labor organizations have done more to eliminate the color line than all other organizations, the church not even excepted," and called other-worldly aspirations inadequate:

I know that in former days you used to sing "Give me Jesus, give me Jesus, you may have all the world, just give me Jesus." But the day has now come that we want a little money along with our Jesus, so we want to change that old song and ask for a little of the world as well. Don't you think so friends?

Davis admitted he had been "thinking so for some time."[28]

IV

Davis' main influence as a union organizer and labor stalwart was felt where he lived and worked—in southeastern Ohio. Mining villages and towns dotted the landscape in Hocking, Athens, and Perry counties. Davis worked there under many disadvantages. Not the least important was the fact that Negroes had first been brought there in large numbers from border-state cities and even the Deep South in 1874 and 1875 to break a bitter strike by Hocking Valley members of the Miners National Association. The strikers had been mostly native whites and British and Irish immigrants. On arrival, some Negroes had refused their assigned role and left, but most did their job and remained on after the strikers surrendered.[29] Racial friction and ethnic mistrust inevitably followed, and coal operators often exploited tensions between Negro and white miners.

Although the history of that region has not yet been carefully studied, certain facts are known about the Negro and white miners. Southeastern Ohio felt deeply the influence of the Knights of Labor and its brand of evangelical democratic trade unionism. Local miners' unions, independent of or affiliated with the Knights, rose and fell before 1890, too.[30] Of the Negro miners little is yet known except from the letters Davis penned in the 1890s. Before the Knights exerted influence, Negro miners suffered severe discriminatory disabilities. Sunday Valley Creek Negroes (Davis lived in that valley) found themselves excluded from all but one mine, and that mine hired only Negroes. A few other mines employed occasional Negroes, but the pattern remained fixed and Negroes suffered. In the "Negro mine," Mine 3 where Davis worked, the screens on which the coal was separated from dirt and rock permitted more wastage of coal than those in the other mines, and its men got no pay for dead work. This meant a lower weekly wage for the same quantity of work that whites performed. The disadvantage lasted through the mid-1880s when Negro miners and the Knights abolished it. The Negroes in Mine 3 protested first to the operator and learned that their screens would be altered to conform with "white" screens but only if whites worked in "their" mine. The men told the operator, Davis remembered, "to put white men in, as they wanted the screens changed. So the screens were changed, and this was the advent of the white men in mine No. 3." At about the same time, the local Knights, including Davis and other Negroes among their members, agitated for wider Negro job opportunity in the entire valley and succeeded in gaining entry for Negroes in other valley mines. Davis recollected these victories and how the Knights had forced "the breaking of the ice." He remembered, too, the anger of certain operators, including one who warned the complaining Negroes that "whenever . . . the colored men demanded the same and caused as much trouble as the whites" the operators would have "no further use" for them.[31]

Integration and improvement in the Negro condition in

southeastern Ohio's mines did not end ethnic discord and employer exploitation of that feeling. In the summer of 1892,
certain difficulties in Davis' town told much about linger-
ing hostilities between Negroes and whites and employer
attitudes toward both groups. The United Mine Workers,
only a few years old, already had made substantial progress
in that region, and Davis served as elected member of the
District 6 Executive Board. His behavior told much about
his attitude toward the race and labor questions and showed
how he, an elected union official, could display much courage
by challenging the attitudes of rank-and-file Negro and white
miners, not to mention the power of local coal operators.

The trouble that threatened the survival of the union
started after a white mine boss quit in July 1892 and was
replaced by a Negro. Angered and unwilling to work under
these conditions, the white miners left the pit. Davis called
a union meeting and tried to soothe "very incendiary remarks" by both white and Negro union men. Though he
thought he had successfully quieted the men, some disturbed
Negroes talked of starting a separate Negro union. Davis
pleaded with both the Negro and white miners:

> We have some men among us who are members of our
> organization only because they are forced to be. These
> men will naturally take any advantage that they can get
> to squirm out of it. Don't think that these are colored
> men alone. . . . Some few of our colored men say they
> will never do any good until they organize to themselves;
> that is, withdraw from our present form of organization
> and get up an organization of their own.

> Well, when I hear stuff as that, no matter from whose
> lips it comes, it makes me nervous [mad], because I
> think that we are far too advanced in civilization to even
> entertain such foolish notions. I have got it fixed up in
> my brain that a man is a man, no matter what the color
> of my skin is, and I don't care who thinks different. I
> think myself just as good as anybody else, although the
> color of my skin is dark. I had nothing to do with the
> making of myself, probably if I had [,] the result would
> be somewhat different.

To those Negroes incensed by the white walkout, Davis reflected on his own mistreatment: "I have had men call me a nigger, but I always call him [*sic*] a fool, so we can keep even on that score." But he warned that the future of the union was at issue and even suggested that ethnic pride be put aside. At the same time, he also urged that white miners abolish all forms of job discrimination:

It is high time for the color line to be dropped in all branches of industry, for until then there will be no peace. The negro has a right in this country; those of to-day were born here, they didn't have to emigrate here. They are here and to stay. They are competitors in the labor market and they have to live, and I think were we, as workingmen, to turn our attention to fighting monopoly in land and money, we would accomplish a great deal more than we will by fighting among ourselves on account of race, creed, color or nationality.[32]

Despite his plea, a number of Negroes, particularly the younger men, remained dissatisfied and expressed continued resentment. At this moment the owners of Mine 3, the William Rend family, long identified with the region and among its most powerful operators, offered to fill Mine 3 once again entirely with Negroes and give them eight or nine months of work each year. Davis still worked in Mine 3, serving as its elected checkweighman. He also sat on its elected union "mine committee." A number of Negroes immediately supported Rend's offer in spite of opposition from F. H. Jackson, another Rendville Negro miner, who explained Rend's strategy: "Of course, I understand this gentleman's idea. The organization is getting too respectable for him, and he probably deems a split in our ranks a very convenient thing. I wish all my race could see through this as I do."[33] Davis made the same point and reminded his Negro adversaries of their condition when they worked separately in the mid-1880s:

Now, what does this move mean? It means simply this, to get up the race fighting among us and finally the dis-

ruption of our organization. . . . I would not be so much
against this thing if men were hired irrespective of color,
but colored men to be hired exclusively and whites to be
turned away I don't like; and it is not right.

Davis pointed out that the national union opposed all such
arrangements and scornfully commented on Rend's promise
of more work for Negroes:

This is the business view of it. Does it stand to reason
that he thinks any more of you or me because of our
color? Not much. He is like the balance; he will get his
coal where he can get it cheapest, no matter whether it
be from white or black. Now, then, do you mean to say
that you can produce this coal cheaper under this plan?

Instead, Davis urged that Negroes be spread among all the
mines. "It does not matter if there are not more than
two or three in a mine; it will go to show that we can
work together."[34]

His forthright defense of interracial trade unionism and
his attack on Rend's proposal caused Davis much difficulty.
Negro critics called him a "traitor" and promised not to
re-elect him to local union office. "I have been given to
understand that my time is not very long at Mine 3," Davis
reported. Not all Negroes opposed him ("We have some
colored men here who are as true as steel, who are as good
union men as ever breathed the breath of life," Davis
insisted), but the choice he had made endangered his local
position. Davis nevertheless did not back away and struck
again at his Negro critics, accusing them of believing that
"capital has a right to the reins of supremacy and that
labor should bow submissively to the bidding of capital."
"I know you don't like me because I tell you of your
wicked ways," he addressed them. "I can't help it, boys."
Of the threat to "down me off the tipple" and force him
to "tramp the ties," Davis responded calmly: "Well, boys,
there is a providence that rules the destiny of nations, and
I think I can make it and my friends, too." Some months
later Davis reported much improved conditions and wrote

of the spirit of "unanimity" among the men. But he offered no details on the pit election. He still defended his earlier actions: "It doesn't hurt . . . to keep up a little agitation now and then and to keep the men in mind of their duty and the reforms needed for the emancipation of the wage slaves. . . . It is our fight, and no one can fight it but ourselves."[35] That year Davis was once again re-elected to the District 6 Executive Board and held that office until he won national office in 1896.

Work as a union organizer took Davis to other bituminous regions, but he did not neglect mining conditions in Ohio valleys nearby. In 1892 he exposed the policies of mine operators in Congo, Ohio, a new mining enterprise one and a half miles from Rendville. "Not the Congo we have so much read of in Stanley's work, but Congo, O[hio]," he first noted. The operators planned to "make a model town of it," and what Davis found there upset him. The company was establishing methods no longer "in vogue" throughout the region. Its house-lease arrangement meant that only men living in company-owned houses could work there, and they had to vacate within five days if they quit work or struck. Davis called the new village "the O.M.P.," the Ohio miners' prison:

> , . . . The place is fenced in all around, with two gates, one at either side, and at each of these gates, so I am informed, they are going to have gate-keepers . . . to keep out all wagons or teams except those belonging to the company. Do you see the point? to keep peddling wagons out. You see they don't want the honest farmer to come in and sell his produce to the miners; no, for that would be competition and the company would not reap the profits accruing to it. . . . Yet this is a free country, eh! Well, if it is, I don't want any of it. . . . I believe in a man having freedom of speech, freedom of thought and freedom of action, and if the present state of things are (*sic*) allowed to exist he [the Congo miner] will have freedom of neither (*sic*). . . .

He found especially wrong the company's separation of Negro from white miners:

> Congo, unlike one of our ancient cities, sits on two hills or ridges with a deep ravine between, access being to either side by means of a bridge. On one of these ridges or hills the white miners' houses are built. I don't know what they call this ridge, but on the other ridge the colored miners' houses are built; they call it Nigger Ridge, see? A distinction is made by the company, and if a colored man goes there seeking a house he is very courteously conducted over on the other ridge, you know. If he wants one on the white folk's ridge, why he is told that he can't get it, and if he insists he is called saucy, and is told that he can get neither house nor work; that's freedom, you know.

> Now, I will leave the houses alone and go down into the mine. Here we have another distinction. On one side all the white men work, on the other all the colored men work. This is called "over in Africa," how is that, eh? Don't suit me.

Such conditions convinced him that "employers . . . keep up a distinction between men for the purpose of breeding strife and dissension in our ranks." Ethnic and religious differences had to be put aside. "Just even horse sense" made it clear that only the operators benefitted from such divisions. "While we are fighting among ourselves, they wag away with the spoils, and what do we get—only the dregs."[36]

Union men soon filtered into Congo ("There are missionaries going there most every day," Davis noted), but it took some time for conditions to improve. The exact causes are unknown, but in 1897 Davis, Congo's most severe critic, called it "the best mining camp in this part of the valley." There, the union had been fully recognized and the men "treated civilly and gentlemanly." A miners' committee adjusted grievances, and the company offered certain primitive welfare benefits. "I say these things," Davis explained, revealing much about himself, too, "in justice to the company because of what I have said in years gone by."[37]

V

All through the difficult 1890s, as a member first of the Ohio Executive Board and then of the National Executive Board, Davis worked as a roving UMW organizer and helped establish new locals, strengthen existing ones, and counsel miners engaged in bitter industrial disputes. Although most of his organizing was done in Ohio, special assignments and particularly severe crises brought him to western Pennsylvania, Virginia, West Virginia, and Alabama. On certain occasions he went only because an organizer was needed, but at times he was sent to an area where the national officers felt a Negro could best appeal to nonunion Negro miners. Organizing nonunion miners was not easy in the 1890s. Employer opposition and miner apathy, fear, or ethnic division hampered Davis and his associates. In the summer of 1897, for example, Davis and other UMW organizers aided by national union leaders such as Samuel Gompers and Eugene V. Debs poured into West Virginia to urge unsuccessfully that its miners join the nationwide bituminous strike.[38] Some West Virginia miners quit work. But the overwhelming majority did not, and of them Davis wrote: "To call them slaves is putting it mildly." Injunctions limited Debs and others. Davis faced other problems. "It was like taking one's life in his hands at times," he wrote afterward. "While we never had any injunctions issued against us, we had men and Winchesters against us which were in most cases just as effective."[39]

That Davis was Negro added to his difficulties as an organizer. In May and June 1892 he worked through the southern West Virginia New River region, an area almost entirely hostile to labor organization. His color exposed him to severe hardship. Davis detailed his trip:

> . . . . A word about the traveling accommodations in this part of the country for one of my race. . . . Had it not been for Brother E. E. Page, traveling salesman of

the West Virginia Cut and Dry Tobacco Co., of Wheeling, and Brother Moran [a UMW organizer] this boy could have seen a hard time of it. . . . We . . . arrived at Peterstown at about six o'clock, in time for supper. After washing and getting ready for eating as I thought, the colored man who worked there came to me and told me that he would show me my room. . . . Well, I went with him, and where do you suppose he took me? Away, away from the main building, out in the wood yard, to an old dilapidated log cabin. I looked in and saw the bed. I turned to the man and asked him if it was intended that I should sleep there. He said yes, that he slept there. I told him that he might sleep there but I wouldn't, that I would walk to Lowell, 30 miles away, that night first.

Page, a white, intervened and convinced the proprietor to give Davis "the best bed in the house." "I would not be afraid to bet that I am the first negro to eat at a table in that man's dining room," Davis remarked. The next day Davis and the others stopped at a Red Sulphur Springs eating place where Davis encountered more personal insults:

I was told that I could not eat in that house. My dinner was prepared outside. I lost my appetite . . . I didn't want anything to eat. We started from there a little after two o'clock and arrived at Lowell at about 8 o'clock. Brother Moran asked the proprietor, could I get supper there, and his answer was, oh, yes, but, lo, when the bell rang and I was to enter the dining room he caught me by the shoulder and told me to wait awhile. Brother Page turned around to him and told him I was with them. He looked as though he was thunderstruck and of course I got my supper.

Davis applauded Moran and Page. "Had it not been for those two white brothers," he believed, "I don't know but that I would have been by this time behind bars."[40]

On another occasion Davis actually feared for his life. In 1894, recent immigrants replaced disaffected native white and Negro miners in Pocahontas, Virginia. Davis went to bolster the Negroes and secretly organized them into "a good little local." But "spy" reports exposed these Negroes, and the operators fired and evicted them. Davis' role became known, too, and made his situation precarious:

> I . . . [was] sitting or standing at different places when maybe two or three strange fellows would come along accompanied by one of the sucks ["spies"?]. . . . When they would get to where I was I would hear one say, there he is, or there is the s—— b——. Not only that, but I have heard myself spoken of in the same way by business men when walking along the streets; besides I have heard threats made as to what they would do to me if I did not leave.

Union adversaries also talked of "doing up" George Harris, a white union organizer, and Davis hastily left Pocahontas, explaining to his critics:

> Boys, I am not yet ready to become a martyr to the cause, and I am confident that had I remained there much longer that would have been the result. . . . Now, you might say, oh, he left because he was scared, but boys, let me say to you that I was then south of Mason's and Dixon's line, and there is but little justice for the black man anywhere, and none at all down there, and for safety I thought it would be best for me to leave and even in doing this I had to be escorted to the station . . . the threats being openly made about doing me up. . . .

The gestures against Harris made Davis even more fearful. "Now, I was born in the State of Virginia, and I know that when they threaten a white man it is an absolute certainty about the negro and he had better make himself scarce, that is, if he values his life any."[41]

Physical discomfort and personal danger were not the only troubles Davis encountered. Other obstacles frustrated or made more difficult his organizing efforts. In March 1892, for example, two local Negro leaders, one a church deacon and the other a Republican Party stalwart, stymied his attempt to convert nonunion McDonnell, Pennsylvania, Negro miners. They condemned interracial organizations, and the deacon explained:

> . . . . While I speak bear in mind that I am speaking in defense of my people. Join that thing and you will rue the day you ever thought of it. Don't you know that if you join that thing you can't get nothing out of the store. I tell you you will starve, you and your little children. I tell you I know just how you people are fixed; you are just like me. I 'aint got but one pitiful dollar and you 'aint got that. Some of you are a long way from home, in a strange land, away from North Carolina. . . . I know what I am talking about. If you don't want to sup sorrow, don't join this 'ere organization.[42]

That same year, racial mistrust blocked Davis' work in West Virginia's New River region ("the whites say they are afraid of the colored men and the colored men say they are afraid of the whites"). But in West Virginia employer hostility, the apathy of the miners toward the union, and their fear of the operators hampered him even more. Davis got permission from the Claremont school trustees to hold an organizing meeting in a schoolhouse, but local operators convinced the trustees to "shut the house up." Unable to buoy the spirit of the men ("they were that badly scared that I could get them to do nothing"), Davis left town. Although the school superintendent in nearby Alaska closed his building to him, Davis planned an open-air meeting. His description of what followed is almost a classic account of the difficulties union organizers faced when confronted with hostile employers and apathetic or frightened workers:

> I notified every man on the place and . . . had them at the meeting. In fact it seemed to be my brightest meeting that I had ever gotten up in the district. We were about to open the meeting and were trying to select a chairman. Nobody would serve. Some of the men were upon box cars and some were upon the ice house. I heard some fellow in the crowd say, "Here comes a chairman; Brown will serve." I didn't know what he was talking

about, but I soon learned that he was one of the head pushers of the place. Well, he came right up in the crowd and ordered the men to get down off the ice house. They didn't move fast enough and he picked up a stone and pretended that he was going to throw it and I tell you they rolled off, all except one colored boy, who remained perfectly still and who had the manhood to tell him that he had better not strike him. After this he went away, so we resumed our efforts in trying to get a chairman and seeing they were afraid, I opened the meeting, starting my talk with [the] boys.

Everything was going lovely. I suppose I had talked about twenty minutes or a half hour when that gentleman returned. I had noticed some of the men shying away, but thought nothing of it; well, he walked right up in front of me with stone in hand, and addressed me thus: "Say, look here, you —— —— black scamp, I want you to get off of these premises right away, move along or I'll knock —— out of you in a minute." I had not very far to go; I just stepped down on the railroad track and told the boys to come on with me, and we would have our meeting anyhow. That wasn't enough, he came again and says: "—— —— your black soul, I want you to move either up or down this track and —— quick." I then gave him to understand that I was not his property, and would not go any further. I tried to get the boys to follow me, but to no avail. They were afraid, and so when I left there I left for home, and that night too.

"Flowery speeches and enthusiasm" would not bring the UMW to West Virginia. Davis argued after this trip that only a permanent resident organizer together with "time and money" might assure some success.[43]

Birmingham, Alabama, tested Davis even more than his work in the Northern bituminous fields and in West Virginia. Alabama coal mining boomed in the 1890s. At the start of the decade, the state counted 8000 miners of whom 3600 were Negroes. When the new century began, the total had increased to nearly 18,000, including 9700 Negroes.

Early efforts to build successful Alabama miners' unions had failed, and in 1894 the United Mine Workers of Alabama, an interracial statewide union, had fallen to pieces after a bitter four-month strike against the giant Tennessee Coal, Iron, & Railroad Company and lesser operators. A pliant Bourbon governor used state militia freely against the new union and substantial numbers of Negro strikebreakers weakened and defeated the white and Negro union miners.[44] Davis visited Alabama, the "so-called Eldorado of the South," in December 1897 and January 1898, and saw little to please him. He found much sentiment for the UMW among the miners but also formidable obstacles to successful organization. "Everything is cheap here but a living," he reported. "Labor is cheap, human life is cheap, but the necessities of life are out of sight, and yet it seems that many of these people are perfectly contented." The reasons were many. The failure of earlier local unions made many miners suspicious of the UMW. Convict labor in competing coal mines nearby weakened the bargaining position of free miners. Widespread illiteracy also added difficulties. Fear among the miners was ever present. Even men Davis had known in Ohio, who now worked in Alabama and retained strong union feeling, remained silent. "All of them are in close touch with us," Davis found. "Of course they can not express themselves here as if they were in the North. Oh, no, to do this would be to discriminate against themselves, and in consequence they do not say very much."

The "race question"—many aspects of it—most hindered Davis. Although he found "a number of good men both white and colored," relations between whites and Negroes caused him to despair. "The one great drawback is the division between white and colored. I do not mean to say all are this way, but a very large number are." The reasons for such division were not simple, and their complexity did not escape him. He focused particular attention on three causes of racial mistrust and conflict. The fact that most Negroes worked as "laborers" for white miners (and some more fortunate Negroes) but not directly for an operator gave Davis a clue to the slow progress of Southern labor organization. A variant of the traditional English subcontract system, this relationship had racial overtones, dividing Negroes from whites as well as "laborers" from "miners." Davis explained it:

> I have often heard the question asked, why is it that the miners of the South will not organize? To me the reasons are plain, and the answer is simply this: For the colored men there has [*sic*] been no inducements, and for the white to organize and be honest he would simply be giving away a good thing. Understand I am now speaking of the past. In the first place, the white miners, when they went into the Southern coal fields, saw an opportunity to make money by hiring colored men to work for them; these people being ignorant of course allowed themselves to become the servant of a servant, working for from 75 cents to $1 per day, and doing all the work thereby making for his servant employer fairly good wages, while he himself only earned a pittance. This custom continued to grow until today not only the whites do this, but the colored gentlemen have adopted the system and they feel proud to stand up and tell you they made say $15 or $25 this week. But ask him, if you please, did he earn it himself, and he will answer, oh, no, I have so and so many laborers. Right here let me say that he honestly does not, for a moment, realize that he has robbed the other poor devil.

Davis found this system at all the Alabama mining camps with one exception, and there the men got rid of it "only . . . recently by giving the company 2½ cents [a ton?] to do it."

Opposition to the UMW by certain Birmingham Negroes also impeded Davis' work. A Negro minister, W. M. Storrs ("one of the most intelligent young colored men we have in the South"), publicly encouraged Davis' organizing efforts, but Davis and the UMW were bitterly condemned by the *Southern Sentinel*, a Birmingham Negro newspaper, which urged Negro miners to form their own separate labor union. Davis pleaded with the *Sentinel's* editor:

. . . . If you continue to follow along the lines that you are now following, then your headlines should be changed to read as follows: "Devoted to the interests of the coal and iron monopolies of the south," for you could not possibly serve them better than you are now doing. You say that you believe in "The Unity of Man," and yet you teach disintegration. I cannot understand your philosophy. Of workingmen in this country we have two races—the white and the black. Of the two the negro constitutes a very small minority. Now I want to know how he can separate himself from the white laborer and live? I am sure that you have intelligence enough to know that an employer of labor cares not what the color of a man's skin may be; he will employ the fellow who will work the cheaper.

The United Mine Workers of America seeks to better the condition of the miners, be they white or black; we seek to place all men on a common level. For heaven's sake, don't seek to further oppress the miner, but rather seek to help him elevate himself. Do this and you will be doing right.

The *Sentinel* printed Davis' criticisms but curtly dismissed them and their author. David found in this newspaper another example of "what we have to contend with down here." Not all opposition to interracial trade unionism came from Southern whites.

Yet it was the "color line" in Alabama—the tradition of deeply felt racial prejudice against Negroes together with the hardening of legally enforced separation—that cast an even grimmer shadow over Davis and other advocates of biracial unionism in the South of the 1890s. Exceptions to the "rule" encouraged Davis but also proved the "rule," and he explained:

In matters of this kind I think it best to be truthful. I found in the South that while white and colored miners worked in the same mines, and maybe in adjoining rooms, they will not ride even on a work-train with their dirty mining clothes on together, nor will they meet in a miners' meeting together in a hall without the whites going to one side of the hall, while the colored occupy the other side. You may even go to the post office at Pratt City, and the white man and the colored man can not get his [*sic*] mail from the same window. Oh, no, the line is drawn; the whites go to the right and the colored to the left.

Now I do not say this is encouraged by all of the whites, for I met quite a number who made it their special business to point out these things to me, and at the same time express their disgust at such a state of affairs, yet they could not help it, though the practice might be ever so distasteful.

Davis hoped for a breakthrough among the Alabama miners and predicted that "in a short while we will get the ball rolling good and strong." But the obstacles to such an advance were too real to be ignored. He ended his January 1, 1898 Birmingham letter sadly convinced of need for dramatic changes in Alabama. "As our people [the Negroes] are celebrating the emancipation proclamation, we will stop now and go out to listen awhile. But we need another proclamation of equal importance, and that one is to emancipate the wage slaves, both white and black."[45]

Davis had frequent difficulties and disappointments as an organizer, and coupled with his frustrations in finding employment, these made his life a troubled one. But the sum of these experiences added up to a deeper commitment to the UMW and to his belief in the redemptive role of biracial industrial unionism. At all times the union commanded his support. Suggestions poured forth to strengthen it. The use of East European immigrant strikebreakers in Virginia convinced him that "a Hungarian organizer . . . be sent there as soon as possible."[46],* Factionalism he called

---

* Davis took pleasure in 1892 in his successes among East European miners. That year he and another organizer went among these recent immigrants, and he reported of one meeting: "Another feature of the meeting was the large number of foreigners present and

"suicide."[48] Letter after letter urged readers to gather a large defense fund and to "attend your local meetings [and] pay your dues."[49] A visit to a mining camp meant an opportunity to canvass for new subscribers to the weekly *Journal.*[50] He found holidays and national crises the occasion to prod the inactive. The Spanish-American War, for example, caused Davis to exclaim: "We are all talking of going over to free Cuba. I would like to see poor Cuba freed, but would like better to free myself, the same with every other American coal miner. Boys, get a move on yourselves, for if you don't the day may soon come when it will be almost too late."[51]

VI

Organizing nonunion miners, particularly Negroes, consumed much of Richard Davis' time in the 1890s, but there was more to his work than just that. If Negroes had often to learn the gospel of trade unionism and labor reform from

what I mean by that is the Polanders, Hungarians, Bohemians, Slavs, etc. One thing that I would like to say about these people is that they were very attentive to the business of the meeting and especially when one of their own number was speaking. I will just here make this plainer. The checkweighman at this mine is a Polander, but can speak the English language quite fluently. After Vice President Miller and myself got through speaking, this gentleman got up and interpreted it to the Polanders, Huns and Slavs in a very able manner. It was quite interesting to notice how they would flock around him while he was talking. . . . Although the meeting was an out-door one, one could almost hear a pin fall while he was talking. After he was through a motion was made that they would join in a body; the vote was taken by the raising of the hands and the motion was unanimously carried, with loud cheers from the foreign-speaking element. At this juncture a secretary was elected from each nationality to take their names as members of the organization. . . . Of the officers chosen, among them were one Hungarian, one negro, one Polander, one Slav and one white, so you can readily see that these people mean business and have started about it in the right way. . . ."[47]

union partisans like Davis, so, too, white unionists and their leaders needed frequent prodding from self-conscious Negroes like Davis when they rejected the "religion of brotherhood" and displayed insensitivity, prejudice, or open hostility toward Negroes. In one sense, then, Davis simultaneously inhabited two worlds: the one shaped by his experiences as a coal miner and the other as a Negro. His life as a trade unionist and organizer exposed him to frequent frustration and even personal danger. But his life as a Negro exposed Davis' white fellow unionists to his recurrent anger over the "color line" and to his zeal for racial democracy within the United Mine Workers. In letter after letter Davis emphasized the need for full integration of Negro miners while the union was still young.

Davis was not a utopian optimist. Personal experience taught him that certain operators used Negro strikebreakers effectively, and thereby increased white hostility toward Negroes. His appeals to white miners therefore frequently emphasized their own "self-interest." And those who viewed Negroes negatively learned from Davis:

> . . . . In this country it must be agreed there are a goodly number of miners who belong to the negro race. These men are certainly following that avocation for the sole purpose of earning a livelihood. . . . In a great many instances the negro has been used as a means of accomplishing the ends desired by capital. . . . Have we been asleep all of this time, instead of educating ourselves upon the necessities of the times? Well, I don't think that all of us have been asleep; no, not by half. Some of us have learned to know that we are men and have certain rights that must be respected, and we are willing to fight for these rights, too.

Self-interest required that white and Negro miners "lay aside petty prejudices and get together, as men." Otherwise, strife and dissension would allow the operators to "wag away with the cream."[52]

Because so many Negroes worked as miners, Davis insistently called for the election of Negro union officers. His arguments varied, but he often remarked that nonunion Negroes found the absence of Negro leadership "proof" that unions benefitted "whites only." After learning that no Negroes had been nominated for national office, Davis exploded in December 1891:

> . . . . These things should not be left for the colored man to mention, but you white men should see that one colored man is elected. Some fellow might say that we can do without that; I wish to say that it is impossible, for take the negro out of our organization, and you have a vast army against you, one that is strong enough to be felt and feared. . . . Let us have one of them and put him to work. Give the poor negro a chance. Its [*sic*] high time this was being done. Remember the white people of this country in 1776 cried out no taxation without representation. I hear that cry today among negroes of this country, and I as a negro say take warning and heed the cry.[53]

Davis continued this appeal. Two years later he urged high office for competent Negro trade unionists. They deserved the prestige and status—as well as the income—that went with national union election:

> Will you admit that you need us in your unions? If so, why should we not hold offices, also? Are we not men? Have we not the same ambitions as you people have? Are we not in many instances as competent as you? Then why should we not hold office? Not office in name, but office in deed; something there is money in that we may cope with our white brothers as an equal.

Davis denied personal interest: "I am speaking in defense of a people who have been down long enough. The day has passed and gone that we, as a people, shall . . . be content with small things."[54] That his plea was answered affirmatively is known. Davis' election to national office and that of other Negroes to lesser offices are a matter of record.

Davis' concern for the place of the Negro worker in the trade union movement extended beyond the mining industry. The rapid growth of Eugene V. Debs's American Railway Union, the fact that like the UMW it was an industrial union, and its bitter controversy with the railroads during the 1894 "Pullman Boycott" made it attractive to UMW leaders, who vigorously supported it. Davis found the ARU "best for railway men in this country" and hoped it would "grow and prosper." But Debs's union, like the railroad brotherhoods, excluded Negroes from membership, and this Davis called a "sad mistake." In July 1894, during the Pullman crisis and after some railroads had used Negroes as strikebreakers, he urged ARU leaders to admit Negro members:

> Surely, gentlemen, you have sense enough to know that we were born here and intend to remain here. We are American citizens and should be treated as such. But what can you expect of the negro with this kind of treatment? Remember that he is as sensitive as any other nationality or race of people. We find that the Hungarian, Polander, Italian, Chinaman, and even the lazy, shiftless Indian can be a member, but an intelligent negro who was born in this country and who was helped to make the country what it is, is considered as naught, and is debarred.

> It is just such treatment as this that has caused the negro to take your places when you were striking. Now, if there is anything that I do despise it is a blackleg, but in places in this country that they will not allow the negro to work simply because of his black skin, then I say boldly that he is not a blackleg in taking your places. He is only doing his plain duty in taking chances with the world. We ask no one to give us anything. All we want is the chance to work and we assure you we want just as much wages as the whites. . . .[55]

A year afterward Davis again criticized the ARU. Condemning Debs's imprisonment, he nevertheless rejected UMW affiliation with the ARU. "I will never be a party to the agreement, nor will any other colored man who has a sense of respect or pride of his race, nor will he if I can bring any influence to bear upon him." "Just think of it . . ." Davis angrily concluded, "I, an American citizen by birth, and many of them are not yet dry from crossing the salt water pond, and yet they have the unlimited gall to say that an American citizen shall not take part in an American institution because of the color of his skin. . . . Away with such rottenness."[56,*]

Not a socialist, Davis was nevertheless radical by the standards of his time and believed deeply that the present and future welfare of Negroes depended on the strength and character of the "labor movement." In 1893 an article entitled "The Colored Race and Labor Organization" offered his most explicit statement on the "race problem." "What . . . should be done with the negro" troubled "the minds of a great number of the American people" so Davis decided to analyze the Negro "condition":

> . . . . It seems . . . plainly evident that he is a citizen of this country and should be treated as such. This, in my mind, is the only solution to the supposedly knotty problem. Less than thirty years ago he was given his freedom, and turned loose to the cold charities of the world without a dollar or an acre of land. Turned loose as he was, is there any nation of people who has made such rapid progress as the negro has made? Search all history and we find them not. During all these years in a said-to-be Christian and civilized country, notwithstanding

* Daniel Wallace, a white Ohio mine leader who favored affiliation with the ARU, answered Davis. He condemned mistreatment of Negroes and urged that the ARU alter its constitution and admit Negro workers. "This is my country," Wallace explained, "every man is my brother and to do good is my religion. . . . I was a member [of the Knights of Labor] when that grand old man Uriah S. Stevens was general master workman . . . and would still be a member if R. L. Davis was general master workman." Wallace condemned all forms of racial injustice, but urged Davis to favor closer ties with the ARU, "put aside nonsensical quarreling," and "stand by our unions."[57]

the rapid strides he has made, he has been looked down upon by both the church and party politics both of which should have been his best friends.

Since most nonrural Negroes labored as wage earners, Davis next considered the relationship between the Negro worker and the trade unions:

> Being poor and used to it, he had to obey the divine injunction, viz.: To earn his bread by the sweat of his brow. In so doing we find him a great competitor with American white labor. It is at this period that we find that the labor organizations, or rather some of them, did that which no other organization had done, the church not even excepted, [and] threw open their doors and admitted him as a full member with the same rights and privileges as his white brother. This, in our opinion, was the first or initiative step toward the equality of mankind, and we are sorry to say that until the present day the labor organizations are the only ones that recognize the negro as an equal and as a man.

He then confronted the suspicion of so many Negroes toward the predominantly white trade unions:

> . . . . It is also true that some of our people have not yet gained enough confidence in his [*sic*] white brother as to trust him very far. And yet, is this strange? When we notice the fact that in our midst we have some as bitter enemies as anywhere else. While we admit that our labor organizations are our best friends, it would be well to teach some of our white brothers that a man is a man no matter what the color of his skin may be. We have nothing but the best of words for labor organizations, and hope they may continue in the same line of actions, and we are confident that they will not only better the conditions of the working classes, but will also wipe out all class and race distinctions, and in the meantime the negro will be found as loyal to labor organizations as his white brother.

Davis looked ahead to those "better days for organized labor with the Negro in the ranks doing his share in the way of emancipating labor." "Confidence" between Negro and white workers was essential because "reform" could come only through "the medium of organized labor." Reform meant changes that would "solve the race problem, better the condition of the toiling millions, and also make our country what it should be, a government of the people, for the people, and by the people."[58]

VII

Richard Davis' election to the National Executive Board of the UMW in 1896 and 1897 was not an isolated example of Negro participation in that union's leadership. Although Davis won the highest position a Negro held in the UMW's early history (and, probably, in any national union before 1900), other Negro miners held elected local, state, and regional offices in the 1890s.* John Mitchell advised the Industrial Commission in 1899 that native Alabama white and Negro miners cooperated in the union. Mitchell admitted that ethnic tensions existed but explained:

> I will say there is no difference as far as our organization is concerned. They [the miners] recognize—as a matter of necessity they were forced to recognize—the identity of interest. I suppose among miners, the same as other white men in the South, there is [sic] the same class differences, but they have been forced down, so they must raise the colored man up or they go down, and they consequently have mixed together in their organization. There are cases where a colored man will be the officer of a local union—president of a local union.

A surprised commission investigator asked Mitchell: "With white members?" And Mitchell replied: "With white people

* Writing in 1909, William Scaife remembered that a Negro miner named Warner held national UMW office before the election of Davis in 1896. I have not uncovered further references to Warner. (*United Mine Workers' Journal*, Nov. 19, 1909.)

in the union."[59] It was the same in other bituminous districts. Negro William Riley served as Secretary-Treasurer of the Tennessee district in the early 1890s and in those years F. A. Bannister was Vice-President in West Virginia.[60] In the competitive fields stretching west from Pittsburgh, Davis was only one of a good number of Negroes in office. Although the exact number cannot be determined, it is clear that Negro leadership was not simply a case of Negro miners electing Negro officers. A Grape Creek, Illinois, Negro miner, S. C. Armstrong, found less than one fourth of his district's men Negroes, yet observed: "I think this one [district] very fair from the fact that our district vice-president, Henry Rector, is colored, and very deeply colored. . . . Not a local in the district is there but has colored local officers. As for myself, I have had more offices than I know what to do with." Armstrong served as elected check-weighman in his mine, but only three of the three hundred men there were Negroes.[61] In Mystic, Iowa, Negro miner O. H. Underwood boasted that "the chasm of prejudice has been bridged with the plank of common sense." "Visit the different locals with me if you will," Underwood insisted, "and [see] all the colored men presidents, secretaries, and members of the executive boards."[62] Milton Reed vigorously led the Kansas miners, and the *Journal* sadly and affectionately noted his premature death in 1901.[63] Two years earlier Thomas H. Rollins, born in Virginia in 1857 and a miner from the age of eleven, gained unanimous election as Vice-President of the new Saginaw, Michigan, district, and white Michigan miners boasted that Rollins had done much to dispel local racial mistrust.[64]

Such widespread Negro participation resulted partly from the union's efforts to counter employer use of Negro strike-breakers. Some Negro miners urged even more Negro organizers, especially in West Virginia, Tennessee, and Alabama. An Indiana Negro, A. H. Harris, pleaded: "In time of trouble, we can . . . get to see them much quicker. . . . If they would put a colored man in each field and let him preach this great organization . . . when trouble arose between any company and its men they would know better than to go." "By doing do," Harris believed, "we can save money, trouble and also lives."[65] The practical self-interest of white unionists, however, only partially explains the active role Negroes played in a predominantly white union. White unionists could have perhaps protected themselves by excluding Negroes entirely. Certain craft unions had adopted this policy by the 1890s. But two considerations, among others, worked against such a strategy. The fact that the United Mine Workers was an industrial union from its start made the notion of exclusion difficult to justify. In addition, early local and especially national leaders of the union deeply believed in the principle of human solidarity and in a kind of evangelical egalitarianism. This mixture of industrial unionism and reform ideology made it hard to exclude Negroes. Anti-Negro diatribes, common in the press and journals of the 1890s, were rare in UMW publications despite the difficulties in organizing Negro miners fresh from rural areas and despite the use of Negro strikebreakers.[66] The older ideology of evangelical reform trade unionism smothered smoldering racial antagonisms and the heat generated by job competition. A by-product, despite much racial friction and even violence, was the active participation of Negroes in union leadership. Difficulties and disagreements frequently arose between Negro and white miners, but Negro activists displayed a deep, fierce union loyalty. The same union, well in advance of other unions, also gave particular attention to the "new" Catholic immigrants and even printed part of its weekly newspaper in Polish. But the Negro miners concern us, and it is sufficient to note only that UMW attitudes toward Negroes probably reflected still deeper attitudes toward the varied ethnic groups that made up the mining population.

The particular importance of the UMW position toward Negroes must also be measured against national developments in the 1890s. C. Vann Woodward and other historians of the "new South" have made clear that the 1890s witnessed the rapid and widespread deterioration of the Negro's political, economic, and social status. Segregation and disfranchisement became more rigid in those years. Violence against Southern Negroes increased, and Northern interest in the Negro condition all but vanished. Few were the whites who felt a deep concern for the increasing plight of black Americans after the Populist debacle.[67] In this setting, the firm (although at times inconsistent) adherence of the UMW to interracial unionism assumes its proper historical significance. Not all white unionists drifted with their "times." Instead, the *United Mine Workers' Journal* saw a close relationship between the deteriorating status of Southern Negroes in the 1890s and the unwillingness of many Negroes to identify with organized labor. In May 1892, for example, the *Journal* pointed to the "unmistakeable pathos pervading the letters of our colored friends" and blamed it, in part, on their condition in the South. Edited by Irish immigrant Martin Kane in its first years, the *Journal* avowed "a feeling of shame and disgust at the frequency" with which Negroes "as a class are outraged and wronged by the barbarous deeds perpetrated on their compatriots by the myrmidons and minions of that fiendishly blind autocrat, Judge Lynch," and found in the growing violence practiced against Negroes sufficient reason for "the tardy and restive progression" of the Negro "to the advances of his pale-faced friends." But it urged Negroes to put aside their distrust of white unionists:

> Point out to us the true member of our United Mine Workers' organization and we will vouch for it that he is a detestor of the things we complain of. We can safely go further and say that the influence of the members of organized labor with those whom they come in daily contact is such that even they are not to be found in the rabble who cling to the coat tails of the remorseless judge. This in itself should indicate to our colored friends where their interest lies.

Labor unions favored the suppression of "monstrous outrages" against Negroes and wanted Negroes to share in "all the things which go to make up a higher civilization." For these reasons, the *Journal* welcomed Negroes into the UMW: "Try it, remain with it, and we have no misgivings as to your decision."[68]

If a significant test of the depth and sincerity of a belief is its relationship to behavior, the UMW's early national officers scored well in this regard. They did more than offer criticism of distant outrages and admonish Negroes to support organized labor. Two incidents involving Richard Davis revealed much about their conception of union power and their attitudes toward race prejudice and discriminatory practices. In June 1892, Davis visited the West Virginia mining fields on an organizing trip and, as seen, encountered much difficulty because of his color so that only the intervention of two sympathetic whites allowed him to manage the trip. The *Journal* noted the "many inconveniences" Davis suffered "on account of his sable complexion" and reminded its white readers: "It doesn't take a very great wrench of the imagination to picture him winding the hills of the Little Mountain state and wondering whether or not he will have to lie in a ditch when he arrives at his destination." Commending those whites who aided Davis, the *Journal* also applauded the Ohio Negro for "compelling some of the insularly inclined hotel proprietors to take the barriers down, if it is only for once."[69]

Three years later, a few months before Davis won election to the National Executive Board, an incident occurred that demonstrated even more convincingly the hostility of white UMW officers to racial discrimination. Davis arranged a miners' mass meeting in Corning in Perry County, Ohio, and on August 22, 1895, national and state officers came to address it. President Philip Penna and Secretary-Treasurer W. C. Pearce, both from England originally and active in Indiana and Ohio union affairs before taking national office, arrived on the forenoon train. So did Michael Ratchford, a Clare County Irishman, then an Ohio union leader and soon to be national President. Other Ohio officials, coworkers with Davis and all of them white, came, too, and Davis met the group at the Corning train depot. They went to the town hotel for dinner. Davis registered at the hotel but quickly learned from a clerk that Negroes could not eat there because certain West Virginia patrons "would get insulted." By that time, Penna, Pearce, Ratchford, and the others had taken their seats and awaited their host. The clerk explained his absence to them. What followed is of great interest. "It was then," wrote D. H. Sullivan, a white Rendville miner, "that our officers showed the true union principle that should characterize all true members of our craft, for they refused to eat dinner and went elsewhere." The incident did not end with this gesture. After consulting a lawyer, Davis entered suit against the Corning hotelkeeper. More than six months later the case came to trial and Penna, Pearce, and Ratchford, together with a few other Ohio white union leaders, testified in Davis' behalf.[70] The results of this litigation remain unknown, but the entire set of circumstances, particularly the involvement of the national leaders, offers telling evidence for the loyalty Davis and other Negroes felt toward their union and for the UMW's successes (despite so many obstacles) in gaining early significant support from Negro miners.

VIII

Other Negro miners joined Davis in filling the *Journal* with letters that explored and exposed their condition and pleaded with Negro and white miners for biracial cooperation. One of them, William Camack, worked in Jellico, Tennessee. Camack was not without humor and asked of those who emphasized racial differences: "I would like for some one to tell me the difference between a negro who has seven-eighths of white blood in him and a white man with one-eighth of negro blood?" Six years before Negroes in large numbers left Jellico for the Illinois coal fields as strikebreakers, Camack explained the difficulties his people faced and fixed the main cause on slavery. "When Uncle Sam was a very small boy and did not know as much as he does at present," Camack wrote in 1892, "he allowed the 'negro' to be brought into his domain, not as the other nationalities came, free, but in shackles." Enslaved because they "happened to resemble Ham a little more . . . than Japeth," Negro labor "built up an aristocracy" in the South. Although in error, Camack's explanation of emancipation was unusual for its time and not without interest to later readers. His argument hinted at a deep sense of betrayal by the party of Lincoln and drained the Civil War of any moral meaning:

. . . . The North had its manufacturing establishments and the South grew cotton. The Southern planter controlled the labor of the black man and the planter could charge whatever price he pleased for his product, and, as the Northern manufacturer was at the mercy of the South, he became mad and jealous and said to himself, "If these black men were free we could control their product and these Southern gentlemen would have to come down a notch." And so the North became very philanthropic and set to work and secured the colored man a nominal freedom.

What followed emancipation did not please Camack either:

So after centuries of primeval existence and years of chattel slavery, we find him turned loose in 1865 without a dollar; ignorant, credulous, yet full of gratitude, and easy prey to the cupidity and avarice of a far worse set of Shylocks than the ones the Nazarene carpenter drove out of the temple of Jerusalem.

Like so many other nineteenth-century American workers, Camack reflected on the past mainly to draw lessons for the present. His conclusion was quite simple: white miners had to understand that "there is no color line but simply the slave line." Drawing from personal experiences, he went on:

I have known men and women of other nationalities who were nearly as black, a great deal more ignorant, and four-fold more degraded than the very meanest "nigger" I ever saw[,] and they were received by some of the kickers against the black with open arms as their social equals. "Oh, consistency, thou art a jewel."

Camack meant to convince white miners "who do not like to sit down in the same [local] assembly as the colored" that slavery, not race, explained the Negro condition. Reminding hesitant white readers of the constitution of the multiracial Knights of Labor, he advised them: "The man who can't stand that kind of doctrine, let him jest get up and git."[71]

Negro union miners did not blame racial friction and union weakness entirely on their white brothers; they found difficulty with nonunion Negroes as well. The frustrations they often encountered in convincing fellow Negroes of the union cause deeply angered them. Soon after Davis faced attack from Rendville Negroes for fiercely condemning their support of employer-sponsored "colored mines" in 1892, the *Journal* published over several issues a lively and revealing exchange among Negro miners on this and other questions. Its tone was sharp and explicit, at times perhaps embarrassing, never defensive, and always deeply committed to biracial trade unionism. An Indiana Negro miner took time out to commend the *Journal* for opening its columns to such a discussion by "colored correspondents." He called that action "a step in advance of any white journal, except those who [*sic*] have done so for selfish gain, and even then it has been only the leaders of the race."[72]

Like Davis' letters, these were the writings of self-educated nineteenth-century workers. Such men were given to flashes of deep insight but not to subtle distinctions or carefully logical and analytic arguments. Their language was often grammatically imperfect: tenses were confused, punctuation misused, and colloquialisms abounded. An argument most often took the form of a series of explicit and blunt statements. Even though the emphasis was this-worldly, evangelical Protestantism reinforced this style and provided a common and deeply felt set of images, analogies, and metaphors. In all of this, the Negro miner sounded no different from the white worker. A well-rounded education, after all, was not a prerequisite for laboring in a nineteenth-century American coal mine. Miners and other workers used the language at hand, and the Bible together with popular political clichés served them well. For the Negro an additional influence shaped his perception—the imponderable and still unexplained effects of slavery. How that experience or the Negro miners' memories of it particularly shaped their views of industrial America cannot be answered on the basis of the evidence examined in these pages. Their letters and other writings nevertheless offer clues to this significant relationship and to an understanding of them as workers and as Negroes groping with their condition, that of their fellow men, and that of a society filled with inequities and in the midst of profound economic and social transformation.

Davis' Negro critics got their sharpest rebuke from William Riley, who opened the 1892 exchange. A minister and a coal miner, Riley had been elected Secretary-Treasurer of Tennessee District 19 earlier that year and had won the votes of all whites and all but a few Negro miners there. A Negro, Riley nevertheless minced no words in attacking Davis' Negro adversaries:

> Did you not know that the worst enemies we have to contend with are among our own race? Did you not know that they will seek more undue advantage over you than anyone else? What? A nigger! He is the worst animal living against his race, and when I say nigger I mean nigger and not colored people.

Riley made much of this distinction and urged Davis to "press forward," make all the "colored and white friends" he could, and not "worry over the niggers and dogs."[73] Another time Riley again complained that "the negro is the worse [*sic*] enemy to one another that [*sic*] they have on top of dirt," but he made clear that his words applied only to those opposing unions:

> Now, let me say to the colored people who are trying to be men second to no man, continue to battle on for the right, seek wisdom and be wise, act honest men and by so doing both white and colored men will love to respect you, and God Himself will bless you. . . . Yes, my people, wake up and ask yourselves these questions: How long am I to live in ignorance? How long am I to be a pullback to my race? How long am I to be a stumbling block for the cause of labor, justice and humanity? Say as the prodigal did: I will arise and join the labor unions and rally for its [*sic*] rights, defend its [*sic*] cause and be known among my own craftsmen as a man among men.[74]

Riley did not back away from his criticism of recalcitrant fellow Negro miners. Accused of being "wrathy at the negroes," he answered: "I do think I made a clean distinction in spelling out those two words. I never wrote any harm about the negro at all, for I have no fight to make against them[*sic*]. But I wrote and will continue to write against the niggers and dogs." His frustration and disappointment spilled out when he explained: "We have tried petting, coaxing and soft words with these curs for years, and we have gained nothing from them[,] only hard names." "My brother," Riley advised a friendly critic, "I live in the South, among these people and know whereof I speak. Of course, there are some good people in the South as there is [*sic*] elsewhere, and again there are some of the worst curs that ever lived."[75]

A Brazil, Indiana, Negro miner identified only as "Willing Hands" found Riley's judgments somewhat harsh and reminded him of the difficulties Southern Negro miners encountered. "I have never seen a white and colored man work together around the mine anywhere in the South as buddies unless it was by the company's order." And then "some hoodlum would be up in arms about social rights." Parts of

Indiana offered little more to Negroes; in Clay County, Willing Hands found "nothing but ignorance and petty-prejudice among them all, both white and colored." But he had only good words for the whites in his mining village:

. . . . Let me say there are not many colored people here but what are treated white by the whites. I am working with a white man of his own accord and have seen several others go buddies[;] also a few respectable families live in double houses together[,] and the closest neighbor I have is white; also where the colored people here merit good treatment from the whites they get it from most all, both men and women of all colors.

The same miner nevertheless expressed deep concern for the generally deteriorating condition of American Negroes and criticized the Knights of Labor and the American Federation of Labor for participating in the Chicago Columbian Exposition which had rejected Negro appeals that it recognize the achievements of their race. Such requests had been "buried so deep that Gabriel's trump" would not disturb them. The South agitated "Willing Hands" even more than the Columbian Exposition. The murder of certain People's Party leaders in Mississippi and Georgia and the electoral successes of the "Bourbon element" that year convinced him that the Bourbons had "about wiped out the negroes" in those states and he asked: "Is the white South civilized? and . . . would it not be wise to emigrate some Christian missionaries there in those fields of labor."[76]

Davis did not remain silent during this exchange but commended Riley and Willing Hands, urging them to go ahead because "our people will begin to think," and then added some observations of his own. He made less allusion to the Negro than the others, choosing instead the general condition of the "laboring classes" as his text. Workers needed "a few more students," for if they studied their "interests as workingmen more" they soon would be "in a better condition." Davis denied "any pretences [sic] of scholarship," but the contrasts between industrial realities, working-class life, and the American Dream tortured him and demanded comment:

> We claim we have a new country, a new age[,] and that
> we need new thoughts and a new method by which to
> bring about much needed reforms. Well, these things
> cannot be brought about unless the people awaken them-
> selves to the full sense of their duties. We cannot expect
> others to do that that we do not do ourselves.

Davis brought together two widely held and popular nineteenth-century American ideas—the theme that knowledge
was power and the notion of "self-help"— in defense of effective labor organization. The "monied kings" would never
"soften their hearts to give us better wages, better homes or
anything else unless we . . . demand and enforce the demands when made."

> Too many men run away with the idea that capital must
> rule, [but] for the life of me I cannot conceive why or
> how a man can be so ignorant . . . We are too indolent
> to try to better ourselves.

American workers had "the power of freemen" but permitted the "enslavement of themselves."

> We boast of this being the home of the brave and the
> land of the free, but can you not see the deception of the
> thing? Now, let us have the truth. Is this not the land of
> the rich and the home of the slave? Truth doesn't hurt
> anyone, and I ask is this not true?

Davis offered these words less than three years before Booker
T. Washington urged upon Negroes at the Atlanta Exposition
a path of improvement derived from eighteenth-century
individualist thought and devoid of a clear assessment of
the realities shaped by a maturing industrial society. Like
Washington, Davis took the American Dream seriously but
saw its fulfillment only through "thorough and compact
organization." Unwilling to accept the permanence of racial
conflict and ethnic division, Davis urged miners to "cast
aside petty prejudices and work together as men." The mean

mixture of race and class that depressed the condition of most Negroes and weakened trade union effectiveness could be overcome only in a collective fashion. "Let us learn," Davis concluded in language alien to Washington and his numerous admirers, "that an injury to one is the concern of all. Until we do learn this, we can hope for no better."[77]

Except for Davis' frequent letters, the flow of correspondence from Negro miners to the *Journal* slowed up after 1892 and did not pick up again until 1898 and 1899, when the use of Negro strikebreakers in Illinois and the ensuing racial violence caused much comment. An exception to this pattern was W. E. Clark, who lived in Davis' town, Rendville, and penned three unusually interesting letters in 1893–94 that told a good bit about the disquiet of certain Negroes concerning their status. Clark first eloquently condemned racial prejudice and advised white miners:

> . . . . Prejudice on account of color is not a natural sentiment. There is a natural prejudice among the civilized nations to certain conditions in life incident to a state of barbarism; there is a natural prejudice to those who are given to immorality . . . but there is not a natural prejudice to a man simply because he is black, brown or yellow. The influence of a man's complexion is not greater than that of his moral and intellectual culture.

Very much of the nineteenth century, Clark insisted that "virtue is the highest influence that move the heart of man, and though it may be clothed in ebony or Parian marble it will command honor, love, obedience and respect in every quarter of the civilized world." But Clark was not an innocent Victorian optimist. Although he believed that prejudice against an individual could be effaced easily, the "removal of prejudice attached to the entire race, incident to a state of slavery," was "a labor of centuries and centuries." However, he unqualifiedly rejected all Negro efforts to form their own voluntary associations:

> There should be no desire to keep up race distinction in this country or in the organization of labor when all

have a common interest in it. No benefit can come to the Afro-American by withholding himself apart from the white people, [and forming] a distinctive negro community, a distinctive negro civilization, distinctive negro organization and social orders. . . . These are not only not desirable, but indeed are reprehensible, for they create class distinction and foster the race prejudices of which we desire to free ourselves.

Immigrants quickly shed their ethnic identity on coming to America and Negroes were advised to follow their examples. Except for "the one black spot on its escutcheon, which has impressed itself upon the heart of the negro, as a hot branding iron," Clark argued, "the Anglo-Saxon civilization . . . by its grandeur and majesty, commands our highest admiration. We desire to live, act and move with such a civilization." Urging racial amalgamation, Clark reminded whites that Ruth had said to Naomi: "Thy people shall be my people, and thy God my God."[78]

Seven weeks later Clark turned his thoughts to the "labor question . . . the supreme question of the hour" and tried bolstering the despair of Negro readers. "We see it often," he admitted, "with horror and alarm, and men, women and even children grapple with it, amidst the progress and poverty of our crowded centers of civilization." The "love of money" was "sucking the very life blood of modern society, impairing its vitality, destroying its better, nobler instincts." But those who despaired were advised to view the condition of the workers, particularly Negro workers, in the light of evolutionary theory. Whites, too, once had been slaves, "helpless slaves," and Clark quoted Tacitus as his authority. The Negro now was adjusting to the status of free labor:

Methinks, I see the negro rising like the white laborer out of the depths in which slavery left him. . . . If we have been slaves, they have been slaves; if we have been beaten, they have been beaten, if we have at times been cruelly murdered, they have also [been] without judge and jury. They have risen; we are rising.

Pessimists were advised of the sacrifices made by Wat Tyler, Robert Emmett, Toussaint L'Ouverture, and John Brown. Clark saw better times ahead. As the Negro improved his social status and found industrial employment, he would soon learn "the value of co-operation and . . . make it a practical part of his varied life."[79]

When Clark wrote again after a silence of nearly eight months, his tone was quite different. "I have been asleep so long," he started. The year 1894 was a bad year for the nation, and Rendville was not different. A nationwide depression cut deeply through the entire society. "Dissatisfaction seems to be the ruling power here now," Clark reported. Personal failure to prevent labor agents for the Northern Pacific Coal Company in the State of Washington from hiring away Rendville Negroes angered him. Only the talk of a new political party by certain national union officials buoyed Clark's spirit. The optimism of his earlier letters was gone:

> My mind has wandered from world to world. My first wonder was, I wonder if the other worlds were inhabited? Did they have the same kind of law and government that we have? and my next wonder was, was this world of ours the hell we read about in the good book? If it is not, how can a man stand the punishment twice, and then live through eternity? They burn men alive, skin them, lynch them, shoot them and torture them. . . .

These outrages convinced Clark that Negroes did not owe existing political parties "a debt of gratitude." But he saw no clear alternative. He urged Negroes to join a new multi-racial party if it "pledged itself to them or adopted a plank in the platform for the protection of its citizens" and would see they were "not discriminated against." But in the same breath, Clark, who some months earlier had favored racial amalgamation and attacked Negro voluntary associations, now wanted "the black man of America [to] form a party of his own." "If you do that," he admonished Negro readers, "you will be recognized as citizens, as it has been said [that] in a body we can elect or defeat."[80] Clark's confusion and own despair were not without cause. The South (not to speak of the United Mine Workers) was in profound crisis in those years, and the Negro fell victim in the cruel defeat of Southern Populism and the vindication of Bourbon power.

Of Negro miners like Clark little is known. But during a bitter West Virginia strike, nine years after he penned these letters, three Negroes, one of them named William Clark and probably the same man, were shot to death while sleeping by local police officials. Chris Evans, a union stalwart as far back as the 1870s, the leader of the great Hocking Valley 1884–85 strike, and for some time Secretary of the American Federation of Labor, investigated the shootings and found "this slaughtering of miners, simply because they are forced to struggle for a just cause . . . a sad commentary on our boasted Republic."[81]

IX

In its early years the United Mine Workers faced serious obstacles in building a multiracial industrial union. Its early leaders, mostly British and Irish immigrants and native whites, had rich trade union experience and high expectations but limited financial resources and a powerful opposition. Not the least of their difficulties was the hostility of most coal operators, particularly large corporate firms such as the Philadelphia & Reading Coal Company, to effective national unions. The diverse ethnic composition of the mining population added other troubles. By 1890 its traditional native white and North European composition had already started to change radically. In Pennsylvania, where most Eastern and Southern European immigrant miners worked, 58,000 of 235,000 coal diggers were of Slavic and Italian origin. Alabama miners counted 2787 native whites, 1492 immigrants, and 3687 Negroes, while the West Virginia coal mines employed 6314 native whites, 1375 immigrants, and

2016 Negroes. These ethnic groups in the coal fields have been inadequately studied, but profound historical imagination is not essential to grasp the difficulties of building a permanent labor organization composed of so heterogeneous and changing a population.

For Negro and white miners to work together was made harder by several additional considerations. Widespread belief in Negro racial inferiority, itself the continuing influence of the historic master-slave relationship, together with the rapid general deterioration of the Negro's social and political status in the 1890s, explained some of the obstacles faced by white and Negro trade unionists. The Southern rural background of most Negroes laboring in late nineteenth-century industry and mining complicated the difficulty. Education was limited for Negroes in the rural South, and deference and dependence more normal in a rural than an urban environment. Although little is known of the early Negro miners, it is possible that their aspirations differed from those of native white miners. They may have viewed their status as workers as a temporary one. In parts of West Virginia, for example, North Carolina, and Virginia Negro farmers worked as miners only in the winter months to accrue income to pay farm mortgages.[82] To such workers, unions often seemed unnecessary. Viewing their industrial work as a means to another way of life, they must have thought the danger of union affiliation unnecessarily risky.* Finally, Negroes, although often ignorant of their mission at its start, were used as strikebreakers on numerous occasions.

Only a romantic or tendentious interpretation of American labor history dares ignore the friction between competing ethnic groups; so much of working-class history between 1890 and 1920 was shaped by that factor. Part of this

---

* This also was true of certain white miners. For the years 1886–93, the Industrial Commission blamed the absence of trade unionism among southern Illinois coal miners, mostly native whites, on the fact that they were "farm laborers who had turned to the mines as a source of ready cash."

97

conflict was inherent in the changing composition of the labor force, but opposition to trade unions often led coal operators to exploit ethnic differences in order to weaken potential trade union solidarity. No ethnic group, including native whites, was free from this role, although recent immigrants and Negroes seem to have served such a purpose more regularly. In 1892, for example, two carloads of Negroes were imported to northern West Virginia from the Carolinas and Virginia. When they proved unsatisfactory a year or two later, employers brought in Italian and Polish workers from Northeastern cities. In 1895 Virginia Governor Charles T. O'Ferrall sent militia to protect four hundred Italians who were replacing striking native miners.[83] But the Negro concerns us in these pages, and his use as a strikebreaker merits attention in assessing the early role of Negroes in the United Mine Workers.

Negroes had been used as strikebreakers in the bituminous fields before the 1890s. In the 1870s Southern Negroes protected by white armed guards came for this purpose to bituminous mining villages in Indiana, Ohio, and Illinois. Not all Negroes arrived as strikebreakers, but their entry in this fashion drew widespread attention to them. The dramatic events surrounding their coming have been recorded for the Ohio Hocking Valley in 1874 and 1875 and for Braidwood, Illinois, in 1877.[84] But little else is known of these early years. In 1880, imported Negroes apparently broke a nine-month strike in the Ohio Tuscarawas Valley, and that year fifty Negroes went to Pittsburgh mines, too.[85] Employer use of Negroes increased in the 1890s as the United Mine Workers gained strength in the bituminous fields. The Henry Clay Frick Coal & Coke Company first imported Negroes as early as 1892 and then again in 1895.[86] In the Southwestern coal district (Arkansas, Kansas, and Oklahoma) Negroes came before 1890 but after the union's early successes arrived in larger numbers. In 1896–97 during a Kansas strike recruiting agents distributed a typical handbill among Birmingham, Alabama, Negroes:

WANTED! COLORED coal-miners for Weir City, Kan., district, the paradise for colored people. Ninety-seven cents per ton, September 1 to March 1; 87½ cents per ton March 1 to September 1, for screened coal over seven-eighths opening. Special train will leave Birmingham the 13th. Transportation advanced. Get ready and go to the land of promise.[87]

The Missouri Pacific Railroad carried 175 Southern Negroes to the struck Kansas mines. As they were unloaded near a stockade white strikers convinced 125 of them not to enter the mines. Some joined the strikers, but most wanted to return to Alabama, and the union paid their way. A federal injunction against the union weakened its further efforts and made it easier to bring in Negroes.[88] In the same years numbers of Southern Negroes went under contract to the Colorado Fuel & Iron Company, too.[89]

But it was in Illinois in 1898 and 1899 that the confrontation with employers using Negroes to weaken the UMW was most severe, and Victor Hicken has told part of that story well.[90] Illinois miners took part in the UMW general bituminous strike that started on July 4, 1897, and as a result the Illinois operators agreed to negotiate with the district union. A joint conference in Chicago in January 1898 led to significant improvements in miners' wages, hours, and working conditions. Wages fixed at forty cents a ton meant an increase of almost fifteen cents a day for ordinary pit workers. Later that year, however, the operators along the Chicago & Alton Railroad south of Springfield protested the wage increase. The Chicago-Virden Company, the state's largest coal company with mines that returned 348 thousand tons a year, headed the group. Their complaint was submitted to the National Executive Board of the United Mine Workers, as provided in the earlier agreement. According to it, the signers promised to accept the Board's decision. But the Board rejected the operators' complaints, and four companies, Hicken finds, "set about to operate their mines with nonunion labor."

Trouble broke out first in Pana. Early efforts to bring in

nonunion whites failed, and, after threatening to import Chinese laborers from the Far West, the Pana operators turned south and sent agents to recruit among Alabama Negro miners. Opposition from the Birmingham branch of the Afro-American Labor and Protective Association did not hinder the agents. Two Birmingham Negro miners testified of their experiences:

> Benj. Lynch and Jack Anderson being duly sworn, upon their oath say they are residents of Birmingham, Ala., resided at Birmingham for 11 years; occupation coal miners; say that on Monday, Aug. 22, 1898, they were approached by two white men and one colored man who represented that they were from Pana, Ill.; that most of the miners had gone to the [Spanish-American] war for two years; that there was a new mine opening there and a great demand for labor, and they wanted 150 men; and there was no trouble there; said about eight or nine months ago there had been a little trouble but that all was settled; affiants said they were working . . . but on being told that they could make from $3 to $5 per day were induced to give up their jobs and go to Pana.

The Pana miners protested the coming of nonunion workers and sent men to meet a trainload of Negroes in Centralia. Some Negroes left but most stayed on the train and headed for Pana—protected by special white police. White Pana businessmen and merchants protested against the Negroes to Republican Governor John R. Tanner, and local Republican and Democratic politicians condemned the operators. But the Alabama Negroes were brought in and housed in a stockade.* A few weeks later violence and even shooting broke

---

* According to *The Public*, a Chicago reform weekly edited by Louis Post, the Negroes first learned of the strike on arriving in Pana. They "complained that they had been deceived by the operators, and most of them refused to go to work," *The Public* reported. But, the same source added, deputies at the mines "are charged with threatening to shoot negroes who attempted to leave." (Quoted in Ray Ginger, "Were Negroes Strikebreakers?," *Negro History Bulletin*, Jan. 1952, 73–74.)

out when angry miners attacked two operators. By the end of September the Illinois national guard was patrolling Pana and had restored order.

Happenings in Virden were even more violent, and numerous deaths and injuries resulted. The Chicago-Virden Company hoped to execute its plan flawlessly. It first constructed a stockade around the mines, and then imported fifty armed white police, mostly ex-Chicago policemen and detectives from a private agency in St. Louis. The miners responded in kind. They set up patrols, some armed, along the railroad tracks into the city and in September prevented a trainload of Negroes from disembarking there. The engineer drove on to Springfield, where district UMW President J. M. Hunter convinced many Negro families to quit. Soon after, Negroes were persuaded to leave trains in other Illinois towns. The company then made a second major effort to bring Negroes to Virden. An appeal to the Governor for military protection failed, but the company went ahead and paid off a number of resident white miners. On October 13 a train filled with Southern Negroes and white guards approached the town. As it stopped near the stockade heavy gunfire broke out between the white guards and the miners. A St. Louis detective found it "hotter than San Juan Hill." The train pulled away without unloading, but the dead remained still on the battlefield. Five guards were wounded and four dead. About thirty miners lay wounded and seven gave their lives. Not a single Negro died, but some suffered wounds. The angered miners destroyed the company store; then the violence abated. No Negroes worked the Virden mines, but at a cost that cannot be measured. As in Pana, the national guard came and stayed in Virden. The Negroes, Hicken found, reached Springfield "in a pitiful condition— frightened, tired, and shamefully disillusioned." They were kept as virtual prisoners aboard the train. District union President Hunter sought to talk with them but was thrown from the train by white guards and badly injured. His second effort proved more successful, and some Negroes left the train. Most went later to St. Louis to find work, and still others returned to Birmingham. The Virden operators had suffered a severe setback, and even though a temporary injunction held back the Pana white miners from "preventing the mines from operating with Negroes" the Pana operators, too, failed in the end. By 1899 the Pana and Virden operators were employing their old hands at the fixed wage rate and under the old contract.

But the tragic violence accompanying the defeat of the Illinois operators strained relations between Negro and white union members. A good number had deserted the operators and all had suffered, but the fact that Negroes had been used and violence and death had resulted shook many white miners. Letters in the *Journal* condemned the Negroes and often slurred their race. Negro unionists also complained of what had happened but tried explaining to white miners the causes of Negro involvement in the Pana and Virden happenings and to both white and Negro miners the benefits of interracial union cooperation.

Three days before the outbreak of the bloody violence in Virden, Richard Davis penned his thoughts on the Illinois crisis. Davis was himself in difficulty. He was black-listed and without work for some time during 1898. "I am indeed sorry to see the state of affairs as it exists there," Davis wrote of the Illinois events, "and yet it teaches us that one lesson seemingly so hard to learn by a great many of us, viz., to organize." The hostility of white union men toward Negroes especially dismayed him:

> I do not mean to organize against the black man, as they are now doing, for that will do no good nor will there any good results accrue from it, and fight it as you may the result will be the same. I have watched it in the past and have never known it to fail. I would advise that we organize against corporate greed, organize against the fellow who, through trickery and corrupt legislation, seeks to live and grow fat from the sweat and blood of his fellow man. It is these human parasites that we should strive to exterminate, not by blood or bullets, but by the ballot, and try as you may it is the only way.

Those whites who attacked the Negro heard sharp words from Davis. "You can't do it by trying to exterminate the negro or 'big black buck niggers,' as they were referred to a few weeks ago through the columns of *The Journal*." His anger was unrelenting. "I assure anyone that I have more respect for a scab than I have for a person who refers to the negro in such a way, and God knows the scab I utterly despise." Davis, who had been in Birmingham in 1897 and seen firsthand the condition of Southern Negroes, attributed to their depressed and exploited status their willingness to serve employer objectives in Northern mines. So long as the South remained a source of cheap labor, just so long would Southern Negroes play that role:

> The negro North has no excuse, or very few excuses, for scabbing, but the negro South has lots of them, and while I give the North a great deal of credit, I fear that I made a mistake, for in many places even in the North, no matter how good a union man he may be, he can not get work [but] only as a blackleg. And in the South he can work almost anywhere provided he is willing to be the other fellow's dog, and I don't mean the employer alone, but the white laborer as well.

"The negro," Davis insisted, "like the mining machine, is here to stay, and you may as well make up your minds to treat them [sic] right." Where Negroes and whites worked together "you seldom or never hear of negroes being brought in . . . to break a strike." He drew only one conclusion: "I say treat the negro right and he will treat you right." But Davis was too strong a union partisan to dismiss the substantive complaints of the white Illinois miners and added, "I earnestly hope to see the miners of Illinois win their battle, for I suppose they are like miners elsewhere. Their pittance is already too small."[91]*

* The conclusions drawn by Davis should be contrasted with those of certain other contemporaries concerned with the relations between Negro and white workers. The Chicago *Public*, for example, found the Virden tragedy "not a race fight at all, but a labor fight." It insisted: "The fact is noticeable that trades unions,

Although Pana and Virden attracted national attention in 1898 and 1899, the neglected importation of Southern Negro miners to Carterville, Illinois, in the same years sheds additional light on the Negro miner and, in particular, on George Durden, a Negro leader of the Illinois miners. Paul Angle has written fully of the Carterville troubles in *Bloody Williamson*, and here we sketch only an outline to make sense of important letters written by Durden.[92] Financed largely by St. Louis and Cincinnati capital, in 1890 Sam T. Brush organized the St. Louis and Big Muddy Coal Company, located near Carterville in southern Illinois, and soon managed one of the midwest's great mines. In 1897, it produced more coal than any other single Illinois mine. Brush bitterly opposed the still young UMW, and, at first, fought it with skill. That year, he raised wages and successfully convinced his men not to join a statewide strike. In 1898, he rejected joint efforts made by the UMW and other operators to persuade him to accept the statewide wage scale. On April 1, 80 per cent of his men quit work, and six weeks later Brush replaced them with 178 Jellico and Coal Creek, Tennessee, Negro miners. Some loyal whites worked with the Negroes. Much bitterness followed Brush's first victory. A Negro later complained that Brush had "dumped unwelcome people in Illinois" to "rob honest men of all that is dear to human existence." After the Tennessee Negroes arrived Brush "deliberately entered the union miners' homes (white) and bundled their beddings, wives and children together and cast them out in the rain and mud."

---

instead of being controlled by race prejudice against negroes, harbor very little of that prejudice. The anti-negro spirit must be looked for higher up." And a Chicago Negro clergyman (who founded the Institutional Church and Social Settlement, a "Negro Hull House"), Reverdy C. Ramson, hoped that white workers would learn from Virden and Pana that "the degradation, by industrial and political serfdom, of the millions of black toilers of this land" menaced "their own industrial independence and prosperity, as well as their political liberty." (Quoted in Ray Ginger, "Were Negroes Strikebreakers?," *Negro History Bulletin*, Jan. 1952, 73–74.)

Brush's success made his the only large Illinois mining company unaffected by the UMW, but his triumph lasted for less than a year. In March 1899, Brush instituted an eight-hour day and raised wages above the UMW scale but rejected a request from some whites and Negroes that a UMW local be recognized. On May 15, a strike started: between 150 and 175 men quit (about half of his force; all the whites and some Tennessee Negroes). Brush decided to replace them with new Negroes. He sent a Negro minister to get more Tennessee Negroes and then hired forty Negroes let go by the Pana operators after they settled with the union. The Pana Negroes added fuel to the fire and especially angered the Negro and white Carterville strikers. When they arrived on June 30 in special Illinois Central Railroad cars, rifle shots wounded twenty and caused the death of the wife of a non-union Pana Negro miner. Brush's loyal hands retaliated that night. Near the Brush mines was Union City—some frame shacks built by the UMW to house evicted miners and mostly inhabited by Negro UMW supporters. Brush's men attacked the encampment and burned it to the ground. A few days later state militia arrived, to remain for nearly two and a half months. Brush brought in more Negroes and was once assaulted by two men, but the region quieted down and the soldiers left on September 11. Only six days passed before bitter violence again erupted and resulted in the death of six loyal Brush Negroes, who with others had marched armed into Carterville and confronted armed white miners. The militia returned to restore order. Two trials followed.

Negro UMW miner George Durden figured prominently in the first of these two trials. Durden, six other Negroes, and two whites were indicted for the June 30 murder of Anna Kerr, and twelve whites were indicted for the September shootings. Durden's group came to trial in early December 1899. Six weeks later the second trial started. Moved to a county nearby, the first trial attracted much attention, as two batteries of lawyers (including a former Missouri lieutenant governor who defended Durden and the union miners) tried to sway an all-white jury of farmers. A white miner, Thomas Jeremiah, and Durden were named as ring-leaders in the June 30 shooting, and the dead woman's husband accused Durden of firing the fatal shot. But the jury freed Durden and the others. The second trial also failed to convict the union miners. In 1906, Brush, who had kept his mines under heavy guard (even using a Gatling gun) in the intervening years, sold out to the Madison Coal Company, and then the UMW won recognition quickly. But it is Durden's letters written while in prison and soon after his acquittal that most interest us.

A testament to his abilities as a trade unionist and an incisive observer of contemporary events, Durden's prison letters exposed the fact that the Negro strikers were held incommunicado in the county jail and eloquently pleaded the cause of increased trade union power. ("The calloused handed miner is a conspicuous figure in the land of civilization. Living and sculptured monuments of heroes dead and gone have no parallel to the tribute paid the miner.") But it is a letter Durden wrote soon after leaving his jail cell that is most important. The union was engaged in a bitter debate over whether to accumulate a "National Defense Fund." Concerned over the increasing use of Southern Negroes to weaken the UMW in the Northern bituminous fields and with the Illinois experience still fresh in his mind, Durden argued for such funds to support striking union men and also to educate "disorganized, pauper, and other labor." He referred here mainly to Southern Negroes. "I am sorry to say that the greater part of this disorganized labor is the man of color." And he favored using funds to "send educators to these dangerous regions [the South] and instill into the hearts of these men the principles of our order." Durden then pleaded the particular case of the Southern Negro and appealed to his white brothers:

. . . . Ask your conscience why it is that this class of labor fails so absolutely to see their interest. This question answers itself when you take into consideration the life, past and present, of the 8,000,000 Afro-Americans.

In the year 1626 [*sic*] the negro was contented roaming the sunny jungles of Africa. There he was kidnapped and in chains and fetters he landed in America, and here he entered a life of shame and death. . . . The man of color had taken on this yoke of slavery and thus burdened he toiled 250 long years in serfdom educating the children of his master and having his own family in ignorance and want. The evident value of the negro can be seen from Virginia even to the Gulf of Mexico. The gigantic oak that once seemed to defy time has not a root left . . . where the wild animal once roamed at will is now the play grounds of the school children. Even statesmen today . . . owe their education to the labor of the sons of toil that was [*sic*] never paid. There were hundreds of thousands of these unfortunates who have been driven to their untimely grave with nothing left to mark their own existence, but a sacred mound of clay. Fathers and mothers have watched their first born sons and daughters sold and borne away from the mother's care, to meet again only on judgment day. The dark secret vaults have been filled with the blood-stained dollars derived from their labor, for which the toiler has never received or asked recompense.

With the tears from their eyes, they have watered the crops, and with the blood from their backs, they have enriched the soil. Thus the public can see and understand why he can toil so earnestly and for so small a sum uncomplainingly. Hence education, labor education, a union education, aided by and with Defense Funds will show my people the pathways of justice. Backed by the independence of the greatest order known to civilization . . . the Southern colored miner will cease to be a factor or a yoke upon the neck of organized labor. The public with our union must remember that the negro is yet a child to our civilization. . . . Educate him to your ways and note the results . . . the heart is as true as steel and his efforts are untiring.[93]

At a time when few Americans thought in such terms and probably as a result of his own experiences as a Negro and a trade unionist, Durden grasped the significant interplay between race and class that would shape so much of twentieth-century American social history.

The tension between Illinois Negro and white union miners did not end after Pana, Virden, and Carterville. That would have been expecting too much from both groups. In July 1899, Danville UMW Negro miners and mine laborers publicly demanded "the right of being employed in any capacity in or about the mines . . . which we are capable of filling without discrimination by either our white brothers or employers."[94] At the Illinois State Miners' Convention in 1900, similar questions arose. Springfield Negro miners complained that five local mines managed by good union men refused to employ Negroes. Cal Robinson, a Negro delegate from Spring Valley, demanded action from the convention and explained, "If you do what is right in this matter, gentlemen, you will have none of your Virden and Carterville riots, and no blood will be spilled. . . . We want to abolish all of those evils, and then we shall not have to get out our Gatling guns; we will have no fights along these lines, and we will have no riots. I hope you will help to abolish this thing here and now." G. W. Williams, a white Grape Creek miner and an Illinois union stalwart since the Civil War, joined Robinson in urging an end to discriminatory employment practices:

> I have been in the union since 1866, and am one of the oldest members. Back in those dark days there were times when black men could not and dared not meet with white men or even attempt to express themselves as being willing to meet. He [the Negro] would have been annihilated by the operators for daring to think of it. But in this progressive age I am astonished. . . . Gentlemen, the time for this is past. I do not expect to hear of such things from young and intelligent men. Those things belong to the time of your fathers, and I hope that you will see this evil is eradicated.

Others spoke, too, and then Durden rose for his turn.

Durden faced a difficult task, one that other Negro union officials had confronted on similar occasions. His sense of the plight and the need of the Negro was without question. Virden, Pana, and Carterville were still fresh in his mind and those of other Illinois miners. So, too, at least for the Negro miners and especially those committed to the union, was the gnawing reality of discriminatory practices against black miners. There may also have been the possibility that frontal attacks on the discrimination a few local unions practiced against Negroes (contrary to explicit national policy) would split the union. What particular ideas turned about in Durden's mind cannot be reconstructed, but he emphasized the benefits Negroes enjoyed as UMW members and not the isolated acts of discrimination they often suffered. His was a plea for a powerful and multiracial union:

.... We have made applications to organizations to help us time and again. You know how even the Masons and Odd Fellows have discriminated against us. There has been no organization that has come to our assistance with such outstretched arms as has the United Mine Workers of America. We are sensitive, it is true. There is a certain class of men in some localities who will not allow the black to work side by side with his white brothers. No such discrimination is made by the Constitution of our organization. There are many places in this State where no color is known when it comes to work. I have seen this organization reach out its arms for my race. They have given them homes and friends; they have helped them when they most needed help. This organization has extended to us more help than we received from any other organization in America. There are places in this State where colored men have been told that they could not stay at all, where when we were without friends, almost without clothes, where the moment we presented our union cards we were taken in and helped and given work. .... Let us have no break between the white and the black. Your constitution has not made any discrimination against anyone. The organization is strong; and we love it and we know that it is only individuals who make objection to our working, and we should not get sensitive over this and attack the union.[95]

Such was the loyalty that the UMW commanded from an Illinois Negro who had suffered in prison, lived still in the shadow of Virden and Pana, and nevertheless pushed aside what he detested in the interest of an organization that had proven itself to him.

X

The evidence gathered in these pages reveals much about the early history of the United Mine Workers of America and, in particular, about that union's attitudes toward Negro workers and the important role Negro miners like Richard L. Davis and George Durden played in its formative years. But the unfortunate absence of a detailed and comprehensive history of the UMW's early decades makes it perilous to claim too much beyond these facts.[96] And yet these are hard truths filled with considerable meaning. Any authoritative history of the UMW surely will tell of the endless and formidable difficulties and frustrations that accompanied early efforts to build this interracial industrial union. It will include grimly detailed pages about racial and ethnic quarrels and even death and violence. But it will also make much of the successful early confrontation between the UMW, its predominantly white leaders and members, and Negro workers. And it will explain why—in a decade that saw the general deterioration of the Negro's condition, North and South, and in which C. Vann Woodward argues "the Mississippi Plan" became "the American Way"—why enormous sacrifices by white and Negro miners made this union a reality.[97]

Even though the available statistics are meager and somewhat suspect, their symbolic value so far as the Negro's direct role and primary importance in building the UMW between 1890 and 1900 is crystal-clear. The essential fact is that about 20,000 Negroes belonged to the UMW in 1900.[98] In its first decade the UMW grew fitfully and mostly among bituminous miners. At its start it had almost 17,000 members and increased rapidly, but before the 1897 nationwide bituminous strike membership had fallen to less than 11,000. Rapid growth followed that strike. In 1900, just before it made its commanding advances among anthracite miners, 91,019 miners paid UMW dues, and John Mitchell embarrassingly chided Samuel Gompers, "We are seriously contemplating the absorption of the American Federation of Labor." Mitchell's amiable jest was not without meaning.[99] The UMW was far and away the largest AFL union in 1900. The Federation counted only 548,000 workers in all of its affiliated unions that year, so that no less than 16½ per cent of its members were miners. And Negroes made up an unusually large proportion of UMW membership.[100] Of its 91,019 members, the UMW included only 8893 anthracite miners and since few, if any, were Negroes, a measure of the Negro's consequence to the UMW should count only bituminous miners.[101] If 20,000 Negro bituminous miners belonged to the UMW in 1900, then 24 per cent of the union's bituminous members were Negroes. Mitchell and other union officials figured in 1899 that Negroes made up between 10 and 15 per cent of the mining population. Leaving aside again the anthracite miners, about 30 per cent of all bituminous miners were UMW members, but between 36 and 50 per cent of Negro bituminous miners belonged to the union. And not without additional interest is the fact that 3½ per cent of the AFL's members in 1900 were Negro coal miners. Further research undoubtedly will adjust these statistics but should not appreciably alter their meaning—a meaning that affects Negro history as well as labor history.

Despite formidable hindrances, particularly in Alabama and West Virginia, the UMW's efforts to organize and to hold Negro members did not end in 1900. Take Alabama as an example. Davis had been overwhelmed and depressed by the "color line" there in 1897 and 1898. But in 1899, 23 per cent of its miners belonged to the UMW, and by 1902 the union claimed 65 per cent of them, a majority being Negroes. In 1904 certain large operators repudiated the Alabama union and caused a strike that lasted two years—"the longest strike on record" to 1906. Court injunctions held back union officers but not union funds. Through its national treasury and its districts and locals, the UMW sent more than $1,000,000 to the Alabama strikers. The Illinois District (where Pana, Virden, and Carterville still remained living memories) alone gave $100,-000. The strike failed, but the UMW held on until 1908 when operators refused to renew expired contracts and also cut wages. A second and larger strike then started and lasted nearly two months. Eighteen thousand miners—all except the convict coal diggers—quit work. Violence and shootings were common; hundreds of union men, Negro and white, suffered. The UMW spent an additional $407,-500 to hold the men together but without success. The power of a hostile governor, himself a former lessee of convict labor who banned public meetings, a state militia that broke up interracial "tent villages" of evicted miners, and a committee of leading Alabama citizens that argued that "the people of Alabama" never would "tolerate the organization and striking of Negroes along with white men" finally ended the strike—and severely impaired the union. A year later the UMW counted 700, not 18,000, Alabama members, and effective trade unionism did not return there until the First World War and then only for a brief time. But that is another story.[102] What matters here is that despite the Alabama setback and the loss of so many Negro members, national UMW Negro membership probably did not decline precipitously between 1900 and 1910 and the union made a vigorous and costly effort to hold districts with large Negro membership.

What, finally, is the import of the successful participation by large numbers of Negroes in the early UMW so far as the general practices and attitudes of organized labor before 1910 are concerned?

Although the subject has been inadequately studied and much misunderstood, it appears that nothing about Negro workers more agitated and angered many white trade unionists between 1890 and 1910 than the frequent use of Negroes as strikebreakers and the "threat" of "Negro competition." The Pana and Virden violence, for example, "proved" to the *Locomotive Firemen's Magazine* (its union excluded Negroes) that "the entire social fabric of the Northern states may crumble before the invasion of hordes of cheap negro labor from the South."[103] In 1900, the year Richard Davis died, Samuel Gompers' annual report to the American Federation of Labor emphasized that unorganized Negroes would be "forced down in the economic scale and used against any effort made by us for our economic and social advancement." He warned that "race prejudice" would become more "bitter" to "the injury of all."[104] Confronted with complaints from Booker T. Washington and other Negro leaders that numerous affiliated unions formally or informally excluded Negroes from membership and therefore jobs, the AFL Executive Council in 1901 did not claim "perfection" for the labor movement but defended its efforts among Negro workers. It criticized Washington for his belief that "the economic, social, and moral progress and advancement of the negro is dependent upon the philanthropic and humane consideration of their [*sic*] employers" but most severely censured Negro strikebreaking as the main cause of "economic bitterness and antagonism between the races":

> The real difficulty in the matter is that the colored workers have allowed themselves to be used with too frequently telling effect by their employers as to injure the cause and interests of themselves as well as of white workers. They have too often allowed themselves to be regarded as "cheap men," and all realize that "cheap men" are not only an impediment to the attainment of the worker's just rights, and the progress of civilization, but will tie themselves to the slough of despond and despair. The antipathy that we know some union workers have against the colored man is not because of his color, but because of the fact that generally he is a "cheap man." It is the constant aim of our movement to relieve all workers, white and black, from such an unprofitable and unenviable condition.[105]

Four years later Gompers harped on the same theme but with a new twist. He argued that the labor movement sought no conflict with Negroes but warned: "If the colored man continues to lend himself to the work of tearing down what the white man has built up, a race hatred far worse than any ever known will result. Caucasian civilization will serve notice that its uplifting process is not to be interfered with in any way."[106] At that moment the UMW was pouring hundreds of thousands of dollars into Alabama to preserve its early advances among Negro and white miners.

Negro strikebreaking and the existence of much racial prejudice among white workers and their leaders were hard realities, but these conditions alone were insufficient causes for the exclusion of Negroes from many organized trades between 1890 and 1910—and even earlier in certain unions. The early history of the United Mine Workers belies such an explanation. It is impossible to measure racial prejudice among white coal miners seventy years ago, but few would deny its existence. "Negro competition" constituted a recurrent threat to the status of established white miners. Negro strikebreakers probably were used with greater frequency in the bituminous mining industry than in any other between 1890 and 1910. And yet (even though Negro strikebreaking surely intensified anti-Negro feeling among white miners in the short run and may even have displaced white unionists) an all-white or racially segregated union did not result. Overwhelmingly white and many of them self-educated British and Irish immigrants, the early UMW leaders, not without formidable difficulties, welcomed Negro members and drew them actively into the union. As a result, an unknown but significant number of Negroes held local and district offices, helped organize both white and Negro miners, diminished some of the racial prejudice and mistrust between Negro and white miners, and stabilized their union in a time of repeated crisis. Rank-and-file Negroes consequently were not to be spotted occasionally throughout the union but added greatly to its strength by their sheer numbers. And after only ten years the UMW functioned as a viable, integrated trade union and quite possibly ranked as the most thoroughly integrated voluntary association in the United States of 1900. Good reason led Negro miner O. H. Underwood to insist in 1899: "I believe that the United Mine Workers has done more to erase the word white from the Constitution than the Fourteenth Amendment."[107]

XI

Was the UMW's experience with Negro workers repeated in one fashion or another by other unions before 1910? Could it have been? Or was the UMW's conspicuous success the result of "conditions" peculiar to the mining industry and its population? The particular preoccupation of most labor historians and others studying relations between Negro and white workers and their unions at that time allows for easy but meaningless answers to these and even more pertinent questions. Critics and defenders of Samuel Gompers and the early American Federation of Labor have studied this subject in a one-dimensional manner and focused almost exclusively at the top level—giving needed attention to the restrictive membership clauses and practices of numerous craft unions and the policy decisions affecting Negro workers by the AFL Executive Council after 1894. From different viewpoints, their findings concur and tell much.[108] The Railroad Brotherhoods and other unions such as the Brotherhood of Boilermakers and Iron Shipbuilders, the International Brotherhood of Electrical Workers, and the International Association of Machinists explicitly excluded Negroes. Certain other craft unions barred them indirectly through narrow apprenticeship regulations, racial "rituals," and other informal but nevertheless effective devices. Some unions, particularly in the South, admitted them but only to separate locals. After 1900 the AFL Executive Council sanctioned separate Negro locals and even central organizations where affiliated unions would not accept Negroes. And from that time the AFL leadership retreated from its earlier declaration that "the working people must unite and organize irrespective of creed, color, sex, nationality, or politics," and from its earlier efforts to uproot racial practices by member unions. By 1910 or so, just before the start of the great Negro migration to Northern cities and industry, the most recent survey of American trade union history concludes: "The labor movement was not only neglecting to organize Negro workers, but it was following a deliberate policy of exclusion of Negroes from many jobs."[109]

And yet while much is known about the racial practices of certain unions and the "impotence" of or "betrayal" by the Federation when challenged by them, a great deal is misunderstood and lost by an exclusive emphasis on *national* policy and on the *intent* of national leaders. The controversy on this matter carried on by certain labor historians and tendentious publicists generates much heat but sheds little light on the relations between Negro and white workers. In another connection, British historian Edward P. Thompson has perceptively criticized such a perspective because it neglects "the tensions and lines of growth in movements which . . . have always been exceptionally responsive to problems of local social and industrial context."[110] Thompson's observation bears directly on our inability to assess fully the UMW experience. The stress in most labor histories means that little is known of the interaction between Negro and white workers, North and South, in particular communities between 1890 and 1910 so that too much is inferred solely from national policies and mere rhetoric. The tradition of Negro craftsmanship that carried over from slavery in many Southern communities, particularly in the building trades, is hardly explored.[111] In addition, although most Negroes lived in rural areas in 1900, seventy-two cities each had more than 5000 Negroes and of them Baltimore, Memphis, New Orleans, New York, Philadelphia, and Washington more than 50,000. In Southern cities such as Baton Rouge, Charleston, Jacksonville, Montgomery, Savannah, Shreveport, and Vicksburg, Negroes outnumbered whites.

The largely nonunion manufacturing industries counted 146,-000 Negroes in 1890 and nearly 350,000 twenty years later.[112] Most urban Negroes labored as unskilled and semiskilled wage earners. But modern scholarship tells inconsequentially little about urban working-class Negroes between 1890 and 1910—about their community life and collective aspirations as well as their interaction with white workers and employers.[113] Where most urban Negro and white workers confronted each other, more than the edicts of national unions affected their behavior. The story was simple if a particular national or local union explicitly excluded Negroes. But where no such barrier was found, local "traditions," particular notions of "self-interest," the conflict between racial attitudes and the egalitarian emphasis of much trade union ideology, and numerous other influences as yet unstudied shaped the behavior and the attitudes of Negro and white workers.[114]

The absence of detailed knowledge of the "local world" inhabited by white and Negro workers between 1890 and 1910 leaves only an obscure and tangled reality—filled with scattered and contradictory but suggestive bits of information. The available evidence deals mostly with craft unions and reveals precious little about the "mass" of unskilled and semiskilled Negro and white factory workers. Some facts confirm deep economic and racial fear of Negroes and their exclusion from local trade unions. But other significant information tells a quite different story, one that can only be hinted at in these pages.

In 1902 the International Longshoremen's Association counted 20,000 members, 6000 of them Negroes, and a Great Lakes officer commented: "We have many colored members in our Association, and some of them are among our leading officials of our local branches. In one of our locals . . . there are over 300 members, of which [sic] five are colored; of these, two hold the office of President and Secretary." A New Orleans Negro longshoreman boasted: "I believe that we are the only craft in that city who (sic) have succeeded in wiping out the color question. Our members meet jointly in the same hall and are the highest paid workmen in New Orleans."[115]

A major citywide building trades strike affected Chicago through most of 1900, and the employment of nonunion Negroes caused some racial strife and even violence.[116] But the Chicago Federation of Labor favored another solution and appealed to these nonunion Negroes:

The frequency with which unscrupulous employers of labor are of late supplanting white men by their colored brethren in times of industrial troubles is a question of most serious moment to the wage earners of this country. In calling attention to this question it is not our intention to arouse sentiment which might lead to race prejudice, or a race war, which would be deplorable in its results, but rather in a friendly spirit to lay before our colored brethren a statement of facts which we hope may convince them of their error. . . . We do not condemn them, believing they are most justly entitled to our sympathy and support. In the slavery days, now happily gone by, when the traffic in human flesh and blood remained a blot on our civilization, the Negro was unable to free himself from the bondage. His white brother rose in arms and declared that the slave should be free. Today the Negro is being used to keep the white man in industrial slavery. The colored man, more simple in his ways, with fewer wants and these more easily satisfied, is contented to work under conditions which are irksome to the white workman, and he is today, perhaps unconsciously, being used to try to drag the white man down to a level lower than was the Negro before he was freed from slavery. . . .

It is to remedy this that we appeal to him, to welcome him into our fold, to elevate him to our standard and to better his condition as well as our own. The trades-union movement knows no race or color. Its aims are the bettering of the condition of the wage earner, whatever his color or creed. In this spirit we appeal to the colored workmen to join us in our work. Come into our trades unions, give us your assistance and in return, receive our support, so that race hatred may be forever buried, and the workers of the country united in a solid phalanx to demand what we are justly entitled to—a fair share of the fruits of our industry.

This appeal did not fail. Many Negroes quit as strike-breakers and became "zealous for the cause of unionism." Although the strike was lost and the unions weakened, more Negroes than ever before, particularly the hod carriers, joined these unions.[117]

In 1906, Negro trade unionist and New Yorker James S. Wallace reported that in his city "many unions, viz., plasterers, carpenters, printers, teamsters, pavers, engineers, drillers, longshoremen, cigarmakers, etc. . . . have a large Negro membership, and they are treated as men." Wallace then served as elected Third Vice-President of the International Union of Pavers and Rammersmen. That union had among its members a substantial number of recent Italian immigrants.[118]

In 1902, responding to pressure (which came mainly from delegates representing white Southern locals at the 1901 and 1902 national conventions) that Southern Negro carpenters be organized, the United Brotherhood of Carpenters and Joiners' President appointed a South Carolina-born Negro, then President of a Savannah local, as a Southern organizer.[119] Much controversy followed, and many Southern white members complained of the "threat" of social equality, said "this is a white man's country," and insisted that whites "revolt voluntarily and involuntarily from a close and intimate association with the negro." One argued that this feeling toward Negroes was "a part of the bone, flesh, and blood of every southern man regardless of his social stratum."[120] Yet the union leadership held firm, and *The Carpenter*'s editor instructed critics that "prejudice on these lines has no standing in the labor movement." A white Savannah business agent supported the union President:

In Georgia they [Negroes] must be organized. I was born and raised among them; my father once owned some of them, and I know them. . . . We are always in competition with them. The contractors prefer them because they can get them cheap. . . . We have 300 white carpenters and 500 negro carpenters [here], and the latter have less unemployed than the whites. The reason is that they are not well organized and can be hired for less wages. So I say we must organize them; for if we can afford to work all day on a scaffold beside them, then we can surely afford to meet them in the hall for an hour or so once in a while. . . . The mere fact that all of the boss builders in the South are advocating leaving the negroes out of the unions is a good reason why we should organize them. . . . Let the good work go on, and let us hope for the day when there will be equal rights to all and special privileges to none. . . .[121]

The white president of Atlanta's District Council, who had lived in the South for fourteen years, also favored the effort and urged his white Southern brothers: "Let us lay aside all our prejudice (I have as much as any southern born white man) and look the question fair and square in the face." He had few doubts. "We want that organizer here in Atlanta for about three months. I believe he can do us more good than anything else."[122] The union did not rescind its appointment.[123]

Reliable information tells us that in 1902 Negroes in Florida unions included 2000 cigarmakers, 1200 building trades laborers, 1000 carpenters, 800 longshoremen, 300 plasterers, 200 painters, and 200 bricklayers. Some Negro women belonged to Florida unions, too. One of that state's Negro union stalwarts wrote of his city's unions:

The Negroes in this city have no need to complain, as white men work, smoke, eat, and drink together with them, meet in a Central Union, and hold office together. I organized and installed the Central Union as General Secretary, and I am a Negro, and have held the same [office] for two elections and was elected by whites who are in the majority. I have presided over the same body, but do not visit their daughters and have no wish [to do so]. The white painters do in a way draw the [color] line, but not openly; the boiler makers also, but none others.[124]

A year later the state AFL started a weekly newspaper in Jacksonville called *The Florida Labor Journal* and an early issue featured a long defense of militant trade unionism by regular local columnist Lynn C. Doyle. Doyle also gave much attention to the Southern Negro and blamed all of the South's racial troubles on Northerners—"the sanctified scum of the earth who first put hell—yes, hell—into the negro of the south . . . and incidently skinned the poor ignoramuses out of all their earnings." Approving lynching and terror against "violent" Negroes and the "use of the gun to suppress riot," Doyle made it clear that "we cannot now, nor ever will, for one moment make them our social equals." And yet even Doyle was not without the contradictory tensions flowing from a commitment to a belief in trade union egalitarianism and a feeling of racial exclusiveness and superiority:

. . . . Right here in our city the spirit of the laws of the A. F. of L. are carried out, even admitting, in some instances, the negro to the white locals. The olive branch was long ago extended, and across the bloody chasm (made by the agitator of the north and the political parasite) the white man and the black clasped hands as brothers in the battle of life. Their foe is a common one —the enemy of all mankind.[125]

Although the *Labor Journal* printed little news about local Jacksonville Negroes in its first two years, what it reported reflected creditably on Negro trade unionists. In January 1903 it urged strengthening three weakened Negro unions, supported extensive organization among Negro workers by white and Negro AFL Florida organizers, and saw in such developments the promise of "a tidal wave of the old union spirit" that would "shake the foundations of autocracy and plutocracy as . . . never before . . . in Florida." A local of Negro women, apparently clothing workers, and the city's largest union, invited the *Journal*'s editor to a meeting chaired by its woman President. He found it "well regulated" and commended it to white and Negro readers:

> It is to the shame of some unions in Jacksonville that they sit back and knock their brethren while these women, who on an average draw less than $3 per week, attend their meetings, keep in good standing, and pay a sick benefit of $2 per week. Too much credit cannot be given to these good women. . . .[126]

A Democratic Party supporter, the *Journal* nevertheless printed a Jacksonville Socialist Party advertisement addressed "To the Colored Voters of Jacksonville" during a June 1903 municipal election campaign. The Socialists appealed to Jacksonville Negroes: "The Democratic Party excluded you (by direct prohibition) from voting in the late primary . . . There is now no place for SELF-RESPECTING MEMBERS of your race to go in the city election except into the Socialist Party. . . . VOTE FOR YOUR OWN INTERESTS. . . ."[127] Six weeks later, without comment the *Journal* reprinted on its front page a commentary on W. E. B. Du Bois' *The Souls of Black Folk*, which first appeared in *Boyce's Weekly*. "This negro question," the Northern labor journal (about which no information has been found) said, ". . . is, in its essentials, a working class question."

> A certain proportion of the white people of the United States are determined that a man with a black skin must be ever and always a hewer of wood or drawer of water. His brain may have the genius of a Dumas or a Frederick Douglass, but if in its veins flows a trace of black blood he is condemned to occupations that stunt and dwarf his mentality.

> North and south alike this condition exists. If the problem seems more acute in the old slave states it is only because its proportions are more commanding. The spirit which condemns the black man to his own restricted

sphere, industrially as well as socially, exists quite as much among the whites north as south of Mason and Dixon's line.

What support Negroes found, *Boyce's Weekly* believed, came mostly from white men "outside . . . the laboring class" and this was "a grave blunder."

Race prejudice is easily transformed into class prejudice. The spirit that says the negro may not hope to become a lawyer, teacher, educator or banker—save for the service of his own race—will soon say the same of the Russian, the Hungarian, the Jew. If a man of surpassing talents and earnest industry may not rise above the dead level of his race, we shall soon find it will be equally hard for him to surmount the boundaries of his class. Indeed, today class spirit no less than race prejudice is becoming characteristic of American society.

White workers therefore had much to learn from Du Bois' book.

If you want to know what this means to the negro of trained intellect get Professor Du Bois' pathetic book "The Souls of Black Folk." To imagine what it may yet mean to workingmen you have only to translate his stories into terms of your own class.

Boyce's Weekly commended those Southern whites in the labor movement who were "taking the negro into full communion" and called such involvement the possible "beginning of the most effective work for the correction of an evil that menaces the rights and liberties and the souls of white as well as black workingmen."[128]

What occurred in Jacksonville was not repeated in all Southern cities, but the few details available show that Negroes were not excluded or separated everywhere. In 1901 the Industrial Commission summed up its findings about Southern unions: "As the unions have grown, separate locals have been demanded. . . . In some places the city central bodies have begun to reject colored delegates. *While there are still many places in the South where negroes and*

*whites meet on an absolute plane of equality in the labor
organizations*, there are others where not only separate local
trade unions but separate city federations have become necessary."[129] (Italics added.) In Atlanta, where most Negro
unionists apparently met in separate locals, the State Federation of Labor nevertheless refused to join the 1898 "peace
jubilee parade" because Negro workers could not parade,
too.[130] Respondents to W. E. B. Du Bois' inquiries that
resulted in *The Negro Artisan* (1902), a neglected pioneering study, gave evidence of much discrimination against
Negroes by Southern unions, but their replies also showed
contrary trends. In Atlanta, Birmingham, Danville, Memphis,
New Orleans, Richmond, and Savannah, Negro union plasterers outnumbered their white brothers and met in locals
that were "often mixed." Masons and bricklayers also had
"mixed" locals in parts of the South.[131] Some Ashville,
Charlotte, and Winston-Salem unions admitted North Carolina Negroes. In Georgia, Athens Negroes combined with
whites in certain unions, while Savannah and Augusta had
several Negro unions. Savannah counted seven separate Negro
locals among the building trades laborers, carpenters, coopers,
lathers, painters, and tinners.[132] New Orleans had the
greatest number of Negro trade unionists in any Southern
city, almost four thousand. The Crescent City had many
unions that admitted Negroes and six powerful all-Negro
unions in the docking and transport industries. The much-
impressed Negro Secretary of the New Orleans Central
Labor Union reported to Du Bois: "By amalgamation of
organizations and through International connections, we expect to have the color line in work removed."[133] Du Bois'
study was not nearly as optimistic. His survey of contemporary trade union practices found much that deserved
criticism. And yet, paradoxically, he could write: "At the
same time, there are today [1902] probably a larger number
of effective Negro members in the trade unions than ever
before, there is evidence of renewed inspiration toward
mechanical trades, and a better comprehension of the labor
movement."[134]

XII

Nothing written in these final pages should be taken to suggest that Negro workers had an easy time in Northern and Southern crafts and factories between 1890 and 1910. This evidence means merely to indicate the difficulties involved in judging the "uniqueness" of the UMW experience and to hint that the full story of the confrontation between Negro workers and organized (as well as unorganized white) labor at that time has yet to be written—and that when examined it must be from "the bottom up." Surely, however, the evidence in these pages tells us that Booker T. Washington (himself a member of the Knights of Labor as a young man) exaggerated when he boasted that "the Negro is not given to 'strikes'" and that trade unionism was "that form of slavery which prevents a man from selling his labor to whom he pleases on account of his color."[135] William Hooper Councill, the Negro head of the Agricultural and Mechanical College for Negroes at Normal, Alabama, and very much a prophet of a subordinate role for Negroes in the "New South," was also wrong in arguing that Southern labor unions "will bring into the South the disorders that will exceed the disturbances of 'reconstruction days'" and that trade unionism would chase the Negro from the South so that "Communism [will] drive the white man's coach, Nihilism cook and serve his food, Agrarianism plow his fields, and the red flag of Anarchy float over every Southern industry."[136] Equally erroneous was Samuel Gompers, who in 1910 could insist that Negroes just did not "understand the philosophy of human rights."[137]

In all of this, it is the problem of perspective and the lack of detailed knowledge that plague us. Much has been written about the trade unions and their national leaders and about their petty and significant quarrels as well as their larger successes and frequent failures, but little is yet known of the quality of life and the complexity of thought and feeling of ordinary white and Negro workers in the early modern era. August Meier has explored painstakingly and well the world of Booker T. Washington and his Negro critics and defenders,[138] but the world of men like Richard Davis awaits its historian. How difficult it is therefore to grasp the response of a Negro worker to the racial sentiment of the older Gompers or to imagine the feelings of a white trade unionist confronted with the anti-labor imprecations of Washington and Councill. When the United Brotherhood of Carpenters and Joiners disturbed so many of its Southern white members by appointing a Negro organizer, the *St. Louis Advance*, a labor weekly, applauded its action and urged further organization of Negro workers:

> It is useless to read homilies on thrift and morality to under-paid labor. . . . More and more the Brotherhoods are opening their doors to him [the Negro], telling him to step in. The labor leaders know that without the Negro their organizations are lop-sided and their movements necessarily failures, and the Negro can see that as a laborer he must ally himself with his brother, or remain as he is now in the South, the poorest paid laborer in the world.[139]

The *Advance* was wrong in its prediction. Although Richard Davis and the early white leaders of the United Mine Workers of America were among those to make such a connection, theirs was not the dominant influence between 1890 and 1910. Davis died in 1900. By 1910 surely only those coal miners, Negro and white workers, who had felt his presence and benefited from his experience and courageous leadership remembered his name.* Historians often

---

* In 1909, William Scaife recorded his memories of the early UMW years. Scaife devoted an entire article to Richard Davis and called him "a heroic fighter." Scaife scorned those who neglected the pioneering efforts of the Ohio Negro miner and reminded his readers of his "unflagging zeal . . . against trials and tribulations that would have daunted and discouraged the best of them." "If he was black," Scaife said of Davis, "he had a heart as white as any man, and a devotion to union principles that

characterize an era by a dominant personality, a figure who looms large over a period of time and leaves more than a momentary impression or in his person symbolizes significant changes. In this sense, the years between 1890 and 1910 did not belong to men like Richard Davis. This was indeed "The Age of Samuel Gompers" and "The Age of Booker T. Washington." Men like Davis were not asked to serve as presidential advisors or as members of federal commissions. *The New York Times* did not query them for their opinions on the "race" and "labor" questions. Instead, their long-range vision and concrete aspirations for democratic interracial trade unionism were stifled by the defensive strategy of organized labor and middle-class Negro leadership as well as the rising tide of racism within the labor movement and throughout the country.

The American people have journeyed far from the Age of Washington and Gompers. One measure of the distance traveled and the losses incurred is that so little is known about working-class Negroes like Richard Davis who displayed so full an awareness of their plight and that of their brothers and who retained and exemplified older traditions of pride and hope and militancy. We know a great deal about the world of Washington and Gompers. But until we know more fully the world of men like Davis, we shall not clearly comprehend the tragedy and the hope embedded in recent American history.

---

was second to no man in the movement. His color he could not help, and I don't know that it matters a great deal anyhow." Scaife found in men like Davis reason not to "erect in the miners' organization a 'color standard,' but one of manhood." "We need more colored men like Dick Davis," he concluded, "and we white men want to treat them right for the common good of all of us." (Old Timer [William Scaife], "Forty Years a Miner and Men I Have Known," *United Mine Workers' Journal*, Nov. 19, 1909.)

Chapter III

THE NEGRO IN SOUTHERN UNIONS

RAY MARSHALL

Since unions are never independent social forces but tend
to reflect their environments, the racial practices of unions
in the South cannot adequately be understood apart from
the region's main political, economic, and social climate. It
is not easy to portray this context both briefly and accurately.
Generalizations must be qualified by the many differences
among various kinds of unions and Southern geographic
subregions, and by the influence of other important, changing factors.

For our purposes, the dominant factors in the South's
history have been slavery and racial segregation. But even
before it became firmly established around 1900, segregation
was being undermined by the impact of industrialization
remolding Southern institutions in greater conformity to the
national image. This essay will discuss union racial practices
in the context of these institutions and changes. Since union
racial practices in the South differ only in degree from
those of other regions, we need not consider in detail the
racial practices of various national unions.*

* This essay is based mainly on my *The Negro and Organized
Labor*, New York, Wiley, 1965, and my forthcoming *Labor in the
South*. Some of the material is also based on research financed by
a grant from the Ford Foundation. I am grateful to both the
Wertheim Committee, Harvard University, and the Ford Founda-
tion for this support. See also my *The Negro Worker*, New York,
Random House, 1967; and *The Negro and Apprenticeship* (with
Vernon M. Briggs, Jr.), Johns Hopkins University Press, 1967.

SLAVERY, THE CIVIL WAR, AND RECONSTRUCTION

Many basic racial customs and attitudes of the South have their roots in slavery. Slavery created an image of the Negro as an inferior person, and competition between slaves and white workers created mutual animosities which persisted after Emancipation. Slavery also led to the plantation system and cotton culture, which made the South's economy relatively static at a time when the rest of the country was experiencing rapid economic development. This led to a divergence of non-economic Southern institutions from those of the rest of the country and further set the stage for the Civil War.

The Civil War and Reconstruction also had a profound impact on the South. Much of the region's capital was destroyed by the war and Emancipation, and the planters' consequent dependence on credit from supply merchants and bankers produced the sharecropping system and forced a heavy reliance on cotton as a mortgageable and salable crop. And the exigencies of cotton growing were such that little food was produced, the diet was poor, the fertility of the soil was rapidly depleted, and farming techniques were relatively static, requiring little more than brute strength from the sharecropper and his family. Sharecroppers also suffered from the fluctuations of the cotton market, large families, and ignorance, all of which contributed to a vicious cycle of self-perpetuating poverty. Whites, who were given no better terms than Negroes in competition for the declining number of positions on the plantations, blamed the Negro for their plight, and one motive for the formation of the Ku Klux Klan during these years was the removal of the Negro as a competitor, especially in the renting of land.[1]

Although Negroes and whites suffered from the same disabilities, it would be a mistake to infer that their conditions were equal. Unlike the Negroes, whites had some control over public officials and were not as restricted if they wished to move out of agriculture. In many areas of the South, Negroes were kept in a state of virtual peonage by local law-enforcement officials and the plantation debt system. Moreover, in those nonagricultural industries associated with the idea of the "New South," they were restricted to certain menial, dirty, or difficult jobs. And since class lines were blurred by the intensification of racial identification during the Civil War and Reconstruction periods, whites had what apparently was to them the important psychological asset of a feeling of racial superiority.

While the Civil War and Reconstruction tended to unify Southern whites, the political tradition of the "solid South" was not established immediately. In the period just after the removal of federal troops, Negroes were not disfranchised and there was considerable competition among politicians for the Negro vote.[2] It even looked for a time during the 1880s and 1890s as if Southern Negro and white workers and farmers might be welded together politically and economically in the Populist movement and the Knights of Labor. The Knights organized Negro and white workers without regard to trade or occupation (except that bankers, lawyers, professional politicians, and other "drones" who did not work for a living were excluded) in every section of the South and formed a political alliance with the Populists, who were active among the region's farmers during the 1890s. However, in spite of the Populists' relatively liberal racial attitudes (never extending to social equality), they were defeated by Negro votes controlled by conservative Democrats in the plantation belts. The Populists therefore became convinced that, to enable them to form a movement emphasizing economic objectives, Negroes would have to be disfranchised. Of course, many whites favored disfranchisement of Negroes because they were afraid that the latter would hold the balance of power if whites split their votes on economic lines. But once the Negro had been disfranchised through white primaries, poll taxes, and other restrictions, demagogues were able to use the race issue to perpetuate the one-party system. The Democratic Party became the Party of the South and Republicanism was equated with "treason to race, country, God and Southern womanhood." Consequently, according to W. J. Cash, the "master class . . . would go on . . . dealing with the government machinery of the South as their private property. . . ."[3]

But just as disfranchisement of Negroes did not occur immediately after the withdrawal of federal troops, it took some time for a rigid form of legal racial segregation to become the pattern in the South. Whether for fear of the return of Yankee troops or fear of the Negro vote, it was about a decade after the end of military occupation before the first segregation laws were passed. In Mississippi, Wharton found that saloons in Jackson served Negroes and whites at separate tables, and the governors of Louisiana and South Carolina went on record in favor of protecting the Negroes' right to vote.[4]

Virtually complete legal segregation had become the accepted way of handling the race problem in the South by 1900, because, among other reasons, there was a feeling in the South that a majority of Northern whites also favored segregation and second-class citizenship for the Negro and therefore would not send the troops back South. This conviction was supported by: segregation in the federal Army and the refusal of many Northern states to enfranchise the Negro, even though they insisted that the South do so; the prevalence of segregation in the North; the acquiescence of Northerners in the political compromise of 1877, which resulted in the withdrawal of federal troops; the use of racist arguments by Northerners to support U.S. policies in the Pacific and Caribbean areas after 1898, making it difficult for them to counter the same arguments when Southerners used them against Negroes; and finally, a series of U. S. Supreme Court decisions between 1873 and 1898 establishing the legality of the "separate but equal" doctrine and denying Negroes federal protection for acts committed against them by private individuals.

By about 1900, therefore, the Negro had become almost

completely segregated by law or custom. He rarely found
it possible to vote. He rode in separate compartments or
in the back of public conveyances, went to segregated public
schools, could not marry a white, ate in separate restaurants,
and was buried in a segregated cemetery. Employment was
also segregated and Negroes were displaced from some occupations they had formerly held; they had great difficulty
leaving agriculture, and were relegated to "Negro" jobs in
manufacturing and other nonagricultural activities.

EARLY SOUTHERN UNIONS

It is against this background that the racial practices of
the South's earliest labor organizations can best be understood. Although the first unions in the South were formed
long before the Civil War, the periods of most rapid union
growth before the New Deal came after 1900.

The oldest labor organizations in the South were the
"mechanics societies" established in the major cities, usually
in seaports, during the eighteenth century. The oldest craft
unions in the region appear to have been the printers'
unions formed during the early nineteenth century, the
earliest-known example of which was the New Orleans
printers' union of 1810. New Orleans printers reorganized
several times after 1835 and were one of the strongest
unions which united to form the oldest national union in
the United States—the International Typographical Union
—in 1852. Indeed, the President of the second national
convention of journeymen printers (1851), which led to
the formation of the Typographical Union, was from Louisville; and New Orleans printers were Presidents of the
national organization from 1853 through 1855. Strong typographical unions were formed in all of the South's major
cities before 1860. Although the Civil War disrupted these
organizations in the deep South, locals in Tennessee and
Kentucky remained affiliated with the national organization
during the war. The Southern unions rejoined the national

organization when the war was over, and many of the Southern organizations, particularly those in New Orleans, Louisville, Memphis, and Nashville, were among the strongest in the country.

Because there were few Negroes in the printing trades, the ITU had few racial incidents in the South. The main exceptions were occasions when Southern ITU locals refused to accept the traveling cards of Negro ITU members from the North. Such incidents in Memphis and Little Rock led the international to rule in 1879 that locals could not refuse to honor the traveling cards of members in good standing. However, the decision concerning the admission of members to ITU locals was left to the locals, which in the South followed the practice of barring Negroes from membership.

Although there were many older local organizations, the union that did most to popularize unionism in the South was the Knights of Labor, which reached the peak of its importance in the region around 1890. In many areas, however, particularly among farmers and agricultural workers, the Knights' Southern assemblies were more political than collective-bargaining organizations. Although the Knights enunciated a policy of racial equality, their leaders made it clear that this policy did not extend to social relations, and Negroes commonly belonged to segregated assemblies in the South.

The screwmen, a group of Southern longshoremen who stored cotton and tobacco aboard ships with jackscrews, were among the earliest and most successfully organized occupations in the region. Before the Civil War, screwmen were almost always whites and many were Irish or German immigrants. After the war, however, Negro longshoremen learned the screwmen's trade and formed separate organizations that entered into work-sharing arrangements with the white screwmen. General longshoremen also became relatively well organized on Southern docks after 1865, but they had more serious racial clashes. Indeed, although work-sharing arrangements were usually worked out between Negro and white longshoremen, until the 1920s, when the unions were almost completely destroyed and Negroes came to predominate, there was a steady undercurrent of racial trouble, which erupted from time to time in race riots. The main causes of racial tension appear to have been interference by politicians, the use of Negro strikebreakers, and Negro dissatisfaction with racial quotas, which almost always gave the better and more permanent jobs to whites.

The underlying reason for the politicians' interference with the racial practices of unions was a feeling that Negroes were inferior people who should be denied better jobs. And although monopoly instincts played a role in prompting most unions to attempt to exclude Negroes, status considerations were also important; thus craftsmen who considered themselves aristocrats of labor felt that the admission of Negroes would lower the prestige associated with their crafts. Southern unions were formed partly as social organizations at a time when it was considered improper to have social relations with Negroes.

As noted in the longshoremen's case, however, the extent to which unions succeeded in excluding Negroes was determined mainly by the number of Negroes already in the trade or the ease with which they could be trained. The oldest building trades unions in the South, like the Carpenters and Bricklayers, found it impossible to exclude Negroes and still maintain their organizations because many slaves had been trained in these occupations. Shortly after the Civil War, for example, white bricklayers in New Orleans struck for higher wages but ignored the Negroes who acted as strikebreakers. Thereafter Negro and white bricklayers in New Orleans formed a united front and have one of the most successful histories of racial harmony on an integrated basis of any union in the South. Some Southern bricklayers' locals are integrated and others are segregated, although there are very few recorded complaints of discrimination from Negroes in the segregated locals.

The experiences of other building trades unions have been much less satisfactory to the colored workers. The

Carpenters followed the practice of organizing Negroes into segregated locals, which restricted the colored members' job opportunities. In some cases whites even struck against the use of Negro union members on building projects outside Negro neighborhoods. Unions like the Sheet Metal Workers, the Electricians, the Iron Workers, the Elevator Constructors, and the Plumbers were almost completely able to bar Negroes from their crafts and from their unions. Whites maintained control of the better jobs in these crafts since they required technical training and these trades first became important after the Civil War, with consequently few Negroes in them. Although there were some licensed Negro electricians and plumbers, they were usually restricted to Negro neighborhoods because whites would boycott contractors who used Negroes in these occupations. These threatened boycotts were effective because building tradesmen change jobs easily and there would not be enough colored electricians and plumbers to supply the needs of a boycotted contractor.

Given their high mobility and skilled positions, most railroad craft unions were organized in the South relatively early. Indeed, a number of unions active among railroad workers (the International Association of Machinists, the Blacksmiths and Boilermakers, and the Maintenance-of-Way Employees) originated in the South. Probably because they were social organizations in part and were organized very early, most railroad unions, including Eugene Debs's American Railway Union, barred Negroes from membership by constitutional provision. Although they always faced indirect competition from Negroes, some of these organizations never had serious racial problems because it was almost unthinkable in the South that Negroes would be hired for such high-status jobs as conductor or engineer. The Trainmen and Firemen had more difficulty because many Negroes had been used in these occupations at a time when the jobs were hot and dirty and therefore "Negro" work. As technological improvements made these jobs easier, and as they became stepping stones to conductors' and engineers' positions, they proved more attractive to whites. As a result, the Brotherhood of Locomotive Firemen and the Brotherhood of Railroad Trainmen (particularly the Firemen) sought to remove Negroes from the Southern railroads by contractual agreements with employers. They were never able fully to realize this objective because, as we shall see, they were prohibited from doing so by the federal courts.

The Blacksmiths, Electricians, Machinists, Carmen, Railway Clerks, and other so-called nonoperating or shop craft railroad unions also sought to bar Negroes, but were not as successful as the operating brotherhoods. The main difference was that in these occupations, the tradition of using Negro helpers, who were usually excluded from union membership, gave employers a ready supply of strikebreakers. Moreover, when these unions attempted to extend their jurisdictions to take in occupations with large numbers of Negroes, they had to work out some arrangements to represent these workers. A variety of techniques were used, including: having the excluded Negroes organized by another union (such as the Firemen and Oilers) which did not bar them from membership; having colored workers organized directly into federal local unions by the AFL; and organizing Negroes into auxiliary locals controlled entirely by whites. All these arrangements were unsatisfactory to the Negroes, who were inadequately represented, and to the unions, which were unable to collect dues or present a united front in bargaining with employers. As a result of the Negroes' dissatisfaction and the anti-union attitudes of Negro leaders in the South before the New Deal period, Negroes entered many of these railroad occupations as strikebreakers, particularly during the anti-labor 1920s, when nonoperating unions were greatly weakened in the South.

As a result of the debilitating effects of their discriminatory racial policies, most nonoperating and shop craft unions were looking for more satisfactory arrangements when a series of measures caused them at least formally to drop their racial barriers. These included: lawsuits brought by Negroes which led to the 1944 *Steele* decision by the U. S. Supreme Court requiring unions to represent Negroes fairly and subjecting them to damage suits for violation of this duty; competition among unions for Negro support in representation elections, particularly after the formation of the CIO in 1935; attacks on the discriminatory practices of these unions by the all-Negro Brotherhood of Sleeping Car Porters, organized in 1925; court decisions and the 1951 amendment to the Railway Labor Act, which denied unions the right to maintain union-shop conditions unless all members of bargaining units were admitted to membership; and the passage of state anti-discrimination laws in the North after the Second World War. Although all these organizations had racist members in the North, the greatest opposition to dropping racial bars came from the South.

Unions were also active at an early date in the South's coal mines, which became increasingly important with industrialization and after the development of the iron and steel industry in the Birmingham and Chattanooga areas during the 1880s. Since labor costs were a high proportion of total coal-mining cost and some Southern deposits were rich and extensive, it became increasingly clear to the United Mine Workers that unionization of Southern miners was essential to its survival. Because of the large number of Negro coal miners and potential strikebreakers, it became equally clear that equalitarian racial policies were essential to successful unionism in the industry.

Between 1900 and the 1920s numerous Southern coal strikes were broken by Negroes. After the defeat of the UMW in the 1920s Alabama coal operators adopted a welfare system and formed an alliance with Negro leaders which kept unions out of the industry until the 1930s.

Despite the use of Negro strikebreakers, however, the official policy of the United Mine Workers was always to organize all workers into the same unions, regardless of race. Although this policy succeeded in some places because coal miners were relatively isolated from the main social forces of the South, in others, Alabama for example, community opposition to unions before the 1930s was based in part on the UMW's equalitarian policies. And even though racial sentiments had changed in the South by the time the UMW reorganized most of the region's miners during the 1930s, local unions in Alabama had trouble with the Ku Klux Klan and other racist elements.

This is not to argue, however, that all of the UMW's trouble was caused by outside groups. There were some complaints from Negroes of discrimination against them by white union members. And relations between Negroes and whites in the Alabama unions during the 1930s appear to have been fairly formal, with segregated seating in union halls. Nevertheless, the UMW's policies always called for nondiscrimination and that organization was one of the earliest and largest examples of a successfully integrated union in the South.

Since the subject is covered more fully elsewhere, we need not say much about the racial practices of the AFL. There can be little question, however, that the apparent change in the AFL's position, from the declaration of racial equality during the 1890s to the acceptance of discriminatory unions in 1900 reflects the general trend in race relations described above. Moreover, after the International Association of Machinists (IAM) was admitted to the AFL in 1895 through the subterfuge of transferring the race bar from its constitution to its ritual, it would hardly have been logical for the Federation to have denied the admission of other unions with race bars or to have prohibited some of its affiliates from inserting prohibitions against nonwhites in their constitutions. But the most important factors at work on the AFL's policies were undoubtedly the general climate of race relations and the desire of AFL leaders to build a strong union movement. The Federation was particularly desirous of organizing the rapidly industrializing South during the early 1890s, and Gompers visited the area during the 1894–95 period, after he had been defeated for the presidency of the AFL, and about the time, incidentally, when the IAM was admitted to the Federation.

AFL leaders apparently thought it more important to organize the South than to attempt to change the prevailing racial views of Southerners. Their anti-Negro attitudes were also influenced by the anti-union alliances formed among employers, Republicans, and such Negro leaders as Booker T. Washington.

Whatever the reasons, the AFL had adjusted to the racial sentiments of the South by 1900. There were some Negro AFL locals in the South that would ordinarily have been eligible for membership in various central labor organizations, but until the New Deal period, many Southern state federations of labor refused to seat Negro delegates. The constitution of the Louisiana State Federation of Labor, for example, provided that "Colored organizations shall be represented by white proxies, but no local shall hold the proxy of more than one colored local." In addition, many Southern city centrals refused to seat Negroes, so after 1901 the AFL followed the policy of chartering Negro central labor organizations. Furthermore, many federal labor unions chartered directly by the AFL refused to accept Negro members. The AFL discontinued these practices during the 1930s, probably because of the competition between it and the CIO for the allegiance of Negroes in representation elections under the New Deal labor legislation. Also, race relations had changed sufficiently in the South by 1935 so that integrated locals were more acceptable than they had been twenty-five years earlier.

Factors Undermining Racial Segregation in the South

Although the pattern of racial segregation and discrimination in the South manifested itself most clearly between 1890 and the First World War, forces were set in motion during this period which gradually undercut that system. Perhaps the most significant was industrialization, which was accompanied by a greater commercialization and urbanization of economic life. We have noted that the racial system adopted in the South following Reconstruction was rooted in agriculture. It is not surprising, therefore, that the diminishing relative importance of the plantation system and cotton culture should have changed the South's social institutions. The Negro could be kept "in his place" only so long as he was isolated and identifiable. His isolation limited his knowledge of alternative ways of living. As we have noted, moreover, the agricultural system required little or no schooling, so most Negroes could not see the real need for improved education and other efforts to meet the requirements of an industrial civilization.

Industrialization worked to undermine this system in a variety of ways. By improving transportation and communications, it gave formerly isolated groups knowledge of alternative systems and focused the attention of others on the plight of these disadvantaged groups. At the same time, industrialization created the necessity for change by making civil rights and improved education essential for survival and advancement in society. In addition, nationwide transportation and communications networks influenced the attitudes of Southern whites by bringing them into contact with national points of view and breaking the information monopolies of local news media and power structures. The vast internal market in the United States led outsiders to invest in the South's economy and produced a certain standardization of ideas and operations. These developments also brought non-Southerners to the South as technicians and managers of the new industries. Thus, the South was edging back into the mainstream of American life from which it had been diverging since about 1840.

Industrialization also tended to undermine the Southern political system, of which segregation had become an integral part. As the American economy grew more complicated and interdependent, the role of the federal government became more important relative to that of the states. And as Negroes migrated out of the South in increasing numbers, beginning at about the time of the First World War, their ability to influence the federal government's policies toward the

South increased, and was reinforced as race issues became more significant in the international contest with the Communists after the First World War. Industrialization also produced important internal political changes within the South. With economic development came a differentiation of political interest which rendered the undemocratic one-party system obsolete. As economic diversification divided the white population along economic lines, the Negro became increasingly important in the political balance of power, as had been the case during the Populist period.

These changes created a real dilemma for the South's political leaders. They wanted to retain control of the political system which they had built on racial fears and customs, but they also wanted the benefits of industrialization. This dilemma manifested itself in the political developments in Mississippi during 1962 and 1963. Realizing that the emerging Republican Party would increase the political power of the Negro vote, some Mississippi Democrats proposed legal restrictions which would make it difficult for the Republicans to operate in that state. These efforts were thwarted, however, when the Republicans fought back and when it was emphasized that many of the entrepreneurs the state was eagerly attempting to attract were Republicans.

Racists also realize that political alliances between unions and Negroes are potentially very powerful. Indeed, in states like Texas, Kentucky, and Tennessee these coalitions have already become important political forces. The segregationists have therefore sought to disrupt these liberal coalitions by infiltrating unions. In some cases where this tactic failed and unions have demonstrated considerable political power, the segregationists have been able to split Negro-labor coalitions by backing pro-labor segregationists like Orval Faubus in Arkansas. Clearly, however, the political influence of both the unions and Negroes is increasing in the South, making the Negro-liberal-labor coalitions important determinants of the region's political future.

These political, social, and economic changes also have had important influences on the South's business community. As noted earlier, the employment patterns established in the South following the Civil War caused employers to hire Negroes for nontraditional jobs only when they would serve as impediments to unionism or when they would accept lower wages than whites for the same jobs. The social ferment of the New Deal period greatly disrupted the traditional alliance between Negroes and employers, because the formation of the CIO and the Roosevelt Administration's encouragement of unions caused many Negroes to switch their allegiance to unions and the Democrats. The employers' other major motive for hiring Negroes was removed when measures were taken to abolish racial wage differentials.

Some economists have argued that forces outside the market are unnecessary to overcome employment discrimination because there is a natural tendency for employers, who are motivated by profits, to hire workers on the basis of merit, regardless of race. But this conclusion is not warranted, since the market does not work as perfectly as some economists imply and decisions are not made in isolation from social forces. There has, for example, been no shortage of unskilled white labor in the South, so many employers have been able to man their operations without using Negroes. Moreover, employees sometimes have hired or upgraded whites who were not so well qualified as some Negroes for fear of adverse reactions from whites. There can be little question that as a logical proposition employers *tended* to hire workers on the basis of their merit regardless of race, but when market forces collided with social institutions these "rational" decisions were not made. Most employers apparently considered it more "rational" not to disturb the region's social customs. However, when federal policies gave them protection from those social customs, they were free to follow merit employment policies. Employers have received added incentives to break the traditional racial system because of a growing realization that that system is incompatible with economic progress and because in the racial atmosphere of the 1950s and 1960s direct pressures from civil rights groups can seriously affect economic development and sales. These factors explain the emergence of the Southern business community as the greatest force for producing conformity with national equalitarian racial policies. Of course, business groups can take equalitarian measures and have a greater impact on Southern institutions than unions because companies are not democratic organizations and are much more powerful than unions. Unions openly favored racial equality much earlier than business organizations, but, compared with the latter, they were relatively impotent.

INFLUENCE OF UNIONS ON
NEGRO EMPLOYMENT OPPORTUNITIES

Although the record of racial discrimination by unions is clear enough, it is difficult to measure the union movement's influence on Negro employment. Our statistics on employment and union membership do not permit precise quantitative analysis of this problem, but unions were clearly only partly responsible for racial employment patterns. In the aggregate, there appears to be no correlation between these patterns and union growth. This is undoubtedly because unions have not been strong enough in the South to have much influence on total employment. In manufacturing establishments the custom of hiring Negroes only for menial and disagreeable occupations was established long before unions came on the scene. There is no evidence, for example, that nonunion firms offer greater employment opportunities for Negroes than those which are organized. The influence of industrial unions has been mainly to perpetuate job segregation by formalizing separate seniority lines and resisting changes which would make it possible for Negroes to be transferred and promoted on the basis of seniority.

The foregoing is not to imply, of course, that industrial unions did nothing to promote and protect the interests of their Negro members. After the formation of the CIO and the racial ferment in the South following the Second World War, the Southern locals of some international unions, notably the United Packinghouse Workers, took positive measures to eliminate job segregation. Although the usual practice of industrial unions in the South was not to challenge prevailing job patterns, some unions like the Auto Workers, the Rubber Workers, and the International Union of Electrical Workers invariably sided with their Negro members in the South when they, with the aid of the NAACP and other civil rights organizations, challenged prevailing job arrangements. Although the international did not itself initiate the action, the Oil Workers even joined their Negro members in legal action against their white local leadership. Older industrial unions in the South, like the Tobacco Workers and unions in the pulp and paper industry, took measures to abolish job segregation only after pressures were put on the employers by the federal government during the late 1950s and early 1960s.

To the extent that they protected all workers from discrimination by employers and raised the wages of lower-paid workers, the unions advanced the interests of their Negro members. Moreover, we shall see that unions in the South were forced in some measure to conform to the equalitarian racial practices of their parent organizations with respect to such matters as holding integrated meetings and challenging prevailing social customs. Indeed, the first integrated meetings attended by many Negro workers in the South were sponsored by unions. State and city central labor organizations have been particularly important in supporting liberal causes in the South. Moreover, the unionization of a work group gives Negroes legal rights to challenge job discrimination that they otherwise would not have. The fact that a union acts as bargaining agent under federal laws imposes upon it the duty to represent all workers in that bargaining unit regardless of race. A violation of this duty subjects the union to restraining orders from federal courts, damage suits, and orders to cease and desist from the National Labor Relations Board.[5] In 1964 the NLRB even ruled that a local union violated its duty of fair representation by not using its bargaining power to abolish the traditional job segregation system.[6]

The stronger craft unions on the railroads and in the building trades have had more influence on job patterns. In the so-called "trowel trades" Negroes have been sufficiently numerous to protect their interests in the South because they can train one another and supply the needs of employers who are boycotted by whites. These trades are also older and employ relatively static methods, making it difficult for unions to exclude Negroes by monopolizing training programs. Unions in the newer occupations like the plumbing and electrical trades have been able to bar Negroes from their unions and from better jobs in the industry through their control of apprenticeship training and their influence with some licensing boards. These and other building trades unions have commonly restricted Negro employment to Negro neighborhoods or to nonunion work, in spite of the fact that unorganized Negro workers pose a constant threat to union standards. Although there has been some token relaxation of the racial restrictions of the Plumbers and Electricians in the South, under pressure from the federal government and civil rights organizations, the basic pattern of exclusion had not been disturbed much by the end of 1964.

In older unionized sectors like longshoring, Negroes have been able to perpetuate their hold on certain jobs because of racial quota systems. Although in 1964 the NLRB declared the longshoremen's racial quotas to be unfair labor practices,[7] it is doubtful that the decision will seriously disturb the Longshoremen's quota system. Negroes are sometimes disadvantaged compared to whites, but they have good jobs in the industry and a strong position within the international union, and unless something happens to change their attitudes, the overwhelming majority of Negro ILA leaders in the South will apparently support the prevailing job system. It is significant that the challenge by the Negro longshoremen which led to the NLRB's decision against

Brownsville, Texas, ILA Local 1367's racial quota system was not an objection to the quota system itself but an effort to increase the Negroes' share of the jobs.

The Railroad Brotherhoods have also limited the job opportunities of Negroes, though they were prevented by the federal courts from completely carrying out their intention to remove Negroes from certain jobs in the industry.[8]

SOUTHERN REACTION TO EQUALITARIAN RACIAL MEASURES

Since union policies tend to reflect prevailing community sentiments, it is not surprising that the racial policies of Southern local unions created considerable anxiety among national labor leaders. The union leaders' problems were intensified because the national trend in race relations made it necessary for them to enunciate racial policies in the North which they feared would not only alienate their membership in the South but might also make union organizing more difficult in that rapidly industrializing region.

With respect to the influence of racial conflict on union organizing, it is the writer's conclusion that this is not a very important problem for unions, certainly much less significant than it was in 1900. Many employers have used the race issue in an effort to deter union organizing in the South, but it would be difficult to demonstrate that race arguments defeated unions in many cases where they might otherwise have been successful. Indeed, it can probably be demonstrated that equalitarian racial policies are more likely to attract Negroes to the unions than they are to deter whites; the unions' racial policies are probably more important to Negroes than to whites. Moreover, in many cases Negroes have formed the balance of power between union and nonunion whites, causing the plants to become unionized. The relationship between unions and the Negro community worsened somewhat following the AFL-CIO merger, but Negro-union relations are still much better than they were in the pre-CIO period.[9] And although there seems to be a slight tendency for unorganized Negroes in the South to support unions less frequently than formerly, this does not appear to be a really important problem.

It is necessary, however, to make a distinction between the influence of racial conflict on central labor unions and local unions. Since the centrals have little economic power and are mainly public relations and legislative bodies, their interests and functions are different from those of collective-bargaining organizations. Indeed, since the formation of the CIO, the state labor organizations have been relatively liberal with respect to their racial policies, a liberalism that stems in part from their need to appeal to Negroes for legislative support and to gain Negro votes in internal union politics. As a result of these policies some of the state federations have had difficulty retaining some local affiliates. This has been a particularly big problem in Alabama and Mississippi, but of only moderate importance in most of the other Southern states, though they all have had some disaffiliations partly for this reason. It should be emphasized, however, that locals are willing to disaffiliate because state federations of labor or city central organizations have very little influence on the local unions' bargaining positions.

Opposition to equalitarian policies of central bodies usually involves community and not trade union policies and was most intense in the period immediately following the Supreme Court's 1954 desegregation decision. In Chattanooga, for example, the Central Labor Union was bitterly criticized by segregationist union leaders for endorsing the local school board's plans to comply with the Supreme Court's desegregation decision. The CLU's action was prompted by a 1954 AFL convention resolution endorsing the Supreme Court's decision, but evoked vicious attacks from segregationist unions led by the Printing Pressmen and joined by the Switchmen, Carpenters, Plumbers, Machinists, Typographical, and Electrical Workers; in all, nine affiliated unions opposed the CLU's actions. The CLU and *Labor World*, the local labor paper, were accused of being dominated by leaders "supporting organizations and sociological theories . . . dedicated to removing the last vestiges of our Southern heritage" and "selling us out for 30 pieces of our own silver" by contributing union money to the NAACP. Local union leaders also were denounced as "alien Communist lovers and socializers who have had their way for a long time." According to the segregationists, the CLU could not deny "some responsibility for the disgusting integration of Negro and white workers in the labor movement in Tennessee."[10]

As a result of this criticism, some locals withdrew from the CLU, some members dropped their subscriptions to *Labor World*, and a meeting was called to reconsider the central body's support of the school board. This meeting, attended by the largest number of delegates of any meeting since the thirties, adopted a resolution which vowed to organize all workers in order to "keep gains of the bargaining table from being taken away by anti-labor legislation," but "because of the highly controversial nature of the issues raised by the Supreme Court's decision on segregation in the public schools, issues which cut across our ranks tending to divide us, it is hereby declared to be the policy of the Chattanooga Central Labor Union henceforth to refrain from involving itself on either side of this issue."

A number of international unions have had trouble implementing their racial policies in the South. The Auto Workers revoked the charter of a Dallas local in 1952 for refusing to follow the international's racial policies, and it has had considerable difficulty with locals in Memphis and Atlanta. The Memphis International Harvester local was placed under trusteeship by the UAW in 1960 after a long series of disputes between the local and the international over racial matters, particularly the local's segregation of facilities in its headquarters and strikes by local whites to prevent International Harvester from upgrading Negroes and using them in nontraditional jobs. The company's firmness, backed by the international, succeeded in forcing local whites to comply with company and union policies, although success was at least partly due to relatively high wages in the plant and the fact that the international was certified as bargaining agent by the NLRB.

The only Negroes in the Atlanta automobile plant organized by the UAW in 1937 were janitors, but local whites refused to accept these colored workers into the local until forced to do so by the international union in 1946. Thereafter Negroes were accepted in the union but seating was segregated, as it was in most other so-called "integrated" unions in the South. During the racial ferment of the 1950s and 1960s this company hired more Negroes and moved them into jobs previously held by whites.

No union has followed equalitarian racial policies in the South more vigorously than the United Packinghouse Workers. This attitude was dictated by the CIO's realization that the large number of Negroes in the industry, many of whom had started as strikebreakers, could not be unionized by any other policy. The UPWA's policies have been opposed by its Southern members and it has lost a few locals for this reason. On balance, however, the union's support from Negroes probably has brought it more members than it has lost by the defections of whites. In 1954, for example, Louisiana UPWA leaders made an effort to get nine sugar locals to withdraw from the United Packinghouse Workers, partly because of the union's racial policies. But the international was able to avert the secession of the five largest, which had Negro majorities, through the appeal of the union's equalitarian position. Four smaller locals withdrew, but two of these returned to the UPWA because they could not survive alone and could find no strong union willing to take them. The UPWA has also encountered opposition in Georgia, Alabama, and Texas because of its racial policies.

It is not easy, however, to determine whether Southern reaction to the UPWA's policies was due to a greater extent to racial prejudice or to a sincere belief that the union's actions were Communist-inspired. There is weighty evidence, which we need not detail, to support the conclusion that both elements were present. The Communists used the race issue to defeat anti-Communist UPWA leaders, and segregationists used Communism to cover their opposition to integration. Southern white UPWA leaders were apparently embarrassed by the fact that their organization followed equalitarian policies much more vigorously than almost any other CIO union.

A number of international unions have had trouble in the South because of a movement among Negroes during and after the Second World War to eliminate racially segregated seniority rosters, which were sometimes supported by racially segregated local unions. The most significant examples of unions that have had this problem include the Oil Workers, the Pulp, Sulphite, and Paper Mill Workers, the Steelworkers, the Paperworkers, and the Rubber Workers. We can use the experience of the paper industry as an illustration, though the Oil Workers were the only other industrial union mentioned to have segregated local unions. As in other Southern industries, Negroes in the pulp and paper industry were commonly hired into labor pools, while whites were hired directly into the operating departments. The main difference between Northern and Southern paper mills was that in the South workers in the labor pool (Negroes) did a lot of the work that was done elsewhere by the operators and their helpers. In the paper industry, as in others, the separate seniority rosters were not invented solely to segregate jobs racially, but also were based on the training needs of the companies involved. The fact that Negroes were hired only for menial, dead-end jobs meant that they were usually not so qualified as whites to move into many higher-paying skilled jobs which could not be filled on the basis of seniority alone.

Desegregation of seniority rosters came later in the paper industry than in steel, rubber, petroleum refining, and a few others, perhaps because paper mills tended to be located in smaller, more remote towns in the South, which are not so conspicuous and not so vulnerable to those forces tending to undermine racial segregation. And although whites have almost invariably resisted desegregation, the resistance was probably stronger in the pulp and paper industry, particularly in view of the fact that it came some ten years after the trend to desegregation had started in other industries. In addition, the international unions in the paper industry are more conservative on racial matters than internationals in the other industries mentioned.

As a result, there was considerable reaction to President Kennedy's Committee on Equal Employment Opportunities (PCEEO) when it ordered the Southern mills desegregated in 1962. The companies apparently were seriously influenced by the PCEEO's threat, because high-ranking company officials supervised job desegregation. Upper-management officials met with unions and supervisory employees, emphasizing the need to integrate in order to keep federal contracts. Some union leaders led protest rallies in an effort to maintain segregation. But while there were scattered acts of violence, and relations between Negroes and whites within the local unions were strained, white union leaders and their segregationist allies in the local communities were frustrated in their efforts to avert integration of the mills; about the only advice the White Citizens' Council could offer the protesting union members was "write your Congressmen."

A meeting of four hundred segregationists in the high school auditorium at Springhill, Louisiana, illustrates the feelings of some paper union leaders in the deep South. The meeting was called by nine local unions of the huge International Paper mill in Springhill and was attended by members of the Louisiana Legislature, White Citizens' Council, and the unions; indeed, union leaders said the meeting was open to "all those interested in maintaining our Southern traditions."[11] One union leader was quoted as saying that local union leaders had met with the company on August 1, 1962, and had been told that the PCEEO had prohibited "the company from using any discretion in hiring employees based on color. He told the segregationists that this action was ". . . a result of the Anti-God, Anti-Christ Kennedys, Inc.," and added, "They may cram it down our throats, but they can't make us agree and like it. Integration is now in Springhill. We don't want trouble and won't agitate trouble, but we are against integration. Our local unions won't be responsible, but we'll stand behind our men."

A number of attempts to form racist labor organizations in the South were made by segregationists in the wake of the Supreme Court's 1954 school desegregation decision. These included the United Southern Employees Association chartered in North Carolina in 1956 and subsequently in Virginia, Alabama, Florida, Georgia, and South Carolina. The USEA sought unsuccessfully to form an alliance with Ku Klux Klan organizations in the Piedmont area. The organization's general objectives included: organizing all workers in order to drive the AFL-CIO out of the South; attempting to work with employers by emphasizing efficiency and good will; promoting the enactment of laws requiring advocates of integration to be "sterilized" so they would be unable to produce "mongrelized offspring"; reversal of the Supreme Court's desegregation decision; the passage of right-to-work laws; and defeating liberal candidates for office by splitting Negro-labor alliances where they existed. The USEA apparently generated more publicity than collective-bargaining contracts. While it was temporarily active in many places, it never succeeded in winning bargaining rights or, apparently, in establishing permanent labor organizations.

Other unsuccessful segregationist ventures included the Southern Federation of Labor, which fizzled briefly in Birmingham in 1956; Southern Crafts, Inc., headed by a railroad engineer from Birmingham; and the Southern States Conference of Union People, formed by a group of Chattanooga unionists. The Southern States Conference of Union People sought to work from within the AFL-CIO in an effort to turn Southern union members away from the AFL-CIO's policies. In addition, various organizations like the Ku Klux Klan and the White Citizens' Councils have infiltrated unions in the South and otherwise opposed the AFL-CIO's policies.

CONCLUDING OBSERVATIONS

The first conclusion that seems to flow from a study of union racial problems during the period of racial turmoil following the Supreme Court's 1954 desegregation decision is that few Southern whites will either withdraw from collective-bargaining unions or refuse to join such organizations for purely racial reasons. The main cases of secession have involved such noncollective-bargaining organizations as the state federations or city centrals and governmental organizations like the American Federation of Teachers, which lost five Southern locals during this period because of their refusal to obey an international's ultimatum to integrate, and the National Association of Letter Carriers, which lost a Louisiana white local for the same reason. (The race question would appear to have had only marginal influence on the organizing of unorganized whites in the South.)

The failure of segregationist labor organizations is probably due mainly to inadequate leadership and the improbability of building a labor organization on purely racist principles. In no case has a regular union leader been willing to leave his position to lead one of the racist groups.

Superior economic conditions also prompt Southern union members to maintain their allegiance to national unions. Most of the important unions of the South are craft unions, railroad unions, or industrial organizations which are extensions of strong power bases outside the regions; unions often use their power in non-Southern areas to force companies to give equally favorable conditions in the South. Southerners who attribute their good pay and working conditions to unions will not lightly abandon those advantages over racial matters.

The ability of a national organization to enforce its racial policies in the South depends upon the relative power of the local and national organizations. A situation where Southern members receive better wages than those prevailing in their area tends to increase the power of the national over the local. Other factors involved in this power relationship include: whether the local or national union is the certified bargaining agent; the ownership of strike funds and other property; internal union politics, especially the political power of the local union; the nature of the market and the need for national coordination of wage policy; and whether there are other national unions with more compatible racial policies willing to admit seceding members or locals. Generally, local unions will not secede for racial reasons and internationals will not expel a recalcitrant local. A number of internationals have decided, however, that locals that defy international racial policies will be placed under trusteeship.

Race trouble in unions is most likely to occur where there is race trouble in the community; where outside groups raise the issue in local union affairs; where national union leaders make widely publicized integrationist speeches, contribute union money to civil rights organizations, or engage in other publicized integrationist activity. Practices which go unnoticed for years will create trouble if publicized, because publicity often causes Southern union members to feel compelled to disassociate themselves from the policies of their national leaders. Southern whites frequently break with Southern tradition when they join unions, but are rarely willing to risk complete ostracism by becoming identified as integrationists.

Chapter IV

THE AMERICAN FEDERATION OF LABOR AND THE NEGRO WORKER, 1894–1949

MARC KARSON AND RONALD RADOSH

In the years immediately after its founding in 1881, the American Federation of Labor subscribed to a policy of nondiscrimination against Negro workers. Its 1890 convention stated that the Federation "looks with disfavor upon trade unions having provisions which exclude from membership persons on account of race or color."[1] Similarly, a later convention urged working people to "unite and organize irrespective of creed, color, sex, nationality, or politics."[2] The National Association of Machinists in 1890 and the Boilermakers and Iron Shipbuilders in 1893 were refused charters by the AFL because they constitutionally barred Negroes from membership. Southern racists in the AFL, and AFL staff members in the South, were critical of the Federation's advocacy of organizing Negroes and whites in the same unions, and warned that such a policy would stand in the way of recruiting white workers.

The first signs of the Federation's change in policy were evident by 1894 in Samuel Gompers' speeches to union conventions, in letters to union leaders, and in a new admission policy permitting unions to receive AFL charters as long as they did not have an explicit constitutional provision barring Negroes. This meant that if a union resorted to an obvious subterfuge to deny membership to Negroes, the AFL would not concern itself. Thus, the International Association of Machinists received its AFL charter in 1895, after removing a formal color bar, although the Secretary of this union could write that "in 1899 the Negro is not admitted to the International Association of Machinists." (One labor leader, asked by the U. S. Industrial Commission if he had ever worked with a Negro machinist, answered: "No sir: I never worked in a shop with a Negro as a machinist. . . . I would not."[3])

At the same time, the AFL decided it would grant a direct charter to Negroes who were not accepted into a white local, since unorganized workers were always a potential economic threat to the wages and jobs of union members. At the 1890 AFL convention, Article XII, Section VI of the AFL constitution was revised to read, ". . . separate charters may be issued to Central Labor Unions, Local Unions or Federal Labor Unions, composed exclusively of colored members, where in the judgment of the Executive Council it appears advisable and to the best interests of the Trade Union movement to do so." The AFL leaders justified this policy with the rationalization that the AFL's existence was contingent upon the *per capita* dues it received from affiliated internationals. The organization would have to compromise its principles of brotherhood if it did not want to alienate many unions opposed to admitting Negroes.

Samuel Gompers made use of his dialectical talents to square the Jim Crowism of the AFL with the historic trade union position of "solidarity forever." On the one hand, he claimed, the AFL did not believe in discrimination but, on the other, it could not determine the internal admission requirements of international unions; the AFL believed in organizing Negro workers but was doing it, in part, through separate "federal" Negro unions; the Negro workers were often to blame for allowing themselves to be used as strike-breakers, and at some future time genuine integration would be realized. All these rationalizations could not hide the fact that moral principles had been sacrificed to expediency, that a growing treasury and white membership meant more than the welfare of Negro workers. This may seem a severe judgment but it must be realized that since employment often required union membership, to deny Negroes entry into an established union meant, in effect, denying them jobs. The fact that Negroes could receive separate charters from the

AFL did not mean that they would find jobs as easily as white unionists, for Negro locals were smaller and less powerful. Furthermore, the fact that apprenticeship training programs in the many building trade unions operated by unions and employers conspired to keep Negroes out meant that the Negro remained an outcast. In addition, when Negro unionists did secure jobs, they frequently were assigned to the lowest positions and paid less than white unionists. The employers knew they could exact a harder bargain from a Negro local, which did not have the same backing from the international that white locals could expect. Finally, the AFL did little in the way of appointing Negro organizers, although recommendations that this be done were adopted by the AFL Conventions of 1902, 1907, 1917, and 1918. For all practical purposes, the AFL did not even aid the unorganized Negroes in gaining entry into the segregated structure which the 1900 Convention had created. The basic American trade union movement had chosen not to become a leader in the fight against segregation but to accommodate itself to and, in fact, incorporate segregation into its own organization. Negroes were to be organized in separate local unions wherever an existing international in the area of jurisdiction would not accept them for integrated membership. In a city where a number of Negro locals existed, they would be formed into a separate Negro trades council.

In 1902 Dr. W. E. B. Du Bois undertook a university study of Negro membership in unions and reported that forty-three internationals including the Railroad Brotherhoods were without any Negro members and that twenty-seven additional unions had only a very small number of Negroes. Of about 40,000 Negroes who belonged to the AFL, more than 20,000 were members of one union, the United Mine Workers.[4] By 1910, AFL unions that excluded Negroes through constitutional provision or ritual requirements were: the Railroad Telegraphers, the Railway Trackmen, the Stationary Engineers, the Railway and Steamship Clerks, the Railway Carmen, the Wire Weavers, the Switchmen, the Maintenance-of-Way Employees, the Commercial Telegraphers, the Machinists, the Boilermakers, and the Iron and Shipbuilders. Other unions denied admittance to Negroes without resorting to constitutional or ritual provisions. This was accomplished by means of "unwritten" practices, high initiation fees, examinations designed to fail Negro applicants, the requirement of special licenses unobtainable by Negroes, and an apprenticeship program that excluded Negroes and thereby prevented them from gaining the skill required to obtain jobs.

The AFL's fear of antagonizing its affiliated internationals led it to deny a direct charter to a Negro local union unless it had the approval of the international which had refused admittance to Negroes. Nor did the AFL venture into the field of education in an effort to lessen the prejudices of its staff, the international's staff, or its rank and filers and thereby begin the long-range effort to end discrimination.

By 1910–12 the great majority of AFL unions had either a few or no Negro members. The industrially structured United Mine Workers stood out with 40,000 members, the Teamsters with 6000, the Cigar Makers with 5000, the Hotel and Restaurant Employees and the Carpenters with 2500 each, and the Painters with 250. The number of Negroes in the remainder of the unions was negligible.[5]

In speeches, in testimony before government commissions, and in the AFL monthly journal, *The American Federationist*, Gompers, after 1900, made many racist attacks on Negroes. He referred to white workers as "Caucasians" who had a character and an ambition above that of Negroes. He threatened Negro strikebreakers with "a race hatred far worse than any ever known," although he failed to put any blame upon the labor movement for failing to organize the Negroes, thereby facilitating their recruitment as strikebreakers.[6] In a statement to the press in April 1901 Gompers acknowledged that the Federation "does not necessarily proclaim that the social barriers which exist between the whites and blacks could or should be obliterated."[7]

As a noted labor historian has written, not only was

Gompers "utterly and completely silent" on the mistreatment that Negroes encountered in America, such as disfranchisement, lynchings, exclusion from jury duty, segregation in schools, colleges, railroads, and other places, but he "employed racial epithets which revealed contempt for the Negro people. He took delight in telling stories in his public addresses that helped to perpetuate the stereotype of the Negroes, whom he referred to as 'darkies,' as superstitious, dull, ignorant, happy-go-lucky, improvident, lazy and, immoral."[8]

The 1917 AFL convention conclusively showed the prevalence of racial prejudice among the organization's leadership and membership. Although a few months before the convention a race riot in East St. Louis had claimed the lives of thirty-nine Negroes and eight whites and the nation was involved in a world war, the AFL convention turned its back on a resolution denouncing discrimination against Negroes in America.[9] The resolution listed a number of offenses suffered by Negroes such as disfranchisement, segregation in transportation, housing, schooling, hotels, theaters, restaurants, and other public places, the lack of representation in local and state government, and the enormous extralegal punishments for crimes and alleged crimes. It asked the convention to direct the AFL Executive Council to influence the President and Congress "to the end that all the political, civic and economic disabilities so offensive and destructive to the rights of Negroes as human beings and American citizens be removed." The Committee on Resolutions presented the resolution to the convention without approval and with a specific announcement disclaiming responsibility for any of the resolution's statements. After it had been denounced on the convention floor, an amendment was attached to the committee's report which rejected the statements contained in the resolution. This amended report, in effect upholding inequality and discrimination against Negroes, was adopted by the convention. The 1921 convention was also presented with two resolutions opposing discrimination, but the Resolutions Committee disapproved on the ground that the AFL "cannot interfere with the trade autonomy of affiliated" unions. Gompers' position was again that the Federation had no power to enforce integration policies upon unwilling internationals.

The efforts of Negroes outside the labor movement to gain the AFL's support against discriminatory practices also met with little success. W. E. B. Du Bois forwarded to Gompers his 1902 study on the Negro and unions (see above) which listed the segregationist policies of AFL unions and described their acceptance by the AFL national leadership. Gompers replied that the Du Bois study was "neither fair nor accurate," and was "pessimistic upon the subject." Dismissing Du Bois curtly, he closed by saying that he had "more important work to attend to than correct 'copy' for your paper."[10]

During the First World War a committee of nationally known Negro leaders met with the AFL Executive Council to voice its criticism of labor's racial discrimination "and neglect of the thousands of Negro workers" who needed to be organized. Gompers defended the AFL's policy of segregated Negro unions by claiming it was at the time the only way in which unions could have been established in the South. He then pointed to the limits of the Federation's power.[11] Six months later Eugene Kinkle Jones, Secretary of the National Urban League, presented several proposals to Gompers on behalf of the Negro committee. The group requested that the Federation issue a statement clarifying its racial position, employ a Negro organizer, and consult from time to time with the Negro committee. The Council did not accept the suggestions. Instead, it reported that "it could find no fault with the past work of the Federation" and it took no further action on the committee's proposals.[12]

The 1924 NAACP convention requested the AFL to form an Interracial Labor Commission, made up of representatives from the AFL, the Railroad Brotherhoods, and the NAACP, to facilitate the admission of Negro workers into *de facto* white unions. This appeal proposed that the interracial commission undertake "to find out the exact attitude and practice of national labor bodies and local unions toward Negroes, and of Negro labor toward unions," and that it "organize systematic propaganda against racial discrimination, on the basis of these facts at the great labor meetings, in local assemblies and in local unions." No action on this plea was taken.[13]

During the period in which William Green held the presidency of the AFL, it continued the policy of discrimination. Even Philip Taft, the AFL historian, admitted that "discrimination against Negroes and other minority groups was tolerated in practice throughout the years."[14] This attitude was not so much the result of neglecting to curb racist elements within labor's ranks as it was the product of the overtly racist views held by the trade union leadership itself. As in Gompers' day, the Federation's policies encouraged racist practices and discouraged the efforts of those who opposed racism. While defenders of the AFL have stated that it had no power to compel international affiliates to obey its pronouncements against discrimination, the AFL actually used its power to coerce affiliates during jurisdictional conflicts, in political struggles, or when confronted by the threat of dual unionism.

A. Philip Randolph, the Negro organizer and leader of the Sleeping Car Porters, was a constant thorn in the side of the AFL leadership as he continuously fought for the end of discrimination. His initial attitude toward the Federation reflected the black worker's great distrust of and skepticism toward organized labor. Originally, Randolph had contended that a new union federation had to be built, restructured on a basis other than trade autonomy and neglect of unskilled workers. "The dissolution of the American Federation of Labor," Randolph had argued, "would inure to the benefit of the labor movement in this country in particular and the international labor movement in general. It is organized upon unsound principles. It holds that there can be a partnership between labor and capital. . . . It stands for pure and simple unionism as against industrial unionism . . . the present American Federation of Labor is the most wicked machine for the propagation of race prejudice in the country."[15]

By 1929, Randolph had decided to ask that the Sleeping Car Porters be admitted to the Federation, although this did not mean that he was going to abandon his fight against its discriminatory policies. At first, jurisdictional claims of the Hotel and Restaurant Employees International Alliance blocked the AFL's ability to grant the Brotherhood an international charter, but at the 1929 Toronto convention a compromise proposal was accepted in which separate charters were issued to the Porters as a temporary arrangement. "We did not agree to their admission as an international organization," the annual report of the Executive Council stated, "but we did agree to issue charters to them as local unions directly affiliated with the American Federation of Labor."[16]

The Hotel Employees argued that they made "no distinction between the white and the colored workers; they enjoy the same benefits and they secure the same working conditions." The union claimed the right to represent sleeping car porters because they viewed them as part of the hotel industry. Randolph argued that the porters were railroad men and not hotel employees, and that Negro workers were beginning to realize that "their place is in the American Federation of Labor, and that they want to play their part in building up this organization." Randolph now viewed the Sleeping Car Porters as "the spearhead which will make possible the organization of Negro workers."[17]

In 1933 Randolph's union numbered thirty-five thousand members, half the total number of Negro workers in the AFL. At the 1933 convention Randolph asked that the Federation go on record as enlisting and employing Negro organizers to carry on the campaign for Negro organization. He emphasized that Negroes were one tenth of the population but that a larger proportion of them worked for a living than in any other ethnic group in the country. Yet the racial barriers of unions were fostering distrust and weakening the unity and strength of the labor movement.

Randolph argued on the convention floor that he raised this problem "because of the great importance at the present time of carrying forward the movement of the organization of the workers," and because he knew employers were pitting white against black in order to weaken all organized labor. Negro workers in the South had to have Negro organizers, because only a Negro organizer could make an effective approach to black labor. Noting that employers would use racial prejudice as a means of escaping from NRA responsibilities, Randolph said labor had to "remove from the hands of the employing class the weapon of race prejudice." This could be done only by organizing black workers "in large numbers." Vice-President Frank Duffy squashed Randolph's resolution. While he claimed that he was not opposing the resolution, he had it referred back to the Executive Council to be "put into effect if the cost will permit."[18]

In 1934 Randolph raised the whole question of the AFL's discriminatory attitude toward Negro workers. He introduced a resolution which noted that the ratio of Negro workers to white workers was higher than the corresponding ratio in the over-all population, and that there was "widespread unrest . . . with the existing status of Negro workers in the American Federation of Labor, and with its policy toward the organization of Negro workers." While convention resolutions were splendid, they did not "frankly and effectively face and solve the problems of organizing Negro workers."

Randolph's resolution charged that all the international and national unions of the Railway Department had either color clauses in their constitutions or racist pledges in their rituals, such as "only sober and industrious white men are eligible for membership." He denounced such bars as "unsound, defenseless, undemocratic, illegal, and un-American." Since capitalists would readily exploit white men, women, and children "with as much severity as they will exploit black men," he proposed that the convention go on record "for the elimination of the color clause and pledge from the constitution and rituals of all trade and industrial unions." Further, he asked for the expulsion of all trade and industrial unions which violated the AFL constitution "by maintaining said color bar." Finally, Randolph proposed that a Committee of Five be appointed to "investigate the question of the status of Negro workers in the national and international unions, federal unions, and the general policy of the American Federation of Labor on the matter of organizing Negro workers, and report to the next convention its findings with recommendations as to future policy in relation to Negro workers."[19]

The AFL Organization Committee, in reporting on Randolph's resolution, insisted that the Federation already practiced a nondiscriminatory policy. The committee claimed that the AFL had "for the last fifty years" made it plain that all workers, irrespective of creed, color, nationality, or political views, were eligible for membership. The AFL could not "interfere with the autonomy of national and international unions. The American Federation of Labor cannot say who are eligible or who are not eligible to membership in national and international unions." These bodies had the right to restrict membership if they saw fit, a right of which unions "cannot be deprived." The committee noted that the AFL's Article XI, Section 6 proclaimed that separate charters could be issued to all Negro unions. Finally, it recommended nonconcurrence with the Randolph resolution.

Randolph answered the argument that separate charters were a substitute for integrated organization by stating that resolutions adopted at previous AFL conventions on the question of Negro membership "have not effected the desired results; in fact they are meaningless because of the fact that they have made certain declarations without any actual attempt being made to translate these declarations into concrete facts." The delegates all knew, Randolph continued, that color clauses and pledges still existed and that "therefore no effort . . . is being made to organize the Negro workers." Because of the clauses a "psychology is being created among white and black workers that makes effective organization of Negro workers more and more difficult."

In fact, there had not even been a systematic effort to develop federal unions of Negro workers. Randolph offered his resolution so that machinery could be created and a committee established to study the status of Negro workers affiliated with the AFL. A study of the condition of black labor would lay the basis for an intelligent policy, and could help to form opinion that would view the organization of Negro workers more favorably. As Randolph put it, "if we go on from year to year and merely concur in the resolutions, saying we are in favor of Negro workers joining the unions and nothing is done to put the resolutions into effect we will not get very far."[20]

William Hutcheson, head of the Carpenters, supported the organization committee but argued that there was merit to the request that a committee be appointed to investigate the conditions of colored workers. Andrew Furuseth, President of the International Seamen's Union, argued that although seamen made no racial distinctions, acceptance of the Negro on a basis of "absolute equality with the white man as to wages and conditions" created a situation whereby the employer hired the white man only and the union could "get no employment for our colored workers if we had to pay the same wages and give the same conditions. The result was that the colored man as a whole left our organization and accepted the employment with less wages." Furuseth therefore favored separate colored organizations. Arguing that race is "the most terrific force in the whole of human life," he claimed that the AFL policy was "fundamentally correct." What it had done in bringing about a feeling of equality was good, and the AFL, in "the interests of the black race itself, in the interests of our Negro brothers, *is bound to go slow*—not to stop, not to cease working for the colored worker, *but to go slow.*" Furuseth wanted any investigation to be carried out by the AFL's own Executive Council since while "we are all entitled to life," there is "something here that has got to be dealt with with some care."[21]

Vice-President Duffy claimed that the AFL had "endorsed

and re-endorsed" the concept of organizing Negro workers, and he was upset that Negro labor was going "a little further" by asking expulsion of discriminatory unions. He also suggested that the proposed investigatory body be the AFL Executive Council itself, and that it submit its own report to the next convention. Rejecting Randolph's proposal, Duffy argued that the AFL had done everything it could to show recognition to the Negro workers and that the question was how to "reconcile the Negro workers" to the Federation. William Hutcheson then suggested that the President of the AFL appoint the Committee of Five himself, with the understanding that perhaps someone outside the Executive Council would be included.[22]

The 1934 convention gave its approval to the Organization Committee's position, and rejected another civil rights resolution introduced by one James P. Dallas. Dallas' resolution asked for the elimination of clauses in union constitutions containing discriminatory provisions, and for the merger of all Jim Crow locals and white locals. John P. Frey, head of the Molders, bolstered it by noting AFL support for the principle of equal pay for equal work. But because the AFL was "without authority to interfere with the internal affairs and administration of affiliated unions," the committee considering Dallas' resolution recommended nonconcurrence, and was upheld by the delegates.

About seven months after the 1934 convention, William Green assigned John E. Rooney of the Operative Plasterers and Cement Finishers, John Brophy of the United Mine Workers, John W. Garvey of the Laborers, Jerry L. Hanks of the Journeymen Barbers, and T. C. Carroll of the Maintenance-of-Way Employees to serve on the Committee of Five to investigate the condition of Negro labor and to report to the 1935 convention. All the appointees were white.

The committee began hearings in late June, 1935, and a circular letter was sent to international unions to find out if they discriminated against Negroes or barred them from membership. At hearings on July 9 and 10, Randolph testified in regard to racial practices of affiliated AFL unions. The National Association for the Advancement of Colored People was represented at the hearings by its chief counsel, Charles H. Houston. Houston reported that signed statements of specific acts of racial discrimination by AFL affiliates were being collected by NAACP branches through the United States for presentation at subsequent hearings to bolster the charges being made by Randolph and others. But Green soon notified the NAACP that he would not schedule any more hearings, because the first Washington hearing had gathered "sufficient information."[23]

The Committee of Five's report was not included as part of the Executive Council's report to the 1935 convention, although the 1934 convention had ruled that it was to be presented the following year. A reading of the report suggests why the ruling was ignored. The Committee of Five asked that all internationals that barred Negroes from membership or had established Jim Crow locals or denied Negro representation at conventions or meetings eliminate these restrictions at their next convention. It urged that AFL charters conform to AFL national admission policies and proposed that "separate Negro Federal Unions shall be discontinued by the AF of L and such membership be transferred to mixed locals of the respective Internationals, where they may have an effective voice in determination of wages and other conditions." The report also requested a campaign on racial education and continuation of the committee.[24]

At the 1935 convention there were more fireworks on the racial issue. The question of discrimination took second place only to the debate on industrial unionism. Toward the end of the long and important convention, A. Philip Randolph rose and stated that delegates were still waiting for a discussion of the Committee of Five's report, a report "so handled as to delay its presentation at this convention until such time when it will not be possible to have a full discussion." Randolph urged that despite the late hour it was important for the convention to hear discussion of the report on discrimination in trade unions against Negro workers.[25]

Randolph charged that the Executive Council's report was "very inaccurate, fragmentary and absolutely unsound and ought to be examined by the convention." He read the Supplemental Report of the Executive Council on colored workers, which declared that only a few national and international unions denied membership to Negroes. In these few instances, the report continued, "special provisions are made to organize the negroes into Federal Labor Unions directly chartered" by the AFL, and in other cases Negroes are placed in separate local unions with "varying rights of membership." The Executive Committee pointed out that because each union had complete autonomy the Negro's welfare would "be best served by a campaign of education" leading toward the "voluntary elimination of all restrictions."

William Green supported this statement, while Randolph argued that it did not meet the issue in any respect, and that the Executive Council had not even followed procedure laid down by the 1934 convention. He scored the Council report for omitting the Committee of Five's recommendations. Without these, he declared, the Executive Council's report was "merely a dignified, diplomatic camouflage." Randolph quoted to the convention from the Committee of Five's call for action, citing its suggestions that: 1) all unions that bar Negroes discuss this at their conventions and then harmonize their constitutions and practices with the AFL precepts on equality; 2) charters be issued only in conformity with declared policy; and 3) the AFL conduct a mass educational campaign in order "to get the white worker to see more completely the weakness of division and the necessity of greater trade union unity between white and black workers to the end that all workers may be organized."

Randolph denounced those unions with color clauses or pledges in the ritual and those which used other devices and subtle ways to bar Negroes. Citing the Executive Council's answer that provision was made for Negroes in federal unions, Randolph stated that "the federal unions that include Negroes are racial unions" and that no justification for their continuation existed. Randolph revealed that Negro freight and express handlers, under the jurisdiction of the Brotherhood of Railway Clerks, had no power to negotiate an agreement concerning rates of pay or working conditions, and that the Brotherhood of Clerks had no machinery through which federal union members could present their grievances. Although the national bodies covering Negroes who were in federal unions claimed that they made agreements on behalf of black workers, Negro laborers had neither the right nor the power to take grievances to the National Railroad Board of Adjustment because their union was an "isolated, separate body" with no legitimacy. Without a national structure they could not make use of provisions established under the Railway Labor Act.

A federal union based on race, Randolph argued, was actually a dual union which held no power under the law. Therefore the federal form that the AFL supposedly provided for Negro workers was "virtually no organization at all." Not one had negotiated a contract with employers, and neither did they have the power to protect the interests of the Negro workers nor did they organize them to any appreciable extent. In effect, the many references to their existence were evidence of the AFL's acquiescence in racist practices, or at best an evasion of the question of real support for the principle of Negro organization.

No organization in the AFL, Randolph declared, had the moral right to compose an agreement for a class of workers and exempt a section of them because of color, or to accept benefits of federal legislation and keep black workers from enjoying that privilege. The "refuge of trade autonomy" was an evasion because the AFL had dealt harshly with affiliated internationals in several other cases. It had forced the building trades unions to accept national structures, and there was no reason "under the sun why an organization of labor which is interested in the organization of workers . . .

should single out the Negro workers and attach to them the stigma of inferiority" by prohibiting them from joining an organization and preventing them from drawing up their own contracts. Correctly foreseeing the future, Randolph said the AFL "will not be able to hold its head up and face the world as long as it permits any section of workers in America to be discriminated against because they happen to be black."

Randolph's remarks did not pass unchallenged. John P. Frey, Molders' chief, moved for approval of the Executive Council's supplemental report, stating that actually he was "in very large agreement" with Randolph's statements and sympathized deeply with "his problems." He disagreed, however, that the Executive's report was evasive and insufficient. He considered that the union movement had done more than any other institution to break down racial prejudice, and that Randolph's words would "create prejudice instead of breaking it down if we make too strong an effort in that direction."*

AFL President Green also took exception to Randolph's charges. Actually 100 out of 105 unions admitted Negro workers to membership, and he expressed disappointment that Randolph desired to compel international unions to provide for admission of Negroes to membership.** Green defended the inability of the AFL to "say to an autonomous International Union how it shall draft its laws" and whom

* Apparently Frey was even more of a racist than his convention remarks indicated. For example, to his friend, the British union leader W. C. Appleton, he wrote: "The English speaking colonies have decided that their standard of civilization made it absolutely necessary that the oriental should be excluded . . . the new countries, which the white man's courage and energies rescued from a wilderness and turned into a civilization, shall and must remain a white man's civilization." (John P. Frey to W. C. Appleton, April 5, 1921, John P. Frey MSS., Library of Congress, Washington, D.C.)

** Randolph disagreed with Green's figures, and told the delegates that actually twenty unions, not five, completely excluded Negroes from membership.

it should admit to membership. Green was personally opposed to unions excluding Negroes, but, he said, the unions had to decide that question for themselves. He held that the AFL could not go as far as Randolph desired, to the point of stipulating that union laws must provide for admission of Negroes to membership. Green rejected the idea of revoking charters, and expressed his faith that education would finally overcome the racial problem in the labor movement. He also defended the existence of federal unions for Negroes in order to "accommodate the needs of the colored workers who come under the jurisdiction of national and international unions that yet retained" exclusionary clauses.

Milton Webster of the Sleeping Car Porters answered Green, arguing that federal bodies did not work and that the Brotherhood of Sleeping Car Porters had been unable to organize Negro workers successfully before they created a national organization. Workers had to be represented in national groups that had the power to write agreements for all classes of workers. Other union leaders commented, acknowledging the existence of discrimination in their unions but nevertheless showing an unwillingness to change this situation. George Harrison, President of the Railway Clerks, emphasized his belief that all affiliated unions had complete autonomy to determine the qualifications of membership and the only way to end restrictions on Negro participation was by education. Referring to his own union, Harrison related that the grievances of Negro workers were handled in the same manner as those of white unionists—that, in other words, the Negro worker was "separate but equal." "We do not admit Negroes to our Brotherhood," Harrison admitted, but the Brotherhood gave "them the same service we must give to the white employees" since "we organized the Negroes into Federal Labor Unions." Harrison argued that the Negro worker "under the Brotherhood I represent has complete economic equality," implying that this precluded any need for abolishing the Jim Crow union structure. The Negro worker would have to wait until the white unionists were persuaded to grant full membership to the

Negro workers. At the conclusion of the debate, the 1935 AFL convention endorsed by voice vote the Executive Council's report and rejected Randolph's position.

John Brophy, a member of the Committee of Five who was bitter at the omission of his committee's report, wrote to William Green that while the Committee of Five had "acted in good faith and in accordance with the definite instructions of the San Francisco convention, the arbitrary action of the Executive Council and yourself in denying us the opportunity to report completely nullified the committee's work and completely nullified the mandate of the previous convention." Moreover, the "maneuvering on the part of the Executive Council plainly indicated that you wanted the 'Committee of Five to Investigate Conditions of Negro Workers' to be merely a face-saving device for the AFL rather than an honest attempt to find a solution to the Negro problem in the American labor movement."[26]

Other members of the Committee of Five had been less determined than Brophy to take meaningful action against discrimination. Thomas C. Carroll wrote to William Green that John Brophy had been

> . . . rather insistent that the committee, in making the report, recommend that all National or International Unions that had any kind of a bar against colored workers . . . be directed to immediately eliminate them. The Committee members endeavored to show Brother Brophy that such a recommendation could not be made under the present law of the American Federation of Labor, that if such a recommendation was to be made, it would first be necessary to amend the constitution and by-laws of the A.F. of L. and take from its component organizations the self-autonomy guaranteed them in respect to their membership and it was, finally, more as a compromise measure that the other members of the committee who signed the majority report went along with Brother Brophy as we did.[27]

Carroll's letter had the effect of informing Green that the committee really did not stand behind its own recommendations. Other Committee of Five members also let it be known that they did not stand behind the proposals. Jerry Hanks was opposed to any action whatsoever, on the basis that the issue of discrimination against the Negro predated the formation of the AFL.[28] This may have encouraged the Executive Council to ignore the committee's strong proposals for action when preparing its annual report.

Resolutions introduced at subsequent conventions urging an end to discrimination encountered by Negro labor were never able to secure approval. At one time William Green asked D. H. Robertson, head of the Brotherhood of Locomotive Firemen and Enginemen, about the Brotherhood's policy on the enrollment of Negro firemen. Robertson wrote that his union bargained collectively for all locomotive firemen, regardless of race. Union committees saw to it that the same wages and working conditions were given Negro workers. "These men," he wrote to Green, "are not promoted to positions of locomotive engineers, with the result that as time goes on they may become the senior firemen and in order that there may be no discrimination against white men, agreements have been negotiated to limit the seniority of colored firemen."[29]

At the 1941 convention Randolph continued his efforts. He introduced a resolution that called for the establishment of a committee to investigate complaints of union racial practices.[30] He related that while the AFL wanted him to appear in Detroit and urge unionization of auto workers, the Negro workers in the Ford plant were taking the position that they should not join the AFL because it "admits that it cannot do anything to remove discrimination practiced by its internationals." Randolph listed case after case in which AFL unions violated the rights of Negro workers.

The business agent of Local 15 of the Bricklayers in Columbus, Georgia, had refused to certify two Negroes who had been sent to work in Columbus upon the request of the international headquarters, while white workers found no difficulty in getting employment. A conspicuous example of denial of employment to Negro workers "which can be attributed almost directly to union influence is found at the Boeing Aircraft Corporation in Seattle," Randolph revealed. Since the start of World War II's defense program, the company explained that its policy of not hiring Negroes was a result of the fact that it had a contract with the Aeronautical Mechanics Union and that the union accepted white members only. The personnel manager had also written a letter to the NAACP stating that his company had another agreement with the Machinists "obligating it to employ only white members."

Moving to a discussion of other areas, Randolph gave many illustrations to demonstrate that unions were preventing Negro labor from entering various trades. In Portland, Oregon, the Boilermakers kept Negro labor from certain jobs, and the union wrote to a particular company that the "available supply of Negro labor in this area can be absorbed as janitors." In Tampa, Florida, union labor was responsible for taking jobs away from Negro workers that they previously held and performed responsibly. Randolph testified:

> After a successful strike for recognition, the Tampa Shipbuilding Corporation signed a union contract. Prior to this time, approximately six hundred Negroes had been employed in the yard in various skilled and unskilled capacities. After the contract was secured, the Negro workers were excluded altogether from the union, or were sidetracked in a separate Negro local, and eventually frozen out of work. Those who were kept at work were given the most menial of unskilled labor, and one instance has been cited of a Negro hoisting engineer being assigned to the job of picking up paper in the yard. The AF of L is supposed to have made an exhaustive investigation of this case, but its report did nothing to relieve the plight of the six hundred Negro shipyard workers who had supported the strike for union recognition only to be frozen out of their jobs after the battle was won.

Randolph described the efforts made to talk to the president of the Tampa Shipbuilding Company and the manager of the Boilermakers local, efforts which produced only a series of evasions. The union told Negro workers that no Negro could join the union unless he was employed in the trade. When the Negro worker went to an employer, he was told that he must be a union member to find employment. "In other words," said Randolph, "he cannot get a job unless he has a union card and he cannot get a union card unless he has a job."

Noting that the International Association of Machinists was keeping Negroes out of Boeing Aircraft, Randolph requested a statement from the IAM President on this question. While national defense necessitated the utilization of all workers, the Machinists were telling the worker "because he is a black man he is not going to be permitted to work." If the Machinists consistently defied Franklin D. Roosevelt's Executive Order on Employment, it was the duty of the AFL to put the Machinists out. But for the time being, Randolph said, he was asking only for the creation of a committee to study the question and to hold hearings. He denounced the Resolutions Committee for characteristically reaffirming positions of past conventions, which meant a continuance of the "old attitude of do-nothing," and he asked that the committee's proposals be voted down since the real questions had been given no careful consideration.

At the end of his talk, the union leaders from major AFL affiliates that he had directly challenged rose to defend themselves. Some admitted he was essentially correct but they claimed they were helpless to alter the situation. Painters' leader Lindelof, said he had desired to create a Negro local in Omaha, Nebraska, and one in Kansas City but had found a charter could not be issued unless the existing white local gave its consent. Although he had tried, his international was unable to gain approval for Negro admission—even in separate locals.

The Molders' leader, John P. Frey, expressed great distress because Randolph had come to "present an indict-ment," and that "considerable research work has been done, and now we have the indictment as part of our record." Frey claimed that "if there is any institution in these United States to whom the colored race owes more than to any other, it is this American Federation of Labor." Frey ac-cused the Negro leader of excluding whites from member-ship in the Pullman Porters, and stated that Randolph was injuring the Negro cause by permitting a biased at-titude to influence him. He went on to argue that racial prejudice had begun before the AFL was born, and that the union movement could not change men's minds and attitudes. Randolph's demand for action only made a cam-paign of education more difficult. Frey urged that the AFL refrain from any action "which would afford a sounding board for the public inflaming of racial prejudice." He climaxed his presentation with the assertion that the Negro himself wanted separate unions because he preferred to as-sociate with members of his own race. "I am familiar with the South," argued Frey. "I spent many years there as an organizer and otherwise, and I know that in some of the denominations the whites go to their church and the colored go to their church buildings, of the same denomination. They get along as Christians should. In fact, the colored members prefer to have the privilege of employing and discharging their own pastors." Comparing these segregation-ist churches to segregated unions and implying that the furor created by a program for integration in both in-stitutions would be worse than the existing segregation, Frey maintained that his comments were meant only "to be helpful to the members of the colored race and to break down racial prejudices which handicap them."

Frey's argument was rebutted by Milton Webster, who pointed out that he and Randolph had not even asked for open committee meetings, but only for a committee within the AFL to investigate the problem, since nothing could be worked out if they continued to shove the question aside convention after convention. Webster asked that a permanent committee be established not to spread propaganda but to sit down with white and Negro members to work out a solution. Delegate Turco from the Newsboys then confirmed that the only time the AFL favored the Negro "is when we need their support," or when a boss used Negroes to take white men's jobs. Mentioning the Harriman strike of 1911, Turco reminded the delegates that when "some of the Negro workers said they wanted to be organized, they did not want to scab, they were denied the right to organize because they were Negroes, and the Harriman strike was lost from the standpoint of unionism."

Matthew Woll, on behalf of the Executive Council, responded that the Resolutions Committee did not favor discrimination, and was anxious that affiliated unions remove whatever degree of discrimination existed. What was objectionable was that Randolph wanted to "infringe upon the jurisdictional rights of our various national and international unions in the matter of discrimination of race," rights which Woll was more desirous of protecting than those of Negro labor. Woll stated that the Resolutions Committee would not recommend this procedure to the AFL, because to interfere with the autonomous rights of internationals on the Negro issue could lead to intrusion on their jurisdictional and autonomous rights in other regards.

To AFL leaders, the issue was not discrimination by unions, but "how far this convention will want to intrude itself upon the rights of autonomous National and International unions." President Green endorsed Woll's approach, and said that the AFL opposed discrimination; it was the white locals that discriminated. Green held that it was unfair to place blame on the AFL for opposition to the organization of Negro labor when it was not responsible, and he wished Negroes would recognize that the AFL could not require locals and affiliates to abide by nondiscriminatory standards. "I ask you," he queried, "if it is the policy . . . to organize these Negro workers into federal labor unions, are we then to be opposed when we attempt to organize them on the ground that we practice race prejudice and race discrimination?" William Hutcheson, AFL Vice-President and Carpenters leader, criticized Randolph for presenting the negative side and ignoring the positive. Hutcheson claimed that the attitude of the Negro worker toward the AFL would have been better if Randolph had "not merely criticized" and told the "things that did not sound so well." If in the future Randolph described all that had been done for the Negro instead of all that could be complained of, "he would do much more good for his race."

Notwithstanding the array of opposition, Randolph did not retract any of his charges. Affirming his own ability to judge the situation, he added that he did not care "anything about the opinion of Brother Hutcheson so far as advising me what I shall do in regard to this resolution." Moreover, he called the AFL's defense "a herring . . . drawn across the issue." He reiterated that he had not stated that the AFL as such discriminated against the Negroes. Negro organizations that attacked the AFL were protesting that discrimination existed within its ranks, that organizations affiliated with the AFL denied Negroes membership, but this did not mean that the AFL itself discriminated against Negroes. The problem was that it was difficult for the public to differentiate between the AFL and internationals affiliated with it. Hence a definite need existed for the AFL itself to provide machinery for the study of discrimination so that policies to rectify discriminatory practices would be instituted. Woll's claim that Randolph's intention was to infringe upon the jurisdiction of international unions was a "pure appeal to the prejudice of the national and international unions in this convention. . . . The assumption is now if the purpose of this resolution is to infringe upon the jurisdiction of national and international unions, 'You national and international unions had better vote against it.'"

This time, Randolph changed his approach. At previous conventions he had always attacked federal unions as a Jim Crow institution. Now, stating that "the American

Federation of Labor does not discriminate against Negroes; you accept Negroes in the federal unions," he used the tactic that because the AFL itself did not discriminate, there was more reason for it to take strong action. He then went on to relate that William Green, "at a large convention," had permitted the Brotherhood of Railway Clerks to take over the freight handlers that were federal unions and enroll the Negro workers in Jim Crow auxiliary unions, where they did not "have the right to vote [or] a voice in the determination of the policy of that international union." Randolph charged that "to that extent the American Federation of Labor has not kept faith with the Negro workers."

The next civil rights debate in the AFL took place at the 1943 convention.[31] Again, Randolph rose to protest the limited scope of that year's Executive Committee report on discrimination, arguing that "racial discrimination should be abolished by every union affiliated with the AF of L, not only for the benefit of the Negro . . . but for the sake of the AF of L itself—to square its practices with its professions." The Federation had to decide whether to eliminate racial discrimination within its ranks or permit it to continue. If it did not make the morally correct decision, "it will, despite its material and economic power, forfeit and lose the confidence and faith of the enlightened and liberal people of America and the world." Material strength with no moral justification was hollow and impermanent. Because of man's lasting struggle for justice, freedom, and equality, the AFL would always hear "the voice of Negroes crying out against the color bar and discrimination in the constitutions, rituals, and policies of certain trade unions." Randolph warned that when he was gone, other Negro delegates would continue to cry out against membership exclusion policies by unions on account of race, color, religion, or national origin until such policies were wiped out.

While union leaders privately stated that they themselves had a "liberal attitude," Randolph proclaimed, they avoided taking any action out of fear that Southern white unionists would be offended. But Randolph reminded the union leadership it had the responsibility to uphold the basic tenet of trade unionism—the worker's right to join an organization of his choice irrespective of his race. The AFL could not "expect the public to give it moral immunity from condemnation for racial discrimination by its International unions on the ground that it is a federated body. If the AF of L claims that it is the house of labor, then it cannot escape criticism for the wrongs committed in that house. If the AF of L is justified in claiming credit for the numerical increase in general union membership, it must bear the guilt for the lack of increase of Negro union membership because of a narrow racial policy."

As in other years, Randolph cited specific cases of racial discrimination. For example, the Bay Cities Metal Trades Council of the AFL excluded Negro workers and organized them into auxiliary lodges which had no representation in the local Trades Council. Thus the black laborer was denied participation in or control over the conduct of the bargaining agency set up by the federal government under Labor Relations Act provisions. Once the government gave a union that discriminated the exclusive right to represent workers in one trade, Negro workers in that trade ended up being denied a voice in their conditions of work. The NLRB mechanism thus was used by the unions as a device to prevent Negro participation in the collective-bargaining process. A closed-shop agreement negotiated between a discriminating union and an employer meant total exclusion of the Negro from employment.

Randolph asked that the NLRB refuse to certify unions that denied membership on racial grounds.* Citing a study conducted by Herbert Northrup,[32] he revealed that a total of thirty international and national unions excluded Negro workers either by constitutional provision, union ritual, tacit consent, or by arranging "representation" in unions that were

---

* In 1964, twenty-one years after Randolph made this point, the NLRB adopted this position.

segregated and had only an auxiliary status. Such unions as the Airline Pilots and Railroad Telegraphers were among those that still had exclusion clauses in their constitutions. The International Association of Machinists typified those that made exclusion part of union ritual; the Glass Workers, Granite Cutters, and Plumbers excluded Negro workers by tacit consent; and the Boilermakers, Iron Shipbuilders, and Maintenance-of-Way Employees were among those which formed segregated auxiliary unions.

Randolph branded auxiliary unions as the equivalent of "colonies of colored people to the empire systems," as a group of "economic, political, and social serfs" who possessed "none of the rights that the white population in the mother country enjoy, except the right to be taxed." Like the colonists, they were used as cannon fodder "in defense of their oppressors when wars break out." The auxiliary members were also taxed without representation, since they had to pay union dues while they were not permitted to elect representatives, bargain for adjustment of grievances, or administer union affairs. Quoting from the Boilermakers' constitution, Randolph showed that local lodges were protected against admission of Negroes by restrictions in the ritual, while the laws of the Jim Crow auxiliaries provided that lodges should be composed only of "colored male" persons. The auxiliary members were restricted to a nominal status; they could not select representatives or control dismissals of men who were arbitrarily ousted by white officers. Most important, a change in the classification of a Negro auxiliary member from a "helper" to that of a higher-salaried "mechanic grade" did not take place unless such classification was approved by the supervisory white lodge. The Negro therefore had no voice in the one body that exercised veto power over his upgrading.

The auxiliary lodge also was not given any vote in the quadrennial union convention, the legislative authority of the Boilermakers, while each white lodge was given a vote proportional to the number of its members. Moreover, the President of the international was allowed to suspend, at his discretion, any auxiliary lodge or member while no provision existed for the use of such arbitrary executive powers against white lodges. Since the Negro auxiliaries could be suspended without formal trial, Randolph stated:

> The net effect of this scheme is to make it lawful for a white local lodge and its business and other bargaining agents at their whim and caprice to permit Negroes to work on union jobs, reserving arbitrary control over their status, upgrading, and even their continuation in nominal good standing. All significant rights of union membership, including all participation in collective bargaining, are denied to the Negroes. In substance, he pays dues and gets in return only a work permit revocable at will. This travesty designed to sanction the inevitable temporary utilization of Negro workmen in these times without conferring any significant status upon them does not merit characterization as union membership.

President MacGowan of the Boilermakers was one of those union leaders who condemned Randolph's presentation and urged protection of the autonomy of international unions. MacGowan opposed Randolph's civil rights demands and stressed that progress was made only by compromise. He noted that it was his own international convention which recommended the institution of auxiliary all-Negro locals, and that this decision resulted from elections based upon free choice.

MacGowan charged Randolph with "one of the greatest disservices that he has ever rendered his people," because they would not appreciate his fight against segregated unionism, and attacked other Negro leaders who had sought to have the government's Committee on Fair Employment Practices instruct the Boilermakers to disestablish the auxiliaries and admit Negroes to full membership. The auxiliary locals did not interfere with the hire, tenure, wages, or conditions of employment of Negro labor, MacGowan claimed, and while he admitted that to a "champion of the underprivileged" the auxiliary local might not be the "entire answer," he urged acceptance of it as a practical measure. Until any international's convention agreed to admit all workers on a basis of equality of membership, separate locals for the races had to be maintained. Mac-Gowan was critical of Randolph for calling the auxiliary local un-American and undemocratic, at a time when the nation was at war and unity of purpose was essential for victory; he contended that national unity during wartime required that the Negro in America call a halt to the civil rights struggle. He ended his speech by attacking the "professional Negro," and suggested that the Negro question would be "handled wisely without the interference of those who would instruct us at this time."

Other white union leaders responded differently. Delegate Bugniazet from the Electrical Workers used the argument that his union did not bar Negroes, and that Randolph's accusation that they were excluded by tacit consent was nonsense. Negroes were not union members because they were not competent workers. "They have got to be competent," Bugniazet stated, "and I could say many things that might hurt the Negro and let him know why he hasn't progressed in our line of industry, but I don't intend to injure his cause." He claimed that the unions had the same problem as the South, that "you can't mix oil with water, even if you want to."

John P. Frey, as in previous conventions, also joined the counterattack. He said that while the AFL had done its best to urge that prejudice be eliminated from the trade union movement, there had been "deliberately" put into the record a statement that depicted AFL policy in the wrong light, one which would prejudice Negro workers against the Federation. This was nothing but a moral crime. Frey argued that he did not see how a representative of the race that was helped more by the AFL than by any other organization could arouse feeling against his friendly allies. The only problem faced by Negro workers was caused by "men of their own race, who endeavor to stir up all the trouble possible." In closing, Frey accused Randolph of having rendered the greatest disservice to the colored race that had ever been rendered since the Negro became a free man.

Randolph answered that MacGowan's emphasis on the need to preserve the international's autonomy was simply a cover for the policy of racial discrimination. He urged the AFL to use only one tenth of the energy in the interest of ending discrimination that it used trying to protect the jurisdiction of international unions. In fact, he pointed out that the AFL had not even used consistent and systematic educational methods to uproot racial discrimination in the labor movement. Randolph had proposed only that a new committee be set up to study union discrimination, and even this minor step was opposed. He challenged Mac-Gowan's advice to accept the auxiliary Jim Crow locals as practical. "Is there anybody in this convention who is going to take the position that the organization of racial unions can be justified?" he queried. MacGowan had not proved that the auxiliary bodies had a voice in the determination of the international's policy, and if the worker had no part in determining wage standards and working conditions, he could not benefit.

To those delegates who implied that criticism of unsound policies is unjustified, Randolph pointed out that when an organization cannot examine its principles and policies, it is moving backward. When Negroes picketed some unions, he said, it was because they "recognize that the Auxiliary Union is a step backward and they want to express their opposition to it." Because fifteen thousand Negroes were in auxiliary bodies did not make them acceptable. After all, Negroes had to buy tickets in Jim Crow railroad cars, and this did not signify acceptance of that practice. Blaming Negro leaders who drew attention to the AFL's racial practices was like "contending that a meteorologist that points out a storm is coming creates the storm." If no one denies that the discriminatory practice exists, why attempt to condemn people who point it out? The auxiliary unions were "mere window dressings . . . simply raised here for the purpose of making it appear that the condition is not as bad as it is." Randolph suggested to the delegates that if they were Negro and gave their blood and lives for the country and yet were not permitted to exercise their skill and ability at home, they, too, would be seeking to change this situation.

Merely disputing the policy of Negroes to fight for their rights, he went on, "is not going to change that policy." It was not the attack waged by Negro leaders that was at issue; the AFL itself was not secure so long as Negroes were not given the same rights that other workers in the Federation enjoyed. The AFL had to develop the courage to say to international unions, although they were autonomous, "Your policy is wrong and it is up to you to bring your policy in harmony and in conformity with the basic principles of the American Federation of Labor as expressed in the constitution."

At the end of Randolph's rebuttal, William Green rose and asked that the convention understand that the AFL was trying to find a "correct solution" to the problem. While he patronizingly asked that delegates "manifest a sense of understanding toward Delegate Randolph . . . because I can understand how he is moved by a deep sense of injustice," Green said that the racial issue could not be solved solely by the AFL. It was a problem to be solved only through understanding and education, through an appeal to the "hearts and minds and the consciences of all classes of people," not through "forced methods or through the presentation of demands that groups . . . comply with said demands." Education was the only sound path to progress. Praising himself for always taking "a most advanced and progressive position upon this subject," Green stated that if he had his way every organization affiliated with the AFL would admit Negroes to membership on the same basis of equality as other workers. He insisted that he had always supported pro-civil rights resolutions at AFL conventions, and argued once again that federal unions chartered by the AFL did not discriminate, and that any representative of the AFL who sought to discriminate would be removed from office.

He defended the auxiliary all-Negro bodies as well. Although these unions afforded the Negro worker only a segregated auxiliary status, Green stated, ". . . these unions accept Negroes into membership." If he had his way they would not be organized upon a segregated basis, "but I have found in life's experience that I don't have my way in a good many things, and many times I have to wait a good while before I can have my way, and sometimes I never get it."

The 1944 convention reaffirmed the 1943 AFL Executive Council's statement on discrimination, and the familiar debate, Randolph versus the Federation leadership, once again took place. A new motion that called for abolition of auxiliary unions was defeated. Randolph cited some successful efforts toward Negro-white unity and urged that the Boilermakers and Electrical Workers not be permitted to get away with the myth that white workers would not work alongside Negroes. These two unions should "be made to toe the line or be put out of the American Federation of Labor."[33]

MacGowan responded that he was tired "of being kicked around by professional agitators when we are striving to do a job." He argued that agitation caused an irritated group to desire restoration of the word "white" members only in their constitution, and that this proved the Negro's goal would be met more quickly without "unfair and unfounded accusations." Delegate Loring from the Tennessee State Federation of Labor argued that the only race problem was Randolph's, and that while he had no complaints against unions that took in Negroes, he did object to being told that "we have to take anybody." Randolph summed up his attitude at the convention: "If anyone thinks that Negroes are going to wait a thousand years in this country to get their rights, they have another thought coming."

Yet union leaders like John P. Frey persisted in looking forward to a "happier period when the members of the

colored race would take the floor and express appreciation
for what the American Federation of Labor had done for
the colored race." Instead, the organization received only
criticism and demands for action. Randolph, Frey complained, practically charged the AFL with complete failure
to do its duty to the colored worker. Frey was actually
opposed to all federal laws that proposed to bring racial
equality closer to existence, because he argued that Americans could not be compelled "to do things that run strongly
against the grain." Race prejudice, he believed, could not
be overcome by edicts, fiats, or demands. William Green,
as on past occasions, commented that "we can only win
through patience . . . good judgment . . . and through re-
lying upon the soundness of our position." It was only
time that would bring a solution of the problem.

Thus, at the end of World War II, the record of the
American Federation of Labor's attitude toward the Negro
worker was a history of the acceptance of segregated unions.
This attitude continued for a number of years after the
war was over. The 1946 convention again defeated resolutions calling for an end to Jim Crow auxiliary locals, and in
1949 a resolution endorsing Federal Fair Employment
Practices legislation passed only after delegates deleted the
words "and labor unions" from a motion, calling for the
"elimination of discrimination in industry and labor unions
based upon race, color, religion, national origin, or ancestry."[34]

Although union leaders all spoke of their friendship for
the Negro, although they all argued that they desired an
end to discrimination against the black worker, they supported policies that enabled racist unions to continue their
discriminatory practices. It is understandable that the
estrangement between the labor and Negro community, so
often referred to in the 1950s and 1960s, had become so
wide. For the Negro worker learned from a long and grim
experience with the American Federation of Labor that the
white union leader did not really believe in the Negro as
his brother in the true union sense of the word.

Chapter V

THE CIO ERA, 1935–55

SUMNER M. ROSEN

Resolved, that the CIO reaffirms the position which it has consistently maintained from the beginning in opposition to any and all forms of discrimination between one worker and another based upon considerations of race, creed, color, or nationality . . . and that the CIO condemns the policies of many employers of discriminating in their hiring and other employment conditions against Negroes. . . .

> Adopted at the 1941 Convention of the CIO

Negro workers, join the CIO union in your industry. The CIO welcomes you. It gives you strength to win justice and fair play. The CIO unites you with fellow workers of all races and all creeds in the common struggle for freedom, for democracy, for a better life.

> "The CIO and the Negro Worker—Together for Victory," CIO publication no. 63

Most people who remember the CIO would probably describe its position on race in language similar to these quotations. The CIO is remembered for its militancy on the burning questions of its era, and the question of racial discrimination was one key to the politics of that period. CIO leaders and literature espoused and elaborated a whole range of progressive attitudes—on taxes, employment policy, social security, planning, health, education, and many more —and racial justice was a necessary, central element in that series. CIO literature was aimed directly at Negro workers. "The CIO and the Negro Worker" boasted of CIO actions and statements attacking discrimination and attacked the craft unions for their racial practices.[1] Other CIO publications dealt vigorously and directly with the problems of racism and prejudice. Southern policies and politicians were excoriated; denial of the right to vote in the South was the subject of CIO wrath and resolution; anti-lynch and anti-poll laws were supported, as was a federal FEPC. The CIO's Committee to Abolish Racial Discrimination—later the Committee on Civil Rights—was headed by such men as George Weaver and chaired through much of its life by James Carey; by 1944 there were eighty-five committees at the state and local level.[2] Affiliated unions had, in many cases, similar committees in operation.

None could doubt the political or rhetorical commitment. But rhetoric is not always an accurate gauge of reality. To what extent did the performance of the CIO and its affiliated unions translate these sentiments into practice, on the job and in the union hall? To what extent could they? How was the commitment to fight racism translated into bargaining and hiring concessions from employers, the government, and affiliated unions? An examination of these and other questions is necessary to assess the degree to which the CIO affected the rights of Negro workers, and the relationship between Negroes and the labor movement as a whole.

A few summary observations, elaborated in the body of this essay, may convey the results of such an assessment.

1. The CIO commitment to racial equality, while unquestionable, was pursued more through CIO influence in the general political process than through direct action. CIO strength supported such progressive measures as were adopted—such as the wartime FEPC—but did not, and probably could not, either innovate or decisively shape any of them.
2. CIO affiliates varied considerably in their devotion to eliminating racial barriers to hiring, promotion, and equal treatment on the job. Some lagged behind the leader-

ship; a few forged well ahead. The latter were not the largest or strongest unions in the CIO.

3. Most advances secured by Negro industrial workers during the CIO's lifetime were due to dominant economic forces, specifically the acute and prolonged labor shortage which prevailed during the Second World War. CIO affiliates gladly capitalized on these conditions to secure concessions for Negro workers from employers; AFL affiliates were in many cases far more resistant to these forces, and did not generally welcome the threat that they posed to traditional racial patterns and practices. Nevertheless, CIO practices altered those of AFL unions, often to a considerable extent.

4. By the time of the AFL-CIO merger the CIO had largely abandoned any vigorous commitment to an improvement in the position of Negroes through direct union action, either in collective bargaining or by internal reform. It did not seriously fight to implant CIO standards of union conduct in the merged organization.

It might be well to consider the last of these points first. In 1955 many people were disappointed that the CIO did not wage a stronger fight to exorcize the racist taint from the merged organization. In part, this failure reflected its relative weakness vis-à-vis the AFL, as well as the fact that merger was as necessary to prevent CIO splits as to save both organizations from a rising tide of public and political opposition to labor unions. However, the CIO seems to have deliberately avoided a fight, against the wishes of some of its leaders. There was no open opposition to the terms of the merger from the floor at the last CIO convention except on this issue. Michael Quill, President of the Transport Workers, delivered a strong and emotional speech on the first day of the convention, arguing that the proposed constitution of the merged organization contained no binding language on the racial practices of affiliates; he also attacked the general posture of the CIO for apparently accepting submergence in the new structure, and for having failed to fight for principles in the premerger negotiations. But this was clearly a minority position. Quill, while a member of the Executive Committee of the CIO, was not a major power in the organization and had few allies willing to jeopardize such autonomy as the CIO had been able to salvage. In the debate he was supported by only one delegate, a Negro from the United Packinghouse Workers of America; in the vote the UPWA delegation supported the official position. President Walter Reuther's rebuttal dealt not with the merits of Quill's case, but with Quill's alleged failure to have stated it during the merger negotiations, which, as a member of the Executive Committee, he could have done. Earlier, in his opening speech, Reuther had praised the new constitution's racial provisions:

> I believe that we will demonstrate, before the gavel adjourns the united labor convention, in a very tangible way that we intend to give meaning and a purpose to the constitutional declarations against discrimination for racial reasons.

The Civil Rights Committee, in its convention report, expressed similar sentiments, but in more circumspect language:

> When this constitution is analyzed, it is evident that this principle [of equality] is protected to the extent that can be defined in a labor constitution for a voluntary federation of labor unions.

This deference to the traditional AFL position tended to negate the committee's assertion that the racial clauses of the new constitution were "stronger than the present CIO constitution."

The near-unanimity was more apparent than real. Clearly many were disturbed at the concessions that necessity seemed to have imposed on the CIO, and it seemed for a time that James Carey might speak for them on this aspect of the merger agreement. For the founding convention of the

AFL-CIO, Carey prepared—but never delivered—a speech that sounded the traditional CIO position. It called on the new Federation to emulate some specific CIO practices such as prohibiting any state or city-wide affiliate from meeting in segregated facilities; it also called for a vigorous civil rights committee, comparable to that which he had chaired in the CIO, with a broad mandate to enforce the constitutional standards. Carey's failure to deliver his speech was a case of discretion serving as the better part of valor, but given his commitment to racial equality, it must have required considerable persuasion to induce him merely to place it in the record. It is worth noting, in passing, that Thurgood Marshall, who addressed the founding convention for the NAACP—presumably a CIO nominee—never mentioned the problem of union racial practices.

The causes of the decline of CIO strength relating to the AFL in the decade preceding merger need not detain us here. What is important is that they demonstrated the degree to which the CIO depended on forces outside itself —in the economy and in the political apparatus—to achieve the kind of change in the economic status of Negro workers to which it was deeply committed in principle. When these forces were favorable, the CIO could defy the AFL and successfully prove that it could deliver, at least to a degree, those improvements which had never had real meaning for the AFL or most of its affiliates. But when these forces lost strength, particularly in political life, defiance became a hollow and possibly a dangerous gesture.

In effect, the AFL won the real victory, whatever the new constitution seemed to promise. Five years after the merger, the formation of the Negro American Labor Council by more than one thousand Negroes active in labor unions seemed to mark the final recognition of this victory by those most directly affected; the presence at the opening meeting of Walter Reuther and the conspicuous absence of George Meany was an ironic accent to this phase of history. Ray Marshall had pointed out that neither Reuther nor

Carey voted to exclude from the new Federation either of the two railroad brotherhoods—the Firemen and Trainmen —which retained racial bars in their constitutions; only A. Philip Randolph voiced his objections, as he had been doing for many years.[3]

The truth was that the most important reasons for the typical CIO policies and attitudes on race had lost most of their significance by the time of the merger. For one thing, the appeal to Negroes had been an important element in organizing some of the key industries on which CIO strength was based, but the organizing drive had spent itself. Indeed, CIO numbers were ebbing in the early 1950s; there were no great new fields to conquer except—as in the South—those in which the unions had been virtually checkmated and had largely abandoned their organizing efforts. Thus the need to speak with a clear voice on the race question in order to win the support of unorganized Negro workers in target industries no longer existed. Secondly, the political climate that had done so much to foster a Negro-CIO alliance had altered dramatically. The heart of the New Deal Democratic Party had been the CIO and the Negro organizations. Their common work had yielded significant gains to both, especially in terms of prestige and influence within party circles. Each needed and worked with the other, extended courtesies to the other, and used its influence for the benefit of the other when needed. In national discussion the two spoke largely with one voice, and they reaped concrete political rewards. However, even before the Eisenhower period began, it was apparent that the center of power had moved elsewhere. Increasingly, both the CIO and the Negro leadership began to define their interests in new and different terms. For the CIO, merger with the AFL became increasingly the center of attention, leading to an inevitable emphasis of those policies, such as militancy on the race question, that had most sharply marked its differences with the AFL. In this way the alliance with such Negro organizations as the NAACP and the Urban

League began to acquire an increasingly formal and rhetorical character, without the substance of past commitment. The Negro groups, too, began to seek influence where it mattered, to place greater emphasis on governmental and business pressure than on the support of the CIO. While the good relations between these organizations never ceased, much of the real meaning of their mutual support slowly eroded. By the time of the merger there was little save nostalgia to put in the way of the CIO's capitulation.

From the very beginning the CIO appeared to the American Communist Party to offer the avenue to mass organization that the Party had sought in vain by various other routes since its formation. The Party had always stressed the importance of the Negro masses for the revolutionary future it foresaw. Its role in the CIO and constituent unions was bound to bring the question into prominence once the actual mass organization of industrial workers had begun. James W. Ford, long a Party spokesman on Negro questions, emphasized the importance of the CIO to the Party's hopes in the presidential campaign of 1936, and it was a dominant theme in party planning through the CIO's early years.[4] The earlier, sterile definition of the Negro question as one of national identity gave way to this more pragmatic and promising strategy.[5]

The part that Communists played in the CIO has been described in detail.[6] The times were ripe for an active role, and Party members achieved considerable influence within the CIO itself, and important—often dominant— positions within constituent unions. This influence persisted until the painful, protracted, but ultimately successful effort to eliminate it that went on from 1948 to 1950. Its effects on the struggle for Negro rights during this period fall into three phases.

I. In the organizing period prior to the war, the CIO enrolled hundreds of thousands of Negroes; nobody knows the exact number. In many cases the unions encountered suspicion and apathy among these workers who had long been short-changed and discriminated against by organized labor.[7] The early sit-down strikes in Detroit were carried out with virtually no Negro participation.[8] But wherever Negro workers formed a significant fraction of the labor force, intensive, persistent efforts were expended to secure their support. This was true whether Communists played a subordinate role or held the key positions of leadership. CIO organizers, both Communist and non-Communist, brought unionism to many thousands of Negro workers. The distinctive feature of the efforts of the Communist organizers was to secure the maximum possible influence for Party members and supporters, a strategy which is no surprise.

Where the Communists were in control, Negroes who received support for leadership positions were generally men who would respond to Party influence. Where Communists did not control, they often sought to elevate to a principle the election of Negroes to leadership positions, making of this question an issue on which to build support among the Negro workers. The most celebrated instance was the concerted campaign to put a Negro on the Executive Board of the UAW, an effort which, though it failed, worked as a chronically divisive factor in the immediate prewar years of that union's life. Similar in purpose was the use of the issue within local unions as the basis for mobilizing support for Party-backed "fractions," a basic Communist technique of organization.[9] In many cases, of course, the goal of placing Negroes in leadership positions was a logical element in the major organizing task in which the unions were engaged, but such consistency was often not the deciding factor for those who wanted to further Party fortunes. Even where an effort to raise the question of Negro leadership roles was likely to hurt rather than help the union cause, it was still emphasized.

What the Party sought in those years was to achieve the greatest possible influence within the unions; its appeal to

Negro workers was calculated to secure and consolidate that influence. Party organs stressed the importance of the new unions to the economic liberation of Negro workers. A Party pamphlet in 1938[10] argued that the advance of Negroes resulted from "the alliance of the Negro people with the progressive sections of the white population"; among these:

> Most important . . . has been the advance made on the economic field. The advent of the CIO and the great advance of militant trade unionism has doubtlessly been a prime factor in breaking down Jim Crow bars and practices in the trade unions, resulting in the participation en masse of Negro industrial workers, on the basis of equality, in the trade union movement of the country.

Clearly the Communists expected and intended their role in the CIO to provide them with a secure and significant position from which to mobilize Negro workers around Party goals and programs.

II. Whatever the timetable for achieving this goal might have been, the Second World War altered matters considerably and, as it turned out, permanently. The Party and its supporters opposed American involvement in the early years of the war, but Hitler's attack on the Soviet Union in June 1941 reversed that position. The war was henceforth characterized as a holy crusade and its successful prosecution became the overriding priority. While Communist literature continued to stress the necessity of rooting out racial injustice, the emphasis changed. In the name of furthering the war effort Negroes were denied their right to full participation in that effort.[11] Labor leaders were judged not on their racial attitudes but on their devotion to the war effort, and Foster was harshly critical of John L. Lewis, once a Party favorite, for his failure in that regard. Party spokesmen criticized Adam Clayton Powell for his insistence that Negro grievances receive attention.[12] This new tendency reached its climax in the *Daily Worker*'s harsh denunciation of A. Philip Randolph for organizing the March on Washington Movement that led to the establishment of the Fair Employment Practices Commission.[13] Ben Davis, dismissing a shameful incident involving the medical neglect of some Negro soldiers, wrote:

> The U. S. General Staff has on many occasions . . . proved that they deserve the full confidence of the Negro people. . . . We cannot temporarily stop the war until all questions of discrimination are ironed out.[14]

The Party abandoned its work in the South and, in effect, its commitment to Negro equality.

This was an important and fateful step. The CIO, in contrast, continued its pressure to improve the economic status of Negro workers and used its influence within the government vigorously. CIO leaders argued that the promotion of racial equality was a necessary war measure, but they continued to stress the moral imperatives involved. They also understood that wartime prosperity offered the most favorable setting in which to improve the economic and legal welfare of Negroes. When the Communists downgraded the issue of Negro rights, the first meaningful differences between the two groups began to become clear, presaging the later open struggle. Union strength continued to grow during the war, and Communists inside the CIO unions grew with it. But the stage was set for a new phase in the relationship.

III. The postwar period saw the decline of Communist influence. Many factors contributed to this decline, predominantly the onset of the cold war. As pressure to purge its ranks mounted within and upon the CIO, the Party and its supporters fought to hold their positions. This effort largely depended on the reaction of the Negro workers. In some cases their response made the difference between success and failure. Kampelman states that the inability of the National Maritime Union to take over the Marine Cooks and Stewards after the latter was expelled from the CIO was due to Negro loyalty to the MCS, based on its solid achievements in improving the economic

welfare of Negro workers in that branch of the maritime
industry:

> The Negroes in the stewards' department on vessels from
> West Coast ports were since 1947 the source of some of
> the strongest union support. Negroes became increasingly
> common on the ships' rosters of stewards. Many Ne-
> groes entered the union and received jobs at a time when
> jobs were denied them by other shipping unions on the
> West Coast. The MCS made much of the fact that it
> was the only organization on the West Coast that came
> to their aid as a union. The union leadership insisted
> that any anti-MCS talk was in fact anti-Negro union
> talk. The union leadership saw to it that Negroes entered
> into the ranks of the leaders. For this reason the NMU
> was unable to use the issue of Communism successfully
> in its efforts to undermine the MCS.[15]

Unfortunately for those who fought against expulsion from
the CIO, this had not been the general rule in those
unions where the struggle took place. The Party's wartime
position had been a strategic error which contributed to
the downfall of those union leaders who, later, became the
targets of the anti-Communist struggle within the CIO.

The Party made further errors. For a short time after
the war its position on the Negro question consisted of a
militant revival of prewar demands. In the face of declining
employment in the war industries, the Party held that
Negroes needed and deserved special treatment including
super-seniority systems to protect them from layoff.[16] Such
demands found a favorable reception among some Negroes,[17]
but there was little opportunity to put them into practice
except in a few smaller unions.[18] While the bulk of the
CIO unions did not take this position—rightly or wrongly
—the Party was unable to dramatize the difference effectively to the mass of Negro workers. Before the effort to
do so had really gotten under way, the Communist position
on the Negro question shifted; the replacement of Earl
Browder by William Z. Foster saw a return to the old
pre-CIO approach, stressing Negro nationalism and all but

abandoning the pragmatic, influence-building strategy of the immediate prewar period. Added to this was a near-hysterical witch hunt for "white chauvinists" within the Party, a desperate and divisive expenditure of energy that served only to divide the Party, isolate the trade unionists within it, and confuse and alienate precisely those Negro masses on whom the Party's fate rested. From 1946 to 1953 this rigid and perplexing purgation continued, weakening the Party and rendering it even less capable of effectively countering the attack that had been launched by those whom Foster called the "Social-Democratic leaders" of the CIO.[19]

It is worth noting that the CIO did not immediately take up the challenge of declining Negro economic opportunity in postwar period. The CIO's entire political position had been greatly altered by the war, and its capacity for bold initiatives weakened. The postwar strike wave had evoked a public reaction that put the unions on the defensive, a position from which, in fact, they never succeeded in extricating themselves. There were more pressing matters to worry about than the problems of Negro workers. Testifying for the CIO about these problems before a Senate Committee in 1947, Walter Reuther said:

No single institution such as the CIO . . . can do more than fight a holding action until the community moves through law to guarantee basic freedoms.[20]

In fairness, one must observe that this approach has not significantly changed in the intervening years.

Yet the Communists could not withstand the challenge; after a bitter struggle the CIO acted to expel or to "cleanse" virtually all the unions in which Communist influence had been significant. The CIO itself was so deeply enmeshed in this struggle that, in these critical years, it had little energy to spare for other things, including the development and application of an effective strategy for dealing with the economic problems of Negro workers. And, to the extent that the unions expelled had been the more militant and devoted advocates of racial justice, the cause itself lost much of its meaning and appeal. The unions under attack had sought vigorously—but ineffectively—to label as racists all those CIO leaders who had become their enemies. But in one of the ironies of this history, those unions that survived the purge with their identities preserved were largely unions with few Negro members.[21]

The net effect of American Communism on the racial practices and achievements of American unions in this period is ambiguous. Clearly the Party's role inside the CIO was to strengthen the rhetorical and political commitment to racial equality, to participate effectively in organizing many Negro workers, and to single out for special attention the problems, grievances, and ambitions of Negro workers in individual CIO unions. These were positive contributions. They took place almost entirely during the early phases of the CIO's life. During the war the Party uncritically subordinated Negro needs to the war effort, thus abandoning a cause that urgently needed intensive work—as it still does. The postwar period saw the Party struggling, weakly and unsuccessfully, to preserve its mass base; in this struggle the needs of Negro workers were brought in primarily for tactical purposes. The struggle itself constituted a massive and tragic diversion of union effort from the real problems of the society and the economy, and thus represents a serious setback to progress in the welfare of Negro workers, which had begun so auspiciously with the formation of the CIO.

It is necessary to recognize the reality of Negro gains during the period under review, and to assess them as carefully as possible. These gains were real. Many opportunities long denied were at last realized; many barriers of long standing were at last broken down. The data show important increases in Negro industrial employment and income. They also show that these gains were not uniform, but varied by industry, occupation, and area.

In 1939 the median income of nonwhite wage and salary

earners was 41 per cent of that of whites; by 1950 it had risen to 60 per cent.[22] Negro wages rose, on the average, faster than white wages during this period. A significant upward shift occurred in the occupational distribution of Negroes, reflecting the large migration from the rural South to industrial areas, and the penetration of Negroes into occupations where manpower shortages were acute. The percentage of male Negro workers in white-collar and professional jobs rose from 5.6 per cent in 1940 to 7.2 per cent in 1950; craftsmen and operatives rose from 16.6 per cent of the total in 1940 to 28.8 per cent in 1950.[23] Along with large numbers of white workers, many Negroes achieved middle-class standards of employment and income.

Robert Weaver's study[24] showed that a large part of this change, the most important since the Civil War, occurred between 1942 and 1945. Negro employment in the war industries studied rose in that period from 5.8 per cent to 8.2 per cent. In iron and steel foundries, where Negroes had always been an important part of the labor force, the Negro share of total employment exceeded 25 per cent in 1945. In other industries important but not spectacular rises were observed in this short period, so that at the end of the war Negro workers constituted an important fraction—ranging from 5 to 13 per cent in most cases—of the dozen or so key war industries. At the same time, Weaver points out, a large share of the total of one and a half million Negro war workers was concentrated in a relatively small number of geographic areas where labor shortages were especially acute,[25] and this period saw virtually no change in the proportion of Negroes occupying professional, managerial, or sales jobs.[26] Retrogression also occurred. The introduction of the diesel engine in railroads made it possible for the Brotherhood of Locomotive Firemen and Enginemen, between 1937 and 1943, "to achieve an objective it had been seeking for over fifty years—namely, the perfection of a plan to eliminate Negro firemen."[27] CIO unions were not immune to racist resistance; even the United Electrical Workers, which took effective initiative in some places to open doors to Negro workers, was forced to accede to resistance from a Pennsylvania local, while the United Steelworkers and the Marine and Shipbuilding Workers met strong rank-and-file resistance to efforts to break down racial barriers.[28] Resistance was of course strongest in the South, and even the tight labor markets of the war years did not, on the whole, open the doors of opportunity to Negro workers in skills and occupations historically closed to them.[29]

These and other facts support the view that, even at the most propitious moments, the power and willingness of unions deliberately to alter hiring and promotional patterns are limited. Though there are exceptions, the dominant pattern is one of accommodation to the prevailing pattern of employment as it has been historically determined by the employers. In some industries, such as iron, steel, and coal mining, Negroes have long been employed in jobs at relatively skilled levels. In these cases the unions accepted and built on the pattern they found, adopting non-racist policies which, whatever their secondary motivation, were calculated to achieve and maintain organizational success. The United Mine Workers and the United Steelworkers both represent this pattern. Both have long and honorable traditions of racial equality; these have their roots in employment patterns that preceded the unions' presence. But the Textile Workers Union, although squarely in the CIO tradition of racial equality, found itself forced to accept Southern patterns of segregation in hiring and assignment as the price of survival in the South.[30]

In the auto industry, Weaver points out, the prevailing employment pattern, confining Negroes to unskilled and foundry work, did not begin to alter until conversion to war production was actually under way.[31] Here the United Auto Workers put its weight squarely in support of equal opportunity and at length—after painful and protracted negotiations—these policies prevailed. Hitherto the union, whatever its desires, found itself with no option but to accept the patterns established in the past. This was, indeed, the general picture in American industry. What differentiated the AFL and the CIO was the difference in their response to the changes the war imposed. CIO unions generally—although not always, and not without internal resistance—supported and worked for egalitarian employment policies, and were actively supported in this by the parent body. AFL unions varied considerably in their responses; some acted honorably and vigorously to open new opportunities for Negro workers, but others actively resisted any Negro inroads. Northrup has described the response of such unions as the International Association of Machinists, the International Brotherhood of Electrical Workers, the Boilermakers, the Shipbuilders, and the Plumbers. At the same time, in industries where both AFL and CIO unions were actively organizing, the CIO zeal for racial progress was often dampened by the presence of an AFL rival prepared to accommodate itself to local race prejudice; in these cases, quite often, CIO unions soft-pedaled their characteristic approach to race and accepted practices they would normally have criticized.[32]

Where the factor of competition was not present, CIO unions often showed themselves ready and willing to press actively for open hiring and promotion policies. The Marine and Shipbuilding Workers, a CIO union, frequently did this, though the results were not always those hoped for.[33] And it must also be said that the AFL unions frequently responded to the CIO challenge by recognizing the importance of opening their ranks to Negroes where Negro employment made a difference in organizing success. This response was part of the general loosening in the strict craft approach to organizing that was forced on AFL unions by the CIO challenge; it had its roots more in a strategy for survival and growth than in any moral or ethical change. Naturally, as some of the older bastions of racism such as the printing trades and the railroads began to decline in economic importance, the balance of strength inside the AFL shifted. Unions with a stake in the principle of industrial organization grew as they responded, under CIO prodding, to these exigencies, and to a degree the pattern of practices inside the AFL as a whole was seen to alter. This change should not, however, be exaggerated. It would not be correct to say that the AFL leadership as a whole underwent any significant change of attitude on race questions during the CIO period. Such changes as have occurred have their origins to more recent events and forces.

General comments tend to understate the real range of response among international unions—and among local unions within a given international—to the rising tide of pressure for greater racial equality. The most blatant, persistent, and deliberate of union policies of Negro exclusion or segregation were to be found in AFL unions; the most determined and far-reaching efforts to combat racism were carried out by CIO unions. At the same time, CIO local unions did discriminate, especially in the South, while some AFL unions won and kept the loyalty of significant numbers of Negro members, even resisting CIO organizing efforts in certain instances. The racism of some Birmingham, Alabama, Steelworkers locals was well known before the merger.[34] Segregated locals have existed at one time or another in such CIO unions as the Amalgamated Clothing Workers, the Oil Chemical and Atomic Workers, and the Textile Workers.[35] (It should be added that the list of AFL unions in this category is far longer.) In such CIO unions as the United Rubber Workers and the United Paperworkers, *de facto* segregated locals were long accepted. In virtually every case these were an accommodation to prevailing patterns and customs. In these unions, and in many others, the leadership sought to counteract reactionary forces, with varying degrees of energy and commitment and with varying results. In many cases the instability of leadership—the dangers of losing strength to a rival bloc or candidate for top office—was an inhibiting factor. It was only when Walter Reuther had achieved unchallenged dominance in the UAW that he was able to move resolutely against Dallas, Atlanta, and Memphis locals. Because the UAW's great strength lies outside the South, Reuther could act without serious risks. By contrast, the Textile Workers have never been able to deal with racism in Southern locals because any attempt to promote equality jeopardizes the union's chances of making inroads where the bulk of the industry now is found.

In some cases CIO unions took considerable risks for the principle of racial equality. The best-known of these situations involved the United Packinghouse Workers (UPWA), where the risks were significant in the North as well as in the South.[36] A large Negro membership from the outset and a strong ideological commitment to equality help to explain the union's position. The UPWA's opposition to racism has been militant, consistent, and thorough. The leadership never ducked the issue. In fact, its position placed in jeopardy its standing with other CIO leaders; protests forced the CIO to investigate charges of Communist influence in the union in 1953.[37] The United Electrical Workers and its CIO successor, the International Union of Electrical Workers (IUE), shared a commitment to racial equality, though they applied it less energetically than did the UPWA. IUE President James Carey was chairman of the CIO Civil Rights Committee, a position that tended to reinforce his role in his own union; at the same time, he had less freedom of action than did the UPWA leaders, because of his closeness to Reuther and because of organizing rivalries with other nations, particularly the International Brotherhood of Electrical Workers. Neither the IUE nor any other union has come close to the UPWA in a thoroughgoing commitment to full racial equality.

Marshall states that the CIO had considerable influence in causing the AFL to "abandon its discriminatory practices and to try to project a more favorable image."[38] Most of the effects of this influence, however, seem to have been felt at the top. They took the form of public utterances by AFL leaders, more determined organizing efforts among Negro workers, greater use of Negro organizers and staff, and convention resolutions on issues of racial justice. Once the postwar Southern organizing drive had lost momentum and sputtered to a halt, there seems to be little evidence that the AFL exerted any real pressure on its affiliates to abandon formal or informal racial barriers. Since 1934 A. Philip Randolph had been making an annual impassioned plea at AFL conventions for racial justice in the unions; throughout the CIO period nothing significant occurred to mitigate the urgency of that plea. In 1959—four years *after* the merger— Randolph's charges of failure to act and his attempts to block the readmission of the International Longshoremen's Association and to secure the expulsion of two unions which retained race bars sparked a bitter exchange with George Meany. The issue was fought publicly in 1959, in contrast to the 1934 refusal even to consider a report on the subject, but the substantive result was much the same.[39]

The events that really altered union racial practices have been of more recent date. For all its devotion to the principles of equality, the CIO did not decisively affect patterns of employment, pay, promotion, or apprenticeship opportunity in the craft unions. It dramatized the issue and made it highly visible, an important achievement. It brought the benefits of union membership to millions of Negroes employed in mass-production industries. It forced the AFL to drop, not its racist preferences, but many of the organizational principles that were required to buttress those preferences. In industry after industry its success stimulated AFL unions to accept the necessity of industrial organization and to expand their membership. This, in turn, weakened the relative strength inside the AFL of the craft groups that had always been centers of white privilege. The ultimate result was bound to be a steady erosion of the historic barriers to Negro equality. But it must be recognized that those whose philosophies had long dominated the AFL resisted these tendencies with great tenacity and endurance. There was no substantial weakening of basic attitudes until the immediate premerger period, when it became necessary to accept the language of racial justice as the condition of reunification. As we have seen, there were few sanctions to give the language meaning, and little disposition in the CIO to fight to get them. Only when the race revolution of our own time began, five long years after merger, did the forces that have now started to change the racial practices and policies of the American labor movement make themselves felt. These forces originate and have their strength outside the ranks of organized labor.

CONCLUSION

CIO influence in American life reached its peak in the war years. It helped to solidify the Democratic Party as the voice of domestic liberalism, the modern instrument through which the state has acted to protect men's rights and promote their welfare. It made organized labor a new force in economic life, and gave it a strong voice with which to support the new role of the state. CIO unions sparked the transformation of American labor from an aristocratic, ineffectual minority into the largest labor movement in the Western world. The CIO transformed industrial relations by breaking the resistance of the great mass-production industries to collective bargaining. It organized hundreds of thousands of Negroes and broke down the historic barriers between Negroes and trade unions. The new generation of leaders developed in the CIO included—for the first time—numbers of Negroes, some of them reaching high posts. All of this constitutes a significant achievement.

Yet the CIO could not—perhaps never wanted to—acquire the influence in political and economic life that many looked forward to in its period of greatest growth. An irony intrudes here. It was largely the full employment brought about by the Second World War that enabled the CIO to reach its maximum membership and influence. Yet the war imposed new priorities on the political systems, forcing the CIO—and most of America—to subordinate all other goals to that of victory. Thus, when Sidney Hillman sought to persuade President Roosevelt to adopt a Fair Employment Practices Commission, he was unsuccessful. It was only

the threat of the first modern March on Wahington by
A. Philip Randolph that forced the President's hand.[40] The
CIO and the Negro organizations gave the FEPC strong
support; AFL members of FEPC did not. When the Commission faced its crisis of survival, CIO pressure alone could
not save it. The story is instructive; the war and the victory of the New Deal had deprived the CIO of any real
freedom of action. It could not consummate its symbolic
triumph over the historic albatross of racism. Nor were other
cherished hopes to be permanently realized. As the CIO
faced internal dissension, stagnation, decline, and then absorption into the merged Federation, the mood of the nation changed and left unfulfilled a host of noble dreams,
preserved as in amber in the records of CIO convention
proceedings. Another era had to arrive before these tasks
were again taken up.

The conclusion seems inescapable that the CIO did much
to change the rhetoric of our society's response to social evils,
but less to alter permanently the substance of this response.
The AFL unions emerged from their prolonged confrontation
with the CIO deeply affected in several important respects,
but the leaders had not basically revised their approach to
race questions. Perhaps more important is the fact that the
economic position of Negro workers in the United States was
changed by forces over which the CIO had little or no
influence. What the CIO did demonstrate was the difference
between actively welcoming the opportunities to better this
economic situation and actively resisting them, between
articulating a challenge and remaining silent. AFL resistance,
however, did not seriously change the balance of power between the two groups. And when the war was over, the CIO
did not find the levers of power that would have enabled it to
continue the historic alteration in the Negro's position which
the war had begun.

Chapter VI

THE ECONOMIC SITUATION
OF NEGRO LABOR

SIDNEY M. PECK

Some fifty years ago Scott Nearing, then professor of political economy at the Wharton School of Finance, wrote a classic work on the monetary rewards for services rendered and from property owned in the United States.[1] He titled his book *Income* and proceeded to differentiate sources of income derived from the ownership of land and capital on the one hand and the rendering of services (productive labor) on the other. In an exhaustive analysis of income and employment statistics, Nearing pointed to the great disparity in the accumulation of wealth between the owners of property (land and capital) and the laboring mass (producers of wealth), and predicted that "with the passing years, the producers of wealth will file a protest of ever-increasing volume against an economic system which automatically gives to those who already have."[2]

Concerned about the concentration of wealth among the few while the many lived in poverty, Nearing argued that minimum wage standards paid to the laboring man merely kept "body and soul together" but did not maintain the health and efficiency of the family.[3] He argued that workers should receive a fair wage standard rather than a scale based on bare subsistence. A fair wage standard for a man and wife and three youngsters living in the industrial cities of the Northeast in 1915 was between $750 and $1000 a year.[4] Today the question is whether a family can keep body and soul together on $3000 a year—or $4000.

Scott Nearing is still writing his pungent analyses in

political economy,[5] and the problem of "rich man, poor man" still troubles the public mind.[6] For in 1963 nearly 36 per cent of the American people lived in poverty or deprivation, at family income levels below $3000 and $4000 respectively.[7]

A whole new literature about the poor has emerged since the late John Kennedy raised the specter of mass impoverishment during the preliminaries to the 1960 presidential campaign. With the publication of Michael Harrington's *The Other America* (1963), the question of poverty in the midst of affluence became firmly rooted in the soil of politics. Studies on income distribution, collected essays on poverty, journalistic polemics, and academic monographs apparently found their mark in the State of the Union message which President Lyndon B. Johnson delivered to Congress on January 8, 1964. "This administration," he said, "today, here and now, declares unconditional war on poverty in America,"[8] and the following March 16 he sent Congress a Message on Poverty pointing to "the great unfinished work of our society." "To finish that work," wrote President Johnson, "I have called for a national war on poverty. Our objective: total victory."[9] He urged that one billion dollars be set aside for the task. Some considered this a small sum indeed, compared to the continued appropriation of billions of dollars for the military budget.

It would be naïve to suggest that the governing Administration has finally bowed to the wishes of reformers and Socialists indignant over the extent of poverty in this nation of concentrated wealth. The fact is that the thirty-four million persons who live in poverty and the thirty-two million more subject to income deprivation constitute the raw social dynamite for politically explosive events. And the struggle for civil rights among Negroes driven to frustration could provide the necessary ideological spark. The Administration was obviously aware that the civil rights movement, North and South, had turned increasingly to the mass base of poor Negroes in the urban ghettos and rural hinterlands. And out of this class of poor Negroes arose new leaders, young, militant, and potentially revolutionary.

If the revolution to destroy color segregation also ignited the struggle to eliminate social poverty, then the Establishment would surely be endangered. It is difficult enough to assert military presence against the "have not" revolutions in Asia, Africa, and Latin America without having to contend with potentially revolutionary "have nots" at home. The current strategy of established power is to increase the supply of butter at home while exporting the supply of guns abroad. The "war on poverty" and the "war in Vietnam" are strategic politico-military responses to latent and manifest challenges of "have not" revolutions. These are wars being fought by the Establishment to channel and contain the thrust for social change so as to preserve the industrial-military complex intact. What is the likelihood that the governing powers will be able to lead the revolution of the poor to victory at home while mounting a military war to put down the revolutionary poor in Vietnam? It is the thesis of this essay that the prerequisites for total victory in the war against poverty necessitate a transformation of the national power structure and the concurrent disengagement of military power abroad. The economic situation of Negro labor in the United States will be considered as the historic case in point.

Following emancipation the great majority of the Negro people turned to the land as small-crop farmers, but the image of a Southern Populist countryside economically based on "forty acres and a mule" did not long prevail. With the restoration of Southern plantocracy to power after a decade of black reconstructionism, Negro farm ownership came under the immediate domination of the planter class.[10] Under a system of farm tenancy and sharecropping, Negroes became rural peons subordinated to the landed power of Southern segregation. In the countryside of the South, Negro laborers were the backbone of the cotton-belt economy as sharecroppers, tenants, or marginal farmers. While the

Southern Negro has been close to the soil for most of his history in the United States, he has rarely been able to make a go of it. Lacking capital, credit, and machinery, Negro farmers in the South were easily displaced. Between 1920 and 1960 nearly 700,000 Negro farm operators disappeared from the Southern land, and in the thirty years since the great depression nearly a half million Negro sharecroppers have been eliminated.[11]

Nowhere has the agricultural revolution had more consequences than in the Southern farming states. In the decade 1950–60 Southern agricultural employment dropped a full 50 per cent. Between 1940 and 1959 the national drop in the number of farms was 39 per cent; in the South the decline was 45 per cent. Negro farms have been the hardest hit, dropping 60 per cent. Total farm employment dropped 41 per cent in the nation between 1950 and 1960, but Southern agricultural employment was cut exactly in half. Fully 1.6 million Southern workers were forced out of farming, out of a nationwide total of 2.8 million lost jobs.[12] The most dramatic change in the occupational and residential situation of the Negro people has been "the disappearance of the southern Negro farmer."[13] Only 15 per cent of Negro labor still farm for a livelihood and they are unable to cope with the advances of agricultural technology. Most of the remaining Negro farm operatives are tenant farmers and sharecroppers.[14]

The great demographic shift of Negro people from the Southern countryside to the urban centers of the North took place during the war years of the forties. The need for industrial labor to supply the military juggernaut continued through the Korean war. The interesting fact is that the total population growth of the ten largest central cities during the period 1930–60 was equivalent to the growth of the Negro population in those cities. During the two decades between 1940 and 1960, more than three million Negroes who had been displaced from the soil relocated in the ten largest central cities of the nation.[15] Nearly two thirds of the Negro population of the North came to live in the great slums of the urban centers. As a consequence of metropolitan residential segregation, an apartheid ecology has emerged.[16]

The vast majority of ghettoized Negroes are wage workers. They constitute the core of what David Danzig has called the new working class.[17] They are essentially a class of factory operative and service workers, fast becoming obsolete. The very same technological processes that have largely emptied our farmlands of people, and impoverished the bulk of small rural landholders who remain, now wreak havoc on the ghettoized workers in the industrial centers.

Because of the rapid introduction of labor-displacing equipment in the mass-production industries, a large segment of Negro workers has become part of a new class of minimal labor value. The economic marks of unemployment, underemployment, and unemployability characterize them as unwanted workers in the great urban centers.

Most Negroes (over 70 per cent of the Negro labor force in 1962) are employed in the blue-collar and service occupations.[18] In blue-collar work, more than four out of five nonwhite workers occupy semiskilled or unskilled jobs. In service work, Negroes are most likely to be employed in low-paying domestic and unskilled service jobs. These are the very jobs which are becoming increasingly marginal to the economy, for it is precisely in these occupational categories that the demand for routine labor will cease as automatic equipment is introduced. And yet Negro entrance into blue-collar and service work continues to increase even though the proportion of jobs in these areas continues to decline. The cybernation of routine industrial and service labor is proceeding at a fantastic pace. Industrialist John Snyder has estimated that 40,000 jobs are being displaced each week. While the work force has decreased in the goods-producing industries, productivity has continued to increase at a growing pace. In addition to the traditional heavy industries, cybernation has also caused large-scale labor displacement in chemical and food-processing areas, in the painting trades, clerical operations, and the burgeoning service industries. Given this continued pattern of job displacement, the AFL-CIO has suggested that the economy must have at least 75,000 new and additional jobs each week for the next ten years in order to have full employment. Yet less than 5 per cent, or about 200,000 new jobs, were provided by private industry during the years 1957–63.[19]

While it is difficult to come by reliable unemployment figures, a reasonable estimate is that over eight million people who would like to have jobs are not working. In an interesting breakdown of data for 1962, the Labor Department found that actually 18.2 per cent of the labor force had been unemployed for a significant period of time during that year. Long-term unemployment continued to be reflected in the 1964 labor-force statistics, which showed that more than one third of the unemployed were out of work for ten weeks or more. In round numbers, at least four million persons had been out of work for nearly four months of the year.[20] The economist Leon Keyserling has observed that "close to two thirds of the poverty in the United States is directly connected with a deficient overall economic performance, of which excessive unemployment is the most important single manifestation."[21]

Early in 1965, experts from the United States, Canada, and a half dozen other nations met in Washington (Organization for Economic Cooperation and Development) and reached these major conclusions:

1. Maximum economic growth alone will not relieve current economic employment levels.
2. Between automation and population expansion . . . the potential job force is growing so fast that present policies won't cut back the current per cent unemployment ratio —and it will probably continue to climb.[22]

The expectation is that fifteen million persons will be unemployed at the end of this decade.

It is also projected that 50 per cent of this future army of unemployed will be under twenty-five years of age, over half will be black labor, and two thirds will be blue-collar workers. Of course, these three categories overlap with one another. The point is that the 1960s have witnessed the emergence of a new laboring class, largely "colored," economically exploited, and outside of the union movement and the main economy. Joseph Zeisel has noted that "The major increase in this squeeze-out from the labor force among nonwhites seems to have occurred after 1958, a year of recession from which there has been only imperfect recovery in many respects."[23]

As S. M. Miller has suggested, it is important to recognize that labor in the U.S. may be moving into a dual economy. In the main economy, fairly stable employment with regular income rises guaranteeing higher living standards may continue to be available for those who remain in it. But in the marginal economy centered upon low-level service trades and occupations, employment is unstable, wages are low, and the standard of living is depressed. Miller has commented that "In this kind of [colonial] situation of a successful white economy and a meager bush economy there are wide disparities . . . for the gains in the main economy do not rapidly trickle down to those in the 'other America.' "[24]

It is estimated that the real unemployment rate among Negroes is about 20 per cent. While Negroes constitute 11 per cent of the labor force, they compose 22 per cent of the unemployed. The color line is also apparent when it is known that proportionately *twice* as many Negro adults as whites are unemployed *whatever the occupation, educational level, sex, or age.* Also proportionately, three times as many Negro teen-agers are unemployed as whites in the same age group, and the same holds true for the twenty-four to forty-four age categories. While the unemployment rate of Negro teen-agers is about 30 per cent, it is also true that in some cities today 70 per cent of Negro youths between the ages of sixteen and twenty-one who are out of school are also out of work. In some of the more depressed urban areas Negro unemployment rates climb to 50 per cent. The pointed statistic is that one out of every nine Negro males is out of work, and in Chicago the proportion of unemployed Negro males is even higher.[25] S. M. Willhelm and E. H. Powell have written that:

> With the onset of automation the Negro is moving out of his historical state of oppression into uselessness. Increasingly, he is not so much economically exploited as he is irrelevant. And the Negro's economic anxiety is an anxiety that will spread to others in our society as automation proceeds.
>
> The tremendous historical change for the Negro is taking place in these terms: he is not needed. He is not so much oppressed as unwanted; not so much unwanted as unnecessary; not so much abused as ignored. The dominant whites no longer need to exploit him. If he disappeared tomorrow he would hardly be missed. As automation proceeds it is easier and easier to disregard him. . . .
>
> The historical transition for the Negro . . . is a movement out of the southern cotton fields, into the northern factories and then to the automated urbanity of "nobodiness."[26]

All of this is immediate and automatic. To paraphrase Harrington, it is done without the intervention of a single racist, yet it is a profound part of racism in the United States.[27]

Since 1954, Negroes have usually constituted between 20 and 30 per cent of all long-term unemployment covering between fifteen and twenty-seven weeks or more. In 1962 *over 46 per cent* of the nearly five million workers who were unemployed for a minimum *period of fifteen weeks* were Negroes.[28] In short, the cybernation revolution has resulted in "structural" unemployment for the American work force; that is, the permanent destruction of jobs rather than cyclical layoffs. When this happens, the blow falls disproportionately upon the Negro worker. As the last significant ethnic group to enter the factory, Negroes have low seniority (in a union shop) and they will be laid off first. As one of the least-skilled groups in the work force, they will have the hardest time getting other jobs. The "older" Negro (over forty) may well be condemned to un-employability for the rest of his life. The young Negro worker has twice as difficult a time becoming employed as his white counterpart.

In an exhaustive review of the literature, O. R. Gursslin and J. L. Roach have examined the extent to which federal programs of job retraining fail to reach into this large category of unwanted Negro labor. In addition to the central fact that there are more job seekers than jobs, they have cited several social-psychological factors related to ghettoized living which inhibit the process of retraining for the demands of an automated economy. Finally, they have concluded that it would be quite unlikely for "any appreciable number of lower-status Negroes to reach the point of working in automation-type jobs."[29]

Not only has Negro unemployment increased but the unemployment gap between Negro and white also continues to grow. Thus, in 1940 the unemployment rates were 13 per cent for whites and 14.5 per cent for nonwhites. Twelve years later the gap had increased tenfold, for in 1962 the corresponding figures were 4.9 per cent (whites) and 11 per cent (nonwhites). The figures for 1964 stood at 5.9 per cent and 12.4 per cent respectively. These statistics demonstrate quite conclusively that semiskilled and unskilled Negro labor have become increasingly obsolete. The long-term unemployment of black labor is the direct consequence of the rapid introduction of industrial cybernation in the major goods-producing and service industries. The impoverished economic situation of the Negro may be generally attributed to his status as a marginal worker on the land, in the factory, and at the service counter. Professor Kenneth Clark has summed up the situation for Harlem Negroes in this way:

> Many of the jobs now held by Negroes in the unskilled occupations are deadend jobs, due to disappear during the next decade. Decreases, or no expansions, are expected in industries in which more than 43 per cent of

the labor force in Harlem is now employed. . . . As the pressure of unemployed white workers in the few expanding areas of unskilled jobs grows, the ability of ghetto residents to hold on to such jobs becomes doubtful. And by 1970, there will be 40 per cent more Negro teen-agers (16–21) in Harlem than there were in 1960.[30]

The most dramatic expression of this displacement of human labor from land and factory is the massive institution-alization of Negro poverty. Unemployment and poverty go hand in hand when one reflects on the fact that two thirds of all Negro families have annual incomes below the $3000 poverty level; that one fourth of all Negro families do not receive more than $2000 yearly; that 41 per cent of all unattached Negro males had incomes under $1000 a year. More than 40 per cent of all Negroes in rural areas have less than $1000 a year income. The income gap between Negro and white is readily apparent when it is realized that only one out of eight families in the United States as a whole falls below the $2000 income level. This gap has been steadily increasing in the recent past and is expressed in the fact that the incidence of poverty among Negroes in-creased to nearly two and a half times the white rate during the period from 1950 to 1962. Professor Robin Williams has commented that "in the midst of continuous reminders of rising affluence, Negroes have not increased their income levels relative to whites for over a decade."[31] Thus, in 1963 more than 43 per cent of all nonwhite families in the U.S. lived in poverty, compared to less than 16 per cent of all white families. In 1954, for instance, the average male Negro worker earned $1623 less than the average white worker. By 1960 this difference increased to $2062. In that same year 75 per cent of all Negroes earned less than the white average of $5981. Hence, the income pattern for Negro families in the U.S. has hardly changed since the early fifties. Herman Miller has stated that "In the last decade . . . there has been no change in income differential between [Negroes and whites]. The median pay of the

Negro worker has remained stuck at about 55 per cent of the white."[32]

In Professor Williams's words, "the color of one's skin influences what share of the nation's wealth one receives."[33] David Danzig had recorded that "between 1952 and 1962, the average Negro income dropped from 57 per cent to 53 per cent of the average white income, and the future looks even darker than the present."[34] A recent survey conducted by the Labor Department showed that the annual income differential between Negro and white for the year 1960–61 amounted to $2320. Siegel's intensive statistical analysis of the color-income differential concluded that in its "net regional, educational, and occupation effects, the cost of being a Negro is roughly a thousand dollars." And further, "about two fifths of the difference in average earnings of whites and nonwhites is what it costs to be black."[35] His research demonstrated that irrespective of regional, occupational, and educational similarities of Negroes and whites, the income differences between black and white are clearly revealed as a thousand-dollar billing for blackness. When it is recalled that two out of three Negro households earn less than $4000 a year, then the financial expense of being Negro is tragic indeed. Residential segregation, long-term unemployment, low incomes, all add to costs that defy translation into mere dollar-and-cents terms. The great mass of impoverished Negroes in the urban ghettos have become human beings unwanted at any cost. As Willhelm and Powell have emphasized:

> Basically millions of Negroes are unwanted . . . so we discard them by establishing new forms of "Indian reservations" called "Negro ghettos." We even make them somewhat economically self-sufficient through an "Indian hand-out." One out of every four Negroes in Chicago . . . receives some form of public welfare assistance. . . .
> Is it an exaggeration to suggest that the deteriorated city has now become the junk heap upon which the economically worthless are thrown?[36]

In Harlem the median income is $3480 as compared to $5103 for all New York City residents. Professor Clark has warned:

> The total economy is threatened by the decay of the heart of American cities, long the creative centers of industry, transportation, communication, education, and by the dangers of Negro unemployment, and Negro concentration in low status menial service jobs. No longer can the potential consuming power of one tenth of the American people be ignored, and the power of consumption be artifically limited by the low wages of Negroes and the heavy load of Negro welfare dependency, a product of broken families caused in turn in large part by male unemployment.[37]

In Greater Cleveland, for instance, the situation of Negro labor is dramatic proof of an apartheid economy which links color to poverty. Data from the 1960 census show that while Negroes constituted 15 per cent of the total population they accounted for 32 per cent of the families with an income under $3000.[38] While the median income for the total population was $6943, it came to $4763 for nonwhites. Negroes made up 33 per cent of the unemployed men in the county although they accounted for only 14 per cent of the male labor force. The unemployment rate for Negro men was 12.6 per cent compared to 4.2 per cent for white men.

During the period 1952–63 the number of blue-collar jobs in Greater Cleveland decreased by eighty thousand at the same time that eighteen thousand more Negro males were entering Cleveland's labor force. The consequence of this displacement is that while the Negro population increased to 16.3 per cent of the county total, they accounted for approximately:

84.5 per cent of all families receiving Aid to Dependent Children;

75.3 per cent of all families receiving City Relief;

64.3 per cent of all families receiving County Relief;

58.8 per cent of all persons receiving Aid to the Disabled; 54.6 per cent of all persons receiving Aid for the Blind.

In Chicago Negro families pay 28 per cent higher rent per month than whites and receive more defective housing in return. In Philadelphia nearly half of the housing used by Negroes is listed as "dilapidated" or "deteriorated" as compared to only 15 per cent of white houses. And in Cleveland the Urban League has rendered the conservative estimate that the "color tax" paid by Negroes for rental units in 1960 was approximately three and a quarter million dollars.[39] In concrete terms this means that "every Negro family renting a house must pay at least one dollar more per month for a sound unit and fifteen dollars more for a deteriorating or dilapidated unit than would be normally paid in an open market."[40] Urban renewal adds to this financial burden, as it forces many Negro families to relocate in high-rental substandard housing units. The evidence is that "Negroes dispossessed by urban renewal pay 10 per cent higher rent after the relocation than before."[41]

In addition to higher costs in housing, impoverished Negroes generally pay more for consumer goods as well. David Caplovitz has demonstrated in detail how the credit system in the black ghetto allows local merchants to exploit poor Negroes in the consumer market.[42] The high rate of illiteracy coupled with the role of the child shopper in single-parent Negro families suggests the possibilities for merchant manipulation of the Negro poor. If the "poor pay more" in general for consumer items, the poor Negro, in particular, is confronted with a "color tax" in the purchase of goods and services.

The real income of Negro labor bound to the apartheid ecology of job, school, and residence is measured in the cost of being a Negro as producer and consumer. Paid $1000 less than whites for labor services rendered irrespective of occupational, age, sex, and educational categories, Negroes also pay more as consumers in the marketplace. And, at the same time, most low-income Negro families must support a larger number of children than whites. Developments in urban renewal, higher education, industrial technology and ecology, and wage standards "injure the Negro poor by reducing their supply of housing, increasing their distance from natural education rooms, creating manufacturing jobs where Negroes are excluded, and sending uneducated Negroes from farms to cities where the number of unskilled jobs is falling as the social minimum wage rises above the marginal revenue product of these Negro unskilled."[43]

It is apparent that the circle of impoverishment that Scott Nearing located a half century ago in an income structure which favors property-owning income over service income is now centered on marginal Negro labor. Little wonder that a leading prophet of the "triple revolution," W. H. Ferry, has observed that:

> We had better make up our minds to basic repairs of our ramshackle economic scheme, which has been held together since the Depression by war and threat of war and is now buffeted, as never before, by the technological typhoon. If others won't make up their minds to this task, the Negroes will make it up for them. As I look around for the historical force that will bring today's chaotic elements into a revolutionary point, the unemployed Negro sails inexorably into view. The un-integrated Negro is the symbol of our democratic failure and the unemployed Negro is the most conspicuous evidence we have of the breakdown of the economic machinery. I do not believe there is any chance that the private self-adjusting economy can provide today's unemployed Negro with a job, the traditional means to dignity and self-respect. Tax-cut and war on poverty not withstanding, most Negroes now without work are not likely to be taken up into the private economy again.[44]

If Ferry is correct in his observation that the established system cannot provide the unemployed Negro with a job, then what is the Negro to do? How can unwanted black labor re-enter the main economy? In the absence of organizational power, where is the displaced Negro worker to turn? To whom can he speak and how should he phrase his demands? If the unemployed Negro has sailed into view as a new historical force, then what is the direction of the winds of change which have blown him on to the scene? Or is the current situation best described as the drift of castaways having no port in view?

One could suggest that the sudden, explosive resistance of individual black workers against acts of political injustice, police brutality, and the like are the expressions of anger vented against an oppressive system by those who have been reduced to powerless despair. But the venting of anger in individual acts against the symbols of oppression is anarchic and desperate conduct. It is action without objectives or goals in view. Yet the basis for a concerted class-consciousness is there. As Willhelm and Powell have stated, ". . . the Negro knows what is happening to him. He knows that the main problem is unemployment and that he is being removed from economic participation in white society. . . . He is aware of the attempt to wall him off, out of sight and out of mind. And he also knows that he cannot let this happen to him."[45] In his study of unemployed Negro workers in the Detroit area, J. C. Leggett concluded that "Employment insecurity continues to be a source of working-class consciousness in the industrial community. The unemployed prove to be more militant than the employed, while a disproportionately large number of Negro workers take militant positions in class matters."[46]

The obvious political problem is for unemployed Negroes to determine what are militant positions to take in matters which affect the class as a whole. In Cleveland, as elsewhere, it is apparent that current trends in industrial technology jeopardize the livelihood of all semiskilled and unskilled workers. Unemployment is not restricted to Negro labor nor is the condition of income impoverishment reserved for black workers. The pocket of poverty in Cleveland's near Westside reflects the increasing number of white workers drawn into the circle of impoverishment. As Charles Rawlings has noted,

"Cleveland's near Westside white residents and the Eastside low-income Negroes have more in common than their racial prejudices reveal."[47] Or as Gabriel Kolko has written:

> . . . It should not be thought that income inequality is primarily a racial problem, for the overwhelming majority of the low-paid are white. Their economic position is due to factors that are far more difficult to cope with than racial discrimination. The vested interests in income inequality, and the economic fabric that support that inequality, are very much stronger than any opposition to better job opportunities for Negroes.[48]

The vicious circle of income impoverishment that engulfs between thirty and fifty million Americans is structured in an economic order dominated by corporate power. It is not enough to demand a legitimate share for the black of skin when whites are suffering in poverty as well. It is not enough to plead for integrated education when the education of the urban poor of all colors is totally inadequate. It is not enough to break down the residential barriers of color when insensitive programs of urban renewal have wrought havoc among all the urban poor. Every knowledgeable commentator on the current American scene knows full well that the solutions to the problems posed by the existence of possibly fifty million American poor must involve major structural changes in the American political economy.

Herbert Gans has presented a series of proposals for the governing administration to adopt in coping with the twin conditions of poverty and unemployment in an automating society.[49] Bayard Rustin[50] and Tom Kahn[51] have pressed hard for a massive public-works program which would rebuild our central cities anew. If carried to their logical conclusion, these are proposals that necessitate fundamental decisions about the allocation of valued resources in the effort to provide a dignified livelihood for all of the American people.

Shall the American economy build one B-70 bomber or five hundred new school classrooms? Shall the government order one new air-to-air missile or construct 26,150 dwelling units at $14,500 each? Shall the administration requisition one Polaris nuclear submarine or twenty-three hospitals of 160 beds each?[52] These are decisions of economic policy that rest upon the structure of national power which dispossessed black and white labor must eventually confront. In the absence of any significant power confrontation, millions of dollars will continue to be spent in the current pork-barrel effort to rehabilitate the great metropolitan slums. These projects, funded by an overlapping involvement of federal agencies and private foundations, are part and parcel of the grand scheme of welfarism which Charles Silberman has so cogently described.[53] The whole effort is illustrative of the great waste of productive energy characteristic of corporate reformism in modern times. While millions of dollars are expended to "cool off" the victims of impoverishment, billions are spent to safeguard "national interests" abroad. The questions, of course, are what shall be the national interests at home and abroad? And who will determine how the national interests are best implemented?

The Establishment hopes to lead the "war on poverty" by funding projects of community action in which the poor are "directly involved" in the local decision-making structure. Thus, the poor are encouraged to participate actively at all levels of organization in those community programs designed to eliminate local poverty. Borrowing a page from Saul Alinsky, this approach gives the poor the opportunity to *confront* the local power structure directly through organizational representation. When two B-52 Hustler bombers crashed on return from a saturation bombing mission in Vietnam, eighteen million dollars went to the bottom of the sea. This loss amounted to several million dollars more than all of the federal money now allocated to fight the war on poverty in the Greater Cleveland community with its Eastside-Westside pockets of poor blacks and whites. How do the spokesmen for the poor confront the local power structure on this matter? The fact is that the war on poverty program has served to fragment the political concerns of the impoverished into local issues of petty consequence which oftentimes lead to further divisions between black and white, as well as between employed workers and the unemployed.

What is apparent to many is the need for an organizational way to unite the automated jobless and the ill-paid marginal labor with harried industrial workers into "new working-class" unions which, in turn, might well provide the political leverage for substantial social change. It is the structure of national power that the poor and their political allies need to confront. The transformation of the national power structure and the concurrent disengagement of military power abroad are requisite to decisions of political economy which aim to reallocate valued resources in order to eliminate mass impoverishment in our society. It is fallacious to conceive that established power in the corporate economy will lead the poor to a total victory in the "war against poverty" without keeping the *poor in their established place*. The economic situation of Negro labor today is a particular case in point.

A full eleven decades have passed since free Northern labor abruptly shifted gears in support of the anti-slavery movement, as the slave system sought to extend to free soil. In an age of nuclear power, automation, and cybernation the white working class is confronted with a decision of similar import. The role of labor as a vehicle for meaningful social change apparently depends on this issue. It depends on the degree to which white workers, and their leaders, will identify with the interests and welfare of the segregated working class living in the great urban ghettos. For it is also the case that white workers have been hit by plant close-downs, technological displacement, and seasonal unemployment. They live under the constant shadow of automation. The facts are that 76 per cent of the long-term unemployed and 74 per cent of the *very long-term* unemployed are white. The total consequence is that trade unionism in the U.S. is losing its basic membership as a result of the new technology. That is why union leaders today have the difficult task of carrying out the ideology and logic of "business unionism" —that is to say, of protecting those not yet fired against the pressures of those not yet hired. Under this policy the contracts negotiated by union officials usually lead to either the outright dismissal of a substantial share of the work force in order to protect the job situation of those who remain, or the protection of job rights for those currently employed while the reservoir of jobs in the economy dries up through natural attrition.[54] Both approaches ensure the fact that new employees will not be hired.

It is apparent that these approaches are mere holding actions that do not begin to deal with the larger consequences of automation and unemployment. Furthermore, these holding actions of official leadership are subject to intense criticism by rank-and-file dissidents. Opposition groups have formed in several international unions over issues of production speed-up and impending labor displacement.[55] In some industries the introduction of measured day-rate pay has set off political disturbances of electoral significance in the union. While the measured day rate eliminates incentive pay, it retains the labor incentive because the worker must now fill a production standard in order to receive full pay for the day. The rate and flow of production, of course, are determined by the company in line with its market situation. The result is a union-sanctioned policy of management speed-up which ordinary workers are unable to block through the grievance procedure. Not only have some union leaders guaranteed higher productivity rates in exchange for job protection through the acceptance of the measured day rate, other union officials have advocated wage reductions in order to prevent threatened plant closure for alleged economic reasons. Oftentimes voluntary wage cuts on the part of the labor force are successful in persuading company officials to postpone or delay decisions to terminate plant operations. But again, this tactic proves to be a mere holding action which fails to succeed in the long run.[56]

There is increasing recognition in the labor movement that collective bargaining with a given company or industry cannot hope to contend with the larger effects of increased productivity and the new technology. As Seligman has phrased it, "No one has yet come up with the idea of 'bargaining' for those outside the gates."[57] The structures of craft and industrial unionism have not as yet adapted to the changed social conditions in the productive sphere. *Once a terminal plant situation develops for particular workers, the union also terminates collective responsibility for the conditions of unemployment.* The archaic pattern of union organization, which excludes the jobless from the bargaining unit, has unwittingly brought into being a new marginal working class. In their discerning manner, R. Bendix and S. M. Lipset once referred to this splintering of the working class as "a major element in the preservation of the stability of the American social structure."[58] The implication of their view is that for workers to unite around agreed-upon class interests would obviously be dysfunctional for the established system of power.

In reviewing the history of trade union growth in the United States, B. Cochran concluded that stages of union expansion were directly related to the struggles of workers in periods of social crisis. His thesis was that in every one of the five major periods of union growth a heavy undertone of radical struggle moved organized labor to specific concerns for social change. Writing in the late fifties, he was moved to predict that American labor in midpassage will once more respond to the developing economic and military crisis with a new stage of determined union militancy.[59] His prediction may hold if the fragmented struggles in the shop are joined with the sometimes anarchic struggles of unwanted workers in the Negro ghettos.

The significant question is whether the potential for class concern becomes expressed in meaningful organization among the jobless, and between the unions and the unemployed. The initiative for organizational involvement will probably arise from the most radical sources of alienated Negro labor. The rumble of social disturbance from below may not take to manipulative channeling by the established powers. While metropolitan police generally serve to block anarchic acts from leading to uncontrolled mass rioting, disenchantment and outmoded approaches to poverty and unemployment in a setting of advanced technology could become expressed in forms of political mobilization resistant to external control. The potential for such mobilization of effort undoubtedly exists and its implications for social power are apparent. The central political problem would be to find ways and means of establishing organizational links with dissident elements in the workshop who have recently been successful in challenging established union policy regarding industrial speed-up and job displacement. Wildcat strikes in the shop may have relationship to wildcat strikes in the street if the objectives of each are bound to the common need for a decent income and a dignified life. Miller has written that "Members of the new working class will increasingly not look to others to produce change for them but will demand and act themselves for change and improvement in their conditions."[60]

But this insight is predicated on the belief that dispossessed workers will act as a class around common power interests. When the impact of structural unemployment goes beyond the bounds of color, it is a dangerous game to play with ideas of quota employment and preferential hiring. It is one thing to press militantly for the abolition of racist job barriers maintained by companies and unions alike. It is quite another matter to ask for the assignment of rigid job quotas as a civil rights demand.

Danzig has made a salient point in his comment that the "inadequacy of the trade-union movement today forces the Negro group into acting to mitigate its own economic plight. Thus the sectarian character of the Negro's economic and political demands can be understood as a consequence of the absence of any political movement in the United States that speaks for the new American proletariat in general."[61] If it is indeed the case that there exists a lack of political leadership from the established trade unions, then it is doubly important for civil rights groups to move into the political void and provide the kind of leadership that will inspire the impoverished of whatever color.

The civil rights revolution, if it be so, is torn between the sectarian nationalists impatiently demanding a "legitimate share" for their striving black bourgeoisie and the integrationists who seek white allies in the common quest for liberal social reform. More than anything else, the freedom movement needs a proletarian perspective that responds to the needs of the working class as a whole. "Black and white—unite and fight" may be an old slogan but it is needed today more than ever to heal the wounds of divisiveness which tend to separate working people into hostile camps. Some thirty years ago the American left worked to create a unity of effort between black and white in the industrial workshops and communities of our land. While they were not altogether successful, the fact is that in the industrial workshops of today many white workers are led by Negroes, and in many plants there is an overwhelming white vote for Negro leadership.

Although it is apparent that individual white workers may hold prejudices toward Negroes that are linked to the prevailing attitudes of the community, it does not follow that at any given moment they will act in accord with these prejudices, or that they cannot act in opposition to them. It is one thing to suggest and document that white workers are racist, bigoted, and prejudiced.[62] Nevertheless, it is quite possible for white workers of varied ethnicity to engage in common alliances with civil rights groups, student groups, peace groups, or radical groups when their interests as workers are at stake. There are potential allies in the white working class which the Negro rights movement has not even begun to tap, mainly because localized rights leadership has very little perspective and hardly any approach at all. The great potential in the labor movement is on the level of rank-and-file involvement. And the rank and file will respond if the issues are openly and honestly communicated to them. In another context I wrote that "the absence of intellect and organization which can appeal to the spontaneous concerns of class-conscious underdogs in the industrial workshops is the most serious void in American politics."[63] That void has yet to be filled, and as a result marginal black and white labor pay more every day in every way. Is it more a hope than prediction to suggest once again that "there is every indication that, with the passing years, the [marginal] producers of wealth will file a protest of ever-increasing volume against an economic system which automatically gives to those who already have"? Possibly not.

In sum, structural developments in the productive sphere have led to changed conditions of industry. These changed conditions, in turn, cause ordinary workers of whatever color to become aware of those technologic forces in society that control their destiny in the labor market. It also throws into sharp relief those archaic union structures which fail to adapt to the new social environment of cybernation technology. Worker dissatisfaction in the shop over conditions of industrial speed-up through measured day-rate schemes has led to open disenchantment with union leadership. Anarchic disturbances and radical politics have come to characterize the behavior of many unwanted workers now ghettoized in the metropolitan center. Class-conscious organizational links between these splintered working-class segments become more probable as the dynamic within the system becomes more obvious in its social and economic effects.

Chapter VII

THE NEGRO WORKER IN THE CHICAGO LABOR MARKET

A Case Study of De Facto *Segregation*

HAROLD M. BARON AND BENNETT HYMER

The President's Council of Economic Advisers starts its 1965 report with a description of the past four years of sustained economic expansion. "As 1965 begins," the Council states, "most Americans are enjoying a degree of prosperity unmatched in their experience, or indeed, in the history of their nation." True enough, yet the Negro worker in the midst of the prosperous urban centers is still suffering a major economic depression—in Martin Luther King's words, "an island of poverty in a sea of affluence."

The paradox of general prosperity and Negro depression can be easily observed by even the casual visitor in Chicago:

Go down Forty-seventh Street on the South Side of Chicago or Madison Street on the West Side. You see the corners crowded with able-bodied Negro men standing around unemployed. At the same time, unemployment rates for white men in Chicago are down to frictional levels and there is a tight labor market.

Go to the northwestern suburbs of Chicago. Out on the prairie you see new plants and offices spring up surrounded by vast plots of moderately priced housing developments. This is where most of the new jobs in the Chicago labor market are coming into being. A brown man's face in office or plant is a rare sight. Inside or outside the places of work for at least a ten-mile radius, Negroes are scarce—only a few live in the small ghettos of the older suburbs, most are confined to the gigantic growing ghetto of the central city.

Go back to the South Side, south of Seventy-first Street. Blocks of well-kept bungalows and three-bedroom Georgian homes attest to the fact that some Negroes are sharing in the prosperity.

Drive down State Street from Fifty-fourth Street to Twenty-second Street. You see the largest stretch of public housing projects in the United States—the largest single concrete reservation for a dispossessed urban peasantry. The apartheid is almost complete—7516 nonwhite families; six white families are the only concessions to tokenism. Almost half of these Negro families are on public assistance, and at least two thirds live in poverty.

"The gains of four years of uninterrupted economic expansion," continues the Council of Economic Advisers, "has brought fuller pay envelopes, greater sales, larger dividend checks, a higher standard of living, more savings, and a stronger sense of security than ever before."

These bird's-eye glimpses portray fantastic paradoxes in the midst of unprecedented prosperity, but a broader panoramic view is necessary to lead us beyond the point of wonder to comprehension.

The experience of the Negro worker in the Chicago labor market* is typical of the experience of Negro workers in urban centers outside the South. The Negro worker in Chicago fares somewhat better than his brother in the cities of the border states and not quite as well as his brother on the West Coast. With relatively little change, the picture just

* The reader should note that when we speak of the Chicago labor market we do not confine ourselves to the City of Chicago. We mean the Chicago Metropolitan Area, which technically comprises the six counties of northeastern Illinois.

described can be applied to any other Northern metropolitan area.

THE SECOND-CLASS STATUS OF THE NEGRO WORKER

Any criterion used to measure the position of the Negro worker in the Chicago labor market testifies that he is systematically confined to a second-class status. To understand this second-class status, we must examine the extent and nature of the major economic differentials between Negroes and whites.

Usually these differentials are not as great in the case of women as for men. This relation is explained by the factors that: 1) all women tend to face job discrimination and ceilings on advancement; and 2) Negro women frequently have an easier time finding and keeping jobs than Negro men. Labor-market comparisons between white and Negro women are further complicated by the fact that white women tend to withdraw from the labor force during the years they are raising a family.

LABOR-MARKET PARTICIPATION

To be counted as unemployed, a worker must be a participant in the labor market. He must actively be seeking employment. Labor-force participation rates measure the number of persons in the labor force, i.e. employed or seeking employment, as a percentage of the total population.

A recent study of labor-force participation in urban labor markets contains data which suggest that in the last generation race has become an important factor in explaining why some labor markets have lower participation rates than others. This trend can be independently associated with most major segments of the potential nonwhite labor force— men twenty-five to fifty-four years old, married women with husbands present, and teen-agers of both sexes. The implication is that within each of these groups the nonwhite position has deteriorated vis-à-vis that for whites.*

Labor-force participation rates are sensitive to the general demand for labor and vary with the opportunities that are available in employment. Several years of high unemployment will drive people out of the labor market; conversely, a tight labor market will attract additional people to seek employment.

Negro males have a lower rate of labor-market participation than whites. Eighty-two per cent of white men over fourteen in Chicago are in the labor force compared to only 77 per cent of Negro men.** A disguised unemployment of Negro men accounts for this differential. After suffering long periods of unemployment, many Negro men will stop seeking work altogether and will disappear from the government unemployment statistics which measure only those actively in the labor market. In previous work we have developed a social concept of unemployment which includes these "discouraged workers" who disappear from the government statistics, but who are still able-bodied potential workers. On the basis of the 1960 census, we estimated that over 5.5 per cent of the nonwhite male population in Chicago were discouraged workers, without jobs and completely out of the labor force.[1]

During the sixties, based on national data, there was a continued growth in the percentage of Negro male discouraged workers. A combination of the four-year-long economic boom and changes in employment practices due to the pressures of the civil rights movement has acted to keep the participation

---

* William G. Bowen and T. A. Finegan, "Labor Force Participation and Unemployment" in Arthur Ross (ed.), *Employment Policy and the Labor Market* (Berkeley, 1965), 115–61.
** Unless otherwise specified, data for the Chicago labor market are taken from the *U. S. Census of Population, 1960.* "Nonwhite" and "Negro" are used interchangeably in the text as Negroes constitute 97 per cent of all nonwhites in the Chicago Metropolitan Area. In the tables, "Negro" and "nonwhite" are used according to their technical definitions.

rates in the twenty-to-thirty-four-year-old range in the same position as they were at the beginning of the decade. But the labor-force participation rates for Negro males, both younger and older than this group, declined. Reacting to higher unemployment rates for his age group, Negro teen-agers evidently have been reluctant to enter the labor force. Since 1960 the labor-force participation rate for nonwhites fourteen to nineteen has declined by a sixth, while that for whites has gone down by only a sixteenth.[2]

On the basis of current data, it is difficult to make estimates of discouraged female Negro workers. Among teen-agers, where the competition for jobs is stiffer, the advan-tages of the white females in the labor market are reflected in a participation rate that is one third to one half greater than that for nonwhites. Between the ages of twenty and twenty-four, participation rates are about equal. However, in the family-raising age range of twenty-five to forty-four, white women tend to drop out of the labor market while an even greater percentage of Negro women seek jobs. There-fore, in this age range, Negro women have a higher participa-tion rate. After forty-five, white women tend to return to the labor market, and the labor-force participation is again roughly equivalent.

UNEMPLOYMENT

During the last fifteen years unemployment rates have risen for all racial and age groups in the economy. In the boom year of 1964 the national unemployment rate was 5.2 per cent as compared to 3.8 per cent in 1956, the last full year of the previous major boom. This long-run trend of rising unemployment was also evident in Chicago. The metropolitan unemployment rates reported in the 1960 cen-sus, which were taken just after an economic peak, were the same as those in the 1950 census, which were taken just after the end of a recession.

The second-class status of the Negro worker has caused

him to bear an undue proportion of the high unemployment that exists in the American economy. The unemployment of nonwhites has increased more rapidly than that of whites. Nationally, in 1948, nonwhite unemployment was 1.6 times that of whites; from the early 1950s to date, nonwhite unemployment has been 2 to 2.25 times that of whites.

Within the Chicago labor market the ratio of nonwhite to white unemployment has been considerably higher than the national average. In 1959, 1960, and 1961 there were three separate measures of unemployment; in each case Negro unemployment was approximately three times that of white unemployment. During the period of high unemployment in the early 1960s, white unemployment rates fluctuated in the neighborhood of 4 per cent while nonwhite unemployment rates ran from 10 to 15 per cent.

In 1965 the Chicago labor market was especially tight. White unemployment was down in the neighborhood of 2 per cent. Nonwhite unemployment fell, but the rate was still a distressfully high 6 to 7 per cent—a level which would be characterized as substantial unemployment by the U. S. Department of Labor.

The large decline in the nonwhite unemployment rate overstates the manpower utilization of Negroes. Low rates of economic growth and high rates of unemployment in the years prior to the current boom drove many Negro workers out of the labor market; they ceased looking for work. The decline in unemployment during the current boom has not been of sufficient duration or intensity to bring these workers back into the market. This point can be illustrated by national data on males in the twenty-five-to-fifty-four-year age range (see Table 1).

An analysis of labor-force data on males in the twenty-five-to-fifty-four-year age range eliminates many extraneous factors that might apply in the case of females, youths, or older workers. Males in this age range consistently have the highest rates of labor-force participation and the lowest rates of unemployment. In comparing the years 1957 and 1964 for whites, we find no substantial difference, either

TABLE 1

UNEMPLOYMENT RATE AND THE PERCENTAGE NOT EMPLOYED
FOR MALES 25–54 YEARS OLD, BY COLOR,
FOR THE UNITED STATES, 1957 AND 1964

	*Unemployment Rate**		*Percentage Not Employed***	
YEAR	WHITE	NONWHITE	WHITE	NONWHITE
1957	2.7%	7.0%	5.3%	11.2%
1964	2.8	6.6	5.6	12.2

* The base for this rate is the labor force.

** The base for this rate is the male civilian noninstitutional population. "Not employed" includes the unemployed and those not in the work force.

SOURCE: Data derived from Susan S. Holland and J. Ross Wetzel, "Labor Force and Employment in 1964," U. S. Department of Labor, "Special Labor Force Report," No. 52 (1965), Table 3.

in unemployment or manpower utilization (as measured by the per cent not employed). For nonwhite males the picture is different. Unemployment was slightly lower in 1964, but the over-all number of those not employed increased by a whole percentage point. Put more succinctly, Negro unemployment for these two years was the same only because more Negroes dropped out of the labor force and the proportion of discouraged Negro workers had increased.

Within the business cycle we find that the fluctuations of nonwhite unemployment are more marked than those of whites. A recent study shows that during periods of economic growth unemployed nonwhites are absorbed into jobs at a rate one fifth greater than that for whites. During downswings in the economy nonwhites are cast into the pool of the unemployed at a rate twice that of whites.[3] Other data indicate that during long booms, like those in wartime or the current one, the nonwhite rate of absorption into jobs increases even more vis-à-vis that for whites.

Negro workers not only suffer a greater incidence of unemployment, but their unemployment is of greater duration. A 1961 study of job seekers in Illinois showed that 36 per cent of the Negro job seekers, as compared to 27 per cent of the whites, had been unemployed for an extended period of time (eight months or more).[4] In 1964 the duration of national unemployment for nonwhites was on the average three and a half weeks longer than that for whites.[5]

Negro youth have particularly met with adverse employment conditions in the last decade. Whereas the unemployment rate for Negro adults in the present boom is roughly comparable to that of the last major boom in the mid-fifties, the unemployment rate for Negro teen-agers is comparable to that for the recession year 1961. The unemployment of Negro youth increased by 51 per cent since 1957, and there has been a drastic reduction in their labor-force participation rates. Partially this is a problem shared by all young people, as white teen-age unemployment also increased by 35 per cent since 1957.

Apologists often try to explain away high rates of Negro employment in terms of the racial differences in education and occupational experience. They point out that the two most important and salable factors that a job seeker brings to the labor market are his training and his work experience, and that therefore the poorly educated and the unskilled will have higher rates of unemployment. The Negro labor force does have a higher proportion of poorly educated workers with a work history in unskilled occupations. While these differences in skill characteristics between the Negro and white labor forces explain part of the racial disparity in unemployment rates, we still find that at every educational level and in every occupational category Negroes have a considerably higher rate of unemployment than whites.

In 1964 the national unemployment rate of all nonwhites was twice that of all whites. However, when persons with high school diplomas and beyond are compared by color, we find that nonwhites had an unemployment rate that was two and a half times that for whites. A more blunt analogy is given in the fact that a nonwhite worker who had completed high school or gone further in his education had no greater chance of being employed than a white worker who failed to finish eighth grade.[6] In a similar manner, Negroes in the more skilled occupations, such as the professional and craftsman jobs, experienced an unemployment rate two and a half times that of their white counterparts.[7] We can conclude that skilled and well-educated Negroes suffer less unemployment than unskilled Negroes; however, this advantage only puts them on a par with unskilled and poorly educated whites.

We have seen so far that there are systematic differences in the rates of employment between Negroes and whites. A larger percentage of Negroes who offer their skills and services in the labor market cannot find a purchaser. High unemployment inhibits young workers from entering the market in the search for jobs and continuous rebuff in hiring discourages established workers to the point of dropping out of the search for jobs. This latter phenomenon is reflected in lower labor-force participation rates for Negroes.

INCOME

Income is the best measure of economic status for individuals. Several factors stand out in a racial comparison of incomes: 1) all incomes have increased over the past twenty-five years; 2) there has been no closing of the relative gap between Negroes and whites since the end of World War II; 3) wartime tight labor markets are the great solvents of racial income differences.

Since 1941, the advent of World War II, the personal incomes of the American population have grown continuously. Even during the last period of economic stagnation, 1957–62, incomes grew, although, at a slower pace. If we compare the earnings of Negroes today with the earnings of twenty-five or fifteen years ago, the improvement is very noticeable. It is equally noticeable that Negro workers in the city are not any closer to equality with whites, for as Negro earnings have increased, so have the earnings of

TABLE 2

MEDIAN WAGE OR SALARY INCOME OF MALES 14 YEARS AND
OLDER, BY COLOR, FOR THE UNITED STATES, 1939 AND 1947–62

| YEAR | *Current Dollars* | | *Constant Dollars** | | *Nonwhite Income as a Per cent of White Income* |
	WHITE	NON-WHITE	WHITE	NON-WHITE	
1939	$1112	$ 460	$2298	$ 950	41%
1947	2357	1279	3030	1644	54
1948	2711	1615	3235	1927	60
1949	2735	1367	3295	1647	50
1950	2982	1828	3558	2181	61
1951	3345	2060	3696	2276	62
1952	3507	2038	3791	2203	58
1953	3760	2233	4034	2396	59
1954	3754	2131	4011	2277	57
1955	3986	2342	4272	2510	59
1956	4260	2396	4498	2530	56
1957	4396	2436	4486	2485	55
1958	4596	2652	4564	2633	58
1959	4902	2844	4830	2802	58
1960	5137	3075	4983	2983	60
1961	5287	3015	5074	2893	57
1962	5462	3023	5182	2868	55

* The purchasing power of $1 during the period 1957–59. (These constant dollars indicate purchasing power of any year's income in terms of 1957–59 prices. Income measurements using constant dollars eliminate those increases in income that reflect only price rises.)

SOURCE: U. S. Department of Labor, *Manpower Report of the President* (March 1964) p. 275, Table H-10.

whites. The net result is that while almost everyone is better off, Negroes are just as far behind.

At the beginning of World War II, after the pall of the great depression had hung over the American economy for a decade, Negro males had national earnings that were only 41 per cent of those for white males (see Table 2). Since at this time Negroes in America were primarily rural and Southern, the racial differential in earnings reflected, to a large extent, the regional and demographic differences between two labor forces rather than the effects of urban racial practices. The wartime economy, characterized by tight labor markets and high demand for all labor regardless of color, narrowed the earnings gap. A secondary effect of the wartime labor shortages was a geographic redistribution of the Negro labor force away from a Southern rural concentration to a more urban base. This demographic shift had a positive influence on Negro earnings over and above any breaking down of racial barriers. Reflecting this wartime influence by 1947, the real wages of nonwhite workers increased by 73 per cent compared to only 32 per cent for whites. The nonwhite male worker in 1947 was earning 54 per cent as much as the white male worker. From 1947 until today there has been no closing of the relative gap. In 1962 the nonwhite male earned 55 per cent as much as the white male.

In terms of the Northern urban population, there has been a further deterioration in the relative position of the Negro worker, which is not directly reflected in the nationwide data cited above. The long-run demographic shift out of the low-wage rural South into the cities has continued so that the latter national figures are more reflective of racial differences within the city than of general rural-urban differences. Within the metropolitan areas the relative earnings of the Negro have declined since the end of World War II. A recent article entitled "The Decline in the Relative Income of Negro Men" shows that in every region the income gap between Negro and white men has increased between 1950 and 1960.[8]

Wartime tight labor markets had the effect of equalizing the position of the races in the economy while peacetime labor markets had the effect of increasing the disparity. A comparison of the relative growth rates of the earnings for these two groups make this point very clearly. The influence of World War II is revealed in the fact that between 1939 and 1947 nonwhite male real earnings grew at an annual rate of 7.1 per cent, whereas white earnings only grew by

TABLE 3

ANNUAL AVERAGE RATES OF GROWTH OF REAL WAGE OR
SALARY INCOME OF MALES 14 YEARS AND OLDER, BY COLOR,
FOR THE UNITED STATES, FOR SELECTED INTERVALS

| | *Annual Average Rates of Growth* | |
Time Interval	WHITE	NONWHITE
1939–47*	3.5%	7.1%
1947–62	3.6	4.3
1953–62	3.2	2.8

* For this interval, the annual average rate was calculated as a
compound interest rate between 1939 and 1947.
SOURCE: Table 2. The growth rate was calculated using constant
dollars.

3.5 per cent a year. Taking the time period 1947–62 as a
whole, we find that nonwhite males still had the advantage
in annual growth rates—4.3 per cent for nonwhites and
3.6 per cent for whites. However, this advantage for nonwhites is achieved only by the inclusion of the Korean war
years. If we examine growth rates for the decade 1953 to
1962, we see that in peacetime the Negro fell behind.
White earnings grew by 3.2 per cent annually and nonwhite
earnings grew by only 2.8 per cent.*

The analysis of national income data obscures some of
the dynamics of income distribution within the urban labor
market such as Chicago. Unfortunately, we only have personal income data for the years 1949 and 1959 for the
metropolitan area, but much can be revealed by breaking
these figures down. We have compared incomes by race
and sex, and by quartile divisions (see Table 4). The first
quartile indicates that 25 per cent of the income earners had
incomes below that figure and 75 per cent had incomes
above it. The second quartile is the median, 50 per cent of
the incomes above and 50 per cent below. The third quartile
indicates that 25 per cent of the income earners had in-

* All of the growth rates are calculated on the basis of real wages.

TABLE 4

QUARTILE DIVISIONS OF INCOME OF PERSONS IN CHICAGO METROPOLITAN AREA BY RACE AND SEX, 1949 AND 1959

Current Dollars

	Male			Female		
	WHITE	NEGRO	NEGRO INCOME AS A PER CENT OF WHITE INCOME	WHITE	NEGRO	NEGRO INCOME AS A PER CENT OF WHITE INCOME
1949						
Quartile I	$2252	$1560	69.3%	$668	$624	93.4%
Quartile II (Median)	3308	2362	71.4	1656	1223	73.9
Quartile III	4378	2990	68.3	2475	1919	77.5
1959						
Quartile I	$3356	$2041	60.8	$762	$769	100.9
Quartile II (Median)	5573	3776	67.8	2118	1810	85.5
Quartile III	7568	5072	67.0	3802	2954	77.7

TABLE 4 *(cont'd)*
Constant Dollars*
(1957-59=100)

| 1949 | Male | | Female | |
	WHITE	NEGRO	WHITE	NEGRO
Quartile I	$2767	$1916	$ 821	$ 767
Quartile II (Median)	4064	2902	2034	1502
Quartile III	5378	3673	3040	2357
1959				
Quartile I	$3304	$2009	$ 750	$ 757
Quartile II (Median)	5485	3717	2085	1781
Quartile III	7448	4992	3742	2907

* Based on Consumer Price Index for Chicago.
SOURCE: *U. S. Census of Population*, 1950, Volume II, Pt. 13 Illinois, Table 87, *U. S. Census of Population*, 1960, Volume PC (1)-15D, Table 133.

comes above that point and 75 per cent had incomes below it.

In 1949 we note that racial disparities for males were least marked toward the lower end of the income scale. The gap was smallest between the middle of the white scale and the middle of the nonwhite scale. The nonwhites at the bottom of the income range (quartile I) were slightly less far behind their white counterparts than were the nonwhites at the higher income range (quartile III).

By 1959 this pattern had reversed itself. The Negroes in the third quartile of Negro income had almost been able to maintain their relative position vis-à-vis the third-quartile whites. Their incomes declined only from 68.3 per cent of the white income to 67 per cent of it. The middle range of Negro income, as measured by the median, showed a greater decline vis-à-vis the whites. They had fallen behind by 3.6 percentage points—from 71.4 per cent of the whites down to 67.8 per cent. In the lower range of income the Negro males suffered a catastrophe. From making 69.3 per cent as much as the lower range of whites they dropped down to 60.8 per cent. In real wages they had virtually no increase in income. As measured in constant purchasing power, the bottom group of Negro men made only ninety-three dollars more in 1959 than they had ten years before. Negro income earners at the lower end of the scale are virtually an urban peasantry, living at a subsistence income, and clearly out of the main stream of the economy.

Interestingly, within the Negro male labor force the spread of income has widened considerably (the same phenomenon occurred among whites but not to the same extent). The bottom group has fallen further behind the top group. In 1949 the income of the bottom quartile was over one half that of the top quartile for Negro males. By 1959 the income of the bottom quartile had declined to only two fifths of the top group. The dollar difference (as measured in constant dollars) between the first quartile and the third quartile rose from $1750 in 1949 to $3000 in 1959. In broad terms, this means that there is a group at the top of the Negro income ladder consisting of 40 to 50 per cent of all Negro men in Chicago who are tenuously participating in American affluence. They are balanced out by a group at the bottom of the income ladder comprising about 40 per cent of all Negro men whose incomes are virtually stagnant and who appear to be locked in poverty in the midst of a wealthy city.

For women the picture is somewhat different. The top group of nonwhite income earners held their own between 1949 and 1959, and the bottom groups gained considerably vis-à-vis comparable ranges among the whites. The improvement of the median and first-quartile gap, however, is basically indicative of changes in the way of white women are being involved in the labor market. There has been a marked increase in the number and proportion of white women working part-time, and accordingly receiving small total incomes. Therefore, as measured in constant dollars,

The Negro Worker in the Chicago Labor Market

TABLE 5

INCREASE OF REAL INCOME* OF PERSONS IN CHICAGO
METROPOLITAN AREA BY QUARTILE DIVISION, BY RACE
AND SEX, 1949–59

WHITE MALE	INCREASE, 1949–59	PER CENT INCREASE, 1949–59*
Quartile I	$537	19.4%
Quartile II	$1421	35.0
Quartile III	$2070	38.5
NEGRO MALE		
Quartile I	$93	4.9
Quartile II (median)	$815	28.1
Quartile III	$1319	35.9
WHITE FEMALE		
Quartile I	$—71	—8.7
Quartile II (median)	$51	2.5
Quartile III	$702	23.1
NEGRO FEMALE		
Quartile I	$—10	—1.3
Quartile II (median)	$279	18.6
Quartile III	$550	23.3

* All calculations are based on constant dollars. (1957–59=100).
SOURCE: Table 4.

here was a decline for the first quartile and no growth in median incomes of white women, (see Table 5). The bottom range of nonwhite females also had a decline in incomes; the middle range had some growth, but significantly below the rate of growth for the top quartiles. This leads us to hazard the judgment that for females participating full-time, all year, in the labor force, the relative gap in incomes between the races remained constant during the decade.

For both males and females a comparison of incomes without regard to age obscures some of the differentials that exist in economic status between the races. The lower end of the white income scale consists largely of teen-agers and persons over sixty-five. In the Chicago Metropolitan Area at the time of the last census, of the white males with incomes of less than $3000 per year, 27 per cent were teen-agers and 30 per cent were over sixty-five years old. In the case of nonwhites, though, only 10 per cent were teen-agers and 15 per cent over sixty-five.

When earnings are compared between whites and non-whites for each age group, we gain further insight into the effects of racial barriers. Among men, the older they get, the greater is the disparity in incomes between the races. For example, in his early twenties, a Negro man makes about four fifths as much as a white man of the same age. By the time he is forty, the Negro is making only two thirds as much as his white peer. This indicates that white workers have greater advantage in advancement and obtaining job security.

For women the picture is more complicated. When all females over fourteen years old are considered, the racial income gap is relatively small and has diminished in recent years. This fact has led one observer to conclude that the Negro women are rapidly gaining in economic status vis-à-vis the Negro male, thus reinforcing matriarchal tendencies in the Negro family.[9] However, within certain age ranges the income differential is just as great for women as for men.

In the age ranges of twenty to twenty-four and forty-five to sixty-five, Negro women have incomes only two thirds as much as white women. Only between the ages of twenty-five and forty-four do Negro women make 90 per cent as much as white women. This factor tells us more about the manner in which white women participate in the labor market than it does about racial differences. Evidently, the white women with higher skills and earnings tend to drop out of the labor market in the years in which they have young children. Since the Negro family is more dependent upon the earnings of women, the more skilled Negro women do not indulge in that luxury.

The somewhat confusing picture of the income differentials among women can be clarified by making comparisons with white women who are seriously dependent upon their labor-market participation. In such a case as the female heads of households, white female heads have as great an income advantage over Negro female heads as do white men over Negro men. White female heads of families tend to have incomes very high in the range of all female income while nonwhite female heads have incomes that are close to the average.

The racial income gap cannot be explained away by the fact that Negroes on the whole have less education than whites. At every level of educational achievement the racial differences in income for men are considerable. The gap is greater at the higher levels of education. In Illinois the non-white male high school dropout makes 73 per cent as much as the white dropout, while the nonwhite college graduate makes only 63 per cent as much as the white college graduate. In fact, the Negro male college graduate makes less than the white dropout.[10]

OCCUPATION

With the continuous introduction into the economy of automation and other technological innovations the un-skilled and semiskilled occupations are gradually becoming smaller. Because a large part of the Negro labor force is concentrated in these occupations, many of the jobs available to Negroes are in the main line of the fire of automation. There is an irony in this for the Negro worker. He may be winning the right to get a job at just the time when the job itself is disappearing. Given the present operation of the labor market, the Negro worker is less likely than any-one else to hold the job he has; he is less likely to get a job in the professional and technical areas; and he is less likely to acquire the skills that are necessary to compete for the jobs that will survive automation.

Harold M. Baron and Bennett Hymer

This ominous portent for the Negro worker exists because his position in the occupational structure is, once again, a second-class one. Historically, racial differentials in the occupational structures of the white and Negro labor forces have followed a pattern of development similar to that for income. In both the Negro and white labor forces there has been an increase in the proportion of workers in the higher-skilled and better-paying occupations. But the relative occupational position of the Negro worker has remained constant in the long run—Negroes are not catching up with whites.

In the Chicago labor market Negroes are notably concentrated at the bottom of the occupational hierarchy. In 1960 three fourths of the Negro males were in the lower-paying unskilled and semiskilled occupations as compared to only one third of the white males (see Table 6).* At the upper end of the occupational hierarchy, in the high-paying professional and managerial jobs, we find only one out of twenty Negro males, while almost one out of every four white males are in these better-paying jobs. In other words, a white male has a five-times-greater chance of being at the top of the occupational scale; while a Negro male has a dubious two-times-greater chance of being at the bottom.

The occupational disparities for women, although marked, are not as great as those for men. In 1960, 71 per cent of the Negro women in Chicago and 35 per cent of the white women were in the lower-paying unskilled and semiskilled occupations. In the high-paying professional and managerial jobs there were 8 per cent of the Negro female labor force and 15 per cent of the white female labor force. The smaller racial disparities in occupation between Negro and white women can be explained by the following factors: women in general tend to be excluded from managerial positions; most female professionals work in governmental agencies where there is usually less racial exclusion than in the

* We have included the low-paying "occupation not reported" in this category.

private business sector; and a high proportion of the total female labor force work is in low-skill and lower-paying occupations.

The fact that Negroes tend to rank lower than whites in the occupational structure of the Chicago labor market can be visualized as an occupational gap, similar to the gap in income. This relative occupational gap can be easily measured by an index. In brief, the occupational index measures by a single number the relative standings of two groups in the occupational hierarchy. If Negroes had proportionately held as many high-ranking jobs as whites, the value of the index would be 100—the lower the index number in a particular year, the further behind Negroes were in the occupational structure.*

The index compares only two racial groups of the same sex in any one year. It does not show how a single group, e.g. white males, fared in one year as compared to a previous year. Therefore the index does not reveal the fact that during this century the occupational structure of all groups, Negro and white males and Negro and white females, has changed so that they all have a higher proportion of more skilled jobs.

In examining the occupational index (see Table 7), we find that the pattern remained amazingly consistent from 1910 to 1950. The index for both sexes was in the range of eighty-two to eighty-five with only one exception. Negro men stood just as far behind white men on the occupational

* In computing the index, greater numerical weight was given to the more prestigious and remunerative occupations. The resulting numerical value obtained by multiplying the occupational weight by the number of persons in the occupation, and summing these weight values give us a standard for measuring and comparing the white and nonwhite occupational structures. A good popular explanation of this index can be found in Herman Miller, *Rich Man, Poor Man* (Crowell, New York, 1964), 99–102. For weights, we used the 1959 median-income of occupations in the Chicago Metropolitan Area. Separate weights were used for male and female.

Harold M. Baron and Bennett Hymer

TABLE 6

PER CENT DISTRIBUTION FOR MAJOR OCCUPATIONS BY SEX,
COLOR, FOR CHICAGO METROPOLITAN AREA, 1960

Occupation	Males			Females		
	WHITE	NEGRO	OTHERS*	WHITE	NEGRO	OTHERS*
Professional, Techn'l and Kindred	12.0%	2.9%	22.1%	11.4%	6.6%	22.0%
Mgrs, Officials, and Proprietors**	11.5	1.9	7.1	3.1	1.3	2.3
Clerical and Kindred Workers	9.4	9.6	8.4	41.2	17.4	26.5
Sales Workers	8.1	1.7	1.8	7.4	2.4	2.5
Craftsmen, Foremen, and Kindred	22.4	9.9	12.4	1.7	1.3	1.6
Operatives and Kindred	19.3	26.4	16.4	17.1	22.5	20.5
Private Household Workers	1.1	.5	.5	2.2	12.8	2.2
Service Workers (except private hshld)	6.0	14.6	14.8	9.0	17.1	6.3
Laborers**	5.1	14.3	2.9	.5	1.5	.8
Occupations Not Reported	6.0	18.2	13.6	6.4	17.1	15.3

* Primarily persons of Asiatic or American Indian ancestry.
** Farm managers, proprietors, laborers, etc. not included.
SOURCE: U. S. Census of Population 1960, Illinois, Detailed Characteristics, U. S. Department of the Census, Final Report, PC (1)-15D, Tables 124 and 122.

ladder in 1960 as they did in 1910, and there had been no variation in this pattern in the intervening years.

The occupational gap between Negro and white women was virtually the same in 1910 and 1950. Only in 1940 was there a deviation in the pattern when the index dropped

TABLE 7
OCCUPATIONAL INDEX FOR CHICAGO: RATIO OF NONWHITE
TO WHITE BY SEX
1910–60

City of Chicago

	MEN	WOMEN
1910	82	84
1920	82	84
1930	83	83
1940	85	75
1950	83	83
1960	84	87

Chicago Metropolitan Area

	MEN	WOMEN
1950	83	83
1960	77	87

SOURCE: Estelle Hill Scott, *Occupational Changes Among Negroes in Chicago* (Chicago, 1939); *U. S. Census of Population, 1960, 1950, and 1940.*

to seventy-five, showing that the great depression had a strongly adverse effect on the occupational position of Negro women.

Between 1950 and 1960 some important changes took place in the occupational structure. If we examine the index in Table 7 for the Chicago Metropolitan Area (which is the relevant area for the Chicago labor market),* we see that occupationally Negro men have fallen further behind white men, and that Negro women have improved their status relative to white women. In the case of Negro men the decline was quite marked, reflecting a much more rapid growth in the proportion of white men employed in professional and managerial jobs. Although both groups upgraded their occupational structures, the white males pulled further out in front.

* Data on occupation by color are not available for the Metropolitan Area prior to 1950.

The improvement in the relative standing of Negro women occurred because the occupational pattern for white women remained constant while proportionately more Negro women moved into higher-standing positions. The increase in female Negro clerical workers was especially noticeable.

Our occupational index does not measure the fact that within each occupation, Negroes tend to be among the lower income earners. By comparing the median income by race in the various occupations, we get a clear picture of this phenomenon (see Table 8). Negro men who are in sales or managerial jobs or who are proprietors are the furthest behind of any occupational classification. They tend to be concentrated in small or marginal businesses serving the Negro community. Very few Negroes are employed by major firms in sales or managerial positions. The income differential is not as great among clerical workers, probably because a high proportion of Negro clerical workers are employed by government agencies. The relatively small income gap between the races in the unskilled and semi-skilled occupations (operatives, services workers, and laborers) is perhaps explained by the existence of minimum wage legislation and the fact that many of these jobs are covered by collective-bargaining contracts with unions that have relatively unrestricted entry. These contracts enforce pay uniformity and strict seniority. In contrast, among craftsmen the trade unions tend to have restrictive entry and to exclude Negroes from better-paying positions. The income gap, therefore, is larger in this classification.

PART TWO
THE DYNAMICS OF SECOND-CLASS STATUS

The types of disparities between white and Negro workers which were described in the first part of the paper have been permanent features of the Chicago labor market since World War I. Prior to the war Chicago had only a small

TABLE 8
MEDIAN INCOMES OF MALES FOR MAJOR OCCUPATIONAL GROUPS IN CHICAGO METROPOLITAN AREA BY COLOR, 1959

OCCUPATION	WHITE MALES	NONWHITE MALES	NONWHITE INCOME AS PER CENT OF WHITE INCOME
Professional & Technical	7648	5226	68.3%
Farmers & Farm Managers	3395	—	—
Managers, Off'ls, and Proprietors (Except Farm)	8524	4834	56.7
Clerical & Kindred	5177	4396	84.9
Sales Workers	6465	3506	54.2
Craftsmen, Foremen, etc.	6632	4614	69.6
Operatives & Kindred	5322	4253	79.9
Private Household Workers	1044	1646	157.7
Service Workers (Except Private Household)	4417	3437	77.8
Farm Laborers & Foremen	2480	2440	98.4
Laborers (Except Farm & Mine)	4382	4023	91.8

SOURCE: U. S. Bureau of Census, *U. S. Census of Population: 1960. Detailed Characteristics, Illinois*, Final Report PC (1)-15D; Table 124: "Earnings in 1959 of Persons in Experienced Civilian Labor Force, by Occupation, Color, and Sex, for the State and for Metropolitan Statistical Areas of 250,000 or More: 1960."

Negro population, largely employed in menial- and personal-service-type occupations. During a tight wartime labor market, aggravated by the cessation of European immigration, many employers began to recruit Negro labor from the South to fill manpower shortages. It was at this point of time that Negroes formed a sizable and distinct ethnic group in the Chicago labor force.

For the majority of Negroes coming to Chicago from the South, their point of entry into the labor market was at the bottom of the occupational hierarchy. Both rural work backgrounds and the emergence of discriminatory policies prevented their movement into higher-skilled and better-paying occupations. Soon after, the racial occupation lines that were emerging became permanently frozen.

Since 1920 there has been only a small change in the status of the Negro worker relative to that of the white worker. While both groups have improved their employment conditions—higher wages, more leisure—Negroes have not been able to catch up and close the gaps in income, occupation, and training. A comparison between Negro and white immigrants to the city further illustrates the inability of the Negro worker to eliminate these disparities. White immigrants in one or two generations were able to disperse throughout society and the economy of the Northern city. Negroes, on the other hand, one hundred years after emancipation and following almost three generations of intensive migration to the North, are still confined to certain sectors of the labor market.

A constantly increasing proportion of the Negro population in Chicago has been born and reared in the North. If Negroes operated only under the same handicaps that European immigrants did, we would expect to find a closing of the gap as the percentage of second and third generations of Northern Negroes increased. Instead, we find that the disparities have become fixed features of the over-all socioeconomic structure. Neither urbanization nor substantial increases in the level of Negro educational attainment have eradicated the disparities in income and occupations between whites and Negroes. In other words, just as the large city has confined Negroes to residential ghettos and segregated schools, so has it locked them into definite (and inferior) sectors of the labor market.

To date, no satisfactory explanation has been offered for the perpetuation of Negro's second-class status in the Northern city. Instead, comprehension of the Negro worker's position in the Northern labor market has been obscured by the myths inherited from America's racial history. In accounting for the Negro's status in the Northern city, Americans have substituted a continuation of Southern economic folklore for fact. Explanations tend to be deduction from myths instead of cold analysis of the urban status quo.

These racial myths originating in the South served to justify the treatment of Negroes as low-cost plantation labor, first under chattel slavery and then under rural peonage. The brand of racism developed by the Southern intelligentsia to defend the peculiar institutions of slavery and its successor, Jim Crow, was based on claims that Negroes were intellectually, biologically, and morally inferior to whites. The doctrine, as explicitly stated by John C. Calhoun, held that slavery was a positive good for "there never has yet existed a wealthy and civilized society in which one portion of the community did not, in point of fact, live on the labor of the other."

These myths accounted for the position of both slave and master. The poor white was included in the picture with the doctrine that he could claim an exalted social status solely because he was white in a racially hierarchical society. "The poor white laborer in the North," said the Southern spokesman DeBow, "is at the bottom of the social ladder, whilst his brother here [in the South] has ascended several steps and can look down upon those who are beneath him at an infinite remove." This racist ideology was in effect a rationalization on the part of the Southern oligarchy as it sought to preserve its control over a low-cost unskilled labor force and to maintain its vested social and political interests by separating poor whites from poor Negroes.

Harold M. Baron and Bennett Hymer

The North's social and economic structure was not based on the exploitation of a particular segment of its labor force. Yet the status of the Negro worker in the North has always been second-class, both socially and economically. In the days prior to World War I, when Negroes were only a tiny minority in the North, their second-class conditions were largely derived from the status of the great mass of Negroes in the South who were held in bondage. This inferior position was rationalized by a somewhat less virulent version of Southern racism.

Modern-day racial institutions in Northern labor markets were forged in the early twenties when Negroes entered the labor force in large numbers. The ideology developed to defend contemporary Northern racial institutions was expressed in psychological and individualistic terms, in contrast to the Southern experience where racism was based upon an entire way of life. Racial attitudes of Northern whites were attributed to factors like prejudice, stereotypes, and discrimination. These attitudes were rationalized by relating the economic plight of the Negro to his specific handicaps and circumstances—lack of education and training, ill-health, weak motivation, and the instability of Negro family life. The gaps in income, occupation, and education, resulting from discrimination and segregation, were interpreted as being the factors that produced the discrimination and segregation.

The emerging pattern of Northern racial differences that was becoming institutionalized was explained by social scientists in terms of the individual preferences of whites to exclude Negroes and the failure of the Negro worker to bring certain acquired attributes to the labor market—education, incentive, skills, and middle-class habits and appearances. The North refused to admit that its own racial practices, like those in the South, formed a well-institutionalized socioeconomic structure of subjugation. Negroes and whites were seen only as an aggregate of separate entities relating to each other within a *laissez-faire* market.

The racial folklore of the Negro worker's experience in

the Northern labor market can now be replaced with a more sophisticated analysis. By utilizing recent findings in the study of Northern race relations and urban labor markets, the disparities between white and Negro workers can be related to institutional factors within the large urban labor market —the existence of barriers that divide the labor market into distinct compartments based upon race.

For expository purposes a blueprint of the typical Northern labor market will be drawn. Although the main point of reference is Chicago, the model is highly applicable to other urban labor markets having a sizable Negro labor force. Basically, the blueprint consists of three generalizations describing the way in which the Chicago labor market generates differences based upon race. These generalizations are:

1. The labor market is divided into two racial components —a sector for the deployment of white labor and a sector for the deployment of Negro labor. Each sector has its own separate institutions and mechanisms for the recruitment, training, and allocation of jobs and workers. Firms are cognizant of this division and have different perceptions of the two labor forces when they shop for labor.

2. The Negro labor force has served as a pool of surplus labor used to fill shortages of white labor that occur during war years or periods of rapid economic growth. A large segment of the Negro labor force has been frozen into positions that are regarded as traditionally Negro jobs. These jobs are usually marginal and low paying; they require little skill or formal training; they often involve physical hazards; they frequently offer only seasonal or cyclical employment; and they are frequently in stagnant or declining industries.

3. Northern *de facto* segregation, in general, is maintained by a complex of interrelated and mutually supportive institutions whose combined effect is greater than the sum of the effects of each institution considered singularly. The racial distinctions and differentiations created

in any one institutional area operate as effective barriers supporting the segregation and status differentiation that occurs in other institutions. The division of the labor market into a Negro sector and a white sector is made more effective by the existence of the barriers in nonlabor-market institutions. These barriers feed back to limit the Negro worker's access in many areas of the labor market.

RACIAL DUALISM IN THE URBAN LABOR MARKET

The racially dual labor markets found in Northern cities have their origins in the earlier system of Southern slavery and rural peonage.* However, if the Negro's subordinate position in the North were merely a historical atavism from his Southern past, it would be expected that race would lose its significance as a social and economic category with the passage of time. Instead, we find that the Negro's second-class status has been effectively institutionalized in the Northern city—far removed from Southern rural conditions.

The marked and systematic disparities that exist between whites and Negroes in regard to income, employment, occupation, and labor-force participation offer *prima facie* evidence that a dual racial labor market exists. The two distinct and enduring patterns of employment characteristics that have been described cannot be explained in terms of a single homogeneous market. The description of these disparities, however, documents the dualism at only a general level of observation.

In more specific terms, a racially dual labor market means

* Both these systems can be considered as forms of social and economic segregation, which made possible the exploitation of the Negro labor force by the Southern landed ruling class. The division of the labor force also enabled many Southern manufacturers to practice wage discrimination, i.e. to pay Negroes less than whites for similar work and to pay Southern whites lower wages than Northern whites.

that there exists a primary metropolitan labor market in which firms recruit white workers and in which white workers look for jobs; side by side with the major market, there exists a smaller labor sector in which Negroes are recruited and in which Negroes look for employment.* For each sector there are separate demand and supply forces determining the allocation of jobs to workers and workers to jobs. Over time, this dualism is characterized by a transfer of jobs from the white sector to the Negro sector as the economy develops and as the Negro labor force expands in absolute and relative numbers.**

To understand the perpetuation of the Negro's second-class status, it is necessary to examine the mechanisms by which the labor market and in a broader sense the general socioeconomic structure have distributed jobs between whites and Negroes. The conception of a division of the labor market along racial lines in a city such as Chicago is an important factor in understanding how racial differences have been systematically maintained.

The racial divisions in the Chicago labor market are visible in many dimensions—by industry, by occupation, by geographic area, by firms, and by departments within firms. In general, Negro workers tend to be hired by certain industries and by particular firms within those industries. Some firms have absolute racial barriers in hiring, with Negroes being completely excluded. Within all industries and even in government employment there is unmistakable evidence of occupational ceilings for Negroes. Within single establishments that hire both white and nonwhites, Negro workers are usually placed in particular job classifications and production units. A good rule of thumb is that the lower the

* In the Chicago area Negro workers comprise one seventh of the total labor force.
** It should be noted that the generalization concerning the dual labor market is made at a high level of abstraction and that there are obvious exceptions at the level of particulars. The need here is to comprehend the process, and comprehension requires some degree of abstraction.

pay or the more disagreeable and dirty the job, the greater the chance of finding a high proportion of Negroes.

Racial concentration by industry in Chicago is shown in the fact that 20 per cent of employed Negro males work for federal, state, or local government as compared to only 6 per cent of employed white males. Six per cent of Negro males are in the primary metal industry as compared to 3 per cent of white males. At the other extreme, 1.5 per cent of white males are in the banking and finance industry as compared to only 0.2 per cent of Negro males. The existence of limited entry for Negroes can also be found in manufacturing—for example, 6 per cent of all white men are employed in the nonelectrical machinery industry while only 2 per cent of all Negro men are in that field.

While an examination of broad industrial classifications indicates certain tendencies toward racial dualism in the labor market, the pattern becomes much more distinct when individual firms and occupations within an industry are considered. A recent survey based on a sample of firms from the membership of the Chicago Association of Commerce and Industry makes this point strongly by showing the percentage of firms in the Chicago labor market that do not employ nonwhites. Seven out of every ten small firms, one out of every five medium-sized firms, and one out of every thirteen large firms do not hire nonwhites. Construction, transportation and utilities, and finance and insurance are the *most segregated* industries. Those small firms that employ any nonwhites tend to have labor forces with a very high proportion of nonwhite workers. While nonwhites account for 10.4 per cent of total employment by small firms, they are confined to 30.9 per cent of the universe of small firms.

Employment of some nonwhites by a firm does not necessarily mean that it has an integrated work force. Within a firm, racial segregation can take place on the basis of production units, branch operation, or occupational classification. Table 9 offers conclusive proof of this point. For each major occupation it shows the percentage of employees working for firms that have no nonwhites in that particular occupational classification. It stands out clearly that within individual firms, four occupations—professional, managerial, sales, and craftsmen—tend to exclude nonwhites. In the case of professionals and managers Table 9 understates the segregation of Negroes, as a high proportion of the nonwhites in these classifications are Orientals.

In some firms that are integrated by occupation, departments within that occupational group may be divided along racial lines. Negroes are especially segregated into hot, dirty departments like foundries and heat-treating shops. Sometimes within the same operation there will be occupational segregation in which the laborers are Negro and the machine operators are white, or in other cases the machine operators are Negro and the higher-paid mechanics are white. A plant might have an integrated semiskilled work force, but it will almost invariably have segregation of its craftsmen and lower-level supervisory employees, even though most of these jobs are filled by within plant recruitment. In general, the lower the position on the occupational scale, the greater the chance that there will be integration for a particular job classification.

TABLE 9

PROPORTION OF EMPLOYMENT SEGREGATION BY OCCUPATIONAL GROUPS AND COLOR

Occupation	Per cent Segregated (NONWHITE)
Professional	43.3%
Managers	75.1
Clerical Workers	27.3
Sales Workers	54.7
Craftsmen, Skilled	66.2
Semiskilled	11.5
Service Workers	8.0
Laborers	11.0

SOURCE: Chicago Association of Commerce and Industry, *Manpower Survey*, 1964, p. 16, Table 11.

The one occupational category in which the barriers between the two labor markets are becoming noticeably lower is in the employment of female clerical workers. Integration of women clerical workers is most noticeable in government, but in the last few years private industry has sought Negro secretaries. Often this is used as a symbol to show that a firm no longer practices racial exclusion in white-collar employment. Some of the integration of female clerical workers can be attributed to the fact that white women tend to have more erratic employment patterns than Negro women, as we have noted earlier. Negro females seem to be filling a labor shortage that exists for stable women clerical workers within the current tight labor market.

Within government employment we find a pattern similar to the private sector, although the lines of separation and the extent of exclusion are not quite as sharp. Lower racial barriers in hiring have made government employment a haven for skilled Negroes. In Chicago an estimated 60 per cent of the Negro professional workers, compared to only 22 per cent of white professional workers, are employed in the public sector of the economy. Even though entry into the preferred occupations in the public sector is not as limited, there are still clear-cut occupational ceilings for Negroes. For example, the federal government has much greater equity in its racial practices than state or local government, yet Negroes are compressed into the bottom occupational categories. In the U.S. government's Chicago Civil Service Region, 19 per cent of all employees are Negro. But 27 per cent of the employees at the lower level are Negro, while only 1.7 per cent of the employees at the higher level are Negroes.[11]

Even where Negroes can advance into supervisory jobs or professional positions, there still tends to be a dual labor market. Negroes in these positions generally service or supervise other Negroes. This pattern prevails in both private and public sectors. The Chicago Board of Education, which is the largest employer of Negro professionals in the area, offers a perfect example of this mechanism. Almost all Negro teachers are in schools with Negro children. Sixteen out of seventeen Negro principals head overwhelmingly Negro schools, while the seventeenth principal heads a school with many Spanish-speaking pupils. Higher-ranking Negro administrators either supervise Negro districts or direct programs that are largely geared to Negro pupils.

In response to this segregated job pattern in the total labor market, Negroes and whites have developed separate patterns of job seeking. Whites do not seek employment with firms that they identify as being totally in the Negro labor market, nor do they seek jobs that they identify as being Negro jobs. In firms which have integration among their unskilled or semiskilled workers, it is the whites in these categories who operate with the expectation that they will be chosen for on-the-job training or considered for promotion.

Negroes, on the other hand, shop in what they consider to be the Negro labor market. Firms are identified as employing Negroes, e.g. in Chicago certain mail-order houses and the Post Office; or jobs, such as laborer or foundry work, are identified as being Negro jobs. The Negro job seeker expects automatic rebuff outside the identified Negro labor market, and he accordingly limits his shopping to the places where he feels that he has some chance of success. Not surprisingly, most jobs in the white labor market are never sought by Negroes.

These segregated job-seeking patterns are reinforced by several practices. Many firms fill vacancies by word of mouth to friends and relatives of employees, thus recruiting from the same racial groups as their present labor force. Labor-market intermediaries—the Illinois State Employment Service, some five hundred private employment agencies, and vocational counselors—tend to operate on the basis of the dual labor market. Negro youngsters in school are encouraged to seek careers in occupations that are traditionally Negro jobs. Nonwhite job seekers are counseled to apply for positions within the Negro labor market. Both public and private employment services, in spite of legal prohibitions, tend to respect the racial lines of the labor market in their referrals.

SURPLUS LABOR SUPPLY

The concept of dualism is a convenient way of describing a major feature of Northern race relations in the area of employment—the segregation and division of the white and Negro labor forces. To understand further the operation of urban labor markets where there is a sizable Negro labor force, it is necessary to describe the processes of how Negroes advance occupationally and how certain jobs are either kept from or allocated only to the Negro labor force.

Our second generalization, i.e. the surplus labor pool, shows that the Negro labor force has served as an excess supply of labor utilized for jobs that whites have recently vacated, or for jobs where there are shortages of white labor, or for jobs that have become traditionally Negro jobs. According to this generalization, the Negro labor force can be broken down into three distinct groups:

1. A Negro *service sector* selling goods and services to the Negro community;
2. A *standard sector* regularly employed by major white-controlled firms or institutions, including government;
3. A *surplus labor factor* that is without work or tenuously employed in low-paying, marginal jobs.

By the Negro service sector we refer to Negroes self-employed or employed by firms, either white or Negro owned, which service the Negro community. In the case of professional services, such as medical or legal, the persons within this sector are usually well paid. At the other extreme are small neighborhood retail establishments providing only a subsistence income to their proprietors. In general, the size of the service sector is dependent upon the amount of money that Negroes have available for consumption expenditures.

By the standard sector of the Negro labor force we refer to workers regularly employed in firms and institutions that supply goods and services to the total economy. Annual earnings in this sector are well above the subsistence level and in many cases are comparable to those for whites. Jobs in this sector are either with major employers or with firms that are competitive with the major companies. Within this standard sector Negro workers are often segregated by firm and within firms by job classification or production unit. The size of this sector is generally determined by the extent to which past or present labor shortages have allowed the entry of Negro workers into areas where previously just whites were hired. Currently, approximately half the Negro labor force is in this category.

The surplus sector of the Negro labor jobs consists of workers occupied in traditional Negro jobs outside the standard sector and workers who are unemployed or are out of labor force, or are in marginal jobs. Workers in the surplus sector who have jobs occupy positions that are at the very bottom of the occupational ladder. These jobs are low paying, involve dirty and unsafe work, are often of short duration, and have little advancement potential. Many of these jobs are assigned to the Negro labor force only as the white labor force advances into higher occupations. Traditional Negro jobs like bootblacks, car washers, busboys, washroom attendants, porters, and servants are positions that through custom have gradually formed an area of employment exclusively for Negroes, or other minority groups, regardless of employment conditions elsewhere in the labor market.

Table 10 provides estimates for each of these sectors of the Negro labor force for 1959. Because earlier data were not available, changes in the relative and absolute sizes of each sector cannot be measured.

Many workers in the surplus sector are dependent upon some form of public aid for their incomes. In Chicago ap-

TABLE 10

ESTIMATES OF THE SECTORS OF THE NEGRO
LABOR SUPPLY IN CHICAGO METROPOLITAN AREA BY SEX, 1959

	MALE	FEMALE
Standard Sector	125,000	57,000
Negro Service Sector	20,000	15,000
Surplus Sector	80,000	53,000
Total	225,000	125,000

proximately one fourth of all Negroes receive some form of public assistance. All persons in this sector have low incomes, close to or at a subsistence level, that cover only the basic necessities. For all members of this sector, both those with and those without work, the level of subsistence income is primarily established outside the labor market by the political determination of welfare payments. The level of welfare payments serves as an effective minimum income. The size of this sector has generally been dependent upon the degree of unemployment in the general labor market and, in earlier years, upon the amount of white immigration.

The concept of the surplus labor supply can also be viewed as a dynamic process occurring over time. Usually some Negro workers are moving from the surplus sector into the standard sector. This movement is often accelerated in periods of rapid economic growth when tight labor markets help break down many discriminatory barriers. Many firms will begin to shop in the Negro labor market when they are confronted by a shortage of white labor. In Illinois these positions are often in declining industries that are losing their labor force to the growth industries.[12] Sometimes this movement reverses itself. For example, many Negroes in the Chicago meat-packing industry were forced back into the surplus sector when displaced from their jobs at the time the packinghouses left Chicago. But usually the breakthroughs in employment that occur are irreversible partly because of social custom, and partly because of seniority and other forms of job security.

The Negro Worker in the Chicago Labor Market

In the last twenty-five years the number of Negro workers who have left the Negro surplus labor sector has increased considerably. However, the Negro labor force is still growing today, primarily through the entry of indigenous teen-agers and secondarily through the migration of Southerners. In the face of this growing labor force the expansion in employment opportunities for Negroes has not been sufficient either to have eliminated or to have reduced substantially the size of the surplus labor pool. Negro teen-agers are frequently trapped in the surplus labor sector because of the inadequate preparation they receive in inferior, segregated schools like those in Chicago. Negro workers displaced from Southern agriculture are even worse off as the gap between the requirements necessary for industrial employment and unskilled Southern rural labor has widened over time.

The concepts of the dual labor market and the surplus labor supply can be more closely related by considering their more general usage. Social scientists who specialize in the study of underdeveloped countries point out that these economies are usually composed of two clearly identifiable sectors: an advanced industrialized sector using modern technology and skilled labor, and a subsistence peasant sector, using very little machinery and containing a large unskilled labor force that has high rates of unemployment and underemployment. We find a parallel in the urban labor market that we have been examining. Here, there is a white labor force which, for the most part, uses modern technology and contains a large percentage of skilled and highly skilled workers; then there is a Negro labor force which, to a large extent, is unskilled and employed in jobs either located in declining industries or providing only marginal types of employment. In fact, the surplus sector of the Negro labor force forms a type of urban peasantry comparable in certain aspects to the subsistence sector in underdeveloped economies. Since this supply of labor is outside the general economy and workers in it live at a subsistence income, they can easily be attracted into regular employment in large numbers without forcing wages to rise.

Harold M. Baron and Bennett Hymer

That racial dualism exists in most urban labor markets and that the Negro labor force has served as a surplus labor pool may explain why unemployment rates in the U.S. have been above those tolerated by workers in the Western European countries.[13] In the U.S. the unemployment rate for Negroes is almost always double that for whites, if not higher, and a much greater proportion of the Negro labor force is concentrated in undesirable jobs. An equitable distribution of unemployment would probably raise the white unemployment rate by at least 1 per cent. In this context, dualism can be considered as a way of minimizing the potential economic and social grievances resulting from unemployment and other forms of economic injustice. Given the tendency of the economy over the last eight years to function at levels where unemployment seldom falls below 5 per cent, white workers are only protecting a narrow economic interest by excluding Negroes from many occupations. Because of a lack of political and social power, the Negro labor force has not been able to impose its own political constraint concerning the level of unemployment it will tolerate. One impact of the current civil rights movement may be to reduce the permissible rate of Negro unemployment.

De Facto BARRIERS

Racial dualism in the labor market is only one of the several major forms in which the system of Northern segregation perpetuates the second-class status of Negro workers in the Northern city. Housing segregation and school segregation restrict them in the acquisition of both skills and jobs. At the same time, the ideology of racism and the lack of Negro political power re-enforce these major institutional patterns. Within the labor market these practices together with employment discrimination act as the barriers that produce and maintain the dualism.

The over-all effect of Northern racial institutions—housing segregation, school segregation, employment discrimination—operating concurrently is not confined just to the labor market. There is an overriding system of race relation characterized by the social and economic subjugation of the Negro via the whole constellation of institutions. In examining the components of this system we find a number of similarities. Discrimination and segregation in the labor market operates in much the same way as residential segregation and *de facto* school segregation. In each case there are no modern laws either regulating or maintaining the practice, yet the institutions operate almost as though they were ordained by a body of statute. Secondly, none of these particular racial practices could persist by itself if there were not an array of re-enforcing social, economic, psychological, and geographical elements supporting it. The various types of *de facto* segregation in housing, education, and employment each make the other types that much more effective and absolute. Consequently a reduction in one barrier—say, employment discrimination—will have only a limited effect unless the other institutions also change. Third, each of these racial barriers considered by itself has fuzzy edges and exceptions. However, when they are examined as a group, they produce an over-all pattern of sharp racial differences and little interracial contact.

The total network of *de facto* segregation in Chicago is so pervasive that the second-class status of Negro workers is passed on from generation to generation. Urban segregation in the Northern city cannot be explained merely in terms of the problems of rural Southern migrants learning to cope with city life—this is only one of many factors. The system of *de facto* segregation breeds its own children within its confines and keeps many at the lowest possible level of income. For example, in 1960, 25 per cent of the Negro mothers on ADC[14] Public Assistance had been born in Chicago—Northern-born women had almost as high a representation on the welfare roles as did women born in the South.

Harold M. Baron and Bennett Hymer

EMPLOYMENT DISCRIMINATION

Firms seeking to discriminate can exclude Negroes in a number of different ways. They can directly turn down Negroes because of race, or screen them out by criteria that appear to be color-blind. Certain job requirements—residence near the job, a stable work record, a high school diploma, and no arrest—will tend to exclude a greater proportion of Negroes than of white applicants. Some of these criteria serve as cutoff points and job-rationing devices, rather than actually being related to job performance.

Individual decision-makers involved in the recruitment and hiring process—personnel men and foremen—will exert their own conscious or unconscious preferences by applying ambiguous and discriminatory hiring criteria—looks, dress, speech patterns—rigidly for Negroes and loosely for whites. Many of the tests used by firms to select workers will contain cultural biases that handicap applicants from low-income nonmiddle-class homes. Finally, a firm may discriminate by shopping only in the white labor market, i.e. not advertising in Negro newspapers or informing Negro placement agencies of vacancies.

Employment discrimination is seldom an all or nothing proposition (as we have noted in our section dealing with dualism). In practice there is a wide range of hiring policies that may be in operation. Although some firms completely exclude Negroes, most big firms will recruit Negro workers for certain occupations or for certain departments and certain job classifications, while still excluding them from others. Often firms that hire Negroes establish job ceilings through on-the-job discrimination in promotion. In general, the hiring and promotion policies of most firms depend upon their immediate manpower requirements and the extent to which the government and civil rights groups are exerting pressure.

An individual firm may discriminate from the irrational

motive of prejudice. In other cases firms may discriminate to placate customers or employees. The discrimination may be secondary, as in cases where union membership is a requirement for employment and the unions exclude Negroes from membership. A firm may also discriminate unintentionally because it is well within the area regarded by Negro job seekers as being part of the white labor market. Some firms may also use racial divisions as a means of weakening unions in organizing and in collective-bargaining negotiations.

In the past some firms may have been able to benefit from the dual labor market by paying Negro workers less than whites for similar work. This point is indirectly suggested by a national study which showed that in 1959 there was a 13 per cent difference in hourly earnings between Negroes and whites having the same individual attributes.[15]

Employment discrimination is not totally regulated by the employers. For certain occupations trade unions have an important voice in hiring procedures. In the skilled trades, especially those with apprenticeships, unions—either solely or in joint councils with employers—determine who can enter the craft. The result has been the widespread exclusion of Negroes from these skilled jobs. After four years of strong criticism by civil rights groups and governmental bodies the Washburne Trade School, which provides the training for most of the apprenticeship opportunities in the Chicago area, has only reached the stage where 2 per cent of its enrollment is Negro.

Even when Negroes have managed to enter the building trades, they have frequently been shunted into Jim Crow locals. These segregated locals and discrimination in hiring-hall procedures in the integrated locals serve as a rationing device in passing out the jobs. Negro bricklayers have difficulty finding employment except in the peak season; in the slack season the available work is shared among the white bricklayers and the Negroes are excluded. In other cases, such as the painters, Negroes are generally confined to working in the ghetto areas while whites can work any-where.

The industrial-type unions, on balance, have had a positive influence in breaking down racial discrimination. This influence has not been of particular importance in the initial hiring procedure. It has been felt primarily through the operation and the strict enforcement of seniority provisions. Seniority rules have given Negro workers job security and greater access to promotion to better-paying jobs that are included in the bargaining unit. Nevertheless, even in industrial union shops Negroes are still grossly underrepresented in the higher-paying skilled jobs.

Housing Segregation

The persistence of housing segregation in Chicago has recently been documented in the Chicago Urban League's *Map of Negro Areas of Residence: 1950, 1960 and 1964.* The map shows that the large Negro ghettos on the South and West Side are expanding in accordance with the long-established Chicago pattern of segregated housing on a block-by-block basis. Residential segregation in Chicago is not on the decline, despite the changes in attitudes of whites concerning the acceptability of integrated housing and despite changes in public and private policies. Professor Karl Taueber of the University of Wisconsin has demonstrated that the intensity of residential segregation actually increased in Chicago between 1950 and 1960.[16] Housing segregation has resulted from the practices and policies of members of the Chicago real estate industry, the Chicago Board of Education's adherence to a narrow type of neighborhood school policy, and the influence of the ideology of racism on individuals.

The effect of housing segregation is to confine the Negro labor force to certain geographical areas of the labor market. The access of Negro workers to many jobs is limited as they can seek employment only within reasonable traveling distances. Even when workers are willing to travel long distances, proximity to the job is often used as a hiring criterion.

Most new jobs in the Chicago labor market are located in areas remote from the Negro ghetto and generally out of reach for Negro workers. Since 1957 there has been a continual movement of plants and offices away from the inner city near the ghetto to the outlying, lily-white areas of the metropolitan region. Between 1957 and 1963 the number of jobs near the Negro ghetto declined by almost 93,000 while the number of jobs in outlying and suburban areas increased by 72,000—generally in the northwestern suburbs farthest away from any sizable Negro population. The residential remoteness of Negroes from new jobs in growing industries re-enforces the pattern of hiring Negroes in declining industries.

SCHOOL SEGREGATION

Racial segregation in Chicago schools creates extreme differentials between whites and Negroes in the skills and training which they bring to the labor market. The system of segregation is highly efficient—in 1964, 85.6 per cent of all Negro pupils were in Negro-segregated schools (90 per cent or more Negro) and 78 per cent of all white pupils were in white-segregated schools (90 per cent or more white). The segregation is more extreme at the grade school level than at the high school level. During the school year 1964–65 there was a decline both in the number of integrated schools and in the number of pupils attending them.

Chicago's Negro schools are definitely of inferior quality. Less money is spent per pupil in them; they have more pupils per classroom and a higher concentration of inexperienced teachers. It is more often the rule than the exception that substitute teachers are not provided in Negro schools when the regular teachers are absent. In economic terms the segregated school system has served as a device for rationing insufficient educational resources to whites on a preferred basis.

The school system has low expectations for Negro pupils, and it graduates them with far less demanding standards. The Negro child tends to incorporate within himself the low estimate that the educational establishments has of Negroes. Accordingly, the segregated school system tends to dampen his motivation and to instill low career expectations in him. Test scores show that formal skills imparted to the Negro child are drastically lower than those given the white child.

The effect of inferior segregated education on the Negro student is obvious. He is less likely to obtain a high school diploma, less likely to score well on a placement test, and less prepared to acquire further skills on the job. The situation was recently summed up in a quip by Professor Kenneth Clark, the distinguished social psychologist: "Personnel managers need no longer exercise prejudicial decisions in job placement; the educational system in Chicago screens Negroes for them."

THE IDEOLOGY OF RACISM

The ideology of racism rationalizes the Negro's second-class status in the labor market and the total society. Racism is generally the rationale that underlies acts of discrimination against Negroes and behavioral patterns of avoiding Negroes. While the ideology of racism can best be conceived as a justification of the racial status quo, it also becomes important in re-enforcing that status quo. It guides individual behavior so that it conforms to the established racial institutions. For example, housing and school segregation is strongly supported by the racist flight of whites when a few Negro families enter a neighborhood.

In the labor market, racism is an important element causing employment discrimination in hiring. Racist ideas about the Negro's mental capacity limit the training and advancement offered to him. Racism is also a very important element in the hostility of many white employees toward their fellow Negro employees.

THE LACK OF NEGRO POWER

As a group, Negroes are without political and community power proportionate to their numbers. Major decisions affecting Negro employment, education, and residence have usually been made by white decision-makers who often live in suburbs far removed from the inner city where the Negro population is concentrated. Power on a city-wide basis is generally derived from the control of large economic or political institutions. Very few Negroes hold positions of authority within industry, government, or unions. There are hardly any large Negro-owned companies. Negroes are singularly marked by an absence of wealth in a society where wealth is power.

The absence of important Negro decision-makers put Negroes at a disadvantage in bidding for new opportunities, good jobs, and lucrative investments. This powerlessness inhibits the removal of existing racial barriers. If Negroes had effective power, changes in segregation patterns would have taken place long ago. Instead, within the political sphere where Negroes are best represented in the formal decision-making opportunities, the general pattern of *de facto* segregation tends to limit the actual power at their disposal. Professor James Q. Wilson, in his study of Negro political leaders in Chicago, makes the point that the very efficient Negro organization within the Cook County Democratic Party is in a secondary position of power and derives its influence from the cohesiveness of the county organization.[17] Although the Negro Democratic organization is very effective in getting out the vote, its influence, as measured by high-level patronage and officeholding, is nowhere proportionate to the number of votes it produces.

In the absence of important Negro power within the

established channels of decision-making, the civil rights movement operates to fill the vacuum. At present civil rights organizations are employing a wide range of pressure tactics to influence those who do wield power. Instead of exerting power by filling well-established and defined roles in a decision-making apparatus, the civil rights movement exerts its influence by mass participation and by disturbing traditional modes of operation.

Whether the movement's current strategy will be sufficient to overcome the complex system of *de facto* segregation remains to be seen. This new form of Negro political power is presently being used to improve the distribution of jobs between Negroes and whites and to raise the lower limits on the quality of education and housing for Negroes.

CONCLUSION

Segregation in the Northern labor market has been as efficient a mechanism for subjugating Negroes to second-class status as segregation in housing and education. In Chicago the process of allocating jobs to white workers is so effectively separated from the process of allocating jobs to Negro workers that year after year the differentials between white and Negro workers are maintained. At the same time, a large segment of the Negro labor force is relegated to the role of an urban peasantry destined to live off welfare payments and white paternalism. The Negro labor force, unlike those of other large ethnic groups, has not been allowed to assimilate into the metropolitan labor market. One hundred years after emancipation and forty-five years after urbanization, Negroes in Chicago are still systematically restricted in both the skills they may acquire and the extent to which they can utilize any given level of skills.

Racial dualism in the urban labor market is a structural phenomenon. While this does not necessarily mean that the social and economic order depends on segregation, it does tell us that our basic social and economic institutions have to be revamped in order to achieve equality. A dual structure based upon race is not merely a slight deviation from some acceptable norm as to how the labor market should function, but an essential feature of urban labor markets and American race relations.

Several implications immediately follow from this conclusion. (1) Programs and policies to eliminate segregation in the labor market have to be more extensive than those that now exist. Changes on the demand side—the removal of discriminatory barriers in hiring—can have only limited impact so long as conditions on the supply side remain stationary: inferior Negro public schools, housing segregation. (2) So long as current programing is continued under the same institutional assumptions—that the labor market is not divided racially—Negroes can make advancements only during periods of exceptional economic growth. Current programs are still applicable only in situations where the labor market is tight. And (3) the current pattern of racial disparities will perpetuate itself so long as only the market mechanism is relied upon as a corrective device and so long as supportive institutions that help shape the supply of labor continue their racist policies. Individual decision-making units in the labor market—the large firm or union—cannot by themselves produce changes in the institutional framework. At most, their policies can result in marginal adjustments. Concerted action and long-range planning by all important groups—employers, unions, placement agencies, and government—are necessary to produce the structural changes for the erosion of the dual structure. The labor market, if allowed to operate only through its own internal forces, does not generate sufficient economic or social pressure to eliminate racial disparities.

Recent events in the labor market can be evaluated against this background. So far the main institutional impact of the civil rights movement in Chicago has been in the area of employment, as both school and housing segregation have remained the same or even increased since Birmingham.

On the demand side of the labor market, there has been a partial lowering of discriminatory barriers as firms seek to comply with new laws and federal executive orders. An even greater lowering of barriers has been brought about by the labor shortages created by the present five-year-long economic boom.

In most major firms absolute racial restrictions have been removed. The biggest changes have been in those firms which are U.S. government contractors and therefore subject to review under the President's Equal Employment Opportunity Program. A few Negroes are now moving into professional and managerial positions for which, regardless of qualifications, they never would have been considered a few years ago. In some firms a fair number of female clerical workers are being hired.

However, these breakthroughs into new job classifications usually involve only a handful of Negro employees. They provide a symbolic token that the firm no longer discriminates absolutely. Most firms are pursuing only cautious programs of integration designed to be easily observable so as to satisfy government enforcement officers and civil rights groups. The current interest of many firms in race relations and the expensive rituals undertaken to indicate this interest still have not produced a major alteration in the employment structure. The openings in the better jobs are still minimal. The National Industrial Conference Board reports on a survey of forty companies: "Negroes, generally, still are being hired for low-paying, low-status jobs. The number of being employed in nontraditional Negro jobs is very small." The NICB further states: "There is a gap between policy and practice in the area of Negro employment. Few of the companies studied are doing as well as they want to do or so well as their top officers think they are doing."[18]

The current status of the Negro worker in the Chicago labor market may be characterized by the statement that although some discriminatory barriers on the demand side have been slightly lowered, most on the supply side still remain. Regarding the employment of semiskilled and un- skilled workers by firms subject to compliance with the President's Equal Employment Opportunity Program, one close observer of discrimination in Chicago comments: "In the past, personnel men used to discriminate against nine out of ten Negro applicants; today they only discriminate against eight out of ten."

POSTSCRIPT

The above analysis predates Watts and the subsequent urban riots in low-income Negro neighborhoods. Since then, the war on poverty and government-sponsored manpower pro- grams have reached maturity and have had an impact. The expansion of the armed forces over the past two years has curbed the size of the pool of younger workers in the labor force. Most important for the study of labor markets, unem- ployment is at its lowest level since the Korean war.

Within the Chicago area, conditions affecting the utiliza- tion of Negro labor have been extremely favorable. The rate of unemployment in the Chicago labor market ranks among the lowest in the country. High demand for almost all types of labor exists in most industries. Among many of the larger establishments, direct racial exclusion, which had been rampant until a few years ago, is beginning to disappear. Moreover, many companies are actively looking to the Negro labor force to fill manpower requirements that the white labor force cannot provide.

Yet when we examine the actual performance of Negro workers in the Chicago labor market, these factors seem to have had little effect on altering the over-all second-class status of the Negro worker. True, there has been an ex- pansion in the number of white-collar and skilled Negro workers, and recently college-trained workers enjoy oppor- tunities that are unprecedented for Negroes. But, on the whole, judging from available data, Negro workers, as a group, still occupy the same relative position vis-à-vis their white counterparts. The gains won by the civil rights movement basically have accrued to the upper half of the Negro wage earners.

The ratio of Negro to white family income dropped from 74 per cent in 1960 to 72 per cent in 1965 in the North Central region of the United States, which includes Chicago. The rate of Negro unemployment is still two to three times that for whites. Nationally, unemployment for Negro workers, which had been on the decline since 1965, began to edge upward in the latter half of 1966 while the white unemployment rate remained constant. We estimate that 20 per cent of the Negro labor force in Chicago is still employed at jobs that provide incomes below $3000, while about 6 to 7 per cent are unemployed. Given these conditions, the problem of the discouraged worker still remains.

Over-all, we find that semiskilled and skilled Negro workers have experienced impressive increases in real income as measured in purchasing power, although their position relative to that of white workers remains the same. On the other hand, unskilled Negro workers have had a hard time holding their own, and in some cases real income has even declined. A recent survey showed that ten Chicago community areas which have the lowest socioeconomic ranking have fared poorly since 1960. Real income for families in these areas, the majority of whom are nonwhite, increased at an annual rate of only 1 per cent, about one third the national average for all families. More accurate U. S. Bureau of Census surveys in Los Angeles and Cleveland show actual declines in real income for comparable neighborhoods.

The differentials in income and occupation that now exist within the Negro labor force will become more important in the near future. It is well to note that recent racial disturbances all occurred in nonwhite poverty neighborhoods. We can expect the rapid growth of political, social, and economic pressures reflecting the needs, aspirations, and expectations of nonmiddle-class Negroes. For low-income Negroes, civil rights represent as much a problem of class as of race. In view of this, our breakdown of the Negro labor force into three groups takes on added meaning.

Despite the current tight labor market, the dual-labor-market concept remains a valid description of how jobs are allocated in the Chicago labor market. Negro workers still look for work, accept employment, and receive training within the confines of a separate sector of the labor market.

A recent analysis of the Chicago labor market by David Taylor of the Massachusetts Institute of Technology shows that unskilled Negro workers earn less than comparable unskilled white workers. He made adjustments for such differences as age, education, and work history. When all these factors were taken into account, he found that Negro janitors earned ten cents less an hour than white janitors, and Negro material handlers thirty-two cents less an hour than their white counterparts. The bulk of this wage differential can be attributed directly to discrimination. The wage differential is further illustrated in a recent U. S. Department of Labor study which indicates that nonwhite graduates of Manpower Development Training programs earn twenty-one cents less an hour than white graduates, even though nonwhites in the program had higher educational levels.

The lowering of racial barriers in Chicago has occurred within the dual-labor-market structure. According to the concept we outlined, integration of certain job activities or the transfer of jobs from the white labor market to the Negro labor market sector occurs during periods when there are shortages of white manpower.

In the current tight market conditions we find that demand barriers have been lowered mostly through the removal of the overt forms of exclusion. Subtle discriminatory methods, such as residence requirements, recruitment procedures, and irrelevant hiring criteria, are still practiced. The major barriers, however, presently exist on the supply side of the labor market. The effects of housing segregation and school segregation are easily seen when the demand for labor is high. Job vacancies exist side by side with high rates of Negro unemployment.

Independent studies by Henri Theil and the Chicago Urban League prove that school segregation in Chicago has increased since 1963. Because of the inferior education provided in Chicago's segregated schools, Negro youngsters still enter the labor force with few marketable skills. They are unable, therefore, to take advantage of many of the changes in hiring practices. Housing segregation has continued at its traditional high level. Its effect on the mobility of Negro labor has become serious enough to warrant the attention of Chicago employers who are having difficulty recruiting nonwhite workers for their suburban plants.

In a recent study John Kain of Harvard University estimated that as many as thirty thousand jobs were lost to the Negro community by 1956 because of housing segregation and the movement of industry from the inner city to outlying areas. This problem has probably worsened in recent years. The centralization of Negro housing in Chicago has continued at the same time that the geographic dispersion of jobs has steadily increased. It is also estimated that as many as 112 thousand unskilled Negro workers might move from Chicago's ghettos to housing near suburban workplaces if they were free to choose locations similar to those available to low-income whites employed at the same workplaces.

In light of the events of the past two years, we can speculate about the future course of progress for Negro workers in the American economy. Should current rates of unemployment be maintained indefinitely, the income and occupational gaps can be narrowed for semiskilled and skilled Negroes. However, the existence of school and housing segregation sets limits to the amount of progress that can occur. On the other hand, even with a tight labor market unskilled workers cannot be expected to improve their relative status unless there are massive programs to offset the joint effects of automation, inferior training, and residential immobility.

However, the chances are extremely slim that the tight labor market will continue indefinitely under peacetime circumstances. If civil rights objectives are made subordinate to other national goals, the position of Negro workers could deteriorate seriously. This was pointed out in a recent speech by a Federal Reserve Board member who cautioned against expecting any future progress in Negro employment should the growth rate fall below its recent 4 per cent level:

> Negro job gains are large and Negro unemployment falls sharply only when the economy is growing at a "real" rate—after adjusting for higher prices—of well over 4 per cent a year as measured by the gross national product, such as the experience of 1964 and 1965 which were the best years in the Negro's employment history and in which the number of Negroes crossing the poverty line was impressive.
>
> Current economic conditions with nearly full employment and inflationary pressures call for a moderation of the growth rate next year to 4 per cent. This may mean not simply a slackening in the pace of improvement but a halt in further progress and even some rise in unemployment for nonwhite workers. Postwar experience shows that a 4 per cent growth in the economy produced a growth in blue-collar jobs of about three quarters of 1 per cent. Yet the recent rate of growth for the nonwhite labor force has averaged about 1.5 per cent a year.*

* Andrew F. Brimmer, *The Quests for Economic Stability and Equal Employment Opportunity*, A Speech to the National Urban League Equal Opportunity Day Dinner, November 18, 1966.

Chapter VIII

(A) THE RACIAL PRACTICES OF ORGANIZED LABOR:

THE CONTEMPORARY RECORD

HERBERT HILL

I

The tension between American labor's early advocacy of working-class interracial solidarity and the widespread pattern of anti-Negro practices within trade unions was symbolized by a proposal made by Samuel Gompers in 1895. In that year the past and future President of the American Federation of Labor* advised the National Association of Machinists (later the International Association of Machinists) that it could be admitted into the American Federation of Labor merely by transferring the color bar then in its constitution to its membership initiation ritual, where it performed the same function. Thus, Gompers developed what was to become the classic labor stance on civil rights, i.e. expressing formal support for Negro equality while acquiescing in overt discriminatory practices. Gompers could state that "the sentiment of organized labor of the country is decidedly in favor of maintaining and encouraging the recognition of equality between colored and white laborers."[1] But the President of the AFL also wrote: ". . . if the

* At the 1894 AFL convention President Gompers was defeated for re-election by John McBride of the United Mine Workers. He was re-elected President at the following convention and held the post until his death in December 1924.

colored man continues to lend himself to the work of tearing down what the white man has built up a race hatred far worse than ever known will result. Caucasian civilization will serve notice that its uplifting process is not to be interfered with in any way."[2]

From Gompers to benign William Green to the current era of sophisticated public relations under George Meany, the disparity between the public statements of organized labor on civil rights and the discriminatory practices of many unions continues. Today, lily-white exclusion clauses in union constitutions have been removed, but colored workers remain excluded from many craft unions by tacit consent. Pious resolutions on civil rights are routinely adopted at AFL-CIO conventions but discriminatory provisions in union contracts and segregated locals continue. At best, there is a minimal strategic adjustment, a token reform as a result of direct action by the Negro protest movement and litigation by aggrieved Negro workers.*

When the American Federation of Labor and the Congress of Industrial Organizations united in 1955, resolutions were adopted committing the merged Federation to the rapid elimination of racial discrimination and segregation within unions. These statements were hailed by the NAACP and other civil rights organizations. But more than a decade later the failure to eradicate patterns of discrimination has invalidated the earlier optimism.

During the AFL-CIO convention in September 1959, A. Philip Randolph, President of the Brotherhood of Sleeping Car Porters and the only Negro on the AFL-CIO

---

* There are a few significant exceptions to this pattern, such as the United Automobile Workers of America (UAW) and the United Packinghouse Workers of America (UPWA). The history of organized labor suggests that discriminatory racial practices were less likely to develop where there was a large early concentration of Negro workers in a given union's jurisdiction, in conjunction with an ideological sensitivity to "the Negro question" on the part of the union leadership. This sensitivity in most instances was rooted in the radical political ideologies of union leadership groups in their formative years, as in the Auto and Packinghouse Workers Unions.

Executive Council, criticized organized labor's lack of progress. He publicly called upon President George Meany and the Federation to take concrete action against segregated locals, discriminatory seniority provisions in union agreements, exclusionist practices, and the systematic barring of Negroes from leadership positions even in unions with large Negro memberships. Randolph also raised the issue of internal union democracy, so closely related to the question of racial discrimination. After a heated exchange Meany lost his temper and, pounding the rostrum, roared at Randolph: "Who the hell appointed you as guardian of all the Negroes in America?"[3] Later Randolph presented to the Federation's Executive Council detailed charges of anti-Negro practices in affiliated unions together with recommendation on ways to eliminate segregation and discrimination within international and local union organizations.

The Federation sharply rejected the charges. On October 12, 1961 the Executive Council publicly censured Randolph because, as George Meany put it, he was responsible for the "gap that has developed between organized labor and the Negro community" and because he had "gotten close to those militant groups." Instead of taking action against racist practices, the AFL-CIO Executive Council publicly blamed the acknowledged spokesman for Negro workers within the labor movement for the dilemma of labor's own making!*

Roy Wilkins, Executive Secretary of the NAACP, on October 13 issued the following statement:

* At the Annual Convention of the Negro American Labor Council, Chicago, Ill., November 10–12, 1961, Richard Parrish, national Treasurer of the Council, voiced the sentiments of the delegates on the Federation's rebuke of Randolph as follows: "Where was David Dubinsky, where was Walter Reuther, where was Joe Curran, where was Jim Carey?" Where were all those liberals on the Council when the vote was taken? This was a show of power to demonstrate to Negro union members that they represent nothing when it comes to setting policies in the labor movement even though they pay dues."

The National Association for the Advancement of Colored People believes that the AFL-CIO's "censure" of A. Philip Randolph is an incredible cover-up. The so-called report made to the Federation's Executive Council by a three-man subcomittee* is simply a refusal to recognize the unassailable facts of racial discrimination and segregation inside organized labor, as well as an evasion on the part of the AFL-CIO leadership of its own responsibility in fighting racism within affiliated unions.

We reject the Federation's statement that A. Philip Randolph caused "the gap which has developed between organized labor and the Negro community." If such a "gap" exists it is because Mr. Meany and the AFL-CIO Executive Council have not taken the required action to eliminate the broad national pattern of anti-Negro practices that continues to exist in many significant sections of the American labor movement, even after five and a half years of the merger and the endless promises to banish Jim Crow.

On October 13, the day after the Federation's censure of Randolph and its rejection of his recommendations, the U. S. Commission on Civil Rights' Report on Employment was issued. The report documented the significant extent of discrimination within organized labor, and concluded that "Existing Federal law has little impact on the discriminatory practices of labor organizations,"[4] and that the efforts of the AFL-CIO had proved largely ineffective in curbing discrimination. The impact of union discrimination, it said, especially in skilled occupations, was a basic factor in contributing to the concentration of Negroes in menial jobs in industry and their virtual exclusion from the construction and machinists' crafts, and accounted for Negro labor's extreme vulnerability to long-term unemployment. The report urged federal legislation to prohibit discrimination by

* This subcommittee consisted of Presidents Harrison of the Brotherhood of Railway Clerks, Walsh of the International Alliance of Theatrical Stage Employees, and Potofsky of the Amalgamated Clothing Workers.

unions and stressed the inability of the AFL-CIO to take action on its own initiative against the broad pattern of union racist practices.

Randolph, who successfully fought for a federal fair employment practices order during the Second World War and is well remembered for his leadership of the historic March on Washington Movement during the war, responded to the Federation's attack by calling upon Negro unionists to join the Negro American Labor Council and to raise their voices within the labor movement in protest against the paternalism of "liberal" white leaders and discrimination by trade unions.

Randolph also endorsed a detailed criticism made by the NAACP of the AFL-CIO civil rights record since the merger in 1955.[5] Addressing the Fifty-first Annual Convention of the NAACP in St. Paul, Minnesota, in June 1961, Randolph commenting on the report of the Association's labor department stated: "It is pertinent to observe that we in the Negro American Labor Council consider the report timely, necessary, and valuable. . . . Moreover, the Negro American Labor Council can without reservation state that not only are the basic statements of the Report true and sound, for the delegates of the Brotherhood of Sleeping Car Porters have presented these facts to convention after convention of the American Federation of Labor for a quarter of a century."

In 1966, more than a decade after the merger, there has not been a significant change in the pattern of racial discrimination in the major AFL-CIO affiliates, especially in those that have a long history of anti-Negro practices. A close examination of what has been called "progress" is most revealing.

The Brotherhood of Railway and Steamship Clerks had traditionally operated segregated locals in many Northern as well as Southern cities. In addition, union agreements provided for separate racial classifications, which limited Negro job mobility and violated the seniority of Negro members. During 1966 in Salt Lake City, Tulsa, and elsewhere, Negroes forced to belong to segregated locals of this union requested the assistance of the federal government through the Equal Employment Opportunity Commission in preventing the Brotherhood of Railway and Steamship Clerks from forcing them out of jobs in violation of their seniority rights.* Between 1960 and 1965 the Brotherhood of Railway Clerks eliminated several segregated local lodges by eliminating the jobs of Negro workers. They did so by reclassifying the traditional Negro job categories and declaring them to be within the jurisdiction of the white locals, which in practice meant, for example, that Negro freight handlers were dismissed from jobs long held and replaced by less senior white workers who had been in the all-white baggage clerks' seniority line.[6]

Another example of dubious "progress" is to be found in the Brotherhood of Locomotive Firemen, a union with a history of notorious anti-Negro practices going back to the 1890s. This union is directly responsible for forcing thousands of Negro firemen off the nation's railroads. It was the defendant in several important federal court cases brought on behalf of Negro firemen and did not remove the provision in its constitution that banned Negroes from membership until 1964. But as Arthur M. Ross, Commissioner of Labor Statistics, stated:

. . . the Brotherhood of Locomotive Firemen . . . removed a Negro exclusion clause from its constitution in 1964, after the railroad "work rules" arbitration had made it virtually certain that few, if any, additional firemen would ever be hired on American railroads.[7]

Among other industries where unions continued overt discriminatory practices a decade after the merger were paper and pulp manufacturing, chemicals and oil refining,

* In 1965 the Equal Employment/Opportunity Commission found "reasonable cause" in a Texas case against this union involving segregated locals and separate racial job classifications. (*Moses LeRoy vs. Brotherhood of Railway Clerks, Local 1534,* Houston, Texas Case #5-8-517, November 1, 1965).

the skilled metal trades, printing, tobacco manufacturing, and Great Lakes shipping—where the Seafarers International Union dispatched Negroes for jobs only in the galley and stewards' departments from SIU hiring halls.[8] In San Francisco the Hotel, Restaurant and Bartenders Union, with the full support of the AFL-CIO Central Labor Council, obtained an arbitrators ruling invalidating an agreement won by civil rights organizations with the San Francisco Hotel Employers Association that opened new job opportunities for Negro workers.[9]

Addressing a trade union conference in Detroit on February 7, 1959, A. Philip Randolph stated: "It is fair to state that racial discrimination is practiced by building trades unions in practically every community in the country, varying in intensity from community to community, and local to local."

Today, in virtually every large urban center in the United States, Negro workers are denied employment in the major industrial and residential construction projects because they are, with some few exceptions, barred from membership in the building trades craft unions.[10] Since these unions exercise rigid control of the hiring process in the industry, denying Negroes union membership effectively denies them the opportunity to secure employment. As progress in eliminating racial discrimination within organized labor ten years after the merger can be properly evaluated only by examining the status of Negroes in those unions that have historically discriminated against them, we shall look closely at the building and construction trades craft unions, especially in the North.

Shortly after the riots in Watts, the Negro ghetto of Los Angeles, Negro leaders and others proposed an end to the discrimination practiced by the AFL-CIO building trades unions in Los Angeles. It was argued that as federal and state funds were to be made available for the reconstruction of Watts, Negroes should be admitted into the unions that would supply the workers. The all-white construction unions rejected the proposal. An official of the Los

Angeles County AFL-CIO Building and Construction Trades Council stated, as reported in the Los Angeles *Times* of September 10, 1965, that "since Watts was not officially designated a disaster area, the unions should not take the initiative in trying to change hiring procedures."[11] Because the unions have exclusive hiring-hall arrangements with the contractors' associations Negroes were barred from new construction jobs within the Watts ghetto and throughout the Los Angeles area. It is ironic that the discriminatory practices of AFL-CIO unions will prevent Negro residents of Watts from participating in the eventual rebuilding of their own community.

A detailed examination of the racial practices of the powerful building trades unions reveals significant truths about organized labor's commitment to Negro equality, since these unions are a large and important group within the AFL-CIO with thousands of local affiliates throughout the country. A comment Gunnar Myrdal made in his *American Dilemma* has as much validity today as it had in 1942: "The discriminatory attitude of the organized building crafts is the more significant at the present, since they dominate the American Federation of Labor—a circumstance which is behind the reluctance of this organization to take any definite action against the exclusionist and segregational practices."[12]

Moreover, these unions are operating in an expanding sector* of the economy, and they have organized their

---

* New construction increased 57 per cent between 1960 and 1964, and is expected to double between 1970 and 1975, according to Commerce Department estimates. The volume of work in construction and repairs is also expected to grow. Thus, the skilled manpower necessary in 1970 will be 35 per cent above the present labor supply. *The Wall Street Journal*, April 10, 1964, in a front-page story stated that "booming construction activity will provide strong support this year for the nation's economy." The report concluded by noting that the general contractors who build highways, housing, office structures and utility facilities generally agree they will have record volume." The New York *World-Telegram* of January 13, 1965, reported that according to Louis Broido, Commissioner of

jurisdictions with *de facto* closed-shop arrangements that give them effective job control. In addition, they have adroitly used their considerable political power, entering into durable alliances with both political parties in many states and municipalities.

The Missouri State Advisory Committee to the United States Commission on Civil Rights reported that in Kansas City Negro membership was "restricted in a number of unions such as plumbers, sheet metal workers, steam fitters, operating engineers, and electricians."[13] Similarly, the Louisiana State Advisory Committee reported that in New Orleans "In some crafts, notably the electrical workers, plumbers, asbestos workers, boilermakers, pile-drivers, elevator constructors, hoisting engineers, glassworkers, ironworkers, sheet metal workers and sign painters, Negroes are completely excluded."[14] The report also noted that segregated Negro locals are maintained by the carpenters' and painters' unions and that in Detroit less than 2 per cent of all craft union apprentices were Negroes.[15] These practices are typical of the discriminatory pattern in both North and South. In December 1963 the New York City Commission on Human Rights investigated and found "a pattern of exclusion in a substantial portion of the building and construction industry which bars nonwhites from participating in this area of the city's economic life."[16]

On occasion one or two Negroes have been admitted into

the New York City Department of Commerce and Industrial Development, there had been a recent increase of twenty thousand jobs in the construction industry in New York City.

On December 13, 1965 the U. S. Department of Commerce reported that outlays for new construction would reach an all-time high of about $72.7 billion in 1966. *Time* magazine, December 17, 1965, p. 88, reported that "labor pirating by firms has broken out in the Midwest as a result of shortages of ironworkers, carpenters and cement masons." The 1966 *Manpower Report of the President* notes on p. xiii that "There are shortages of machinists for the metal working industry throughout the country, and shortages of building trades craftsmen in many areas."

an all-white local as a result of litigation by Negro workers or as token compliance with a state fair employment practice law. Among several such examples are Local 38 of the International Brotherhood of Electrical Workers (IBEW) in Cleveland and Local 8 of the Bricklayers in Milwaukee. But this is essentially a limited accommodation to community pressure and represents very dubious "progress." Certainly the token admission of a few Negroes into an electrical workers' union in Cleveland* can no more be regarded as integration than can the token admission of two or three Negro children into a public school in Mississippi.

The record of the repeated efforts of Negro workers to breach the color bar in the craft unions in Cleveland in the decade following the merger between the AFL and the CIO illustrates the very limited nature of progress since the merger in Northern cities.

In 1955, charges were filed with the Cleveland Community Relations Board against Local 38 of the International Brotherhood of Electrical Workers which adamantly refused to admit nonwhites into its membership. The fight to open this union's membership rolls to Negroes had begun in 1940 when nonunion Negro journeymen electricians requested the assistance of the international union in an effort to be admitted into Local 38 which has traditionally maintained a rigid control of all hiring for new construction.

In 1957 in the case of a Negro electrician, Theodore Pinkston versus Local 38, the Cleveland Community Relations Board found the union guilty and ordered it to admit Negroes. The union refused to admit the plaintiff Pinkston,

---

* Cleveland together with many other Northern cities has experienced a very significant increase in the Negro population. According to the 1960 Census Negroes constituted 38 per cent of the population of Cleveland. For an analysis of Negro urbanization and data on recent developments in Negro labor force participation see, Herbert Hill, "Demographic Change and Racial Ghettos: The Crisis of American Cities," *The Journal of Urban Law,* Vol. 44, Winter 1966, University of Detroit.

but admitted two other Negroes. In 1966, eleven years after the original charges were filed with the Cleveland Community Relations Board, Local 38 had admitted two Negro journeymen electricians into membership.[17]

On August 6, 1963, after months of mass picketing at the Cleveland Municipal Mall construction site, a Negro worker, Gilbert Foster, was hired by the A. Nabowski Company, the sheet metal subcontractor, to meet the demands of the NAACP and the other civil rights organizations that Negroes be employed on the public construction project. Immediately upon the arrival of Mr. Foster at the worksite, members of the all-white Sheet Metal Workers Local 65 walked off the job refusing to work with a Negro.[18]

As a result of the mass demonstrations at the Cleveland Municipal Mall construction site, an agreement was entered into on August 4, 1963, between Plumbers Local 55, the City of Cleveland, the United States Department of Labor, and the United Freedom Movement consisting of NAACP, CORE, and other local civil rights protest groups. Local 55 agreed to admit Negroes and to sign labor agreements with Negro-owned contracting companies and furthermore to admit Negroes into the union-controlled apprenticeship training program. Local 55 admitted one Negro plumbing contractor with his four journeymen employees but soon thereafter refused to admit other qualified Negro journeymen.[19]

Hearings before the United States Commission on Civil Rights held in Cleveland, Ohio, April 1–7, 1966 revealed the following information regarding the status of Negroes in certain major building trades craft unions in Cleveland:

International Brotherhood of Electrical Workers, Local 38, with a total membership of 1258 had two Negro members.

Iron Workers Local 17, with a total membership of 1786 had no Negro members.

Plumbers Local 55, with a total membership of 1482 had three Negro members.

Pipefitters Local 36 with a total membership of 1319 had one Negro member.

Sheet Metal Workers Local 65, with a total membership of 1077, had forty-five Negro members.

At the end of a decade of mass demonstrations, the filing of complaints with FEPC agencies, and the repeated attempts to secure enforcement of federal anti-discrimination executive orders, the five craft locals had four Negro apprentices.[20] This analysis confirms the statement of Roy Wilkins that,

> given a continuation of present rates of advance, it will take Negroes 138 years or until the year 2094 to secure equal participation in skilled-craft training and employment. Surely this condition will not be accepted by Negroes and we hope it will not be countenanced by others.[21]

The events in Cleveland* and elsewhere indicate that there are many instances in which unions have removed the racial exclusion clause from their constitutions as a public relations gesture but continue to exclude or limit Negroes as members and apprentices by tacit consent.[22]

Apprenticeship programs provide from one half to two thirds of all the skilled workers needed to replace older craftsmen and to meet the needs of industry. Unions, however, have the power to fix the number of apprenticeships, and they deliberately maintain an effective shortage of the skilled labor supply on the theory that this enhances their power at the bargaining tables. By restricting to sons and relatives the right to become an apprentice, the construction unions automatically exclude Negroes, since few have ever belonged. Union members view these provisions as a source of job security, and proclaim they do not discriminate against Negroes, but only against nonmembers. Yet this

* On August 8, 1967, The U. S. Department of Justice filed a lawsuit against Local 38, IBEW, in the U. S. District Court in Cleveland, charging violation of Title VII of the Civil Rights Act of 1964.

particular form of "security" results in the systematic exclusion of Negroes and Puerto Ricans as a group.

Donald Shaughnessy in his study of racial discrimination in the building trades unions for the New York State Advisory Committee to the United States Commission on Civil Rights describes how labor unions discriminate against Negroes applying for admission into union-controlled apprenticeship programs:

> For a union to engage in the "volley ball" technique, it helps to have two offices. Then the Negro applicant for the apprenticeship program can be sent from one office to the other, on some pretext, until he becomes discouraged or cannot afford any more time. If two offices are not available he can be called to appear at the one office on repeated occasions until the same effect is achieved. The "G-plan" technique is somewhat simpler. After the Negro applicant has filled out an application for the apprenticeship program, it is immediately disposed of ("G" for "garbage") and no reply ever sent. If the applicant has the temerity to call or make further inquiry about his application, he can be required to come down to the office and fill out another application form. Several such trips usually discourage even the most persistent applicant. The only requirement for the successful use of the "full house" technique is a thick pile of papers resembling application forms on one's desk. They can be pointed to or waved in the face of any applicant, indicating there are at least several hundred, if not thousand, applications already on file. If he nevertheless insists upon filling out a form, the "G-plan" technique can be put into effect.[23]

An accurate description of the way many trade unions control admissions into apprenticeship training programs and deliberately use such control to exclude Negroes is to be found in a study made by the Joint Legislative Committee on Industrial and Labor Conditions of the New York State Legislature. This staff report entitled "Discrimination in Employment and the Operation of the New York State Commission for Human Rights" (mimeo, December 1964) provides an excellent case history in its analysis of how Local 28 of the Sheet Metal Workers, AFL-CIO, excluded Negroes for seventy-eight years from union membership, from union-controlled apprenticeship training programs, and from jobs in the industry. The study states:

> For all practical purposes entry to the union and trade are synonymous. This is institutionalized in existing union-management arrangements and further sanctioned by the Department of Labor. . . .
>
> Restrictive admission policies sometimes led to acute labor shortages. When union members were not available, Local 28 called on other locals in the International from out of town and allied trades in the Building Trades Council. Occasionally even these additional sources proved inadequate. When this occurred the Local did not hesitate to refer a small group of non-union specialty men. All this occurred while Ballard and other Negro applicants were denied admission.
>
> A similar pattern existed with the Iron Workers in the Albany area. In the shortage of state-certified welders in 1958–59, James Bolton and other qualified Negroes were denied union permits and union membership, while the Union sent out non-union men to fill jobs for which there were not enough union members. It is clear that protection of union standards was not involved here.*

On March 4, 1964 the New York State Commission for Human Rights ruled that Local 28 had "automatically excluded" Negroes over the entire seventy-eight years of its existence, held this to be a violation of New York State Law Against Discrimination, and later issued an order for the union to end job discrimination.[24]

In 1948 the Commission had ordered the local to desist from "executing and/or maintaining constitution or by-law

---

* Pp. 18–19. James Ballard, a twenty-two-year-old Negro Air Force veteran initiated a complaint against the local in 1963 before the New York State Commission for Human Rights. The Civil Rights Bureau of the State Attorney General's office also intervened on Ballard's behalf against the union.

provisions which exclude Negroes." But while the union removed the "Caucasian only" clause from its constitution, apparently for public relations purposes it did not admit any Negro members.

Sixteen years later, when the local refused to comply with the new order, the Commission was forced to go to court to get it enforced. On October 14, 1964 Justice Jacob Markowitz of the State Supreme Court sustained the action of the State Commission and ordered the adoption of a new set of standards: "Apprentices will be selected on the basis of qualifications alone, and all applicants will be afforded equal opportunity under these standards without regard to race, creed, color or national origin . . ." (43 Misc. 2nd at 970, 252 NYS 2nd at 661).[25] (In a letter dated August 28, 1964, to Donald Slaiman, the Director of the AFL-CIO Civil Rights Department, the NAACP national office requested that the Labor Federation inform affiliated unions of this important legal precedent and suggest compliance. To the best knowledge of the NAACP, the Federation has taken no action in this important matter.)*

Local 26 of the International Brotherhood of Electrical Workers in Washington, D.C., is a typical example of how labor union power can be used to exclude Negroes from employment in federal construction projects. For many years Negro workers have been attempting without success to secure admission to Local 26, which controls all hiring for electrical installation work in the nation's capital. Thus, Negro mechanics were not permitted to do electrical work on the construction of the AFL-CIO national headquarters

---

* On December 29, 1966 the New York State Supreme Court issued a restraining order against Local 28 at the request of the State Commission when the union scrapped the results of a test for admission into the apprenticeship training program because Negro applicants received "phenomenally" high scores (Peter Millones, "High Marks Upset Metal Union Test," *The New York Times*, December 29, 1966; also Murray Kempton, "The Test," New York *Post*, January 3, 1967).

building and other private and public building projects in Washington. The 1961 Employment Report of the United States Commission on Civil Rights stated that "Local 26, like the majority of construction locals in the District of Columbia, has no Negro members. . . . Local 26 has a virtual monopoly on electrical jobs in commercial construction work in this area."[26] The report also noted that:

> None of the construction unions surveyed have racially restrictive provisions in their constitutions or bylaws. Most, however, require that an applicant for membership be approved by the local before acceptance. It is clear that the absence of Negro members in the "lily-white" construction locals means that few, if any, Negroes will be employed in these highly paid craft jobs on union construction projects. Obviously then to the extent that union membership practices are discriminatory, they deny employment opportunities to Negroes on racial grounds.[27]

The Employment Study of the Commission also stated that some locals

> openly practice racial discrimination in their membership policies. Local union officers have been known to explain the absence of Negro members in the following terms: " 'Nigras' are all afraid of electricity"—"Jews and colored folks don't want to do plumbing work because it is too hard."[28]

After years of avoiding conflict with the politically powerful building trades unions, the Pennsylvania State Fair Employment Practice Commission, beginning on July 9, 1963, held public hearings involving six major unions that had long engaged in anti-Negro practices, and finally issued a series of orders against them. On February 24, 1964 the New York State Commission for Human Rights made its first important step in prohibiting employment discrimination by building trades unions. It found Plumbers Local 373 of Spring Valley guilty of maintaining a pattern of anti-Negro practices. Harold Mitchell, a member of the NAACP in Spring Valley, had filed a complaint against Local 373 of the AFL-CIO Plumbers Union in Rockland County with the State Commission for Human Rights (previously the State Commission Against Discrimination). The union, he alleged, had forced him out of a job he had held for more than ten years after it had entered into a collective-bargaining agreement with his employer and refused to admit him into membership because of his race. Mr. Mitchell also charged that the union was lily-white in its membership and had never admitted a Negro into the apprenticeship program it controlled. The State Commission handed down an order requiring re-employment for Mr. Mitchell, payment of some back wages, and admittance into the union.[29] Fair employment practice commissions in other states have recently invoked anti-discriminatory laws against building trades and other unions for the first time as a result of demonstrations and other pressures from the Negro protest movement.

There is also frequent discrimination against Negroes despite union membership, as in the racially segregated locals of the Carpenters in the North as well as in southern cities. For over a half century the United Brotherhood of Carpenters and Joiners has been among the most important of the unions in the building trades, and, with few exceptions, organizes Negroes and whites into separate locals, when it permits Negroes to join at all. In the South there seem to be no exceptions to this rule and it is often followed in Northern cities as well. In Memphis, Negro carpenters in a segregated local union found that members of the white local refused to work on the same job with them. The 1961 Employment Report of the U. S. Commission on Civil Rights refers to similar practices in Atlanta and other cities.[30]

Wherever segregated locals exist in the building trades, the white locals are in control of the union hiring halls and frequently, because of arrangements with municipal and county political machines, all hiring for major public as well as private construction projects is done through these union halls.* In some instances white locals have imported white workers from other cities rather than allow local Negro members to share in attractive work opportunities.[31]

Frequently Negroes are excluded altogether from work in white neighborhoods. This means that Negro mechanics are restricted to marginal repair work within the Negro community or as maintenance electricians and seldom permitted to work on the major public and private new construction projects. The disparity between the wages of construction electricians and maintenance electricians in industry varies between three and four dollars an hour. In New York City construction electrical workers earn $7.70 per hour, for bricklayers the base wage is $7.74 per hour. Wages for the crafts in the building trades unions average about three times the general industrial wage.[32]

The protest against racism in the building trades union goes back to the early twenties. And in the summer of 1963 the Negroes of Philadelphia, New York, and other cities, plagued by rising unemployment, took to the streets to protest the widespread refusal to admit them into union membership and jobs on the many large publicly financed construction projects.**

On June 13, 1963, the day Medgar Evers was killed in Jackson, Mississippi, demonstrations against racial discrimination by New York City's building trades unions began at the Harlem Hospital construction site, in the heart of Manhattan's Negro ghetto. One picket, injured in a scuffle with police when he attempted to block a truck from de-

---

* Daniel P. Moynihan has written, "I would note that 20 years ago the Taft-Hartley Act outlawed the closed shop, and that today the closed shop is probably more completely in effect in our building trade unions than ever in history." "The Politics of Stability," *The New Leader*, October 9, 1967, 8.

** Some 465 thousand man years of employment were produced by programs assisted by the U. S. Department of Housing and Urban Development in 1966. This is only a small part of the jobs created by federal, state and municipal agencies in public construction. For additional information on employment in public construction, see NAACP Labor Manual, Revised 1968 edition, 124–26.

livering materials to the site, said: "Before I went to picket today I heard on the radio of the assassination in Jackson, Mississippi, of Medgar Evers, and I felt, if he could give his life, then what happened to me was of very little importance." Many pickets carried radios as they walked the line. To them the atrocity in Mississippi and the denial of jobs in New York were closely related problems in the struggle for racial justice and equality. The demonstrators, led by the Joint Committee for Equal Employment Opportunity (JCEEO), included members of the NAACP, CORE, the Urban League, Negro American Labor Council, Association of Catholic Trade Unionists, and the Workers Defense League. The demonstrations, the first in a summer-long series of actions against discrimination in the building trades unions, spread to other construction sites throughout New York and later to other major cities across the nation.

In New York the pickets were also protesting the failure of Governor Rockefeller and Mayor Wagner to enforce state and city anti-discrimination laws that provide for cancellation of contracts in all public construction projects where employment discrimination based upon race, religion, or nationality exists.[33] The nonenforcement of civil rights statutes and executive orders has directly contributed to the growing civil rights crisis in New York and other Northern cities. In the year preceding the racial disturbances in Harlem and Bedford-Stuyvesant, Negroes in New York and Brooklyn repeatedly attracted nationwide attention through a series of intense but unsuccessful demonstrations to get the laws against discrimination on public works projects enforced. The rights they were seeking are non-negotiable legal rights that exist at the federal level (Executive Orders 10925 and 11114, superseded by Executive Order 11246), at the state level (New York Law Against Discrimination, Section 296; New York State Labor Law, Section 220-e), and at the city level (New York City Administrative Code, Section 343-8.0). State and municipal authorities, as well as federal officials responsible for enforcement of executive orders through the President's Committee on Equal Employment Opportunity, have refused, apparently for political reasons, to enforce these laws in the construction industry. They have refused, despite repeated documentation of discrimination by the U. S. Commission on Civil Rights, the Mayor's Action Panel, the New York City Commission on Human Rights, and reports from the NAACP and other groups. Neither the findings of these groups nor the many demonstrations at construction sites have produced any significant employment gains for Negroes. The failure to enforce this extensive body of civil rights law constitutes a classic example of the administrative nullification of anti-discrimination statutes and executive orders.

The irony is not lost upon the residents of the Harlem community, where the unemployment rate in 1963 and 1964 was more than double the rate in the rest of the city. They have noted that high government officials who piously demanded "law and order" during the disturbances in Harlem and Bedford-Stuyvesant during the summer of 1964 were the same public officials who refused to enforce the laws against discrimination in employment.

The four hundred delegates attending the national convention of the AFL-CIO Building and Construction Trades Department at the Americana Hotel in New York City on November 6, 1963 were greeted by pickets, walking in the rain, carrying signs demanding "Full Integration of the Building Trades Union," "Job Equality for All," and "Full Enforcement of Federal, State, and City Anti-Discrimination Laws—NOW!"

At the convention Governor Rockefeller, who the previous July had hailed AFL-CIO building trades union leader, Peter J. Brennan, as "fearless in his leadership to achieve equal opportunity," was more adroit than Mayor Wagner in avoiding statements on civil rights that might offend the union leaders. He said that civil rights and equal job opportunities are "an overriding must" and that labor, management, and government must do "a little more planning" in order to solve the problems of employment discrimination. After the Governor and the Mayor had spoken, but while the latter was still on the platform, AFL-CIO leader Brennan, who had been chairman of the Labor for Rockefeller Committee during the Governor's campaign for reelection the previous year, told the delegates: "We're not going to have people outside dictate to us, when half of them don't know how to run their own affairs." He criticized the demonstrators and bitterly assailed the Negro protest movement. (During July, when demonstrations at construction projects in New York were most militant, Brennan had exclaimed: "We won't stand for blackmail . . . we had it from the gangsters and Communists in the 1930s and we fought it . . . and if we have to fight integration by blackmail today, fine, we'll fight it." Later that month he angrily accused the demonstrators of attempting to "blackjack" the unions and called for an investigation of "some of the questionable characters on the picket lines."[34]

U. S. Secretary of Labor Willard Wirtz made it clear, in his address to the convention, that the federal government opposed quotas or preferential treatment for Negroes and that it had no intention of interfering with the "private administration" of apprenticeship programs, all of which were highly sensitive questions to the union leaders. On the preceding July 17 the U. S. Department of Labor had issued a directive entitled "Non-Discrimination in Apprenticeship and Training," which evoked angry protests from the building trades unions and construction industry employers. The new regulations required that selections of apprentices be based on objective standards which permit review, presumably by an impartial governmental agency, to ensure that they are not discriminatory. A few days after the July 17 directive was issued, the Construction Industry Joint Conference, a national union-management group, demanded that the Secretary of Labor suspend implementation of the new regulations, stating that they were not acceptable to the industry. The Conference developed its own "voluntary" program to ensure nondiscrimination in apprenticeship programs and, on October 20, after many meetings between this committee and representatives of the Department of Labor, Secretary Wirtz withdrew the original directive and issued revised and weakened regulations that eliminated those sections found objectionable by the union-management group.

In his speech at the convention Secretary Wirtz urged the unions to correct the "acknowledged wrongs" of the past and said that where lists of applicants for apprenticeship training had no names of Negroes because Negroes "knew they didn't stand a chance," the lists should be opened on a fair basis.*

* On September 18, 1967, the NAACP (charging that the Bureau of Apprenticeship and Training of the U. S. Department of Labor had never enforced departmental regulation Title 29 CFR. Part 30, Nondiscrimination in Apprenticeship and Training) revealed a confidential memorandum dated April 20, 1967, from Hugh C. Murphy, Administrator of the Bureau, to all B.A.T. Regional Directors. The memorandum stated "This will confirm our telephone instructions . . . in which we requested that you and your field staff do not take any further action against program sponsors in the B.A.T. states relative to the letters sent them on compliance . . . I repeat, do nothing in the field of compliance follow up until you are given further instructions from the Administrator's office."

In response to an inquiry from a member of Congress, Mr. Murphy confirmed that the Bureau had never decertified a single apprenticeship program.35 Mr. Murphy is a former official of the Bricklayers Union in New York City. The deputy administrator of the Bureau is George Sabo, a former official of the International Association of Machinists in Nashville, Tennessee.

By March 6, 1967, 636 union-controlled apprenticeship training programs had not complied with the anti-discrimination regulation. Among these were affiliates of the International Typographical Workers Union in New Jersey, Texas, Missouri, Nebraska, Illinois, West Virginia, Arkansas; the Amalgamated Meat Cutters and Butcher Workmen in St. Louis, and more than sixty locals of the Plumbers Union. On March 30, 1967, the *Wall Street Journal* reported that Peter Schoemann, President of the Plumbers Union had ordered affiliated local unions ". . . to disregard the compliance command until they checked with him."

AFL-CIO President George Meany praised Brennan for his efforts to integrate New York City's building trades unions and supported his rejection of quotas or preferential treatment for Negroes, asserting: "We cannot visit injustice on the white boy to make up to the black boy for the injustice done to him in the past." At a press conference following his address Meany said that the AFL-CIO was making progress in the field of civil rights, but that some civil rights organizations wanted the millennium and they wanted it "yesterday."

An interesting example of how a major labor union, notorious for its history of anti-Negro practices, defends and rationalizes these practices is to be found in an open letter appearing in the Plumbers Union *Journal* addressed to the U. S. Secretary of Labor. The President of the union, Peter T. Schoemann, wrote:

> Sponsorship and favoritism are phenomena of American political and business life. Indeed, one may wonder whether they are not inherent in free, democratic society. . . . Mr. Secretary, in attempting to regulate sponsorship out of apprentice selection, you may regulate members of apprentice committees into being very angry men and fairly sophisticated liars. Until American society as a whole accepts the proposition that employment and promotion should be based exclusively on merit, if indeed it ever will or ever should accept such a proposition, the United Association [of Journeymen and Apprentices of the Plumbing and Pipefitting Industry] will neither endorse nor support any effort by the federal government to regulate out of existence systems and practices of

---

According to *"Negroes in Apprenticeship"* (Manpower/Automation Research Monograph No. 6 published by the Manpower Administration of the United States Department of Labor, August 1967) Negro participation on federally supported construction projects was 2.2 percent. The report significantly notes that "Indeed, the 1960 census showed only 2191 Negro apprentices in all trades throughout the country. That figure was one more than had been recorded in the 1950 census" (7).

sponsorship in the selection of apprentices. . . . If the Bureau [of Apprenticeship and Training] really believes in this kind of angelic objectivity [the use of objective standards as the basis of selection] we suggest that it will find more than enough to keep it busy in those institutions supposedly most representative of free and democratic society, beginning with the Administration, then the Congress, followed by the Armed Services. . . . We will support you as we have already pledged to do, but please don't try to reform the building trades.[36]

Organized labor's relation to the civil rights movement is clearly revealed in the events surrounding the action of Plumbers Local 2 in New York City during the summer of 1963. Like other craft locals, that union exercises job control through rigid hiring-hall procedures in *de facto* closed-shop arrangements.

When a local contractor, operating with a municipal contract, hired one Negro and three Puerto Rican plumbers who had previously been refused union membership, union plumbers walked off the job claiming it was a union dispute provoked by the hiring of "scab labor," although the non-white workers were ready to join the union. But reporters at the construction site wrote of how the white plumbers used racial epithets and talked to them of "white men's jobs" and how God had made whites separate from blacks.[37] New York papers were united in calling the white plumbers' walkout a racial issue. In contrast, New York's "liberal community" and union leaders maintained an undignified silence. Finally, on May 15, Meany made the following statement:[38]

They walked off the job, and as far as I'm concerned they are going to stay off. This union won't work with non-union men. If they were to go to work with these non-union men, I'd resign from the union and join some other union. [Local 2 is George Meany's "home" local. He still holds membership in this local, in which he had been business agent for many years.]

Meany proposed a settlement in which tests should be given the Puerto Rican and Negro plumbers, supervised by the City Commission on Human Rights and civil rights leaders. If the men passed the tests they would be granted membership in Local 2 and the dispute would be ended. On May 16 he held a press conference in which he reiterated that the dispute was only a union, and not a racial, issue. He proposed to give the men journeymen's tests, administered by a five-man board of journeymen plumbers, containing written questions. If they passed, Local 2 agreed to accept and expedite their membership. "Ironically," *The Times* commented, "the plan is much the same as one voted down by the local at a May 6 meeting."

Meany again stated:

> The reporting on this thing has indicated that the union refused to work with these men because of their color. This was not the reason. . . . This is the practice of American labor—to work with union people. Union men don't work with nonunion people.

But as *The Times* wrote, although the contractor is not legally barred from hiring qualified nonunion men under the collective bargaining agreement with Local 2, "it is a tradition to hire through the union hall." Meany claimed that the men never came near the union. In reality, they had tried for several years to gain union membership. Meany's statements brought immediate opposition from Negro civil rights leaders. Morris Doswell, President of the New York chapter of the Negro American Labor Council, commented that "this action on the part of George Meany demonstrates that he is an outright prejudiced individual and cannot serve everyone in the American labor movement." Whitney Young, Jr., Executive Director of the conservative Urban League, urged repudiation of Meany's position by other AFL-CIO leaders. But no such repudiation was forthcoming.

At first, however, the Negro and Puerto Rican workers stated that they would not consent to Meany's proposal and would not take the tests. The major objection was that it was illegal for a labor union to give job-qualifying tests to prospective employees, as such tests violated the National Labor Relations Act, which establishes that job competence may be determined only by the employer. The men first considered demanding a court test of the traditional practice under which Local 2 and other craft unions determined who was qualified to work on public construction projects. Martin Kroll, a lawyer for the workers, stated that "unions should not control hiring, particularly unions which have used this system to exclude Negroes and Puerto Ricans."* Nonetheless, the men finally decided to take the test.

Actually, the Meany-Wagner agreement would have gained entry into the union only for these four plumbers, if they had passed the test (which they did not). The agreement did not provide for the establishment of the permanent right of qualified Negroes to belong, nor did it make certain that all qualified minority group members seeking jobs would be referred to jobs by the union. The

---

* The National Labor Relations Board found Plumbers Local Union 2 guilty of unfair labor practices in this case. The investigative report of the trial examiner concluded that "By causing and attempting to cause employees to be discriminated against in violation of Section VIII (a)(3) because of their nonmembership in it, Respondent engaged in and is engaging in an unfair labor practice within the meaning of Section VIII (b)(2) of the Act, and by thus restraining and coercing employees in the exercise of their rights under Section VII of the Act, Respondent engaged and is engaging in an unfair labor practice within the meaning of Section VIII (b) (2) (A) of the Act." The NLRB ordered the union to "cease and desist" from further violations of the National Labor Relations Act. (United States of America Before the National Labor Relations Board. Division of Trial Examiners, Washington, D.C. Case No. 2-CB-4024, Case No. 2-CB-4024-2, Case No. 2-CB-4024-3. Local Union No. 2, of the United Association of Journeymen and Apprentices of the Plumbing and Pipefitting Industry of the United States and Canada, AFL-CIO, et al.) The full Board sustained the report of the trial examiner and entered his conclusion as "A decision and Order" of the NLRB. The union unsuccessfully appealed this action.

answer of the NAACP was given in the letter to *The Times* published on May 20 by Robert L. Carter, general counsel of the NAACP. Carter indicated that the workers' failure to pass the test did not demonstrate that they were not plumbers but only that they were unable to explain on paper what they could easily do with their hands. The major issue, he wrote, is "where responsibility ought to lie for establishing and enforcing standards for qualifying for jobs made available by public funds. Should any private group have ultimate power to select and pass upon those allowed employment on work paid for out of taxes imposed on all the people of the City of New York?" Carter suggested that state and city authorities might be at fault in failing to impose and enforce standards ensuring that all craft workers have qualifications determined in a standardized examination, given at stated intervals by an impartial public agency. He noted that "any union that looks upon fair and impartially imposed standards on public construction as a threat to union security is being dangerously and foolishly shortsighted."

Other examples of discriminatory racial practices by building trades unions in several cities with large and increasing Negro populations: ——On December 17, 1964 the Cleveland branch of the NAACP charged that the AFL-CIO building trades unions in that city "had imposed a "lily-white" closed shop in federal construction work," and appealed to the federal government to stop this discrimination by canceling United States government contracts. A telegram to Secretary of Labor W. Willard Wirtz signed by leaders of the Cleveland NAACP branch and the Association's national office asked that the President's Committee on Equal Employment Opportunity conduct an on-the-spot investigation of the "deliberate and systematic policy of Negro exclusion from skilled craft employment on the $32,000,000 federal office building in Cleveland." The telegram charged that Presidential executive orders banning job discrimination "are widely violated as a result of anti-Negro practices of building trades unions in the Greater Cleveland area."

Further, the telegram said, the federal office building "will be constructed by an all-white work force as the result of intransigent racist practices of local unions, thus contributing to the high rate of permanent unemployment and poverty within the Cleveland Negro community. The U.S. government will be a direct party to racial discrimination in violation of federal executive orders if procedures for contract cancellation are not begun immediately." At a news conference local Negro leaders said that there would be massive demonstrations at the construction site if remedial action was not soon forthcoming.*

——On January 20, 1965, in Newark, New Jersey, Negro workers began picketing the Rutgers University Law School construction site after ten months of futile negotiations with AFL-CIO building trades unions. On February 9 Rutgers, the State University of New Jersey, filed formal complaints with the New Jersey Division on Civil Rights (the agency charged with enforcing the state's anti-discrimination statute) against five locals and the International Association of Bridge Structural and Ornamental Iron Workers and Local 24 of the United Association of Journeymen and Apprentices of the Plumbing and Pipefitting Industry of the United States and Canada. (George S. Pfaus, Director of the Division on Civil Rights, on January 31, 1966 issued an order in the case of *Rutgers University v. Iron Workers, et al.*, directing the respondents to show cause on February 15, 1966 why they should not be restrained from using the qualifications and testing procedures for the selection of apprenticeship trainees until the legality of these

* On December 15, 1966, the Urban League and the NAACP withdrew from a federally funded pre-apprentice training program in Cleveland charging that the building trades unions had for the second time broken agreements to admit Negroes and that the U. S. Department of Labor had failed to enforce anti-discrimination regulations. *The New York Times*, "Rights Units Quit a Project in Ohio," December 11, 1966.

procedures is determined by Civil Rights Division or the courts.)

——On August 10, 1965 the Cincinnati branch of the NAACP conducted an all-night sit-in at the headquarters of the AFL-CIO Cincinnati Central Labor Council. This demonstration occurred after futile efforts, made over a three-year period, to eliminate bias against Negroes practiced by the city's major building trades unions. More than fifty Negro and white pickets were arrested when they demonstrated at public construction sites at which Negroes were barred from employment, after the building trades unions and the AFL-CIO Central Labor Council had refused further negotiations with the representatives of aggrieved Negro workers. As of December, 1965 NAACP investigation of Negro membership in AFL-CIO building trades unions in Cincinnati revealed the following: the Electrical Workers —no Negroes; the Plumbers—no Negroes; the Pipe Fitters —no Negroes; the Sheet Metal Workers—no Negroes; the Asbestos Workers—no Negroes; the Structural and Ornamental Iron Workers—no Negroes; the Millwrights—no Negroes. Negro workers are limited to membership in the unskilled trowel trades unions, in the Cincinnati Carpenters local, which has a membership of three thousand six hundred white persons and eleven Negroes, and a small number in the Operating Engineers and Roofers. Cincinnati was beginning to experience a vast expansion in building activity as a result of new public construction programs. On September 9, 1965 the Cincinnati Chamber of Commerce announced that two billion dollars' worth of new construction was anticipated in the next few years.

On August 6, 1965 the Cincinnati branch of the NAACP together with the Association's national office charged in a telegram to President Johnson that the unions were "adamant in refusing to admit Negroes into membership thereby denying colored citizens the opportunity to secure employment on federally financed construction projects," and requesting the withholding of public funds from Cincinnati pursuant to Executive Orders 10925 and 11114 which prohibit discriminatory employment practices in federally financed construction.[39]

Racial discrimination in the craft unions has become deeply institutionalized. A form of caste psychology impels many workers to regard their own positions as "white men's jobs" to which no Negro should aspire. These workers and, often, their union leaders regard jobs in their industries as a kind of private privilege to be doled out or denied as they see fit. Often Negroes are not alone in being barred from such unions, which attempt to maintain an artificial labor shortage. In many craft jurisdictions AFL-CIO affiliates do not function as labor unions in an advanced technological society, but operate as protective associations with much the character of medieval guilds. On the local level the inertia that sustains racial discrimination is to be found among craftsmen in the North almost as commonly as in the South.[40]

The status of Negroes as journeymen members within the building trades unions of Pittsburgh is significant as it is typical of the pattern in Northern urban communities. As of September 1, 1965 the NAACP's investigation revealed: Asbestos Workers—no Negroes; Boilermakers—no Negroes; Bridge and Iron Workers—no Negroes; Carpenters —no Negroes; International Brotherhood of Electrical Workers—no Negroes; Plumbers—no Negroes; Roofers—no Negroes; Sheet Metal Workers—no Negroes; Steamfitters—no Negroes; Elevator Constructors—no Negroes; Tile Setters— no Negroes; Terrazzo Helpers—no Negroes. In the Bricklayers Local 2 there were two Negroes; in the Cement Masons Local 526, eighteen Negroes; in the Painters Local 6, three; in the Construction and Common Laborers Local 373, thirty-five; and in the Tile Layers and Helpers Local 20, four.

Title VII, the section of the Civil Rights Act of 1964 that forbids employment discrimination by both labor unions and employers, went into effect on July 2, 1965. Title

VII is a compromise measure and was among the most fiercely challenged portions of the entire Civil Rights Act. Indeed, its enforcement was postponed for one year. But while some parts of Title VII provide for unfortunate delays and awkward enforcement procedures, it must be recognized that whatever its shortcomings, the Equal Employment Opportunity Act established for the first time a clear statutory basis for invoking the power of the federal government in eliminating job discrimination.

Specifically prohibited in Title VII are discriminatory practices by labor unions. Confronted by the new statute, union leaders responded in a variety of ways. *The New York Times* of July 3, 1965 quotes one of the leaders of a craft union in New Jersey who bluntly stated, "It's the law. We've got to let the Niggers in." Peter T. Schoemann, the President of the Plumbers Union, in a statement that appeared in the Union's *Journal* (April 1965) wrote that his prescription for dealing with applications for union membership from Negroes was to "take them in, provided they are qualified."* However, even where national trade union leaders called for compliance with the law, little or no change was observed in the day-to-day practices of affiliated local unions where there has been a long tradition of anti-Negro practices.

A typical example of adamant refusal to admit Negroes into membership and into a union-controlled apprenticeship training program, two and a half years after the enactment of the Civil Rights Act of 1964, is to be found in New Rochelle, New York, where construction unions prevented the employment of Negroes on a four-hundred-million-dollar urban renewal project. The New Rochelle Human Rights Commission, an official agency of the municipal government,

---

* Since Title VII went into effect, many craft unions have begun using qualifying tests, both written and oral, an effective means of excluding Negroes and circumventing the law. The sudden proliferation of such tests has caused the Equal Employment Opportunity Commission to initiate an investigation of testing procedures.

found "that seven months of private conferences had failed to induce Local 501 of the Electrical Workers Union, Local 86 of the Plumbers Union, and Local 38 of the Sheet Metal Workers Union to hire Negroes." The Commission asked the Mayor and the City Council "to halt all construction at the Mall which is part of a 68-acre program, until the unions relented," and requested "appropriate action under federal Law."[41] Similar anti-Negro practices by major craft unions continued in many cities with large public construction programs, as in San Francisco and Buffalo, where the Equal Employment Opportunity Commission initiated formal complaints against several construction unions in January 1967.

It is evident that labor unions such as those in the building and construction trades, in the printing industry, among the metal crafts, and elsewhere have become narrow protective associations engaged in a variety of restrictive practices. Given union control of hiring and of apprenticeship programs, it is no longer possible to regard racial bias by labor unions as simply a private matter involving "voluntary associations" or a "quasi-sovereignty," as Robert M. Hutchins describes American unions today. Such discrimination is a barrier to the welfare of the entire Negro community, no less serious than segregation in the public schools, which the U. S. Supreme Court has declared to be unconstitutional. Clearly, the intervention of the society through the use of enforceable legal sanctions has become necessary to remove discriminatory practices by labor unions as well as by employers.*

* On February 7, 1966 the U. S. District Court in St. Louis, Missouri, in response to a lawsuit initiated by the U. S. Department of Justice, issued a temporary restraining order against the AFL-CIO Building and Construction Trades Council and affiliated unions in St. Louis. The court ordered the unions to return to work at the Gateway Arch, a federal construction project at which they had refused to work because three Negroes had been hired in response to previous action by the U.S. government. The NAACP also filed unfair labor practice charges with the NLRB against the unions.

In another case the U. S. Department of Justice on December 15, 1966 filed an action in the Federal District Court in New Orleans seeking an injunction against the International Association of Heat and Frost Insulators and Asbestos Workers Union, AFL-CIO, because of discriminatory racial practices. Other cases brought by Negro workers against labor unions are pending in several federal courts. Among the most significant of these are the suits against the United Steel Workers of America in Alabama charging that the separate racial lines of seniority and promotion in union contracts constitute a violation of Title VII of the Civil Rights Act of 1964.

At the conclusion of 1966 many complaints against labor unions were pending with the Equal Employment Opportunity Commission charging violation of Title VII of the Civil Rights Act of 1964. Negro workers charged AFL-CIO affiliates with a variety of discriminatory practices including negotiating separate racial seniority provisions in collective-bargaining agreements, maintaining segregated locals, exclusion from membership because of race, and refusal to admit Negro workers into union-controlled apprenticeship and other training programs.

Among the unions named as respondents were units of the International Association of Machinists, International Brotherhood of Pulp, Sulphite and Papermill Workers, United Papermakers and Paperworkers Union, Brotherhood of Railway Clerks, Tobacco Workers International Union, Brotherhood of Firemen and Oilers, United Steelworkers of America, Brotherhood of Railroad Trainmen, Brotherhood of Maintenance-of-Way Employees, Association of Heat and Frost Insulators and Asbestos Workers, United Cement, Lime and Gypsum Workers, United Brotherhood of Carpenters and Joiners, International Brotherhood of Electrical Workers, Brotherhood of Painters, Decorators and Paperhangers, Amalgamated Meat Cutters and Butcher Workmen, Brotherhood of Railway Carmen, International Longshoremen's Association, and United Association of Journeymen and Apprentices of the Plumbing and Pipe Fitting Industry of the United States and Canada, among others.

The National Labor Relations Board in recent cases has taken the position that it has both the power and the duty to protect Negro workers from racial discrimination by unions. The NLRB dealt with the basic issue when on July 1, 1964 they found in the *Hughes Tool Co. Case* that discrimination by labor unions is an unfair labor practice. For the first time in the history of the NLRB the Board ruled that racial discrimination by a union in membership practices—such as exclusion or segregation of Negroes—is a violation of the duty of fair representation under Section 9 (a) of the National Labor Relations Act. Consequently a new principle in administrative labor law was established. *The Hughes Tool Co. Case* represents a fundamental turning point in the Board's slow

Two Views of Racial Attitudes and Practices

In the decade following the merger of the American Federation of Labor with the Congress of Industrial Organizations, some of the industrial unions founded during the rise of the CIO generally continued their nondiscriminatory practices. It should also be noted that the American Federation of Teachers expelled its segregated locals in the South in the course of developing a successful policy of racial integration and the American Federation of State, County, and Municipal Employees organized a significant number of Negro workers employed in the public sector of the economy. But taken as a whole, organized labor adamantly resisted Negro demands for a fundamental change in the traditional racial practices of many of its largest and most important affiliates, and ten years after the merger the AFL-CIO had become increasingly conservative as a social institution.* In response to this development, Negro

---

evolution to an affirmative policy in protecting the rights of Negro workers.

Among the several other significant cases in which the NLRB issued orders against the discriminatory employment practices of unions was in *Master Stevedores* involving Local 872 of the International Longshoremen's Association; in *NLRB vs. United Rubberworkers Local 12 and NLRB vs. Plumbers Union Local 2.*

* The AFL-CIO and many of its affiliated international unions are bitterly resisting the efforts of the Equal Employment Opportunity Commission to eliminate discriminatory seniority provisions in union contracts. On May 5, 1966 a group headed by William Schnitzler, Secretary-Treasurer of the AFL-CIO; Thomas Harris, General Council of the AFL-CIO; and the Director of the Federation's Civil Rights Department, Donald Slaiman, met with the Commission at its headquarters in Washington, D.C., and together with the representatives of several major unions insisted that the Commission refrain from acting affirmatively on complaints filed by Negro workers involving discriminatory job classifications and seniority provisions in union agreements. The AFL-CIO and several affiliated unions have also attempted to exert political pressure on this matter. For a detailed analysis of this problem, see William B. Gould, "Employment Security, Seniority and Race: The Role of Title VII of the Civil Rights Act of 1964," *Howard University Law Journal*, Vol. 3, Winter 1967, pp. 1–50.

workers are increasingly mounting an attack upon the discriminatory practices of organized labor through public protest, litigation in federal and state courts, and the use of administrative agencies such as the National Labor Relations Board, as well as organizing Negro caucuses within labor unions where there is a significant concentration of colored workers.

II

If the racial practices of building trades unions are representative of the conservative "old-line" craft unions in the AFL-CIO, an examination of the operations of the International Ladies Garment Workers Union will reveal the social consequences of the policies and practices of a union that has a "progressive and liberal" reputation.

With some important exceptions, such as District 65 of the Retail, Wholesale and Department Store Workers Union, the American Federation of State, County and Municipal Employees, and Local 1199 of the Hospital Workers Union, no significant large-scale efforts have been made by AFL-CIO affiliates to organize the tens of thousands of Negro and Puerto Rican workers who have entered the New York labor market in the past decade. (In 1965 District 65 of the Retail, Wholesale and Department Store Workers Union conducted a successful strike involving over two thousand employees in the New York textile converting industry for the specific purpose of opening new job opportunities for Negro and Puerto Rican workers. No other union in the New York City area has resorted to strike action for the same objective.) Instead, as the unskilled labor force in New York City rapidly becomes Negro and Puerto Rican, there is a corresponding expansion in the membership and number of local unions operated by independent, corrupt labor organizations. These gangster-ridden independent unions in league with greedy employers with whom they sign "sweetheart" agreements are victimizing many thousands of workers in a variety of marginal shops in cheap-production industries.[42]

In 1957, as a result of several indictments by the New York County District Attorney and other law-enforcement agencies, together with public exposure by the Association of Catholic Trade Unionists of the widespread operations of racket unions, the major New York City labor unions established the AFL-CIO Committee on Puerto Rican Affairs. In 1958 the Mayor's Committee on Exploitation was established with representation from the AFL-CIO Central Labor Council, the ILGWU, and other powerful labor organizations. These committees, whose leaders publicly pledged to drive labor racketeers out of New York almost a decade ago, have had little or no effect. A clue to the reason for this failure has been provided by Morris Iushewitz, Secretary of the New York AFL-CIO Central Labor Council. When Iushewitz was asked if the AFL-CIO Committee on Puerto Rican Affairs would ever initiate unfair labor practice charges with the NLRB against an employer or independent racket union jointly engaged in exploiting Puerto Rican workers, he stated that it would not do so.[43] The conclusion is warranted that expansion of these gangster-controlled unions is in large measure due to the conservative policies and practices of such major AFL-CIO affiliates in New York City as the ILGWU. Rather than engage in expensive and troublesome organizing campaigns, these unions prefer to enjoy the wealth, power, and prestige they achieved many years ago. In response, workers who are the victims of racket unions grow increasingly distrustful of all labor unions—including the International Ladies Garment Workers Union.*

* The 1964 New York State Labor Relations Board Report indicates that of its thirteen hundred cases approximately four hundred were brought by "independents." Not all of these are racket unions but the evidence suggests that disreputable independent unions are successfully expanding their jurisdiction. See also the New York State Labor Relations Board press release, December 22, 1959.

The ILGWU is one of the richest and most powerful unions in the American labor movement and is unique in many respects. It operates in the basic manufacturing industry of New York City, and by virtue of its control of the New York State Liberal Party and its large financial contributions to the national Democratic Party, it is a force in New York municipal, state, and national political affairs.

It is also one of the most bureaucratically controlled unions, and there is a direct connection between the lack of internal union democracy and the depressed status of Negro workers within the union and the industry. Members of the ILGWU are not permitted to engage in internal political activity and are prevented from participating in the formulation of union policy on matters vital to their interests. They are specifically denied the right to have clubs, groups, or caucuses within the union except for a designated period of three months before the conventions held every two years, or with the formal approval and permission of the General Executive Board of the International union. How can workers gain support for choices contrary to those of the union administration unless they are permitted to organize to discuss their own interests and press for the election of candidates responsive to their needs? The answer is that without permission in writing from the General Executive Board they are specifically forbidden to do so by the ILGWU constitution, which prohibits all internal union caucuses, groups, and clubs,[44] an incredible denial of the democratic rights of the workers.

Although the membership of the ILGWU is denied the same right to internal political activity that is accepted as commonplace in the United Automobile Workers, the Typographical Workers, and other major labor organizations, the union leadership functions every day, using the dues money of all of its members to maintain itself in power. To be eligible to run for President or Secretary-Treasurer, a member must be a delegate to the national convention, a condition that immediately limits the number eligible to approximately a thousand of the union's 442,318 members. Eligibility rules further require that a candidate for these offices must have been a member for ten years and a paid officer for at least five. In order to be a candidate for the General Executive Board, a member must be a delegate to the convention, a member of five years' standing, and a paid officer of three.[45]

An analysis of the composition of the delegates to the last three ILGWU conventions indicates that out of the 442,318 union members, the number eligible to run for the General Executive Board is less than three hundred. Those eligible for the post of President or Secretary-Treasurer number less than two hundred. Thus, of the membership of the ILGWU less than one fifth of 1 per cent are eligible to run for the General Executive Board and less than one twentieth of 1 per cent for the presidency or the secretary-treasurership.*

For the more than 145 thousand Negro and Puerto Rican members of the ILGWU the situation is even worse. As a result of the restrictive requirements, *no more than four or five nonwhite persons are eligible for the General Executive Board, and virtually none at all for the top leadership positions.* This explains why there is not a single Negro Vice-President or member of the General Executive Board of the union and why the local managers, who are usually

---

* The Bureau of Labor Management Reports of the U. S. Department of Labor during 1963 investigated a complaint from an ILGWU member in New Bedford, Mass. The Bureau found improper election practices by the ILGWU and ordered a new election. Unfortunately the federal agency has not acted in regard to the election practices of the international union. In another but related case the U. S. Department of Labor moved in a federal district court to set aside the 1966 election within the National Maritime Union because the international union eligibility requirements for union office violated, it was charged, federal labor laws stipulating that any member in good standing can run for office in a union. See George Home, "Curran Attacks Lawsuit by U.S.," *The New York Times*, January 3, 1967.

hand picked by the union leadership, include no Negroes or Puerto Ricans.†

The ILGWU constitution makes possible a rigid bureaucratic control of the entire union organization. Rank-and-file members have no chance to organize opposition caucuses or participate in policy decisions. For all practical purposes ILGWU elections are simply plebiscites to ratify appointments already made by the leadership. (A further indication of the bureaucratic control of the ILGWU is found in the fact that union officials have been forced to deposit signed, but undated, resignations with the president of the union. Brief for Petitioner, 5, ILGWU, 131 NLRB 111, 1961. See also Charles Halpern, "Recognition of a Staff Union of Business Agents Under the National Labor Relations Act," *Yale Law Journal*, Vol. 72, No. 5, April 1963, 1076–87.)

In New York City, where the largest part of the garment industry is still concentrated, the ILGWU has introduced a form of rationalized control over the relationship among the manufacturers, jobbers, and contractors, which comprises the foundation upon which this otherwise chaotic industry operates. Thus it has established an unusual form of labor union power. Dr. Kenneth Clark, Director of the Social Dynamics Research Institute of the City College of New York, has written:

> The ILGWU is probably the most decisive force in the ladies' garment industry in New York City because it has rationalized and established industry practices and established union control over a scattered multiplicity of small, highly competitive shops. Both employers and workers regard the union as the major power in the industry.[46]

† After public criticism of the ILGWU's racial practices, a Puerto Rican representative was appointed to the union's General Executive Board in March 1964. However, there is still not a single Negro who is a General Executive Board member or an officer of the international union.

Dr. Clark has also cited the plight of the nonwhite worker in the International Ladies Garment Workers Union in New York City as "a significant example of the powerlessness of the Negro worker in a major trade union with a 'liberal' reputation . . ."[47]

It is the ILGWU's position that it attempts to keep the garment industry from moving out of New York, in order to maintain the jobs held by its members in the city. In reality the union has used its extensive power to regulate the industry in solving the problems of the employers rather than in advancing the interests of the great mass of workers, who continue to exist in a condition of poverty. This is especially true for the thousands of Negro and Puerto Rican workers who are concentrated in the low-wage sectors of the industry in New York City. A dynamic union with the ILGWU's financial and other resources could engage in vigorous organizing efforts outside New York City. However, the ILGWU has adopted a different course. It becomes increasingly clear from an examination of ILGWU contracts that the union attempts to keep the garment industry in New York City by maintaining low wages and minimal standards for the majority of workers, who do not have an opportunity to vote upon this matter and are not consulted on this and related policy decisions directly affecting their immediate welfare, but form the large dues-paying membership that constitutes the base of the union's extensive political and financial operations.

Soon after the Second World War the ILGWU adopted a policy of wage restraint, that contrasted sharply with its earlier wage policy. This approach coincided with the rapid increase of nonwhites in the garment industry labor force. Thus in January 1967, when the Dressmakers Joint Council of the ILGWU began negotiations with employers the union reported that the minimum weekly wage was $52.50 and the average weekly wage $77. The Dressmakers Joint Council has a large concentration of Negro and Puerto Rican workers in its membership.[48]

Early in 1963 the important research study known as the HARYOU Report was released and further confirmed this analysis of the status of Negroes within the ILGWU. This research project, jointly financed by U.S. government and New York City funds, was conducted for over eighteen months and published under the subtitle "A Study of the Consequences of Powerlessness and A Blueprint for Change." The report states:

> The status of Negroes in the power councils of organized labor in New York City is most tenuous if not nonexistent. The persistent pattern of racial discrimination in various unions, including some which still enjoy the reputation of being liberal, reflects the essential powerlessness of Negroes to affect the conditions of their livelihood. HARYOU's difficulty in finding a suitable representative of labor for its Board of Directors highlighted the fact that there is no Negro who occupies a primary power position in organized labor in New York City. There are a few Negroes who are constantly referred to as representatives of labor, but upon careful examination it is found that these Negroes, for the most part, hold their positions at the pleasure of more powerful white bosses or leaders. Even in those unions where the bulk, or all, of the workers are Negroes, and Puerto Ricans, the top overt or covert leadership is almost always white. There is evidence that under these circumstances the union leaders are not always above entering into sweetheart contracts, or other types of conspiracies with the bosses, to the disadvantage of the Negro and Puerto Rican workers.

The ILGWU, as the largest and most influential union in the city, is certainly a major factor in perpetuating this condition.

The record of the ILGWU in the fight for a $1.50 minimum wage revealed its interest in keeping New York City a low-wage community. The proposal for a $1.50 city minimum wage was first made in 1959 by several civic groups, including various Negro and Puerto Rican organizations. When it was initially discussed by the AFL-CIO

Central Labor Council of New York City, the ILGWU representative, Charles Zimmerman, (a Vice-President of the ILGWU) informed the Council that the ILGWU opposed the plan and that it would withdraw from the Central Labor Council if that organization supported it. Harry Van Arsdale, President of the New York Central Labor Council, in an effort to avoid an open conflict with Zimmerman, would not permit the question to be voted upon. Subsequently, after public pressure had been brought to bear, the Central Labor Council voted to approve the proposal, but Zimmerman was absent from those later meetings.

In 1961 Mayor Robert F. Wagner refused to support the Isaacs bill for a $1.50 minimum wage. Again, in January 1962, six Democrats and two Republicans on the City Council sponsored a bill that would have instituted a $1.50 minimum wage with no exemptions by January 1963. The bill was referred to a committee. Wagner made no comment but his spokesmen in the Council opposed the bill on the grounds that it was unconstitutional, dealing with matters pre-empted by the state and federal government, and that it would have an adverse effect on business.

A Citizens' Committee for a $1.50 Minimum Hourly Wage was formed in February 1962, including A. Philip Randolph, Roy Wilkins, James Farmer, Juan Mae, President of the Federation of Spanish Societies, David Livingston, President of District 65 of the Retail, Wholesale and Department Store Workers; and several influential clergymen and representatives of other trade union groups.

In April the Mayor announced plans to establish a Citizens' Commission on the City Economy. He named as its Chairman Louis Broido, City Commerce Commissioner and Co-Chairman of the Liberal Party Committee-at-Large. The business members were John Snyder, President of U. S. Industries; Lloyd Dalzell, Chairman of Dalzell Towing Company; and, as alternate, Ralph Gross, Executive Vice-President of the Commerce and Industry Association. The labor members were David Livingston of District 65, Retail,

Wholesale and Department Store Workers Union and Luigi Antonini, first Vice-President of the ILGWU, with Howard Molisani, Manager-Secretary of ILGWU Local 98, and Sol Barkin, Research Director for the Textile Workers as alternates. The public members were Edward Lewis, Director of the New York Urban League, and Hector Bunker of the Banco Popular de Puerto Rico, with alternates Douglas Pugh of the Brooklyn Urban League and Dr. Francisco Trilla, President of the Puerto Rican Hispanic Leadership Forum.

It might be assumed that the business representatives would be opposed to raising the minimum wage and the labor spokesmen for it and that the public members and the Chairman would therefore decide. However, with Broido, a well-known Liberal Party leader, and ILGWU Vice-President Antonini both against the $1.50 minimum wage, the chances for an affirmative report were not good, even if both members supported a higher wage. (In May representatives of the New York Teamsters Union Joint Council 16 accused the ILGWU of adopting "a conscious policy of artificial restraint of wage increases." A letter from the Teamsters to the Democratic majority on the City Council was made public, asking for the removal of Antonini and Molisani from the Commission, and declaring, "Surely you must or should know that the ILGWU has a vested interest in the perpetuation of exploitation, low-wage pockets, and poverty in New York City.")

The Commission began by studying the desirability of a $1.25 city minimum wage, although the bill before the Council called for $1.50. In June, Wagner declared that he was giving top priority to drafting a law to establish "a $1.25 minimum wage for all employment in New York City, authorizing necessary exemption." The exemptions included workers employed by firms in interstate commerce (garment workers), domestics, and employees of voluntary agencies, including nonprofit hospitals.

Arnold Witte, General Manager of the Commerce and Industry Association of New York City, writing in the

October 5, 1962 New York *World-Telegram & Sun*, cited the ILGWU's opposition to the city minimum-wage bill. He noted that "the garment workers, the largest union of the largest industry in the city, has refused to indorse this legislation." A. Philip Randolph charged that Wagner was "perpetuating a hoax," declaring this was further proof that the Commission "was set up merely as a public relations device to forestall action on the bill for $1.50 minimum which has been pending before the City Council since January 9."

Finally, after long delay, Commission Chairman Broido drafted a report which did not even mention the $1.50 minimum, and submitted it for approval to David Dubinsky, President of the ILGWU, and Alex Rose, President of the Hatters Union, before other committee members had received it. It recommended a $1.25 minimum effective October 1963, a month after the federal $1.25 minimum was set to go into effect. However, Livingston of District 65 persuaded Snyder to vote against the report and it was rejected by Livingston, Snyder, and the two public members. The majority drafted a new report in favor of the $1.50 minimum wage and covering workers in inter- and intra-state commerce, as well as domestics and employees of voluntary agencies. It was reported unofficially that the ILGWU's Molisani was against it, but the record listed him as abstaining.

Murray Kempton commented:

The Liberal Party . . . is a despotism of David Dubinsky sometimes tempered by Alex Rose. Louis Broido, an organizer of the Liberal Party, was chairman of the Mayor's Committee to investigate the minimum wage; he was dubious about $1.25 and absolutely against $1.50. Howard Molisani, the ILGWU's deputy on the committee, abstained from voting at all. How marvelous is the ILGWU. It has a position on Vietnam and Algeria; but it has no position on wages in its hometown.[49]

The City Council passed the bill; the Board of Estimate passed the bill; and the Mayor signed it. But when the

New York State Court of Appeals voted four to three to confirm a lower-court ruling declaring the law invalid, Wagner announced that he would not carry the case to the U. S. Supreme Court.

On February 12, 1963 a mass demonstration was held at the state capitol in Albany in support of legislation establishing a $1.50 minimum wage law. Several major trade unions participated, as did the NAACP, the Negro American Labor Council, and many other groups. The ILGWU was conspicuous by its absence. (In 1965 Governor Nelson Rockefeller vetoed a $1.50 statewide minimum wage law enacted by the legislature.)[50]

Periodically, workers' discontent with the union's practices erupts and receives public attention. In 1957 four hundred Negro and Puerto Rican members of the ILGWU employed at a plant in the Bronx picketed the offices of the union in protest against the ILGWU's failure to represent them adequately as the collective-bargaining agent. These workers later filed a petition with the National Labor Relations Board seeking the de-certification of the International Ladies Garment Workers Union as their representative. In their request to the NLRB the workers documented a series of charges against the union. Although the ILGWU succeeded in voiding the de-certification procedure, the case is significant, as it represented a spontaneous effort of Negro and Puerto Rican workers to secure a measure of democratic rights within the union and to stop collusive practices with the employer.

Demonstrations also occurred in 1958 when Puerto Rican members of ILGWU Local 62 (third largest in the international) employed at the Q-T Knitwear Company in Brooklyn marched around the factory with placards reading, "We're Tired of Industrial Peace. We Want Industrial Justice." A New York *Herald Tribune* reporter noted after interviewing the strikers that the wildcat strike was a protest against their boss and "more important, against the workers' own union."[51]

Workers have publicly protested on other occasions against

the union's practices, as did the employees of Plastic Wear, Inc., located in the Bronx. In this 1958 case two hundred members of ILGWU Local 132 demonstrated in front of the international union headquarters with signs reading: "80% of our members speak Spanish. A meeting conducted in English is a farce." Demonstrators shouted, "Mr. Dubinsky, we don't want your contract!" Other demonstrations have occurred when union members protested against "back-door deals" which they describe as "helping the bosses more than the workers."[52]

The degeneration of this union is all the more significant because of its early pioneering radicalism. This spirit was expressed in the preamble to the 1918 constitution, which reads:

> Resolved that the way to acquire our rights as producers and citizens and to bring about a system of society whereby the workers shall get the full value of their products, is to organize industrially into a class conscious union represented on the various legislative bodies by representatives of a political party whose aim is the abolition of the capitalist system.

In the early history of the ILGWU the preamble was more than a ritualistic concession to a politically conscious rank and file. The union, as an institution, encouraged the development of a progressive social consciousness among its members and was committed to social causes beyond the immediate economic concerns of garment workers. The contrast between the ILGWU's radicalism in the past and its present political conservatism and bureaucratic manipulation of workers dramatically illustrates the moral and social decline of the American labor movement.

Nevertheless, tradition and heritage are not easily extirpated. The ILGWU leadership is still obliged to pay homage to the spirit of its militant origins and to project the image of an enlightened, socially conscious union. Its sensitivity to attacks by civil rights leaders on the union's discriminatory practices is evidenced by the vast sums it has spent in recent years in advertising campaigns that attempt to create the impression that the ILGWU continues as a militant, equalitarian organization. It is this continuing verbal commitment—even if inconsistent with its actual practices—which provides some hope that the criticisms leveled against the union by workers and civil rights activists may have a positive effect.

The conservative transformation of the ILGWU is most significantly evidenced by the status of nonwhite workers within the industry and the union in New York City. The nonwhite proportion of the population in New York increased from 13 per cent in 1950 to 22 per cent in 1960. By 1970, based on projections of the Department of City Planning, Puerto Ricans and Negroes will account for at least 30 per cent of the city's population. In the past two decades the number of Negro and Puerto Rican workers in the garment industry has been rapidly growing, and they now constitute a significant part of the work force. Many ILGWU locals have a majority of nonwhite members, but with some rare exceptions these workers remain concentrated in the lowest-paid unskilled and semiskilled job classifications with virtually no opportunity for promotion to other categories. A study of wages in New York City released by the Bureau of Labor Statistics of the U. S. Department of Labor on June 27, 1962 indicates that the city had become a low-wage area, and that between 1950 and 1960 wages for apparel workers there fell from second place among sixteen industry categories to eleventh place and dropped below the national average for all manufacturing. The wage rates of unskilled and semiskilled garment workers, most of whom are nonwhite, were found to be below subsistence levels as indicated by the 1960 Interim City Workers Family Budget for New York City ($5048) established by the Bureau of Labor Statistics.[53]

In 1960 the average wage of all unionized garment workers in New York City was $2.40 an hour. In March 1963 the average was $2.39, a decline in hourly wages of a penny an hour and a decline in real wages of nine cents an hour at

1959 price levels, according to data from the Bureau of Labor Statistics. It should be noted that the statistical data, significant as they are, are deceptive since the median income figure includes the wages of highly paid cutters and pressers who earned over $4 an hour and are almost exclusively white. (In March 1966, according to the Bureau of Labor Statistics, the wage-spread in the New York garment industry was between $1.25 an hour and $8 an hour.)[54] In 1963 between 15 and 20 per cent of the ILGWU membership in New York City was earning less than $1.50 an hour.* All the available data indicate that this group consisted almost entirely of Negro and Puerto Rican workers. Thus, a significant percentage of Negro and Puerto Rican ILGWU members in the period between 1960 and 1965 not only experienced a drop in real earnings but also received an income that was below the figure which the Bureau of Labor Statistics rates as the poverty level for an average family in New York City. Commenting on this development within the ILGWU, Murray Kempton in the *World-Telegram & Sun*, July 27, 1965, wrote:

> It is a source of sadness and not of mockery that after 60 years of labor statesmanship, the real wages of their members could be declining a little year by year and that one out of every seven could well be an element in the city's poverty statistics.

It was perhaps also a source of sadness for David Dubinsky, who was obliged to admit the reality of "many" low-paid organized garment workers. Thus, in an interview with

---

* It is significant to note the shift in the rank of average hourly earnings among industrial workers in Birmingham, Alabama and New York City during the ten year period between 1950 and 1960. In 1950 New York ranked tenth and Birmingham thirty-third among forty-six cities in relation to average hourly earnings of production workers. In 1960, New York City had fallen to thirtieth place and Birmingham was tenth. See "Employment, Earnings, and Wages in New York City, 1950–1960," Bureau of Labor Statistics, Middle Atlantic Regional Office, New York, June 1962, Table 6, 24.

A. H. Raskin, Dubinsky stated: "Here is our union, a pioneer in pensions, welfare, paid vacations. We led everyone else in factory wages only a few years ago; now we are being criticized because our wages are too low. And it is true, many of them are low; that has affected me deeply. Where did we go wrong?"[55] (In June 1966 Dubinsky at the age of seventy-four, after thirty-four years as President of the ILGWU, resigned and was succeeded by Louis Stulberg, the union's Secretary-Treasurer.)

The powerful opposition of the ILGWU to training programs in the garment industry under the auspices of the federal anti-poverty program indicates the harmful social consequences of this union's restrictive practices.

As a result of demands by the International Ladies Garment Workers Union and the Amalgamated Clothing Workers of America (both AFL-CIO affiliates), federal agencies refused to provide funds for manpower training programs in the apparel industry operating within the New York metropolitan area. A typical example of this development is the fate of the training program proposed by the United Community Corporation, the anti-poverty community action agency for Newark, New Jersey. This group operated under Title II, the Community Action Program of the Economic Opportunity Act of 1964. When representatives of the Newark agency requested an explanation for the refusal of the Office of Economic Opportunity to provide funds for an apparel trades job training program for 545 workers (200 of whom were welfare recipients), they were told by officials of the Department of Labor that the basis for the rejection was the refusal of the two unions to approve the job training program.

On August 22, 1963 the Department of Labor, which administers the Manpower Development and Training Act, received a fourteen-page statement of the "position of the International Ladies Garment Workers Union and the Amalgamated Clothing Workers of America, on the question of subsidized training programs in the apparel industry of the United States." In this document, signed by Lazare

Teper, Research Director of the ILGWU, and Milton Fried, Research Director of the ACWA, the unions argued that

> It is our considered judgment that the subsidized training of apparel workers under the Manpower Development and Training Act is unnecessary . . . on the basis of our many years of experience in the apparel industry we are convinced that such training of apparel workers is not only a waste of federal funds but sets in motion forces detrimental to the health and stability of our industry." [Union document, p. 2.]

They also stated that

> the hiring of inexperienced workers by the industry is central to its functioning.
>
> . . . training and the possession of a specific apparel skill is not an essential requirement for employment in the apparel industry and . . . the training of inexperienced workers by the employer is a normal phase of the apparel business.
>
> Since skill has never been and is not now a precondition of employment in the apparel industry, government subsidization of the training of apparel workers is not required to provide employment in the apparel industry.
>
> . . . finally government subsidies for training apparel workers encourages increased instability in a highly unstable industry.

The report concludes:

> These considerations apply to government financed training programs under the Area Redevelopment Act, as well as the Manpower Development and Training Act. We, therefore, respectfully urge that the Department of Labor as a matter of policy not sponsor or approve any training program for apparel workers under the Manpower Development Act.

Both the ILGWU and the ACWA have used their considerable political power to prevent in Newark and elsewhere the same sort of training programs that are operating with public funds in many other industries.

The union argument, that there is no need for training skilled workers, is directly contradicted by statements made by officials of the ILGWU including Gus Tyler, the Assistant President of the union. Mr. Tyler has written:

> There is a shortage of skilled sewing machine operators. Nobody knows this better than the ILGWU. Some employers have either closed shop in New York or threatened to fold up for lack of skilled operators.[56]

In the same article he also referred to the "advanced skills" required by the ladies' garment industry. In addition it should be noted that some ILGWU contracts provide for a "learners" status of ten months and several union agreements require that a year shall pass before a new employee is entitled to the full rate of pay. The statement of the apparel labor unions is also contradicted by recent manpower data on the industry. According to the "Occupational Training Needs Survey," Research Series No. 18, September 1964, prepared and compiled by the State of New Jersey, Department of Labor and Industry, Division of Employment Security:

> By 1965 there will be a shortage in three of the six semi-skilled occupations surveyed. These occupations are: machine presser in the garment, laundry, and cleaning and dyeing industries. By 1968 [in addition to those occupations expected to be in short supply in 1965] there will be shortage of sewing machine operators and hand pressers in the garment, laundry, cleaning and dyeing industries.

These data are extremely significant as they directly relate to the proposal submitted to the Office of Economic Opportunity for funding by the Newark anti-poverty council. Furthermore, Newark has been officially declared a depressed area with extremely high unemployment among Negroes. Recognizing the acute needs of the Negro community, the federal agency was attempting to provide training for two hundred welfare recipients. Such job training programs, which will enable the long-term unemployed to leave the relief rolls by obtaining jobs as a result of newly acquired skills, is the essence of any real war against poverty.

The insistence of the two apparel unions that there is no necessity for training workers in the garment industry and their ability to prevent new training opportunities under the anti-poverty program have a special implication for Negro workers. Negro applicants for jobs in the garment industry are often asked if they have had previous experience. Because they have been denied the opportunity to obtain such experience, they are either denied work or employed only in menial and unskilled jobs. How often have Negroes plaintively expressed it thus: "If they don't give me a job so I can learn, I will never get experience, and without experience nobody will hire me." The ILGWU's restrictive practices are to a large degree responsible for the acute lack of job mobility among Negro garment workers.

In its presentation to the federal government, the ILGWU repeatedly insisted that manufacturing plants are small and that the industry does not require skilled workers. But at the September 1965 meeting of the ILGWU's General Executive Board, President Dubinsky announced the establishment of a new Master Agreement Department. According to *The New York Times* of September 8, 1965, this new department will "deal with the giant apparel companies that have burgeoned in the women's garment industry in recent years." *The Times* report observes that

> While the average garment concern is still a small one, union officials say that in less than a decade the big companies have grown to a point where they now produce a fifth of all women's apparel. They operate across product lines, link plants in many states, regions, markets and union divisions, and often employ thousands of workers under a single management, the board said.

The development of many large companies with modern production methods that require new skills has been evident for some time. But even though nonwhites constitute a potentially large source of skilled-labor recruitment for this industry, they have been effectively denied such opportunities mainly as a result of restrictive labor union practices. Secretary of Labor Willard Wirtz stated on March 1, 1966 at a meeting of the National Board of the Coat and Suit Industry: "Industry reports show that companies were having difficulty finding people with skills. In terms of fully prepared people there is a shortage." He also noted that the impending shortage called for preparations to take care of the expanding needs in industry and asked for support of the on the job training program.[57] David Dubinsky, according to *Women's Wear Daily* of March 2, 1966, in response to the Secretary's statement "scored the Administration's assistance programs for on the job training as they applied to the coat and suit industry."

In the Harvard University study, *Made in New York: Case Studies in Metropolitan Manufacturing* (Harvard University Press, 1959) it is noted that Negroes and Latin Americans

> were largely to be found in the less skilled lower paid crafts and in shops making the lower price lines and in this industry their advancement to higher skills was not proceeding very rapidly. In the higher skilled coat and suit industry the new ethnic groups have hardly made an appearance.

> In short, Negro and Puerto Rican women, who are on the lower rungs of the city's economic ladder, have become important in the New York garment industry, but they work mainly in the more standardized branches, and with few exceptions, unlike the Jewish and Italian men of earlier days, they do not become highly skilled tailor system workers on dresses or "cloaks." As a result, a shortage of skilled sewing machine operators is developing.

The New York Times of June 7, 1967 reported that "15 girls in a Lower West Side branch of the Neighborhood Youth Corps armed themselves with cherry cream pies and soft drinks yesterday to retain the sewing machines they love." This was another instance where the ILGWU attempted to abruptly terminate an apparel trades training program in New York City operated at several locations by the Neighborhood Youth Corps with federal funds provided by the Office of Economic Opportunity. The programs involved groups of teen-age girls mainly Negro and Puerto Rican high school "dropouts" who bitterly defended their sewing machines and their right to learn a craft.[58]

This apparel training program was finally saved only by private donations which made possible the delivery of new machines and bolts of fabric to the community training centers after the federal funds were withdrawn. On June 13, 1967 the New York *Post* quoted Jerry Kolker, project director of the local Youth Corps training program, who said that "Neither the government nor the union will cooperate with us. But now we have enough machines and money to keep going, even if they come to collect them again." Kolker added: "We have asked them [the unions] for their help in developing training programs and working out a solution to this problem but the ILGWU won't answer." Ironically, those labor unions which in the past were important vehicles for improving the economic condition of workers now use their power to prevent the entry of certain groups of workers into the labor market or to lock these groups permanently in unrewarding menial and unskilled job categories.

The New York Times of August 18, 1962, reporting on the testimony of Moe Falikman, Business Manager of Cutters Local 10, before a hearing of the Subcommittee of the House Committee on Education and Labor stated, "Mr. Falikman explained that Local 10 had no formal training program for cutters and no apprentice system." That led Congressman James Roosevelt to observe that "with the changing pattern of population in New York it seems to me you would have gone to some lengths" to provide training and jobs for members of racial minorities.

"We are not an employment agency," Mr. Falikman replied.

"But you are," Mr. Roosevelt declared. "I'd have greater

faith in you if you would face this situation honestly and say, yes, this needs looking into."

After consulting with a union attorney, Falikman did agree that he would look into it.

The New York Times of August 25, 1962, in reporting Mr. Dubinsky's appearance before the House Subcommittee stated that he denied that it was the union's responsibility to upgrade Negroes and Puerto Ricans, "as much as we would like to see them go to higher brackets. The union," he said, "is not an employment agency." Other ILGWU officials appearing before the Subcommittee insisted that upgrading and promotion was not the union's responsibility. "We are not an employment agency," they all said.

But in the testimony reprinted in the October 1, 1962 issue of the ILGWU newspaper *Justice*, in reply to a question as to why Negroes and Puerto Ricans do not advance in the union or in the industry, Dubinsky is quoted as saying, "We are doing everything under the sun on this score."

Either the ILGWU is "doing everything under the sun" or "we are not an employment agency, it's not our responsibility." The union cannot have it both ways.

After many complaints from Negro workers against the ILGWU, and the filing of charges of racial discrimination against the union with the New York State Commission for Human Rights,[59] an investigation of the status of non-white workers within the garment industry and within the ILGWU was made by the Committee on Education and Labor of the U. S. House of Representatives during 1962. As part of the Congressional investigation a series of public hearings were held in New York City and Washington, D.C. At the request of the House Committee on Education and Labor, the author, the NAACP's Labor Secretary, functioned as a special consultant to the Congressional Committee.

An additional factor prompting the Congressional investigation was that the National Labor Relations Board in 1962 had found the ILGWU guilty of unfair labor practices in relation to a union of its own employees.[60] The ILGWU unsuccessfully opposed an NLRB order for a certification election among its employees and then refused to recognize and bargain with the Federation of Union Representatives (FOUR) after that union won the election and was certified as the collective-bargaining representative. The ILGWU was found guilty of coercing members of FOUR and was ordered on several occasions by the NLRB to cease reprisals against employees who support the Federation of Union Representatives, but the ILGWU for years has conducted a campaign of harassment and dismissal against FOUR supporters and has spent vast sums in litigation appealing NLRB orders. It is interesting to note that other important international unions have recognized unions of their own employees but the ILGWU remains adamant in its refusal to recognize FOUR.*,[61]

One of the revealing consequences of the public exposure of racial practices within the ILGWU was the action taken by the union's General Executive Board to cancel an agreement with the Workmen's Circle Home for the Aged in New York City because of the discriminatory admission practices of that organization. After the union with much fanfare announced the project (see June 1, 1961, issue of *Justice* with headline over masthead reading "ILG Wing

---

* It is not only union representatives who had legitimate grievances against the Dubinsky leadership. The 650 office employees, organized in their own union (Local 153 Office and Professional Employees) went on a one-day strike on December 16, 1965. The immediate issue over which the long-dissatisfied office workers struck concerned a notice by the ILGWU, which had heretofore paid all the Social Security payments of these workers, that it would pay only 50 per cent after January 1, 1966. Employers normally pay only 50 per cent, but since in this case the union's payment of the whole amount was built into the office workers' wage levels, the workers interpreted the notice as a wage cut. After bargaining and achieving little satisfaction, they walked off their jobs. To our knowledge, the only serious account in the daily press appeared in the trade paper of the garment industry, *Women's Wear*, December 17, 1965.

of 'Circle' Home Opening June 11"), Negro union members protested the use of union funds to build a facility not available to them. After the congressional investigation the Dubinsky leadership became more sensitive to public criticism and canceled the discriminatory agreement.

According to the Report of the General Executive Board to the Thirty-second Convention of the ILGWU, Miami Beach, Florida, May 12, 1965,[62] the union in 1959 began the construction of an ILGWU wing at the Workmen's Circle Home in the Bronx for retired union members at a cost of $1,300,000. After the ILGWU wing was dedicated on June 11, 1961, ". . . the Workmen's Circle Home refused to process several applications of non-Jewish ILGWU members,"[63] even though the wing was built with the dues money of all union members. Anticipating public exposure, the ILGWU leadership canceled the discriminatory agreement with the Workmen's Circle.[64]

Among the several examples of discriminatory practices cited at the hearings is that of the status of the "push boys" auxiliary unit known as 60-A. Local 60, the Pressers' local, controls jobs that on an hourly rated basis are the highest-paying jobs in the garment industry in New York, the average wage in 1962 being almost five dollars an hour. According to testimony, Local 60 had an all-white membership. Sixty-A was and is simply an appendage to Local 60. Its members are almost entirely Negro and Puerto Rican, and work as shipping clerks, push boys, and delivery men, earning in the vicinity of fifty dollars per week. Yet 60-A, with twice the membership of Local 60, has never been chartered by the international as a separate local, and the manager of 60, who is a presser, also functions as the manager of 60-A. In the annual reports filed with the Bureau of Labor-Management Reports of the U. S. Department of Labor, a joint report is filed for 60 and 60-A, although every ILGWU local union files individually. In addition, one must note that all the business agents for Local 60 are elected by the local's members, but the three Negroes who perform similar functions in 60-A are appointed and designated as "delegates" rather than business agents.[65]

Also cited in the hearings was the case of a Negro worker, Ernest Holmes, against Local 10 of the ILGWU, then pending before the New York State Commission for Human Rights. On April 4, 1961 a complaint was filed against Local 10 of the International Ladies Garment Workers Union with the New York State Commission for Human Rights. On May 18, 1963, twenty-five months later, in the case of *Holmes vs. Falikman*,[66] the ILGWU entered into a stipulation agreement upon which the complaint was finally withdrawn. In the settlement obtained by the Commission the union agreed to admit Holmes into the Cutters local of the ILGWU, to assist him in seeking employment and in gaining training experience as an apprentice cutter. This is precisely what the State Commission had ordered the ILGWU to do a year before when a finding of "probable cause" was issued by the investigating commissioner. *The New York Times* of July 2, 1962, in a report headlined "Union Told to Get Job for a Negro," stated:

A garment cutters' union has been ordered by the State Commission for Human Rights to arrange for employment of a Negro at union rates commensurate with his skill and to admit the Negro into union membership if his work is satisfactory.

The Times story also stated: "With regard to the union, the decision found that 'the evidence raises serious doubt as to its good faith to comply with the State Law Against Discrimination in the matter of this complaint; and that there was "probable cause" to credit the allegations of the complaint.'" On September 14, 1962 Rupert Ruiz, Investigating Commissioner of the New State Commission for Human Rights, in a letter to Emil Schlesinger, Attorney for Local 10, stated that the Commission had "repeatedly requested and for a period of eight months tried to obtain data pertinent to a resolution of the charges of discrimination against Amalgamated Ladies Garment Cutters Union—Local 10. These efforts were unsuccessful. The failure of representatives of that local to cooperate in the investigation, despite their promises to do so, left me no alternative but to find 'probable cause to credit the allegations of the complaint.'"

The ILGWU was involved in a previous case before the State Commission brought by a Negro union member on the issue of separate nationality locals. Nationality locals have been illegal since 1945 in New York under the State Anti-Discrimination Law. Title VII, the Equal Employment Section of the Civil Rights Act of 1964 further requires the elimination of such locals and some unions have moved to disband them. On May 18, 1966, at a tempestuous meeting of the New York Furriers Union Joint Council (affiliated with the Amalgamated Meat Cutters and Butcher Workmen, AFL-CIO) the forty-year-old Greek Fur Workers' local was dissolved. The fifteen-hundred member local union went out of existence and its members transferred to other locals affiliated with the Furriers Joint Council, as a result of action by the international union to comply with Title VII. According to *The New York Times* of May 19, 1966:

> After lengthy hearings and an impartial finding by Professor Samuel Bader of the Brooklyn Law School, the council's parent union, the Amalgamated Meat Cutters and Butcher Workmen, decided that the continued existence of the local violated at least the spirit of the Federal Fair Employment Act.

Although the Furriers Union and other labor organizations have moved to disband nationality locals because of the requirements of Title VII, the International Ladies Garment Workers Union continues to maintain two Italian language locals in New York City: Local 89 designated as the Italian Dressmakers Union and Local 48 designated as the Italian Cloakmakers Union. According to the Report of the General Executive Board of the ILGWU dated May 12, 1965, Local

89, the largest local in the international union, has a membership of 20,898 and Local 48 has a membership of 8047.

In 1946 a formal complaint was filed with the State Commission by a Negro member of Local 22 who was barred from higher-paying jobs controlled by Local 89.[67] After the Commission had notified the ILGWU that the existence of nationality locals was a violation of state law, a conference was held on January 22, 1947, at which the ILGWU entered into an agreement with the Commission that it would not bar Negroes, Spanish-speaking or other persons from membership in the Italian locals. Twenty years later not a single Negro or Spanish-speaking person holds membership in the two Italian locals which have control of some of the highest-paying jobs in the industry and the ILGWU has taken no action to comply with the state law.

A major factor to be understood about the status of Negro workers in the ILGWU is the relationship between Negro powerlessness within the union and economic exploitation. In 1956 the average weekly wage for garment workers in New York City was $55.60. The average over-all manufacturing wage for the city was $74.76. Extensive interviewing of Negro and Puerto Rican workers by the author and other investigators indicates that these workers were and remain concentrated in the lowest-paid categories of employment, with very little, if any, job mobility. During 1956 (a boom year in the garment industry) Negro and Puerto Rican workers took home as little as $2500, but for the highly skilled cutters and pressers, virtually all of whom were white, $8000 was not unusual.

For many locals in New York City in which the overwhelming membership is Negro and Puerto Rican, the wage schedules provided in the collective bargaining are a disgrace to the American labor movement. In these agreements the so-called "minimum wages" are in fact most frequently the maximum wages. In this category are floor girls, shipping clerks, trimmers, and sewing-machine operators in the low-priced dress field and in the so-called "miscellaneous locals" with their large concentrations of Negro and Puerto Rican workers.

The basic contract between Local 98 and the Manufacturers Association in effect until August 14, 1963, provided the following minimum wages—p. 7, Article 4(a):

Floor girls	$1.15 an hour
Operators	1.20
Shipping Clerks	1.20
Cutters	1.20*

Wage scales of other ILGWU contracts in force until 1963 in those locals with a high concentration of nonwhite workers were as follows:

Local 32: Pressers, operators, cleaners, examiners	$1.15
Local 40: Operators, shippers, floor girls	1.15
Local 62: Operators, ironers, examiners, finishers	1.15
Local 91: Operators, ironers, cleaners, finishers	1.20
Local 98: Operators, shipping clerks, cutters, floor girls	1.15

Several new contracts were negotiated at the expiration of those cited above. As a result of the increase in the federal minimum wage to $1.25 an hour there was a small upward adjustment of wage scales. However, the pattern described above remains intact. (On February 20, 1967 a new three-year agreement covering eighty thousand dressmakers employed in ILGWU shops became effective. According to the AFL-CIO *News* the new contract provided for the following weekly wages, ". . . $68 for examiners, $75 for drapers, $65 for cleaners and others, $67 and $72 for shipping clerks."[68])

The Baltimore *Sun* and other major newspapers across the country carried a North American Newspaper Alliance report datelined New York, June 4, 1964, under the headline "Most Garment Worker Paychecks Are Below Johnson Poverty Level." The report began:

* These are cutters of plastic material who are not under the jurisdiction of the Cutters Local 10.

A majority of the 800,000 members of two garment unions, usually ranked among the "most aggressive" in the country, average less than the $3000 yearly in take home pay that the Johnson Administration has declared is the poverty level.

The unions are the Amalgamated Clothing Workers and the International Ladies Garment Workers Union.

After describing the low average wages earned by members of the Amalgamated Clothing Workers, the report went on:

Most ILGWU members fared worse. The ILGWU's 1964 contract with women's apparel manufacturers for floor workers (common laborers in other industries) provides for an average of $1.50 an hour with skilled machine operators drawing $1.90 an hour. These two categories account for close to 90 per cent of the ILGWU membership of more than 400,000. . . .

A huge majority of ACW and ILGWU members are Negroes and Puerto Ricans which are the principal groups singled out for help in the "war on poverty" in the cities.

On April 16, 1967 the New York Congress of Racial Equality (CORE) held a press conference to protest the 1967 agreements signed by the ILGWU and stated that the "ILGWU has for years permitted conditions to exist which keep the vast majority of black workers in the lowest-paying jobs and has denied black workers a policy-making voice in the union through restrictive constitutional provisions."[69]

In announcing that CORE was engaged in the "formation of a black caucus to fight bias and powerlessness is the ILGWU" Roy Innis, chairman of Harlem CORE, stated:

The growing number of black workers coming to Harlem CORE to lodge complaints against the ILGWU and the disgraceful contracts signed in 1967 make it imperative that immediate action be taken. CORE is now assisting black garment workers of New York City in organizing for the right of black people to participate in basic policy-making for their own protection. With the help of

CORE a black caucus is now being organized to fight for the basic democratic rights of all nonwhite workers and eliminate racial discrimination in one of the richest and most powerful unions in the world.[70]

In reality there are two categories of workers in the ILGWU: a relatively small number of highly skilled white workers with seniority and stability of employment who earn high wages and for whom the union performs a variety of protective functions, and the great mass of unskilled low-paid workers, mostly Negro and Puerto Rican, who exist in a permanent condition of semipoverty and are the base of the industry's work force as well as of the union's membership in New York City. As a result, the city must subsidize the low-wage garment industry. The extent of the public subsidy which the substandard garment industry in New York requires is indicated in part by unemployment compensation payments. In 1956, unemployment compensation payments in New York City totaled $127,686,000. It is significant that in that highly profitable year for the industry over thirty million dollars, or 24 per cent, went to workers in the ladies' garment industry who as a group accounted for only 3½ per cent of the city's total work force. The garment industry, as well as other low-paying industries, is subsidized by federal, state, and municipal agencies in a variety of other ways. But in each case, as the city's largest low-wage manufacturing industry, it receives a highly disproportionate share of these subsidies.

Perhaps it is axiomatic that any serious exposure of the anti-social practices of an entrenched bureaucracy, such as that of the ILGWU leadership, would be met with anger and resentment. Yet the ILGWU response has been so extreme that it reveals much about the union leadership and its allies in the liberal community. Instead of making an honest effort to deal with criticisms both before and after they were made public, the ILGWU attempted to smear its critics. Union spokesmen charged the critics with being "Communist agents," "racist slanderers," and anti-Semites.[71]

The Jewish Labor Committee, which consists largely of ILGWU officials, distributed a memorandum by Emmanuel Muravchik, National Field Director, dated November 16, 1962 which repeated the union's charge that the NAACP's criticism of the racial practices of the ILGWU "contributes to anti-Semitic feelings" but makes no attempt to deal substantively with the real issue of racial discrimination and the denial of democratic membership rights within the ILGWU.

To Muravchik's charges, Roy Wilkins responded in a letter dated October 31, 1962 as follows:

> We assert with the greatest emphasis that nothing, absolutely nothing, in Mr. Hill's recent or more remote statements can be construed as anti-Semitic. This is a grave charge to make. It requires more substantiation than your flip reference in a part of a sentence. The charge is not only against Mr. Hill, but against the NAACP itself. We do not deign to defend ourselves against such a baseless allegation. Its inclusion in the resolution, as well as in the statements to the press . . . is unworthy of an organization like the Jewish Labor Committee which, in the very nature of things, must be concerned with the seriousness of such a charge and with the evidence required to give it substance. No such evidence has been submitted in this case beyond the citation of the use by Mr. Hill of one word, "ethnic," out of a total of 4500 words in his testimony before the House subcommittee. The relevance of his comparison of the ethnic composition of the membership of the ILGWU can hardly be questioned in this context. . . .

> We reject the proposition that any segment of the labor movement is sacrosanct in the matter of practices and/or policies which restrict employment opportunities on racial or religious or nationality grounds. We reject the contention that bringing such charges constitutes a move to destroy "unity" among civil rights groups unless it be admitted that this unity is a precarious thing, perched upon unilateral definition of discrimination by each mem-

ber group. In such a situation the "unity" is of no basic value and its destruction may be regarded as not a calamity, but a blessed clearing of the air.

In this connection, it is well to reiterate a facet of this discussion which appears to have escaped the attention of the various reviewers and resolution writers. It is that Herbert Hill, our Labor Secretary, has one duty and that is to serve the interests of the Negro worker through the NAACP. Other groups, including trade unions, have powerful machinery to protect their principal interests. Mr. Hill is employed to maintain anti-discrimination work in the employment field as his top and only priority. He is not for trade unions first and Negro workers second. He has no divided loyalties.

Wilkins indicates that the whole concept of a Negro labor coalition is worthless to Negroes, if such a coalition means a gentlemen's agreement to refrain from attacking racial discrimination within labor unions.

In his letter Wilkins also pointed out that many copies of the Muravchik memo had been sent to unions with the request that they adopt resolutions condemning the NAACP, all based upon their own "bare statement and interpretation" of the NAACP's charges, ignoring the factual accuracy of the assertions. Therefore the Jewish Labor Committee was spreading "a climate of hostility to the NAACP."

When you declare in 1962 that the NAACP's continued attack upon discrimination against Negro workers by trade union bodies and leaders places "in jeopardy" continued progress toward civil rights goals or endangers the "unity" among civil rights forces, or renders a "disservice" to the Negro worker, or raises the question "whether it is any longer possible to work with the NAACP" you are, in fact, seeking by threats to force us to conform to what the Jewish Labor Committee is pleased to classify as proper behavior in the circumstances.

Wilkins cited the NAACP's awareness "that the trade union movement can be a strength to the Negro population of our country whose employed portion is largely in the working class," but noted that for too long and "almost too faithfully" the NAACP followed "the procedure of waiting and working in every possible way to resolve union-race situations without open breaks." But care and respect born of concern for the long-run welfare of Negro workers, as well as concern for the unions as protection for all workers, "should not be regarded as foreclosing a frontal attack, irrespective of the opponent of the Negro worker." Wilkins noted that in 1959 the NAACP had offered to meet with officials of the ILGWU to discuss complaints from Negro garment workers who were also NAACP members, but that the offer was dismissed in a summary fashion by the union leadership.

The NAACP's fundamental attitude toward organized labor was further delineated in a letter from Wilkins to George Meany on December 7, 1962. Wilkins wrote that "there is no difference of opinion between the NAACP and the AFL-CIO upon the desirability of a harmonious relationship among all those who are sincere in their desire to serve the cause of human rights. . . ." However, he stated that while Meany had assured the NAACP that the AFL-CIO did not hold that unions are beyond the legitimate range of criticism, a scanning of NAACP reports from the 1930s on revealed that organized labor had repeatedly rejected and "denounced thoroughly legitimate and soundly based criticism of discriminatory policies and practices of unions in the organized labor movement." Moreover, the evidence showed that opposition to the AFL-CIO policy of nondiscrimination was not centered in only "a few local unions and their members," as Meany claimed. Mr. Wilkins added:

> We do not believe these charges of discrimination are untrue. We do not believe an enumeration and a substantiation of them constitutes an "attack" upon organized labor. In our view, the conditions covered by these charges constitute a formidable barrier to the enjoyment by millions of Negro workers of employment opportunity and of greater security in our economy.

Going on to cite the discriminatory practices of affiliated AFL-CIO unions and stressing that they constituted a national pattern that had the approval of various international unions, he continued:

> It remains our view that no collective bargaining agreement which provides for separate racial seniority lines can be said to be nondiscriminatory. It is our further view that where this type of agreement is kept in effect over a period of years, despite repeated protests and requests for alteration, the union has forfeited its right to bargain collectively for all the workers and that the proper agency, the NLRB, may fairly be petitioned to revoke the certification.

But Wilkins noted that invoking decertification procedures and court action in the campaign to eliminate discriminatory practices was a last resort, since the destruction of unions is *not* the NAACP's objective, "despite accusations to the contrary." It is only "the precarious situation of the Negro worker," Wilkins emphasized, which "spurs our impatience." He ended:

> The conclusion is inescapable that desegregation in the labor movement has proceeded at no more rapid a rate than the disgraceful crawl of public school desegration in the South. When it is considered that unions are declared opponents of segregation through numerous resolutions and policy statements, whereas the Southern states are declared proponents of segregation, the matching snail's pace understandably raises eyebrows in the Negro community.

The exposure of the status of nonwhite workers in the ILGWU, together with the revelations about the monolithic control of the union, provoked a debate that had widespread repercussions in the "liberal-labor community." Typical of the comments from those who had accepted the image of the ILGWU as a progressive and democratic union were: "Why does the NAACP single out the ILGWU?"

"Aren't there unions with far worse records than this one?" These questions are usually asked by those who will candidly acknowledge that the charges are justified in large measure, but bridle at concentrating so much fire on an allegedly progressive union which passes fine resolutions on civil rights and contributes to worthy causes. This approach is unwarranted for the following reasons:

1. The ILGWU, the largest union in the largest manufacturing industry in the nation's largest city, directly affects the economic welfare and dignity of hundreds of thousands of Negro and Puerto Rican men, women, and children in New York.

2. The "go soft on Dubinsky [or Stulberg]" line has the disagreeable connotations of "Uncle Tomism": it suggests that the liberal and Negro community should be appreciative of small favors and not attack "benefactors" even if those friends aren't perfect. The documentation reveals that in reality the ILGWU has bestowed no "favors" on the Negro and has acted in a discriminatory manner—hidden under the rhetoric of its liberal past.

3. The question "Hill is really right but why make such a fuss over a progressive union?" is asked by those who substitute sentimentality for thought, and wish fulfillment for reality. The progressive label is only a nostalgic hangover from a dead past. The word suggests militancy, internal democracy, and social vision. On none of these counts does the ILGWU qualify.

4. The ILGWU leadership is greatly concerned with presenting a progressive and liberal public image, without a critical examination of the social consequences of its policies and practices. Perhaps the most dismal factor in the entire situation is its inability to admit that anything at all is wrong. But, as I have already pointed out, since the ILGWU leadership does care greatly about its public image, it is possible that vigorous public pressure might have salutary effects.

There are indications that as a result of exposure and criticism of the ILGWU some Negroes and Puerto Ricans have obtained better-paying jobs and that the operational bar against their entering leadership positions will eventually be breached. After the NAACP's activity a Puerto Rican for the first time was appointed to the union's General Executive Board, Negroes have been employed in hitherto "lily-white" staff positions within the union, and ILGWU officials are less arrogant in their daily treatment of the Negro membership. Eventually the ILGWU may feel obliged to do something about the substandard wage levels in the industry which victimize primarily the Negro and Puerto Rican workers.

Ten years after the merger the pattern of racial discrimination by labor unions in many important jurisdictions, especially in the skilled craft occupations, remains intact. Some instances of isolated progress have occurred as a result of actions before the National Labor Relations Board, the filing of complaints with federal and state anti-discrimination agencies, the securing of court orders and organized public pressure from the Negro protest movement. But this "progress" does not represent a basic elimination of the patterns of racial discrimination practiced by major sections of organized labor.

There has recently occurred a fundamental change in the immediacy of the goals and in the level of aspiration that Negroes hold in relation to all the institutions of American society, including labor unions. Virtually all the concessions made by "liberal" whites, including union leaders, are forthcoming only as a reaction to Negro protest, to Negro anger, and each concession quite properly creates the realistic basis for the next demand. Labor union leaders, in common with many others, are tragically incapable of understanding the dynamics of contemporary Negro protest. Thus, they express petulance and bitter resentment at increasing Negro demands and frequently are most indignant because "Negroes don't appreciate what we are doing for them."

Across the country many powerful labor unions are an important part of the "liberal labor" coalitions that are in control of municipal governments. The fundamental failure of this coalition, nationally and locally, is expressed most sharply in the deteriorating condition of the Negro in the cities, and the vast expansion of racial ghettos and urban rot. Furthermore, labor unions with vast treasuries that control banks and real estate, purchase high-yield securities on the stock market, and engage in a variety of enterprises are not using union funds for socially desirable purposes.

Organized labor has not used its political influence and financial power to eliminate segregated slums and to alter the dehumanizing status of Negroes locked in the racial ghettos of the urban North. When the building trades unions directly prevent Negroes from working on highly visible public construction projects or when unions such as the International Ladies Garment Workers Union prevent training opportunities for unemployed Negro workers in their jurisdictions, they are directly contributing to the growing racial crisis of the cities.

In a period of racial upheaval and vast dislocation in the urban centers, labor unions whose base is in the cities have become part of that political coalition attempting to maintain the status quo, a status quo that can no longer be tolerated by the urban Negro. Data released by the U. S. Department of Labor on September 5, 1967, indicate that more white workers were employed than at any previous time in the nation's history, but that during the same period more Negroes were unemployed than ever before. At the same time that white workers are earning the highest wages in the nation's history, the economic status of Negro wage earners is deteriorating and the differential between the income of white and Negro workers continues to increase.

As the polarization between the white working class, which shares in the affluence of American society, and the black sub-proletariat, which is kept outside of the labor force and is fundamentally alienated from the social order, increases, organized labor as a social institution becomes more conservative.

A most hopeful development is the significant rise in Negro caucuses inside certain labor organizations and the growth of independent "black unions." These include the Independent Alliance of Skilled Crafts in Ohio, the Maryland Freedom Labor Union, and the Allied Workers International Union in Gary, Indiana, among others. The public attack made by Walter Reuther, President of the United Automobile Workers Union, against the conservative leadership of the AFL-CIO may also become important. In resigning from the Federation's Executive Council, Mr. Reuther denounced the Meany leadership as "the complaisant custodians of the status quo," and prominent among Reuther's criticisms of the Federation's policies and practices was the failure to develop a meaningful commitment to the cause of civil rights and job equality. Emil Mazey, Secretary-Treasurer of the United Automobile Workers Union, resigned from the Civil Rights Committee of the AFL-CIO and denounced its failure to eliminate racist practices in organized labor.

As the racial situation does not change for the overwhelming majority of Negroes and as the economic status of colored workers continues to deteriorate, the entire Negro community becomes increasingly aware of the profound disparity between promise and performance. Thus, there is a new impatience and a rejection of token adjustment and of the "Uncle Tom" who represents racial shame and white paternalism. The dramatic events of recent years in the North as in the South clearly indicate that only the sharpest confrontations with discriminatory institutions can bring change and progress for colored workers, that the white man listens only after the Negro has created a crisis. This is as true for organized labor as for most other institutions in American society.

A consequence of this development is the steady deterioration of relations between the Negro protest movement in its diverse forms and the vague arrangement of groups assembled under the worn banner of "liberalism," a liberalism that has been in retreat and decline for over a generation. White "liberals" in the North can no longer deflect the Negro attack away from their own discriminatory practices, from their own neighborhoods and institutions, by expressing outrage at Southern racism. The white groups traditionally identified with "liberalism" in the North are facing a crisis over their own racial practices, and the so-called "Negro-liberal-labor coalition" is repeatedly subjected to stresses and tensions.

Today, more so than at any time in the past, the order of priority on social issues is vastly different for whites and Negroes. As very real differences and conflicts over programs and tactics develop between the Negro movement and the white liberals, the coalition is increasingly weakened and loses operational meaning. It is hoped that after the debris of the past and present is swept aside, a new constellation of forces may develop in which the Negro can share responsibility and leadership, a new movement in which the interests of colored people are not subordinated to "other considerations" and where there is a genuine appreciation of the unique social experience of the Negro in American life. But such an alliance can develop only when organized labor sheds its bureaucratic conservatism and becomes a dynamic force, capable of organizing millions of unorganized workers in the South and elsewhere, and prepared to challenge the status quo. Thus, the struggle for racial equality and internal democracy within labor unions is a struggle for the regeneration of organized labor as a significant social movement within the United States.

Chapter VIII

(B) CONTEMPORARY LABOR'S ATTITUDE TOWARD THE NEGRO

GUS TYLER

A massive explosion in post-1964 America may arise from expanded rights for Negroes in a society of diminished opportunity for all. Although "rights" and "opportunity" are closely linked, they are separate problems. A man may have the right to a job, but in the absence of jobs there is no real opportunity. A family may have the right to live in any neighborhood it pleases, but in the absence of income it has no real opportunity to move out of the slums. A child may have the right to a good education, but in the absence of a wholesome home environment there is no real opportunity to learn. The problem of the Negro worker is dual, involving "rights" and "riches." The problem of rights involves *de jure* and *de facto* access to the voting booth, to a job, to a decent home, to a proper education, to public accommodations. The problem of riches involves the *reality* of a job, of fair income, of suitable housing: the tangibles that give body to the intangible rights.

While each of these questions is separate, they affect each other. In a society of *expanding* economic opportunity for all, it is easier to win civil rights for Negroes and obviously much easier to fill the *right* with *realities*. Vice versa, in a society of diminishing economic opportunity, tolerance tends to shrink, tensions mount, and hard-won rights merely sharpen appetites at a bare table. Just as economic growth is helpful and meaningful for genuinely improved living among Negroes, so, too, can civil rights move the nation toward the "great society." The application of civil rights can make the Negro worker a better-educated, more skilled, more creative contributor to our national wealth. The fuller and wiser use of the ballot by the Negro can add strength to the progressive political forces in America engaged in enlarging *real* as well as *equal* opportunity for all. Because the American labor movement is innately aware of the duality of the Negro question, the trade unions wage war on a double front: for *equal rights* for Negroes in a society of *greater opportunity* for all.

Let us first consider the first front: civil rights.

"The AFL-CIO is for civil rights—without reservation and without delay.

"The labor movement is dedicated to those truths that were self-evident to the authors of the Declaration of Independence. The rights so eloquently affirmed in 1776 are a sacred birthright of all in America not subject to modification or denial because of race, creed, or national origin.

"Unfortunately, to the shame of the nation, discrimination still exists. It must be wiped out if the United States is to be truly the champion of freedom in a world where nonwhites are an overwhelming majority.

"Mere acknowledgement, mere lip service to equal rights is not enough. The labor movement is committed to a positive program for translating principle into reality on every front. This means on the job, in the schools, at the polls, in housing, and in all places of public accommodation —restaurants, hotels, everywhere."

The above paragraphs were written by George Meany, President of the American Federation of Labor-Congress of Industrial Organizations, as part of a lead editorial in *The Federationist*, official publication of the AFL-CIO, in March 1964.

In 1893 the constitution of the American Railway Union —a militant and class-conscious organization headed by Eugene Victor Debs—stipulated that it would include "all railway employees *born of white parents*." (Italics added.)

The difference between the Debs of 1893 and the Meany

of today is not a difference between men or belief but a difference in time. At the turn of the century many American unions—including a segment dedicated to the oneness of labor and even to the Socialist society—counted few or no Negroes as members. The reasons were prejudice, control of the job market, and craft status. Denial of membership because of prejudice existed primarily in those locals whose membership came from geographic areas where anti-Negro feeling was intense: i.e. mainly areas of the South. Exclusion arising from a desire to control the local labor market was directed against *all* "outsiders" who might bloat the labor supply in some given craft, but inevitably hit Negroes hardest where the latter were newcomers to the labor force. The barring of Negroes occurred in some trades where super-proud craftsmen looked upon their union not simply as an economic instrument in the struggle with employers but as a professional society, conferring a special status on its members, and were dedicated to withholding the "mysteries" of the trade from all except the chosen few. Added together, the obstacles to Negro inclusion were sizable, although the view that the "colored" should be denied membership was always a minority position in the *official* labor movement.

The present forthright and outright position of the AFL-CIO as stated by George Meany and in the statements and resolutions of Executive Council meetings and conventions is the product of three great changes in American society since the turn of the century: 1) a changed national climate, reflected in popular mood and in accumulating legislation on equal rights; 2) a changed labor force; and 3) a changed labor movement.

The changing national climate is most dramatically recorded in the years running from President Franklin D. Roosevelt's proclamation of a Fair Employment Practices Committee during World War II down to President Lyndon B. Johnson's victory over the "backlash" in 1964. In the interim the Supreme Court established its landmark decision on school integration; a score of states passed fair employment practices acts; and, in 1964, Congress passed and the President signed a Civil Rights Act that was the culmination of efforts earlier expressed through the less ambitious acts of 1957 and 1960. Indeed, the changing and changed mood of America on civil rights might well be charted in the political evolution of one sensitive man in America: LBJ!

The nature of the labor force in America changed basically in the decade immediately following World War I. "In manufacturing, the relatively young automobile, chemical and electrical industries contributed a disproportionate share of the increase in output, employment and payrolls," noted Leo Wolman in his *Ebb and Flow of Trade Unionism.* "Outside manufacturing, substantial new sources of employment were created in the rapidly expanding public utility industries, throughout the distributive trades, and in the whole range of services." The disproportionately rapid growth of these industries opened job opportunities for Negroes who had little luck in the older skilled crafts of building, construction, railroading, printing. Entry into the labor force was made easier not only by the growth of these new trades but also by the simplification of work in basic industries, thereby making possible the employment of the less-skilled Negro worker. This dual development—new trades and simplified skills—continued right through World War II, bringing millions of Negroes into manufacture, services, public utility, and—more recently—into public employment.

This changing labor force left its impression on the composition of the American labor movement. From 1897 to the end of World War I the trade union movement was dominated by a cluster of three union groups: the extractive industries of mining, quarrying, and oil; building and construction; transportation and communication. While the first of these in the extractive industries was an "industrial" union, the other two were craft unions to which access was not easy for new workers, least of all for Negroes. In 1897 these "big three" composed half the total labor movement; by 1914 they composed about 60 per cent. In the period after the war other trades and industries grew. And as these were organized, especially in the great "industrial union" push from 1935 on, the composition of the labor movement changed. Unions in manufacture, distribution, services, utilities, and public employment grew. As these trades were organized, a mounting number of Negroes came into the labor movement. These new unions with their new membership mix changed the complexion and the attitude of organized labor.

The changes in national climate, labor force, and union personality were all brought to a head by the civil rights movement to produce a profound change in both labor and nation.

The efforts of top trade union leadership to open the doors to the Negro worker, however, do not date from the 1960s. At the time when the American Railway Union, with Debs as its first President, was writing its "white only" clause into its constitution, Samuel Gompers, President of the AFL, was busy trying to persuade the machinist unions—largely of Southern origin—to admit their black brethren. The Report of the Proceedings of the Tenth Annual Convention of the AFL (1890) noted that the Federation from the beginning "looked with disfavor upon trade unions having provisions in their constitutions excluding from membership persons on account of race and color and they requested they be expunged." In line with this, Gompers called upon the machinists to call a unity convention "for the purpose of forming a national union which shall recognize no color line." He found the exclusion clause to be "objectionable and unmanly" and noted, too, that it "accomplished no good." Despite his plea, Gompers failed.

The present pleas of George Meany have also failed to win total compliance. "It would be futile to pretend," he wrote in the spring of 1964, "that the 13½ million members of the AFL-CIO unions are without exception devoted to the cause of civil rights. They are a cross section of America and they reflect the diversity of the nation."

The dilemma of both Gompers and Meany—their dedication to the principle of equal rights, yet their inability to swing the total labor movement into line behind this principle—stems from the structure of the AFL and now the AFL-CIO. The parent body of American labor—the AFL—is not really a parent with parental authority. It is structurally much closer to the Thirteen Colonies under the Articles of Confederation than to the United States under the Constitution. If a national union wishes to secede from the Federation it may do so, unlike the States of the Confederacy, which were told that they did not have the right to disrupt the Union and that the full military force of the United States would be used, as it was, to deny the right of secession. National unions—whether strong or weak—have the right to and do secede from the Federation, as the cases of machinists, miners, garment workers, clothing workers, lithographers, and others prove. The power of the Federation is moral, resting on consensus and persuasion.

Gompers was in the habit of referring to his beloved Federation as a "rope of sand." This loose quality was its vice and virtue, its weakness and strength. The weakness lay in the fact that no convention of the Federation could make firm policy for any of the great national or international affiliates. The Federation could order neither the terms of trade contracts nor the political posture of its highly autonomous members. The strength lay in the fact that, by the grant of such autonomy, it was possible to maintain a continuing liaison and hopefully a growing consensus among the unions and, simultaneously, to stimulate a sense of self-reliance and creativity among the workers of the different trades, crafts, and industries.

The policy of the AFL-CIO is to create a consensus on civil rights policy by 1) avoiding expulsion of national unions wherein discrimination exists; 2) passing legislation for fair employment to include union practices; 3) putting pressure on affiliates through the civil rights committee of the Federation; 4) setting an example through the statements and acts of national unions and actual labor bodies; 5) involving local unions in actions for civil rights.

The AFL-CIO has been most reluctant to expel national affiliates that are out of step with Federation policy on civil rights. The reason lies in the limited effectiveness of this sanction. The Federation feels that expulsion does not change the policy of the excommunicated affiliate and that such severance may indeed freeze the undesirable policy. Hence, where an affiliate has refused to go along with convention decisions on civil rights, the Federation has sought to persuade, to pressure, to educate, to cajole—but not to expel.

To some, this policy of nonexpulsion appears to be hypocritical in view of the Federation's readiness to expel national affiliates tainted by Communism or "corruption." In explaining this apparent inconsistency, President George Meany argues that there is a difference.

> Corruption—like Communism—seizes the leadership of a union and works down to lower levels by perverting the union's democratic procedures. The rank-and-file members are not consciously affected in their daily lives. They don't know what's going on, and they tend to dismiss published charges against the leadership as just another attack by a normally hostile press. Expulsion was the only way to convince the membership of this domination by corrupt elements. . . .
>
> But there is a big difference between corruption and discrimination. Discrimination is resisted at the top but perpetrated below. Discrimination represents the wrongheadedness of rank-and-file members; it is often maintained by unimpeachable democratic processes. Would we be better off to cast out these misguided members and remove them from the influence of the mainstream of the labor movement; meanwhile expelling in the same action the national leaders who deplore and fight discrimination? I think not. I think we can do more toward educating them if they're in the Federation, with their own leaders getting broad AFL-CIO support toward the same end.

In another major respect, there is a difference between unions controlled by Communists or crooks and those infected by racism. The reds and racketeers are part of a "movement," an aggressive conspiracy with inner lines of communication and action, that—unless lopped off—could threaten the very character of the total labor movement. The Communists have their "underground" and the organized corruptionists have their "underworld." They are not content to run a local their way or even to run a national union. They are out to "take over." They don't just dirty the house of labor; they want to boss it. In this respect, they are unlike the segregationists in the labor movement who have no inner ties, no separate power structure, no urge or desire to remake the labor movement in their parochial image. At worst, the segregationists are a vanishing relic, an annoying cultural lag.

Because the AFL-CIO has been so keenly and painfully aware of the limitations imposed upon it by its structure, the Federation has turned to federal legislation as its primary instrument for wiping out discrimination in unions. It is now an open secret that the fair employment practices section of the Civil Rights Act of 1964 was written into the law because of the bullheaded insistence of the AFL-CIO. Early drafts omitted this vital section because it was feared that addition of this tough clause might overload the bill and make passage impossible. It was the AFL-CIO that demanded inclusion. Several times in the course of legislative passage there were moves to lose the burdensome proviso. The AFL-CIO refused to let go.

Testifying before Congress as early as January 23, 1962, Meany noted that he was appearing not to "ask for special exemptions for unions; quite the contrary." He was seeking a fair employment practices act that would "cover the whole range" written into the AFL-CIO constitution. He pleaded that the act "also apply to apprenticeship programs of every kind."

The depth of AFL-CIO feeling on fair employment legislation rests on three logical and one emotional ground.

Logically, labor backs the law because it is 1) morally imperative; 2) needed to tap the untapped skills of the nation; 3) desirable to clean up the image of American democracy before the world. Emotionally, the AFL-CIO feels especially strongly because, as the Federation head complained, "we have been bitterly attacked for failing to achieve what is beyond our power—equality of opportunity in employment."

The AFL-CIO commitment to strong federal legislation on civil rights was not a reaction to the demonstrations following Birmingham. In April of 1960, Meany blasted Congress for its milquetoast version of a civil rights law:

> The Civil Rights Act of 1960 does not fulfill the hopes of the AFL-CIO for a truly meaningful bill. Once again, a small minority in the Congress has succeeded in thwarting the will of the vast majority of Americans who believe in, and wish to implement, the basic constitutional rights which properly belong to all Americans regardless of race or color or national origin.
>
> We regret that the Administration did not at least stand firm for its own very moderate proposals. If it had, the Congress might have retained Administration proposals that would have aided in the desegregation of schools, and would have given statutory authority to the President's Committee on Government Contracts. Similarly, we regret the failure to include Part III.
>
> Whatever little good remains in the new law is due to the conscientious and dedicated work of a relative handful of legislators in both parties whose efforts prevented still further scuttling of the proposed legislation. Unfortunately, they were outnumbered too often by a strange coalition of Southerners whose position was at least understandable, if not commendable, and other members of the Congress whose vacillation on civil rights was completely inexcusable.
>
> It is our hope that despite its obvious shortcomings, the new law will in fact bring some progress in the extension of democracy to millions of our Americans. This will depend in large part on the determination of the executive branch of the federal government to press forward

vigorously in the full enforcement of civil rights laws, both old and new. Such enforcement has fallen short of the mark in the last few years.

The struggle for full freedom in America has never enjoyed a moratorium, from the very first days of the republic to the present. With enactment of the Civil Rights Act of 1960, there must again be no moratorium. The AFL-CIO will be back again asking the 87th Congress to reinforce and to build on the foundation that has been laid so slowly and so weakly.

When Meany returned to the subsequent sessions of Congress he pleaded for strong legislation not to throw stones at "others" but to clean up the house of labor. "The labor movement," he noted in his testimony before the House Judiciary Committee, "has not been the only advocate of civil rights legislation during the last decade; there have been the church groups, and, of course the Negro organizations themselves. But I think it is fair to say that we are the only ones, among the civil rights forces, which has openly called for legislation for the correction of shortcomings *in its own ranks*." Lest there be any mistake as to intent, Meany rubbed in his point before the Senate Committee with the blunt statement, "I want to state emphatically that we want unions covered by equal opportunity legislation."

In taking its stand for equal opportunity—within the trade unions and within the community—the labor movement has had to face the dilemma of long-run versus short-run self-interest. In the long run, self-interest dictates a firm stand for equal treatment to all persons regardless of race. To exclude any group of people from participation in labor's ranks because of origin can only—in the long run—weaken the movement. Unions do depend upon unity. To divide and separate workers—including Caucasians and excluding Negroes—must obviously injure individual unions and, ultimately, the entire movement. A policy of exclusion—pursued consistently—can only create a legion of "dispossessed," driven by hunger and desperation to turn against the unions, a standing army of scabs. And should the excluded ever organize they would do so in a separate and rival trade union movement based on color.

In the short run, however, the stand of the labor movement for equal rights could and, in some respects, has hurt the unions. Southern organizing drives have been slowed down by labor's insistence on integration. Employers have repeatedly appealed to white prejudice to defeat unions in representation elections. In the areas of intense racial conflict, unions have organizationally been hurt by their efforts to wipe out the color line. To protect themselves against these vicious yet effective appeals, unions have asked the National Labor Relations Board to invalidate elections where such racist appeals were involved. In one famous case, a photograph showing electrical workers' union President James Carey dancing with a Negro was the employer's mightiest weapon to turn the "white" vote against the union. Despite union efforts to bar such "unfair" appeals, they continue and continue to be effective.

In the short run, too, labor's stand against discrimination has also been hurtful in producing severe anti-labor legislation, backed by Southern Democratic Congressmen out to punish the trade unions for their support of civil rights legislation. The Landrum-Griffin Act—an extra turn of the Taft-Hartley screw—was one such slash at labor. In the many maneuverings to pass Landrum-Griffin, the Southern delegation was in a pivotal position. Several Southern Congressmen held the balance of power and would have preferred not to go along with the "conservative" coalition in passing the unduly harsh anti-labor act. But to oppose it, these Congressmen needed some assurance from labor that the unions would ease up in their push for civil rights legislation. And when the *quid pro quo* was not forthcoming, the Southern Solons closed ranks as a geographic unit to join their conservative Republican colleagues to enact Landrum-Griffin.

The labor movement was not unaware of the dangers implicit in its equal rights policy. In 1955–56 the headquarters of the AFL-CIO received more than ten thousand individual letters protesting the stand the Federation had taken in support of the Supreme Court decision on school integration. Every one of the letters was answered, stressing one major line of reasoning with the trade union people. The people behind the White Citizens' Councils, argued the AFL-CIO headquarters, are the same people behind the drive to stop unionism: in both cases they were trying to block the progress of working people, denying union rights and denying civil rights. "This message," according to Meany, "opened up the eyes of a great many."

Despite this direct message and despite a massive education campaign, Meany had to admit that "we still have a problem in our ranks." And to meet this problem, the Federation is operating along several fronts. At the Fifth Constitutional Convention of the AFL-CIO, the Secretary-Treasurer of the organization described some of these operational efforts in reporting on the work of the Standing Committee on Civil Rights. As he ticked off the items of progress, each seemed small. But cumulatively they indicate the direction and method of the American labor movement in the push toward integration.

One significant item involved the Brotherhood of Locomotive Firemen and Engineers. On January 7, 1960, Meany wired the President of the Brotherhood: "Earnestly request that you bring to the attention of your convention, now in session, the matter of amending the constitution of your Brotherhood in order to bring it into compliance with the AFL-CIO policy against racial discrimination." Two weeks later Meany was able to "congratulate" the convention on its action that "eliminated the discriminatory constitutional provisions. . . . The trade union movement cannot—and will not—rest until the civil rights battle has been won and the Brotherhood has scored a significant victory in this campaign." The Firemen and Engineers was the *last* international union formally to eliminate the "whites only" clause. The Brotherhood formally recognized the brotherhood of labor that even Eugene Debs was unprepared to grant in the railroad industry some six decades earlier.

Despite this, however, there still were in July 1963, 172 segregated locals among AFL-CIO affiliates out of a total of fifty-five thousand local unions. Of the 130 international union affiliates, 111 had no segregated locals at all. The segregated locals were concentrated among nineteen international unions, where solution of the problem was doubly vexatious because in many cases where integration did not exist the resistance came from Negro locals.

Where all-Negro locals have refused to go along with integration efforts, the labor movement hastens to point out that the motivation can hardly be ascribed to "discrimination." There are other reasons. A local may not wish to be gobbled up by a larger white unit. There are problems of separate funds, of status, of distinct representation at conventions. There are institutional problems: the desire of a leadership not to play second fiddle, nor to lose its role in the community, nor to surrender its special arrangements in the trade or industry. Whatever the reasons —and they are generally either good or understandable— these racially separated locals do constitute a majority of the standouts in the efforts to integrate at the local level.

In the drive to integrate, the most significant advances took place in the South—where separation was most prevalent and most difficult to overcome. In Danville, Virginia, two locals of the United Textile Workers were merged. In the tobacco industry, where segregation was the pattern of employment, the Tobacco Workers integrated ten locals in Richmond, Virginia; in Reidsville, North Carolina; in Louisville, Kentucky. The same union announced favorable progress in Winston-Salem, North Carolina. Two segregated locals of the carpenters in Knoxville, Tennessee, were merged. In Memphis two locals of the American Federation of Government Employees were merged. Aluminum workers reported mergers in Richmond, Virginia, and Sheffield, Alabama. In Atlanta, Georgia, two locals of the American Federation of State, County and Municipal Workers were merged. Among the Pulp, Sulphite and Paper Mill Workers, where segregation was common in the South, there were mergers in Lufkin, Texas; in Savannah, Georgia; and in Calhoun, Tennessee. In the spirit of the new times, when the union chartered locals in Crossett, and North Little Rock, Arkansas, and in Atlanta, Georgia, and in Dallas, Texas, they started life as integrated organizations. The Oil and Chemical Workers merged segregated locals in Beaumont and Port Arthur, Texas.

These individual local mergers represent a drop in the bucket of fifty-five thousand local unions in the AFL-CIO. But, measured against the background of the 170 segregated locals, these itemized mergers, plus others outside the South, are significant in themselves and even more significant as a sign of intent and effort.

A major declaration of policy in this area was the statement of the Building and Construction Trades Department in June 1963, adopted by the General Presidents of the international unions affiliated with the AFL-CIO. In a four-point program they stated:

1. In order to avoid discrimination, local unions are urged to accept into membership any applicant who meets the required qualifications regardless of race, creed, color, or national origin.

2. If a local union has an agreement which provides for, and operates, an exclusive hiring hall, all applicants for employment are to be placed upon the hiring list in accordance with the applicable law and their collective-bargaining agreement. There is to be no identification of applicants as to race, creed, color, or national origin, and they are to be referred without discrimination as their turn comes up on the hiring list, if their qualifications meet those required by the employer.

3. If the local unions do not have an exclusive hiring hall, but do have a referral system set forth in their collective-bargaining agreement, qualified applicants for employment are to be referred without discrimination as to race, creed, color, or national origin.

4. With regard to the application for, or employment of, apprentices, local unions shall accept, and refer, such applicants in accordance with their qualifications and there shall be no discrimination as to race, creed, color, or national origin, and the local unions shall adhere strictly to their apprenticeship standards.

Resolutions and even merger of once-segregated locals do not, however, mean that discriminatory practices have been eliminated in the American labor movement. Resolutions passed at the high level are often ignored at the low level. Many locals that are not formally segregated may be so in fact, simply barring the doors to Negroes. In pleading with the editors of the labor press, Meany urged that they carry on an educational drive among their readers because "there is still a lot to be done. We know that the passing of a resolution by an international union, and I mean in all sincerity, does not guarantee that there will not be pockets of discrimination at the local level. And even if you eliminate it from the structure, you still have the problem of discrimination on the job where you have segregation in fact even though you do not have it in name."

To reach down to the bottom level, the AFL-CIO made two major moves in addition to its other advances through legislation, executive action, national union policies, and broad education. The first move was a directive to central labor bodies to "hold no conventions, meetings, conferences, or educational institutes" that exclude delegates on the basis of race, creed, color, or national origin. This was part of a general move to have the trade unions play a more active role in the local community for civil rights. Following a meeting with President Kennedy in July 1963, the AFL-CIO set up a five-man special committee composed of AFL-CIO Secretary-Treasurer William F. Schnitzler; Walter Reuther, President of the Industrial Union Department; C. J. Haggerty, President of the Building and Construction Trades Department; A. Philip Randolph, President of the Sleeping Car Porters; and President Meany, who chairs the committee. The purpose of the committee and its special task force is to "initiate local community action or give its full support to collective action initiated by other responsible local leadership." To give the task force an extra push, the AFL-CIO called a nationwide conference on civil rights at the height of the national election campaign. The meeting had a dual purpose: to ready the affiliates for the community action effort and to counteract the propaganda in labor's ranks that was aimed at capitalizing on the backlash. International union affiliates were asked to name a top official responsible for keeping an eye on civil rights developments in the unions, especially in regard to nondiscrimination clauses in contracts; affiliates were also asked to make staff-men available to give counsel and guidance to local bodies that were ready to move at the community level.

In addition, international union affiliates were advised 1) to use collective-bargaining confrontations as an opportunity to press for nondiscriminatory hiring and promotion; and 2) to help workers in nonunion employment to make use of the Fair Employment Practices Provisions of the Civil Rights Act as well as state FEPCs. Although the task force reports work in progress in many communities, it is still too early at this writing to make an evaluation of this ambitious effort.

Despite all these efforts—and further drives to come—there are many local unions that have either no Negro members or so few as to count for none. The problem in such locals is especially tough, not because the local discriminates against Negroes but because such locals generally do *not* discriminate against Negroes. The problem in many of these locals is not racial but economic.

The impact of "new workers" on established trade union standards is one of the oldest and least understood problems in labor relations.

In general, the arrival of a new body of workers tends to weaken standards already established by a union. The reason is obvious. It is the old law of supply and demand. A hungry supply of new workers, competing for jobs with those already

373

employed and already organized, obviously puts the employer in a position to pit the newcomers against the older groups.

This inherent friction between the old and the new worker is particularly keen where the available jobs are not growing in number. The difficulty is doubled if the number of available jobs is actually falling. In such situations the newcomer can get the job only *at the expense* of the old-timer.

From the employer's view, it often makes sense to dump the old-timer and replace him with a new man. The latter is younger, probably ready to work for less to begin with just to get the job, and normally less attached to the union. The employer would also like to use the new job applicant as a threat against the worker on the job.

To counter the competitive threat of a surplus number of workers competing for given jobs in a given area, many (not all) trade unions in America have evolved a double practice: first, to guarantee job protection for the union member and to back it up with a seniority clause so that the old-timer will not be "bumped" off the job by the newcomer; second, not to admit a new man to the union unless there is a job opening.

The evolution of this policy has nothing to do with whether the newcomer is black or white, Jew or Gentile, native or foreign. The men on the job—whether they are Negro Pullman porters or white hod carriers—try to protect their jobs by union contracts that prevent an employer from "bumping" an old union member off the job by hiring a newcomer and by union practices that try to avoid over-loading the union membership rolls with more members than there are jobs.

In many cases the newcomers who are trying to get into the union or to replace union men on the job come from exactly the same ethnic group as the old-timers. This makes little difference to the union man who expects that the union will provide job security. Sometimes the newcomers are from a new ethnic group—from another country, another part of the country, another religion or race. In such cases the difficulties faced by the newcomer in breaking into the trade, especially where the number of jobs has been diminishing, looks like discrimination.

The problem is complicated by the fact that in some unions the membership does practice discrimination against new ethnic groups: Jews, Italians, Negroes, Chinese, etc. In such practices these trade unionists are unfortunately reflecting the mores of their communities. And where this does exist, it is a problem in civil rights. But, by and large, such cases are few and far between. The over-all problem, for a new man or woman trying to break into a job in a unionized industry where job openings do not exist, has nothing at all to do with racial or religious discrimination. The problem is simply this: a man on the job will not step out of the job or even share his income with a newcomer—regardless of race, creed, or color. This is a problem in economics—and not in civil rights.

Because nobody is ready to step out of a job in order to make way for someone else because of race, religion, or national origin, the labor movement has consistently opposed any system of preferential hiring or the establishment of racial quotas on jobs. They oppose this in principle because, after many years of effort to persuade employers—and unions —to be color-blind, any proposal to hire on the basis of color would once more reintroduce skin pigmentation as a factor in employment. More practically, however, the unions would find it impossible to establish and enforce any such plan. It would be necessary, for instance, to bypass those waiting for jobs in order to move a Negro to the top of the list. What would the reaction of the white worker be who is left without a job only because he is white? The union would have equal difficulty in determining just how great the racial quota should be. Should the percentage be set at the per cent of Negroes in the local or national population, or the per cent in the trade, or the per cent seeking to enter the trade? If any local union officer should somehow manage to solve these almost insolvable problems, he would have to be a political magician to hold office in his local union against the outraged screams of old dues-payers who would find themselves disemployed because they are white.

Fortunately, this problem of preferential hiring and job quotas has, for the moment, been settled by the Civil Rights Act of 1964, which specifically forbids any such system of hiring or employment.

Still unsettled, however, is the question of how a Negro is to get into a trade or local union where new jobs are few, if any. In such situations there can be a token solution: the admission of a meager but symbolic number of Negroes. But while tokenism may be acceptable as an expression of good will, it is hardly acceptable as substantive relief for the large army of unemployed Negroes in America.

In an unusually tough-minded and realistic editorial, appearing in the official publication of the plumbers' union, its President Peter T. Schoemann proposed a formula to local affiliates that would compose a "compromise" between the "custom of giving preference to sons and others, and the legitimate aspirations of minority groups to end discrimination." In a remarkably blunt statement, Schoemann declares that the plumbers' union "has not tried to conceal or apologize for the system of preferring sons in the building trades. We have campaigned for the right of our programs to select apprentices in the same way that any private business might select employees, or that an elected public official selects his political appointees." Nevertheless, adds Schoemann, the union has a responsibility simultaneously to promote employment and apprenticeship for hitherto-excluded minority groups. The end result should then be something like this:

"If you want to run a patronage system, then go ahead, but show us what patronage you are reserving for members of the minority group."

If, continues Schoemann, the union should prefer a kind of civil service system, where admissions to the apprentice-ship program are strictly on an open competitive basis, then such objective choice should be "followed to the letter." This means, "no point chiseling and no loophole hunting in favor of the member's son, the contractor's nephew, the mayor's brother-in-law, or anyone else."

This formula for total objectivity or for balanced selectivity assumes good faith on the part of those who administer the program locally. And such good faith is least likely when jobs are scarce and most likely when jobs are plentiful.

The only real answer is *more* jobs. In the absence of more jobs, unions are not likely to throw their doors open to new members, nor are they likely to encourage larger apprenticeship programs for anybody—black or white. "It is totally unrealistic," argues the Building and Construction Trades Department, for instance, "to train people in particular crafts in greater numbers than can reasonably be employed." In his report to the Fifth Constitutional Convention of the AFL-CIO (1963), Schnitzler pointed out that the number of apprenticeship openings was on the decline. In the first years of the decade beginning with 1950, there were about 168,000 apprentices per annum. At present, the number has fallen to 100,000. Even if Negroes were to get their mathematical portion of these new apprenticeships (about 10 per cent of the population), this would add only up to 10,000 openings—a drop in an ocean of Negro unemployment.

(It ought to be noted, importantly although parenthetically, that the problem of unions with no Negro members, although real, is generally overstated. The difficulty is limited to skilled trades in crafts with minimal employment turnover historically operating under closed shops. In industries where labor turnover is sizable, as in manufacture, service trades, distribution, public employment, no such restrictions exist. Here the closed shop was never part of the tradition; the doors are normally wide open with workers coming and going. Through these doors have come most of the more than a million Negroes who are members of trade unions. It should also be noted that, all in all, the American trade unions compose, through their membership, only about 30 per cent of the total nonagricultural labor force in America. At best, then, those local unions that have tight controls over new membership—applications for admittance, preapprenticeship requirements, apprenticeship, waiting lists based on seniority—cover a very small part of the total nonagricultural labor force. The number of *new* jobs in these locals per annum composes a trickle into the labor market.)

To open up new apprenticeships, to open up new jobs, to open up union doors—to do all this requires new jobs.

It is for this reason that the labor movement couples *fair* employment with *full* employment. Attempts to move Negroes into jobs and unions in shrinking areas of job opportunity can only create racial conflict. The struggle then becomes a matter of what race is employed.

This does not mean, of course, that Negro integration into certain presently *exclusive* crafts and trades must await the day of full employment in America. It does mean that a meaningful solution is hastened by *expanding* employment aimed at full employment.

A case in point is West Germany, where, for a variety of reasons, the economy has enjoyed an expanding market. As a result, there is a manpower shortage in Germany. To meet this shortage, semiskilled workers were trained by companies to do skilled work. Unskilled were taught basic skills. Workers were brought in from Turkey, with no knowledge of the language and with no special skills at all, to be taught both linguistics and mechanics.

A similar economic growth in America would throw the doors open: factory doors, union doors, the doors of opportunity.

To the American labor movement, full employment is not some unspelled utopia. The unions *do* have a program operating at two levels: unions and government.

At the union level the idea is to up wages and spur purchasing power; to abbreviate the work week to bring more workers into the active labor force; to negotiate supplementary benefits to provide buying power or its equivalent in services during periods of distress, such as illness, joblessness, old age.

At the government level the idea is to use the taxing and

borrowing powers of government as conscious instruments in spurring industrial growth; to fill great social needs by public investment in school construction and teaching, in medical plant and the training of medical and paramedical personnel, in libraries, roads, beaches, parks, housing; to lift the income of the impoverished through extended minimum wages, through training for useful employment, through more adequate social security, through adjustments in unemployment insurance.

Because the labor movement believes that full employment in America can not be achieved through any single act at any one time, the unions are dedicated to a program of continuing political action to enact a many-sided socioeconomic program, intended ultimately to make a job available to anybody who has the will or the way—white or black. It is in the realization of such a program that Negroes and the trade unions have their closest tie. Together they have, for many years, composed two of the major pillars in America's liberal political coalition. That coalition was tested in the great referendum of 1964. The attempt of the Goldwater campaigners to split worker from Negro, to turn unions against civil rights people, to whip wage earners into a racist frenzy under the backlash turned out to be a reverse backlash. The attempted strategy served only to persuade both unionists and Negroes to close ranks and to turn out their maximum strength for an America rich in goods and rich in good will.

The events of 1964—the Negro movement, the Civil Rights Act, the stand of the unions on fair and full employment, and the great liberal victory at the polls— may well serve as a mold for the second half of the twentieth century.

Chapter IX

TRADE UNION RACIAL PRACTICES
AND THE LAW

ROBERT L. CARTER AND MARIA L. MARCUS

The chasm between the average income of Negro and white wage earners has been increasing consistently since 1951.[1] In 1962 the median wage or salary income for nonwhite workers was 55 per cent of that received by white workers. The ability of a Negro to do the same work as a white does not result in the same earnings. Among factory workers, bricklayers, carpenters, and most other occupations there is a substantial difference between white and nonwhite earnings; the Negro college graduate can, on the average, expect less salary over a lifetime than the white who did not go beyond the eighth grade.[2] In 1963, nonwhites comprised 11.7 per cent of the population and 11 per cent of the labor force, but 21 per cent of the unemployed.

Since about eighteen million of the nation's seventy million workers are covered by collective-bargaining agreements, the internal and external practices of labor unions exert a significant effect on the employment opportunities of minority groups, as documented by the United States Commission on Civil Rights, Book 3, Report on Employment 127, 137, 161 (1961). The conduct and policies of both industrial and craft unions have, in many instances, operated to discriminate against Negroes and to prevent hiring and advancement.

Industrial unions organize both the skilled and unskilled and depend on numerical strength within a plant to provide bargaining power. Since the collective-bargaining process in an industrial plant begins only after the work force is established, the union seldom plays a substantial role in hiring. However, through control of the arbitration and grievance machinery and through its authority to negotiate and administer seniority provisions of contracts, the union exercises a significant influence over the future of any employee in the plant. It controls seniority, layoffs, promotion, transfer, recall rights, distribution of overtime, shift preference, and eligibility for vacation and welfare plans. By negotiating collective-bargaining agreements with separate lines of seniority based upon race, some industrial unions confine Negroes to the unskilled and worst-paid positions in the plant. The "Negro" line of seniority generally runs up only through the more menial jobs, and the "white" line of seniority begins at the more skilled level.

The craft unions organize workers according to their skills and the tools they use, rather than by the plant where they work. They strive to control the jobs in their respective skills through union hiring halls, where employers hire only workers referred by the union. Usually they bargain with contractors' associations, and fix uniform wages and working conditions for the particular craft within the union's geographic district. In the construction field each craft union supplies workers in its own skill; since the building contractors' needs for employees vary greatly from day to day, few, if any, maintain a full crew of skilled craftsmen, but instead rely upon the construction unions as their sole or primary source of labor. Because union membership or referral by the union is a practical necessity for obtaining employment on the majority of commercial construction jobs, exclusion of Negroes by craft unions precludes hiring them. Also precluded is apprentice training in these trades, which is usually union controlled and designed to lead to union membership. The previously cited report of the United States Commission on Civil Rights affirmed, on pages 129–31, that there is a uniform pattern of exclusion in some areas of the country by craft unions such as the Iron Workers, Steamfitters, Plumbers, Electrical Workers, and Sheet Metal workers. The purpose of such membership restrictions, which have been of long duration, is described in Northrup, *Organized Labor and the Negro:*

> To exclude Negroes, these craft unionists have found, is a convenient and effective method of limiting the number of sellers of a particular type of labor or skill, and that, in turn, enables the white craftsmen to obtain a larger share of the available work for themselves and/or higher wages.[3]

In the railroad industry, craft unions such as the Brotherhood of Locomotive Firemen and Enginemen exclude Negroes from membership and have a history of attempts to induce the railroads to discharge Negro employees. See *Steele v. Louisville & Nashville R.R.,* 323 U.S. 192; *Tunstall v. Locomotive Firemen and Enginemen,* 323 U.S. 210; and *Howard v. Brotherhood of Railway Trainmen,* 343 U.S. 768

Discrimination by management also contributes to the picture. In manufacturing and industry, where management retains the hiring prerogative, the Commission on Civil Rights noted that in both the North and South some employers tend to hire Negroes only in unskilled nonproduction jobs and to make apprenticeship for skilled positions available solely to white workers.[4] However, in cases where management demonstrates determination to eliminate discrimination, unions may support the policy since they are freed from fear that the company will use the dissension within the union on the racial question in order to weaken the union's bargaining position.[5]

Another factor has been the conduct of state and local officials toward management and union racial bias. In states without fair employment legislation, state officials often abet private discrimination. Some public employment offices, for example, openly base referrals on traditional employment practices in the community—even where federal funds and United States government contractors are involved.[6] In states such as New York where employment discrimination is prohibited by law, lack of enforcement may render the legislative intent sterile. In New York City, for example, the City Commission on Human Rights investigated the building trades and found in December 1963 "a pattern of exclusion in a substantial part of the building and construction industry, which effectively bars nonwhites from participating in this area of the city's economic life"; this situation was found to be partially attributable to "government failure to enforce regulations barring discrimination."[7] Yet more than 980 million dollars in state and city funds is disbursed annually for public construction, although labor in certain skilled crafts on such projects is supplied solely by discriminatory unions. Section 220-e(a) of the Labor Law of New York requires that on public construction projects neither the contractor nor anyone acting on his behalf discriminate racially in hiring, and §220-e(d) specifies that contracts may be canceled if this requirement is breached; however, no contract has ever been canceled under this provision.*

Somewhat analogous to the power of the public officials to curb exclusionary union practices through law is the authority of international unions to deal with such practices through internal regulations. In most instances throughout the country, union discrimination occurs at the local level. International unions, many of which have expressed adherence to equalitarian principles, generally have the power under their constitutions to fine locals, suspend their charters, or to take over their control.[8] In certain instances, internationals have acted forcefully to prevent discrimination; the United Auto Workers placed one of its Southern

---

* When evidence indicated that the plumbers', sheet metal workers', and electrical workers' locals in Cleveland, Ohio were discriminating against Negro applicants for apprenticeship, the United States government (through the President's Committee on Equal Employment Opportunity) determined that no contracts would be awarded to five construction firms which dealt with these unions, until resolution of the situation. *The New York Times*, February 3, 1965, p. 23, col. 1)

locals under trusteeship. The Commission on Civil Rights comments that the examples set by unions such as the Auto Workers demonstrate that internationals can compel their locals to adhere to the civil rights policies of the parent body. However, as might be anticipated, such measures have been taken only by unions which have declared equal opportunity to be one of their goals and usually by unions with a significant number of Negro members "which renders it safe and perhaps even necessary for the leadership to take a firm anti-discrimination stand."[9]

In cases where aggrieved Negro workers cannot obtain redress through internal grievance procedures, a solution must be sought through administrative bodies such as the National Labor Relations Board or in the courts.

The cornerstone of the present protection of Negro workers against discriminatory union contracts and practices is the duty of fair representation, a doctrine which originated in *Steele v. Louisville & Nashville Railroad,* supra, where the United States Supreme Court made an apt analogy between a legislative representative and a union which is a statutory bargaining representative. It was held that the Railway Labor Act (governing employer-employee relations in the railroad industry) imposes on the statutory representative of a craft as exacting a duty to protect equally the interests of the members of the craft as the Constitution imposes upon the members of a legislature to give equal protection to their constituents. The court enjoined performance of a discriminatory contract between the union and the railroad, and ruled that a union which gains statutory prerogatives has a statutory duty to represent non-union or minority union members of the craft "without hostile discrimination, fairly, impartially and in good faith." *Steele* was followed by other cases decided on similar grounds under the Railway Labor Act. See *Tunstall v. Locomotive Firemen and Enginemen,* supra; *Conley v. Gibson,* 355 U.S. 41; *Howard v. Brotherhood of Railway Trainmen,* supra. The same reasoning was applied to cases arising out of the National Labor Relations Act (which regulates aspects of all industries affecting interstate commerce except rail-roads and airlines) in *Syres v. Oil Workers, Local 23*, 350 U.S. 892, and *Wallace v. National Labor Relations Board*, 323 U.S. 248.

While *Steele* and its successors explained the rationale through which the duty of fair representation was read into the Railway Labor Act and the National Labor Relations Act, they did not clarify the question of what—aside from flagrantly hostile discrimination such as an attempt to terminate the jobs of Negro employees—constitutes evidence of unfair representation. Nor were the courts always able to implement these decisions effectively.

An administrative body such as the National Labor Relations Board, with its daily contact with labor problems, has had a better opportunity than the courts to evolve definitions of fair representation in specific situations. The purpose of the National Labor Relations Act in part was "to protect the rights of individual employees in their relation with labor organizations whose activities affect commerce."[10] That the Board should concern itself with racial discrimination as well as with discrimination on the grounds of union activity or inactivity is the logical consequence of the Board's duty to supervise the exercise of federally granted privileges. Much of the present power of labor unions derives from the provisions of the act. Where the union is a majority representative, the employer must bargain with the union,[11] and may not restrain employees in the right to negotiate collectively,[12] nor encourage or discourage union membership.[13] Where the union is certified by the Board, no new election may be held within twelve months,[14] if the union and the employer sign a contract of three years or more, the Board will not hold an election for three years, under the decision in *General Cable Corporation*, 139 NLRB 111 (1962). A large number of unions seek the certified status in order to gain these "no raiding" advantages, although a union may still be a bargaining agent without certification.

The Board had stated for almost twenty years that it

would "police" its certifications to ensure that they would not be used to perpetrate discriminatory acts. In *Larus and Brother Co.*, 62 NLRB 1075, 1083 (1945), the Board said that the statutory bargaining agent must represent all employees in the bargaining unit without racial discrimination. See also *Veneer Products, Inc.*, 81 NLRB 492, 494 (1948). However, in these very cases it was held that segregation and exclusion of Negroes from membership do not indicate or constitute unfair representation. *Atlanta Oak Flooring Co.*, 62 NLRB 973 (1945). The Board continued to issue joint certifications permitting segregated locals to represent workers in the same bargaining unit.

On October 25, 1962 the General Counsel's office of the National Association for the Advancement of Colored People sought to obtain reversal of these cases by bringing a proceeding on behalf of a Negro local of the Independent Metal Workers Union in Houston, Texas, to rescind the certification of the all-white Local 1 of the same union. Local 1 was jointly certified with the Negro local to represent employees at the Hughes Tool Company. The white local had sole bargaining power, and carried its segregated membership policies over into the bargaining contract under which white employees held the more skilled jobs while Negroes were confined to the unskilled work and excluded from apprentice training programs. In 1961 this contract was put into effect even though the Negro local would not sign it. The white local refused to process the grievance of a Negro employee deprived on racial grounds of the opportunity for apprenticeship. It also resisted the attempt of the company to institute a nondiscriminatory policy after the receipt of a United States government contract.

The argument of the NAACP with respect to rescission was that segregated unionism is inevitably accompanied by discrimination in collective bargaining. Racial exclusion is both the symptom and the cause of unfair treatment of Negro workers. On the one hand, it is the attitude of racial discrimination that leads to the establishment of racial criteria for full membership. On the other hand, the fact that Negroes have no role in the formulation of bargaining policies in an all-white union leads to discrimination in the contract and its administration. Thus, segregation or exclusion from membership is incompatible with the duty of fair representation, and is cause for rescission of a union's certification. The National Labor Relations Board's Trial Examiner adopted this view, and recommended that the certification of Local 1 be rescinded.

On July 2, 1964 the National Labor Relations Board affirmed the Examiner's report and held that it expressly overruled all prior decisions which had held that unions excluding employees from membership on racial grounds could obtain or retain certified status under the act—*Independent Metal Workers Union, Local No. 1 and Hughes Tool Company*, 56 LRRM 1289 (1964). The Board also based rescission on Local 1's negotiation of racially discriminatory contracts, citing the prior case of *Pioneer Bus Co., Inc.*, 140 NLRB 54 (1962).

The decision in *Hughes Tool* was a landmark not only in dealing with the Board's powers to strip unions of the advantages of certification, but also in applying the unfair labor practice sections of the act to racial discrimination. The Board has broad powers to order injunctive and affirmative relief against unions which commit one of the unfair labor practices described in Section 8. The proscribed practices involve restraints on the organizational rights of employees.* Prior to 1962 these sections had been held by the Board and the courts to relate only to discrimination based on union affiliation or nonaffiliation, and to have no application to racial discrimination.

This rule was abrogated in *Hughes Tool*. The Board

---

* Section 8 (b)(1)(A) forbids a union to restrain or coerce employees in the exercise of the right to bargain collectively or the right to refrain from bargaining collectively. Section 8 (b)(2) prevents an attempt by a union to cause an employee to discriminate against an employee for membership or nonmembership in a union. Section 8 (b)(3) requires the statutory representative to bargain collectively with the employer.

dealt with the conduct of Local 1 not only in the context of rescission of certification, but also in relation to Section 8 offenses. It held that a statutory bargaining representative may neither refuse representation to employees on racial grounds nor make bargaining decisions on the arbitrary basis of race, and indicated that racial segregation in membership and the negotiation of racially discriminatory contracts constitute unfair labor practices. In so ruling, the Board was in effect reading the duty of fair representation into the unfair labor practice sections, and thus extending its enforcement powers in racial discrimination cases beyond rescission of certification.

Once it had been ruled that separate lines of job progression grounded on race were violative of the act, the union was obligated to extinguish racial seniority considerations and to merge the two lines. The practical problem was the basis of the merger. If plant seniority was to govern, Negroes would be permitted to qualify for skilled positions on the formerly white line if they had been employed in the plant for a longer time than those on the white line. However, if departmental seniority was to govern, Negroes seeking promotion to a skilled department would have to take a position at the bottom of the white line regardless of their length of service in the plant. In addition, they would lose their old departmental seniority and so be vulnerable to layoff. The problem was solved at the Hughes Tool plant by agreement that the merger would be substantially on the basis of plant seniority.

In the absence of such an agreement, however, the question whether previously segregated Negro workers have a legal right to retain the equivalent of plant seniority is still debatable. The court in *Whitfield v. United Steelworkers,* 263 F. 2d 546 551 (5th Cir., 1959), cert. denied, 360 U.S. 902, found that a union had acted unlawfully in refusing Negroes the opportunity to qualify for skilled jobs, but that the illegality was cured by allowing Negroes to transfer to the bottom of the white line of promotion.

An opposite conclusion was reached in *United Auto Workers and Hugh McRoberts*, 57 LRRM 1298 (1964). Here, a predominantly Negro union sought to put white employees transferring from one department to the other at the bottom of the ladder as to seniority. The rationale of the union was that these white employees had accumulated seniority only through the previous system of segregation. The Board held that this was an arbitrary deprivation of seniority rights which could not be permitted, and the transferring workers were permitted to carry over their seniority. In future cases the Board will undoubtedly be asked to formulate its position on the question in light of the sterility of a transfer right at the cost of all previous seniority.

Further ramifications of the Board's authority to deal with union bias were spelled out in *Local 1367, International Longshoremen's Association, and Galveston Maritime Association, Inc.*, 57 LRRM 1083 (1964), a case following *Hughes Tool*. The union maintained segregated longshoremen's locals. The white local established a 75-25 per cent work distribution between the two, allotting three fourths of the work to its own members, and also maintained a "no doubling" arrangement, forbidding the assignment of white and Negro gangs to work together in ship hatches. The Board found unfair labor practices in the failure to bargain fairly on racial grounds, and held that the duty to bargain was owed not only to the employer but also to the employees the union represents. A union cannot exercise good faith toward an employer while simultaneously acting in bad faith toward employees in regard to the same matter.

Hughes Tool and *Local 1367* were concerned with protecting the rights of Negroes to participate in the collective-bargaining process, and these decisions recognized that the opportunity for membership is of critical importance. Once the union representing the majority has made a contract with the employer, members of the bargaining unit are deprived under the doctrine of *J. I Case v. National Labor Relations Board*, 321 U.S. 332, of any right to bargain for themselves or to obtain mutual aid or protection through any source other than the union.

The desire to ensure responsiveness of union leaders to the membership was the legislative motive behind the passage of the Labor-Management Reporting and Disclosure Act (Landrum-Griffin), which established standards of union democracy. Senate discussions (see Senate Report No. 1684,4) concluded that the best guarantee of fair representation is free and periodic elections.

Periodic elections are of value to Negro employees only when they are members with the right to vote for officers. Membership will ensure their opportunity to present their views and the possibility of reforming the union from within. In addition, the recognition by union officers that the support of a minority may be pivotal in a future decision will help to assure fair treatment.

However, discrimination against Negroes may sometimes continue even after they become members, where the officers of a union make decisions on a racial basis in order to win favor with the white majority. Guarantees in the union constitution of Negro representation among the officers, which is sometimes suggested as a solution to this problem, has the drawback that quota systems seem inconsistent with the goal of achieving nondiscrimination. The case of *Local No. 12, United Rubber Workers*, 57 LRRM 1535 (1964) sought to develop the needed safeguards for minority union members. The NAACP represented Negro members of the Rubber Workers Union at the Goodyear Tire and Rubber Company in Gadsden, Alabama. The union had maintained prior separate seniority rosters on a racial basis, and skilled jobs had been allocated to white employees only. After the company received a United States government contract and had covenanted not to discriminate racially, the union agreed orally in March 1962 to cease interpreting its contract as authorizing racial discrimination in jobs and seniority. However, at the time of trial the union still refused to process a grievance concerning back pay for Negro employees who had been laid off (under the prior unlawful application of the collective-bargaining agreement) while white employees with less or no seniority continued on the job. In addition, there was plantwide segregation in toilet, restroom, and dining facilities, and a plant golf course for employees excluded Negroes. The union not only rejected a grievance concerning plant segregation, but stated that it would "actively oppose" any attempt to integrate the facilities. The Negro employees appealed to the President of the international union, who directed the local to process the grievance, but this direction was not followed.

The Trial Examiner found no unfair labor practice in Local 12's conduct, ruling that the union's position was justified by the "wide range of discretion" allowed to a statutory bargaining representative in determining the demands to be made and when to make them.

The National Labor Relations Board reversed the Trial Examiner, holding that the range of discretion allowed to a union included only consideration of factors such as relevant skills and seniority, and that there was no "discretion" to discriminate on the clearly arbitrary and hostile basis of race.

On the issue of segregated plant facilities, the Board made a thorough analysis of the effect of such segregation on equality of opportunity, finding that it limited job and promotional chances for Negroes. Studies were cited to show that the financial cost to an employer of installing and maintaining segregated facilities for Negroes constitutes a barrier to hiring them for jobs other than those already open to Negroes; such a barrier is equally present in promotions and transfers.

The United States Court of Appeals for the Fifth Circuit, in a landmark decision, granted enforcement of the Board's order. *Local 12, United Rubber Workers v. NLRB,* 368 F. 2d 12 (5th Cir., 1966). The court cited past decisions which affirmed that when individual employees are required by federal law to surrender their right of self-representation to an exclusive bargaining agent, this agent has a duty to refrain from hostile acts against them. The Fifth Circuit was the first federal court to go one step further and answer in the affirmative the controversial question of whether a violation of the obligation of fair representation in itself constitutes an unfair labor practice. Under this ruling, the Board is given sanction to use its powers of injunction against discriminatory unions. A contrary conclusion arrived at by the Second Circuit in *NLRB v. Miranda Fuel Company*, 326 F. 2d 172 (2nd Cir., 1963) was rejected.

The court also faced squarely the question of whether discrimination which has no relation to union affiliation or lack of affiliation can be treated by the Board as a violation of Section 8—i.e. does a union member receive the same protection from the misuse of union power as a nonmember? It was held that a broad construction which would include members was mandated both by the language of the National Labor Relations Act and by the need to protect the right to fair representation in the area of union administration of the bargaining agreement.

Local 12 of the Rubber Workers has filed a petition for writ of *certiorari* in the United States Supreme Court, asking for review of the Fifth Circuit's decision. The case has caused widespread uneasiness among labor unions, which have criticized the role of the NAACP. The NAACP's program, however, has not been based on hostility to collective bargaining or self-organization; on the contrary, it has been concerned with developing genuine solidarity and cooperation on an equal basis between workers of both races. The National Labor Relations Board decisions should strengthen the power of international unions to deal with discriminatory locals, since an illegality in the activities of such locals would furnish a logical ground for intervention or trusteeship.

In summary, present interpretations of the National Labor Relations Act provide that union discrimination against a

Negro employee—when based solely on that employee's race—may lead to rescission of certification and the issuance of injunctions against such conduct. Cases of this kind will probably be tried before the Board rather than in the courts because, by virtue of the United States Supreme Court's decision in *San Diego Building Trades Council v. Garmon*, 359 *U.S.* 236, matters which are "arguably subject to Section 7 or Section 8 of the Act" are reserved for National Labor Relations Board adjudication. The decision of the United States Court of Appeals in the *Rubber Workers* case supports this view. However, the Fifth Circuit made clear that as to cases filed before the Equal Employment Opportunity Commission (EEOC), jurisdiction would be concurrent and complainants would be at liberty to seek redress either before the Board or before the EEOC.

Certain categories of cases, however, might be viewed by the Board as outside the ambit of National Labor Relations Act precedent. The protection of Negro workers under the act derives primarily from the duty of fair representation. Thus, where the complainant is not working for the employer with whom the union is dealing and is not a member of the bargaining unit, the union has no duty to represent him. For example, where craft unions discriminate racially through membership restrictions which foreclose the opportunity to be hired, the discriminatee is outside the closed circle, and the Board's decisions dealing with racial bias may be inapplicable. Unfair labor practice charges could be grounded on the theory that a hiring hall may not refuse referral because of nonmembership in the union, but the discriminatee would remain a nonmember. Moreover, where such a union rejects an applicant for apprenticeship on racial grounds, there is no recourse under the act. Thus, legal challenges in such instances of racial exclusion must be brought in the courts, before state administrative bodies, or before the Equal Employment Opportunity Commission in Washington.

In the case of *Todd, et al. v. Joint Apprenticeship Com-*

mittee, et al., 223 F. Supp. 12, 21–22 (N.D. Ill. 1963), vacated for mootness, 332 F. 2d 243 (7th Cir., 1964), a union that did the hiring for certain crafts on the construction of a United States courthouse discriminated against Negro apprentice applicants. The General Services Administration of the United States, which let the contract, had attempted to eliminate the discrimination. Nevertheless, it was held to have ". . . aided in the perpetration of the Joint Committee and unions' discriminatory policies . . . by making it possible for the Union and Joint Committee to function on a Government Building Project." This governmental participation gave the federal court jurisdiction and the contractor was ordered to hire the qualified Negro applicants.

A broader attack, also based upon governmental responsibility, was launched in the New York State courts in *Gaynor v. Rockefeller*, 15 N.Y. 2d 120, 204 N.E. 2d 627, 256 N.Y.S. 2d 584 (1965). There, Negro journeymen and apprentice applicants in various construction crafts had been denied admission by the unions, which had a monopoly on the learning and utilization of the applicants' respective skills. Since these unions were the sole source of workers on public construction projects in the New York City area, plaintiffs brought suit to challenge the expenditure of public funds on such projects. Defendants were the state and city officials responsible for the disbursement of these funds, and nine unions whose geographic area was New York City. The allegation that the crews in certain skilled crafts on these projects were all white was not denied, nor could it be contended that this resulted from the unavailability of qualified Negroes. The central legal issue was whether there is prohibited "state action" under the equal protection clause of the Fourteenth Amendment to the United States Constitution when public funds are channeled to private discriminatory organizations. The federal courts have answered this question in the affirmative whenever such expenditure of public monies is intended for the accomplishment of public purposes and is thus performed under the aegis of the state.*

The New York Court of Appeals rejected these analogies, holding that there was no governmental responsibility because the unions were not state agents or repositories of state power. Also rejected, without explicit analysis, was the plaintiffs' argument that since governmental officials are accountable for discrimination of lessees in public facilities (*Burton v. Wilmington Parking Authority*, 365 U.S. 715), they should also be accountable for discrimination by the builders of such public facilities; in both situations there is mutual interdependence and a public purpose. The decision of the Court of Appeals was also based on the discretion permitted public officials in the making or canceling of construction contracts, and on the existence of what the court felt was an adequate remedy before the State Commission for Human Rights. The court enumerated the "cease and desist" and affirmative powers of the Commission, which was created to enforce state anti-discrimination laws.

What was sought by the plaintiffs in the *Gaynor* case was to accomplish in one lawsuit the desegregation of all public construction projects where labor was recruited by the nine defendant unions. The ruling of the court in effect confined such suits to a project-by-project and union-by-union desegregation procedure. Within this more limited framework, the Attorney General of New York has been successful in dealing with some individual unions that maintained racial barriers.

An outstanding case of this kind was *Lefkowitz v. Farrell, et al.* [*Case No. C 9287–63*, brought before the State Commission for Human Rights], affirmed sub. nom. *State Commission for Human Rights v. Farrell*, 43 Misc.

---

* See *Simkins v. Moses H. Cone Memorial Hospital*, 323 F. 2d 959 (4th Cir., 1963), cert. denied, 376 U.S. 938, where a private hospital discriminating against Negro physicians and dentists received federal funds; and *Pettaway v. County School Board of Surry County, Va.*, 230 F. Supp. 480 (E.D. Va., 1964), where public funds financed segregated private schools.

2d 958, 252 N.Y.S. 2d 649 (1964), which was decided while the *Gaynor* case was in litigation in the state courts. Air Force veteran Ballard, a Negro, had been denied admission to the apprentice training program of Local 28 of the Sheet Metal Workers Association AFL-CIO. This union had in the past maintained express prohibitions against the admission of Negroes in its constitution. These prohibitions were nominally dropped some years previous to Ballard's application, but tacit barriers remained in effect. Ballard was rejected while whites applying later were accepted. A violation of Executive Law 296(b) was charged, and trial before the State Commission established that the reason for complainant's rejection was racial. The union was ordered not only to admit Ballard, but to alter all policies designed to exclude Negroes as a class. The decision was affirmed by the Appellate Division of the Supreme Court, which worked out a remarkable settlement setting up procedures whereby admission was to be governed by the time of application and the score on an objectively graded citywide test. Pursuant to action by the Attorney General and the Commission, a later decision in the same case rejected the union's attempt to limit and reduce the size of its apprenticeship class after the reorganizing process had guaranteed nondiscrimination in its apprenticeship admissions—*State Commission for Human Rights v. Farrell*, 60 LRRM 2179 (1965). The case is unique because of its effective reorganization of the whole process of Local 28's selection of apprentices.

An interesting sequel to this decision occurred when the Workers Defense League began to give tutoring to Negro and Puerto Rican applicants for sheet metal apprenticeship. The young men came to class every evening and all day Saturday for a total of seventy-five hours of instruction by a teacher who had previously given classes for gifted children in Yonkers. They did so well on the entrance examination that the union tried to destroy their test scores, calling them "statistically improbable" for persons of the educational background which these Negroes and Puerto Ricans had. The Attorney General and the State

Commission for Human Rights were parties in subsequent litigation brought in the state Supreme Court to enjoin the union from rejecting the tests. The NAACP, as *amicus curiae*, submitted an affidavit of the distinguished psychologist Dr. Kenneth Clark, countering the assertion that mental ability is "crystallized in childhood." Dr. Clark brought out the dramatic developmental changes which can be achieved by a gifted instructor working with highly motivated young people. The state Supreme Court totally rejected the contention of Sheet Metal Workers Local 28 and the Joint Apprenticeship Committee that they were justified in refusing the Negro applicants because of theories of "probability" suggested by an official of the New York University Testing Center. The court, and subsequently the Appellate Division, established that since there was obviously no fraud or misconduct involved on the part of anyone, the results must stand.

Other state commissions throughout the country will be under pressure to evolve meaningful remedies for discrimination, because of the provisions of the Civil Rights Act of 1964. Title VII of the act creates the Equal Employment Opportunity Commission, to which reference has previously been made. The EEOC has the power to conciliate cases of racial discrimination by labor unions and employers in industries affecting commerce. If the discrimination occurs in a state which has a fair employment law, the complainant must first file his grievance with the appropriate state commission; the federal commission will take no action until it has notified the proper state officials and given them a reasonable time to remedy the complaint under state or local law—Section 706(c).

If the state commission does not act, the EEOC then begins its negotiations. No enforcement powers have been granted to the EEOC. As originally envisioned, however, the EEOC (like the National Labor Relations Board) was to have been authorized to prevent discrimination through "cease and desist" orders, to award back pay, and to order reinstatement—see H.R. 405, 88th Congress, First Session,

Section 9(j) (1963). However, crucial changes made in the bill before its passage, denied the Commission the right to go to court—see Section 706(e)—and transformed it into a conciliatory and advisory body.

Thus, the legislation as it now stands gives primarily a private remedy. Thirty days after the Commission notifies a grievant that it has been unable to obtain voluntary compliance with Title VII, the grievant has the right to apply to the federal courts for relief under Section 706(e). Such a suit is a somewhat difficult and expensive proposition for the litigant, since the Commission (unlike the National Labor Relations Board) does not assume expenses nor does it provide attorneys. However, "in such circumstances as the court may deem just," an attorney may be appointed by the court for the complainant under Section 706(e). The public interest in the enforcement of Title VII is represented by the Attorney General, who may bring a civil action in the United States district courts for injunctive relief against any persons responsible for a pattern or practice of discrimination outlawed under the act. Thus, the effective enforcement of Title VII of the Civil Rights Act will in great measure depend upon the policies of the President of the United States and his instructions to the Attorney General and the Justice Department.

The strictures of the Civil Rights Act will be particularly relevant to discrimination by the craft unions, since Section 701(e)(1) provides that a labor organization is deemed to be in an industry affecting interstate commerce if it maintains or operates a hiring hall which procures workers for an employer. For the first time, craft unions in Southern states—or Northern states without anti-discrimination policies—will be legally accountable for rejecting applicants for apprentice training on racial grounds—Section 703(d). It is the opportunity for training which will be of vital significance to Negroes seeking to avoid relegation to unskilled positions that may be eliminated by automation.

Thus, federal and state laws in combination have now established fair standards of union activity in racial situations. The articulation and enforcement of such standards will not ultimately damage unionism. Employees when weighing a commitment to racial segregation and exclusion against the possibility of losing the higher wages and other advantages accruing from bargaining collectively have often chosen to give up discriminatory policies.[15]

Unions themselves are aware of the change in their status since the early cases which held that a labor organization was, like a social club, a private association with the right to determine its own eligibility requirements. *Mayer v. Journeymen Stonecutters Association,* 20 *Atl.* 492 (Ch. 1890). A social club has no control over the working conditions of nonmembers—the only benefit it offers and can withhold is that of membership itself. By contrast, a statutory bargaining representative, in its execution and administration of collective-bargaining contracts, has powers which resemble that of a legislature. With these powers comes the responsibility of fair representation and its legal concomitants.

ADDENDUM

Since the writing of this chapter the United States Supreme Court has refused to review Local 12, *United Rubber Workers v. National Labor Relations Board, supra.* This means that the decision of the Court of Appeals for the 5th Circuit, cited above, that a violation of the obligation of fair representation in itself constitutes an unfair labor practice under Section 8 of the National Labor Relations Act, stands. This seems to be the trend of the law. The Court of Appeals for the District of Columbia in *Truck Drivers and Helpers, Local Union 568 v. National Labor Relations Board,* 379 F.2d 137 (1967) has interpreted the reach of the act to the same effect. It is difficult to speculate as to why the Supreme Court declined to review this case, but it probably concluded that the issues raised had been decided in *Vaca v. Sipes,* 386 U.S. 171 (decided last term, February 1967). In that case the Court assumed without deciding that the National Labor Relations Board might properly find a breach of the duty of fair representation to be a Section 8 violation of the act. The main issue before the Court, on which it divided, was whether the Board's jurisdiction in cases of this kind was exclusive. In this respect a majority of the Court disagreed with the view of the Court of Appeals for the 5th Circuit in the *Rubber Workers Case.*

The other important decision was *Ethridge v. Rhodes*, 268 F. Sup. 83 (S.D. Ohio 1967) in another action brought by the NAACP. There the court enjoined the state of Ohio from entering into a contract for the building of a medical center on Ohio State University grounds. The *ratio decidendi* of the court's decision was that the state was barred by the Fourteenth Amendment from entering into a contract for public construction until and unless the state was assured that the contractor secured and obtained his labor supply from a non-discriminatory source. In short, what had been unsuccessfully sought in *Gaynor v. Rockefeller, supra* was obtained in this case. It should have very definite effects on the future development of the law against discrimination in employment.

NOTES

CHAPTER I

1. Sterling D. Spero and Abram L. Harris, *The Black Worker* (New York, 1931), 1–23, 31; Charles H. Wesley, *Negro Labor in the United States* (New York, 1927), 157–62.

2. Wesley, *Negro Labor in the United States*, 173.

3. W. E. B. Du Bois, ed., *Economic Co-operation Among Negro Americans* (Atlanta, 1907), 152–53; African Methodist Episcopal Church *Review* VII (April 1891), 351–56; George Freeman Bragg, *Men of Maryland* (Baltimore, 2nd. ed., 1925), 94–98.

4. *Proceedings of the Colored National Labor Convention . . . 1869* (Washington, D.C., 1870), 37–40, 45–46, 11, 17–19, 30–31, 20.

5. *New National Era*, Jan. 19, 1871.

6. Spero and Harris, *The Black Worker*, 28–30.

7. Wesley, *Negro Labor in the United States*, 163.

8. Herbert Gutman, "Peter H. Clark: Pioneer Negro Socialist, 1877," *Journal of Negro Education*, XLIV (1965), 413–18.

9. Frederick Douglass, *Three Addresses* (Washington, D.C., 1886), 11–12.

10. John R. Lynch, "Should Colored Men Join Labor Organizations?," African Methodist Episcopal Church *Review* III (Oct. 1886), 165, 167.

11. Cleveland *Gazette*, July 17, 1886; Washington *Bee*, Feb. 27, March 20, 1886; Sidney Kessler, "The Organization of Negroes in the Knights of Labor," *Journal of Negro History* XXXVII (July 1952), 273.

12. *Christian Recorder*, Dec. 3, 1885; Indianapolis *Freeman*, Dec. 2, 1886.

13. D. A. Straker, *The New South Investigated* (Detroit, 1888), 194–95, 74, 91, 94, 168–69, 174, 185, 186–87, 189.

14. T. McCants Stewart, "Popular Discontent," African Methodist Episcopal Church *Review* VII (April 1891), 365–69.

15. T. Thomas Fortune, *Black and White* (New York, 1884), 3, 4, 34–36, 238, 239.

16. Ibid., 140–41, 173–74, 223, 150–51.

17. Ibid., 174–75, 235–36, 241–42.

18. New York *Freeman*, March 20, 1886.

19. New York *Age*, Dec. 13, 1890.

20. Ibid., Jan. 2, 1892; Aug. 8, 1907.

21. Bernard Mandel. "Samuel Gompers and the Negro Workers, 1886–1914," *Journal of Negro History* XL (Jan. 1955), 234–60.

22. *Christian Recorder*, July 19, 1894.

23. Cyrus F. Adams, *The National Afro-American Council . . . A History . . .* (Washington, D.C., 1902), 7.

24. Washington *Colored American*, Oct. 8, 1898.

25. A. P. Drucker, et al., *The Colored People of Chicago* (Chicago, 1915), unpaged.

26. Washington, *My Larger Education* (New York, 1911), 76–77, 73–74. For analysis of Washington's ideology see August Meier, *Negro Thought in America, 1880–1915: Racial Ideologies in the Age of Booker T. Washington,* (Ann Arbor, 1963), chap. VII.

27. Telegram from Washington to St. Louis *Post-Dispatch*, Nov. 18, 1910, Washington Papers. Actually it is unlikely that Washington ever belonged to the Knights. He worked as a coal miner before 1872, while the Knights, which began as a secret order in 1869, did not expand into West Virginia until several years later.

28. Washington, *Up From Slavery* (Garden City, N.Y., 1901), 68–69.

29. Washington, *The Future of the American Negro* (Boston, 1899), 78–79.

30. Washington, "The Best Free Labor in the World," in *Southern Estates Farm Magazine*, Jan. 1898, 496–98; clipping in Washington Papers.

31. Washington, "The Negro and the Labor Unions," *Atlantic Monthly* CI (June 1913), 756–57.

32. Du Bois, *The Philadelphia Negro* (Philadelphia, 1899), 368–84; Du Bois, *The Negro Artisan* (Atlanta, 1902), 23.

33. Du Bois to I. M. Rubinow, Nov. 17, 1904, Du Bois Papers. (All references to correspondence and manuscripts in the Du Bois Papers are to Francis L. Borderick's notes on the Du Bois Papers, on file at the Schomburg Collection of the New York Public Library.) Du Bois, "Socialist of the Path," *Horizon* I (Feb. 1907), 7; Du Bois, "The Economic Revolution in the South," in Washington and Du Bois, *The Negro in the South* (Philadelphia, 1907), 116; Du Bois, "The Negro and Socialists," *Horizon* I (Feb. 1907), 7; Du Bois, "A Field for Socialists," MS, Du Bois Papers, ca. 1907.

34. Niagara Movement, *Declaration of Principles* (leaflet), 1905; Washington *Bee*, July 22, 1905.

35. Mary White Ovington to Du Bois, April 24, 1903; Du Bois Papers; Elliott M. Rudwick, *W. E. B. Du Bois: A Study in Minor-*

ity Group Leadership (Philadelphia, 1960), 110; Du Bois, "Niagara Movement," *Horizon* VI (Nov. 1909), 9.

36. Rudwick, *W. E. B. Du Bois*, 118; Du Bois, "Talk No. Three," *Horizon* IV (Aug. 1908), 5–7, "The Negro Vote," *Horizon* IV (Sept. 1908), and "Talk No. Five," *Horizon* IV (Sept. 1908), 7–8.

37. *Proceedings of the National Negro Conference . . . 1909* (New York, 1909), 80–87.

38. *Crisis* IV (July 1912), 131; XV (March 1918), 216.

39. Ibid., IV (July 1912), 131; XV (March 1918), 217.

40. Ibid., II (Oct. 1911), 254; VI (May 1913), 39; VI (June 1913), 71, 91; VI (July 1913), 144.

41. Ibid., XIII (Jan. 1917), 115, 134–35.

42. Elliott M. Rudwick, *Race Riot at East St. Louis* (Carbondale, Ill., 1964), 23–24; *Crisis* XIV (July 1917), 114.

43. Rudwick, *Race Riot at East St. Louis*, 74–94; *Crisis* XIV (Sept. 1917), 215–16, 220–21, and XV (March 1918), 216.

44. Washington *Bee*, July 14, 1917; Cleveland *Gazette*, July 21, 1917; California *Eagle*, July 17, 1917; *Crisis* XV (March 1918), 243; XVIII (Sept. 1919), 239–41; *Minutes of the NAACP National Board*, 1918–19, passim.

45. For a treatment of the ways in which racial advancement organizations have dealt with the racist policies of trade unions since the First World War see August Meier, "Approaches of Civil Rights Organizations to the Problem of Negro Employment," in Arthur M. Ross and Herbert Hill, eds., *Employment, Race, and Poverty* (New York, 1967).

CHAPTER II

1. Robert V. Bruce, *1877: Year of Violence* (Indianapolis, 1959), 292–94; Andrew Roy, *A History of the Coal Miners of the United States* (Columbus, 1906), 353.

2. "Testimony of John Mitchell, April 11, 1899," *Report of the Industrial Commission*, VII (Washington, D.C., 1901), 51–53.

3. Ibid., 31–32, 51–53.

4. "Testimony of W. C. Pearce," ibid., 101.

5. Ibid., 30–58, 101, 136, 149.

6. See the tables and other statistical materials in Sterling D. Spero and Abram L. Harris, *The Black Worker: The Negro and the Labor Movement* (New York, 1931), 209, 215; and in Herbert R. Northrup, "The Negro and the United Mine Workers of America," *Southern Economic Journal* (April 1943), 314.

7. *Report of the Immigration Commission. Immigrants in Industries*, VI and VII, (Washington, D.C., 1911), passim; *Report*

of the Industrial Commission, XV (Washington, D.C., 1901), 405–7 and passim; Frank Julian Warne, *The Coal Mine Workers: A Study in Labor Organization* (New York, 1905), passim, and *The Slav Invasion and the Mine Workers: A Study in Immigration* (Philadelphia, 1904), passim. The Industrial Commission made interesting but as yet unexplored observations about the impact of ethnic diversity on American trade union organization. "This problem of mixed nationalities," it concluded, "results in at least one novelty in the method of organization of American labor unions compared with those of other countries, namely, branch organization based on race." The Commission found that this pattern tended to disappear as "the races assimilate or the needs of the industry dictate." In the UMW, it found disappearance of this form of organization by 1900. Whether or not this "principle" affected unions that organized Negroes into separate locals before 1900 has not yet been studied fully. But the Commission found, for example, that in 1886 the Chicago hod carriers first formed an ineffective "mixed" union of all nationalities. In 1896 it set up a "council" that included representatives from four locals: A German-speaking local with a few Negro members, a Bohemian local, a Polish local, and an English-speaking local that included Italians and Swedes along with 250 to 300 Negroes. (*Report of the Industrial Commission,* op. cit., 313, 426–28.)

8. Brief biographical sketches of Davis are found in the *United Mine Workers' Journal,* April 23, 1896 and January 25, 1900 (hereafter cited as *UMWJ*).

9. Richard L. Davis to the editor, *UMWJ,* Feb. 28, 1895 (hereafter cited as RLD).

10. RLD to the editor, *UMWJ,* April 30, 1896.

11. RLD to the editor, ibid., Feb. 11, 1897.

12. RLD to the editor, ibid., Sept. 10, 1896.

13. "Editorial Note," ibid., Sept. 10, 1896.

14. RLD to the editor, ibid., Dec. 17, 1896.

15. RLD to the editor, ibid., May 19, 1898.

16. "Old Dog" to the editor, ibid., May 12, 1898.

17. RLD to the editor, ibid., Dec. 8, 1898.

18. Ibid., Jan. 25, 1900.

19. Ibid., Jan. 25, 1900.

20. Ibid., Feb. 21, 1895 and April 23, 1896, and RLD to the editor, Feb. 28, 1895.

21. Ibid., April 23, 1896.

22. In 1897 Davis got 124 votes and the candidate ahead of him netted 156 votes (ibid., Jan. 21, 1897). Details on the 1898 election appear in ibid., Dec. 22, 1897 and Jan. 20, 1898.

23. Ibid., April 23, 1896.

24. RLD to the editor, ibid., April 30, 1896.

25. RLD to the editor, ibid., Feb. 11, 1897.
26. RLD to the editor, ibid., March 3 and 10, 1898.
27. RLD to the editor, ibid., Aug. 15, 1895.
28. RLD to the editor, ibid., April 18, 1892.
29. Herbert G. Gutman, "Reconstruction in Ohio: Negroes in the Hocking Valley Coal Mines in 1873 and 1874," *Labor History* III (Fall 1962), 244–64.
30. Some clues about the union life of Ohio miners in the 1880s are found in Roy, op. cit., 221–32.
31. RLD to the editor, ibid., Aug. 4, 1892.
32. RLD to the editor, ibid., July 21 and 28, 1892.
33. F. H. Jackson to the editor, ibid., Aug. 11, 1892.
34. RLD to the editor, ibid., Aug. 4, 1892.
35. RLD to the editor, ibid., Aug. 11 and Oct. 2, 1892.
36. Davis wrote four letters about the Congo mines in ibid., Sept. 15 and 22 and Oct. 6 and 20, 1892.
37. RLD to the editor, ibid., March 11, 1897.
38. See, e.g., Chris Evans, *History of the United Mine Workers of America* II (Indianapolis, 1918), 464–69, 492–95.
39. RLD to the editor, *UMWJ*, Sept. 9, 1897.
40. RLD to the editor, ibid., June 9, 1892.
41. RLD to the editor, ibid., May 24, 1894.
42. RLD to the editor, ibid., March 24, 1892.
43. RLD to the editor, ibid., June 30, 1892.
44. Spero and Harris, op. cit., 215; and Robert D. Ward and William W. Rogers, *Labor Revolt in Alabama. The Great Strike of 1894* (University of Alabama, 1965), passim. This recent study contains much useful information about Alabama coal mining and relations between employers and Negro and white miners before 1895. Although it is marred by superficial analysis, it nevertheless deserves attention.
45. Davis wrote three letters from Alabama and another from Rendville about his Alabama experiences, and they appear in *UMWJ*, Dec. 16 and 23, 1897 and Jan. 6 and Feb. 10, 1898.
46. RLD to the editor, ibid., May 24, 1894.
47. RLD to the editor, ibid., March 3, 1892.
48. RLD to the editor, ibid., March 14, 1894.
49. See, e.g., RLD to the editor, ibid., Nov. 22, 1894 and March 3, 10, and 24, 1898.
50. RLD to the editor, ibid., June 23, 1898.
51. RLD to the editor, ibid., March 24, 1898. A year earlier Davis had urged the celebration of yet another holiday: "You forget the day I love most, and that is emancipation day. By all means let us celebrate the day when the shackles were cut loose and 4,000,000 of black men were liberated from the galling yoke of chattel slavery." (RLD to the editor, ibid., March 11, 1897.)

52. RLD to the editor, ibid., Aug. 25, 1892.

53. RLD to the editor, ibid., Dec. 24, 1891.

54. RLD to the editor, ibid., June 1, 1893.

55. RLD to the editor, ibid., July 19, 1894.

56. RLD to the editor, ibid., Aug. 1, 1895. Davis appears later to have sympathized with or respected Debs. In 1899 he visited Princeton, Indiana, to help its miners celebrate the need for an eight-hour day. A speech by a local minister impressed Davis, who noted: "In fact, Debs could hardly have handled his subject better" (RLD to the editor, ibid., April 13, 1899).

57. Daniel Wallace to the editor, ibid., Aug. 15, 1895.

58. RLD, "The Colored Race and Labor Organization," ibid., May 26, 1893.

59. *Report of the Industrial Commission,* VII, op. cit., 53.

60. William Riley to the editor, UMWJ, Sept. 29, 1892, and Henry Stephenson to the editor, ibid., Aug. 3, 1899.

61. S. C. Armstrong to the editor, ibid., Nov. 10, 1898.

62. O. H. Underwood to the editor, ibid., July 20, 1899.

63. "In Praise of Milton Reed, Negro Organizer," ibid., July 25, 1901.

64. Ibid., June 8, 1899.

65. A. H. Harris to the editor, ibid., Sept. 21, 1899.

66. Rayford W. Logan, *The Negro in American Life and Thought. The Nadir 1877–1901* (New York, 1954), 159–69, 239–74.

67. C. Vann Woodward, *Origins of the New South 1877–1913* (Baton Rouge, 1951), 321–95.

68. UMWJ, May 5, 1892.

69. Ibid., June 9, 1892.

70. D. H. Sullivan to the editor, ibid., March 12, 1896.

71. William Camack to the editor, ibid., May 5, 1892.

72. "Willing Hands" to the editor, ibid., Sept. 29, 1892.

73. William Riley to the editor, ibid., Aug. 28, 1892.

74. William Riley to the editor, ibid., Sept. 8, 1892.

75. William Riley to the editor, ibid., Sept. 29, 1892.

76. "Willing Hands" to the editor, ibid., Sept. 29 and Dec. 22, 1892.

77. RLD to the editor, ibid., Oct. 27, 1892.

78. William E. Clark to the editor, ibid., Nov. 9, 1893.

79. William E. Clark to the editor, ibid., Dec. 29, 1893.

80. William E. Clark to the editor, ibid., Aug. 9, 1894.

81. Chris Evans to the editor, ibid., March 5, 1903.

82. Charles W. Simmons, John H. Rankin, and U. G. Carter, "Negro Coal Miners in West Virginia, 1875–1925," *Midwest Journal* (Spring 1954), 64. This article contains much information on the West Virginia coal fields, but its authors failed to consult

the *United Mine Workers' Journal* and their findings are quite limited.

83. Woodward, op. cit., 267–68.

84. Bruce, loc. cit., and Gutman, loc. cit.

85. Spero and Harris, op. cit., 210.

86. Ibid., 210, 212.

87. Ibid., 210–11.

88. Ibid., 211.

89. Ibid., 213.

90. The details in this and the following three paragraphs draw largely from Victor Hicken, "The Virden and Pana Wars," *Journal of the Illinois State Historical Society* LI (Spring 1959), 263–78.

91. RLD to the editor, UMWJ, Oct. 13, 1898.

92. Full detail on the Carterville strikes, the violence, and trials that followed is found in Paul Angle, *Bloody Williamson, A Chapter in American Lawlessness* (New York, 1952), 89–116, 281–83. Angle exhausted local sources but did not use labor sources, and important additional information is found in unsigned letters, probably written by George Durden in UMWJ, July 20 and Oct. 9, 1899.

93. G. A. Durden to the editor, ibid., Oct. 9 and especially Nov. 25, 1909.

94. Ibid., July 6, 1899.

95. Parts of speeches by Robinson, Williams, and Durden appear in the "Official Proceedings of the Illinois Miners' Convention," ibid., March 18, 1900.

96. The works of Evans, Roy, and Warne, previously cited, are entirely unsatisfactory accounts of the early UMW history. Additional information can be found in Norman Ware, *The Labor Movement in the United States, 1860–1895* (New York, 1929), 214–22; Philip Taft, *The A.F. of L. in the Time of Gompers* (New York, 1957), 137–40; and McAlister Coleman, *Men and Coal* (New York, 1943), passim. There remains a serious need for a full, scholarly history of the UMW.

97. Woodward, op. cit., 321–49.

98. This figure is quoted widely in the standard sources. See, for examples, Spero and Harris, op. cit., 76–78; and Ira DeA. Reid, *Negro Membership in American Labor Unions* (New York, 1930), 101–3. It seems originally to come from W. E. B. Du Bois, ed., *The Negro Artisan* (Atlanta, 1902), 158. Du Bois wrote that "the figures as to Negro membership [in 1900] are reported to us by the unions." Efforts by this writer to secure independent sources that verify this important fact have not been successful.

99. *Report of the Industrial Commission*, XVII, op. cit., 184–85; John Mitchell to Samuel Gompers, April 12, 1900, as cited in Philip Foner, *History of the Labor Movement in the United States*, II (New York, 1955), 345. See also Ware, op. cit., 214–22.

100. Taft, op. cit., 233.

101. For a reasonable explanation of the absence of Negro anthracite miners, see Spero and Harris, op. cit., 207.

102. Woodward, op. cit., 362–65; Spero and Harris, op. cit., 352–57; Northrup. op. cit., 319–21; Roy, op. cit., 430–32.

103. *Locomotive Firemen's Magazine* XXV (Oct. 1898), 378–79.

104. *Proceedings of the Twentieth Annual Convention of the American Federation of Labor . . . 1900*, 22–23. See also Gompers' testimony before the Industrial Commission in 1899 (*Report of the Industrial Commission*, VII, op. cit., 647–49) and his early recognition that exclusion of Negroes would encourage strikebreaking in Taft, op. cit., 308–12, and Bernard Mandel, *Samuel Gompers* (Yellow Springs, Ohio, 1963), 142–45.

105. "Trade Union Attitude Toward Colored Workers," *American Federationist* VIII (April 1901), 118–19. See also Logan, op. cit., 149–50.

106. Quoted by Ray Marshall, *The Negro and Organized Labor* (New York, 1965), 19.

107. O. H. Underwood to the editor, UMWJ, July 20, 1899.

108. See, for examples of widely different explanations of national craft union behavior and especially policy decisions by the AFL Executive Council, Taft, op. cit., 308–17; Philip Taft, *Organized Labor in American History* (New York, 1964), 665–70; Marshall, op. cit., 14–33; Foner, II, op. cit., 347–61, and III (New York, 1964), 233–55; Mandel, op. cit., 142–45 and 234–39; B. Mandel, "Samuel Gompers and the Negro Workers, 1886–1914," *Journal of Negro History* XL (Jan. 1955), 34–60; Gerald Grob, "Organized Labor and the Negro Worker, 1865–1900," *Labor History* I (Spring 1960), 164–76; Herbert Hill, "In the Age of Gompers and After. Racial Practices of Organized Labor," *New Politics* IV (Spring 1965), 26–46; Herman D. Bloch, "Labor and the Negro, 1866–1910," *Journal of Negro History* L (July 1965), 163–84. Taft finds that the Federation "retreated from its earlier position" concerning Negro workers and stresses the importance of craft autonomy and the widespread opposition to integrated unions in the South. The policy of separation, he finds, was "the only one which would make possible the retention of unions in the South." Grob calls the AFL shift "simply a part of a larger development that came to characterize all areas of American life." Foner finds in these years "proof" of a "deliberate conspiracy between employers and the craft unions" to exclude Negro workers and uses this explanation (a "conspiracy") seven times in less than two pages (Foner, II, op. cit., 353–55). Hill argues from scattered evidence that "at the turn of the century the AFL had fully capitulated to a policy of chauvinism and overt discrimination." Bloch stresses that "local" interaction between Negro and white workers shaped discriminatory patterns more than

Notes for Chapter II

national decisions but infers this without examining much local source material. Much of this dispute is tendentious since these writings generally ignore what E. P. Thompson calls "the goings-on 'in the provinces'" and view local labor history "as shadowy incidents or unaccountable upheavals on the periphery of the national scene" (Asa Briggs and John Saville, eds., *Essays in Labour History* [London, 1907], 276–77). Until the national and local pictures are put together—and this only after yeomanlike digging in Northern and Southern sources—little more can be written of the relations between the Negro and organized labor, 1890–1910.

109. Taft, *Organized Labor in American History* (New York, 1964), 670.

110. E. P. Thompson, "Homage to Tom Maguire," in Briggs and Saville, eds., op. cit., 276–77.

111. Woodward, op. cit., 360–61. At the end of the Civil War, Negro artisans far outnumbered white craftsmen in the South and then their number proportionately declined. "Early in the twentieth century," Woodward writes, "there was much comment upon the disappearance of the Negro from trades he had traditionally monopolized, or very largely so."

112. W. E. B. Du Bois, op. cit., 91, and John Hope Franklin, *From Slavery to Freedom* (New York, 1947), 393, 429.

113. An exception is the standard work: W. E. B. Du Bois, *The Philadelphia Negro* (Philadelphia, 1899).

114. Much can be learned about methods for approaching this subject from the recent work of British labor and social historians. See, e.g., "Conference Report," Society for the Study of Labour History, Bulletin IX (Autumn 1964), 4–9; Eric Hobsbawm, *Labouring Men* (London, 1964), passim; and in particular E. P. Thompson, *The Making of the English Working Class* (London, 1963), passim.

115. Du Bois, ed., *The Negro Artisan* (Atlanta, 1902), 158, 160–61. In 1899, however, trouble developed between Negro and white longshoremen in Newport News, Va. ILA locals there were entirely Negro. White workers refused to join them, and only after some time did the Negro unionists agree to separate locals for the whites.

116. This important strike is discussed at length in Ernest L. Bogart, "The Chicago Building Trades Dispute of 1900," in John R. Commons, ed., *Trade Unionism and Labor Problems* (New York, 1906), 87–36.

117. The Chicago Federation of Trades appeal appears in R. R. Wright, "The Negro in Chicago," *Charities* XV (Oct. 7, 1905), 69–73. Much else of interest about Negro workers in the meat-packing industry and Negro teamsters is found in Wright's article which is reprinted, in part, in Herbert Aptheker, ed., *A Doc-*

umentary History of the Negro People in the United States (New York, 1951), 838–42.

118. James S. Wallace to the editor, *New York Age*, July 12 and Aug. 30, 1906, reprinted in ibid., 843–44.

119. "Editorial," *The Carpenter* XXIII (Jan. 1903), 3–4.

120. Critical letters from Southern white union carpenters appear in ibid. (April 1903), 6–7.

121. Savannah, Georgia, carpenter to the editor, ibid. (Sept. 1903), 3, 6.

122. H. B. Adolphus, President, Fenton County, Georgia, District Council, to the editor, ibid.

123. Spero and Harris, op. cit., 66.

124. Du Bois, op. cit., 111–12, 177.

125. Lynn C. Doyle, "Education That Don't Educate," *The Florida Labor Journal*, I (Feb. 6, 1903), 1–4.

126. Ibid. (Jan. 30, 1903), 14–15.

127. Ibid. (June 12, 1903), 9.

128. "Black and White," *Boyce's Weekly*, n. d., reprinted in ibid. (July 24, 1903), 1–2.

129. *Report of the Industrial Commission*, XVII, op cit., xxviii–xxix.

130. Ibid., 36–37. See also the testimony of Du Bois, ibid., XV, 175. Asked what he knew about the extent of Negro labor organization in the South, Du Bois remarked: "Not very much. I simply know that in most building trades the negroes can join, and considerable numbers have joined. They sometimes meet in the same hall, the whites on one side and the colored on the other." Useful information about Negro union bricklayers and their different status in various parts of the country is found in the testimony of John Healey, ibid., VII, 162–63. Data on the complex relations between Negro workers and organized labor in Georgia, which can only be evaluated after additional research in local Georgia materials, are found in ibid., 236–38, 242, 542, 547–48, 554–55, 560, 564–68.

131. Du Bois, ed., *The Negro Artisan* (Atlanta, 1902), 162–63.

132. Ibid., 114–15, 137.

133. Ibid., 127–28.

134. Ibid., 158. Du Bois' observation must not be exaggerated and must be read in the context of his detailed criticisms of trade union discriminatory practices (ibid., 153–78). Yet labor historians have frequently ignored the evidence of Negro participation in Southern trade unions that the Du Bois study brought to light.

135. Quoted in Woodward, op. cit., 364.

136. W. H. Councill, "Negro Labor and Labor Organizations," *The Tradesman* (Chattanooga), Jan. 1900, reprinted in the *Locomotive Firemen's Magazine* XXVIII (March 1900), 197–98. A

vivid sketch of Councill is found in August Meier, *Negro Thought in America, 1880–1915* (Ann Arbor, 1963), 209–10. Councill's paper appeared in *The Tradesman*, a leading Southern commercial publication, as a part of a symposium on "the South and its future." Other contributors included the secretary of Huntsville Chamber of Commerce and Southern Industrial Convention, N. F. Thompson, and a former Georgia governor who found in the Negro "one of the South's best undeveloped resources . . . if properly trained." He urged Northern capital to come into the South whose "labor" made that section "a stranger to riots, strikes and ugly uprisings among the people . . ." Thompson argued for legislation that would "make it a crime to inaugurate a strike that in any way affected the general public." (*The Tradesman*, loc. cit., 195–97.) That same year, Thompson, who had also spent five years in Johnstown, Pennsylvania, and been secretary of the Birmingham, Alabama, Commercial Club, at another time, warned the Industrial Commission that Birmingham Negroes "are being taken into the unions practically on the same basis as all others." Thompson complained of "a deficiency of collective education among the masses" and that "the educational influence of the labor organizations" had gone unchallenged in the South for twenty-five years." He even favored the use of violence against outspoken union activists (*Report of the Industrial Commission*, VII, op. cit., 755–59). John P. Coffin, Vice-President of the Southern Industrial Council, urged that Negroes be used as "a reserve force in case of strikes." "I believe," he told the Commission, "that in the negro labor of the South lies the panacea for the wrongs frequently committed by organized labor, and a reserve force from which can be supplied any needed number of workers when the time shall come that they will be needed." Before they would "submit to unjust domination by unions," Coffin predicted, the "Southern people" would "negroize their industries." An amazed Commission investigator pressed Coffin on this point and only the Mad Hatter could entangle what followed:

"*Q.:* That would bring negro domination in industry then, would it not? *A.:* It will bring negro domination of the labor market if labor is unjust.

Q.: And the white man will dominate the social and political conditions of the South, and the negro will dominate the labor market of the South? . . . If they dominated white labor, white labor would be suppressed? *A.:* No; they would never dominate white labor. He [*sic*] will take their places, but domination will rest with the whites. There is no fear of negro domination in the South.

Q.: I do not mean domination over the employer, but domination over the white labor. They would be eliminated, would they not? *A.:* No; the employer would dominate the labor, not the negro. The negro will never dominate the Anglo-Saxon. He may take his

place in work under certain conditions; but the Anglo-Saxon was not created to be dominated. . . .
Q.: Is it not really, then, to be held up as a menace over the white labor to make them understand that they must not make unjust demands, but that they must submit to the employer in all things? A.: . . . I believe in white labor as far as possible; but I also believe in justice." (Ibid., 790–91.)

137. Quoted in Woodward, op. cit., 361.

138. Meier, op. cit., passim.

139. St. Louis *Advance*, n. d., reprinted in *The Carpenter* XXIII (April 1903), 6–7. See also the letter of a Texas trade unionist, probably white, who wrote to Du Bois: "The Negro question is the one drawback to the success of the labor movement today [1900–1], especially is this true in the South. The Negro has always been the stumbling block in the way of success in many cases; this, however, is not the fault of the Negro, but until the white men realize that it is with the organization and assistance of the Negro, that they can and must win, the labor movement will not be as successful as we hope for." He went on: "They are laborers, in a larger percentage, than their white brothers; they are the ones used to whip the white men into line when striking for their rights or demanding recognition from their employers, whereas, if they were organized, no inducement could be made to cause them to falter in their duty to mankind" (unidentified letter from Texas, quoted in Du Bois, op. cit., 178).

CHAPTER III

1. James McBride Dabbs, *The Southern Heritage* (New York, Knopf, 1959), 107.

2. C. Vann Woodward, *The Strange Career of Jim Crow* (New York, Oxford, 1957), 40.

3. W. J. Cash, *The Mind of the South* (New York, Knopf, 1941), 33.

4. Vernon L. Wharton, *The Negro in Mississippi, 1877–1880* (Chapel Hill, University of North Carolina Press, 1947); George B. Tendall, *South Carolina Negroes, 1877–1880* (Chapel Hill, University of North Carolina Press, 1952).

5. *Steele v. L. & N. Rrd.*, 323 U.S. 204 (1944); *Hughes Tool Co.*, 147 NLRB No. 166 (1964).

6. *Local Union No. 12, United Rubber Workers*, 150 NLRB No. 18 (1964).

7. *Local 1367, International Longshoremen's Assn.*, 148 NLRB No. 44 (1964).

8. See *Steele v. L. & N. Rrd.*, 323 U.S. 204 (1944); *Graham v.*

Brotherhood of Locomotive Firemen, 338 U.S. 232 (1949); and *Richardson v. T. & N. Rrd.*, 242 F. 2nd 230 (1957).

9. See my "Unions and the Negro Community," *Industrial and Labor Relations Review*, Jan. 1964.

10. *News-Free Press* (Chattanooga), Aug. 3 and 20, 1955; Chattanooga *Times*, Aug. 21, 1955. For a more detailed discussion see my "Union Racial Problems in the South," *Industrial Relations*, May 1962.

11. Springhill *Press & News-Journal*, Oct. 10, 17, 1962; Shreveport *Times*, Oct. 13, 1962.

CHAPTER IV

1. Proceedings of the tenth Annual Convention of the American Federation of Labor, Detroit, Dec. 8–13, 1890, 20, 29.

2. Proceedings of the Fourteenth Annual Convention of the American Federation of Labor, 1894, 25.

3. W. E. B. Du Bois, *The Negro Artisan*, Atlanta University Publication No. 7, 1902, 169–70.

4. Ibid., 151–88.

5. Frank E. Wolfe, *Admission to American Trade Unions* (Baltimore, 1912), 122–24.

6. *American Federationist* XII, 9, (Sept. 1905).

7. Samuel Gompers to the press, April 19, 1901, AFL Correspondence file, Washington, D.C.

8. Philip S. Foner, *History of the Labor Movement in the United States*, II (New York, 1955), 359–60.

9. For a detailed study of the 1917 East St. Louis race riot, see Elliot M. Rudwick, *Race Riot in East St. Louis, July 2, 1917* (Carbondale, Ill., 1964). Eugene V. Debs referred to the riot as "a foul blot upon the American labor movement. . . . Had the labor unions freely opened their doors to the Negro instead of barring him . . . and in alliance with the capitalist class, transpiring to make a pariah of him, and forcing him in spite of himself to become a scab . . . the atrocious crime at East St. Louis would never have blackened the pages of American history."

10. Samuel Gompers to W. E. B. Du Bois, Jan. 5, 1903, AFL Correspondence.

11. Philip Taft, *The AF of L in the Time of Gompers* (New York, 1957), 314–15.

12. Sterling Spero and Abram Harris, *The Black Worker* (New York, 1931), 109–10.

13. Charles H. Wesley, *Negro Labor in the United States* (New York, 1927), 275–77.

14. Philip Taft, *The AF of L, From the Death of Gompers to*

the Merger (New York, 1959), 439. Taft's account of AFL policy toward the Negro minimizes the actual extent of discrimination in the labor movement, and seeks to justify the AFL leadership's acquiescence in this discriminatory policy.

15. *The Messenger*, May–June 1919, 7.

16. Report of Proceedings of the Forty-ninth Annual Convention of the American Federation of Labor, Toronto, Oct. 7–18, 1929, 75.

17. Ibid., 136–39, 384–85.

18. Report of Proceedings of the Fifty-third Annual Convention of the American Federation of Labor, 1933, 268–69.

19. Report of Proceedings of the Fifty-fourth Annual Convention of the American Federation of Labor, Oct. 1–12, 1934, San Francisco, 330–31.

20. Ibid., 331–32.

21. Ibid., 333. See Philip Taft, op. cit., vol. 2, 442. In his discussion of this convention, Taft obliterates Furuseth's comments on the need to go slow, and presents him as one who supported the AFL nonconcurrence in Randolph's resolution, but also agreed with the spirit of Randolph's argument.

22. Ibid., 333–34.

23. Herbert Hill, "Labor Unions and the Negro," *Commentary*, Dec. 1959, reprint, 4.

24. Report to the Executive Council by John E. Rooney, John Brophy, T. C. Carroll, John W. Garvey, cited in Philip Taft, op. cit., II, 443.

25. Report of Proceedings of the Fifty-fifth Annual Convention of the American Federation of Labor, Atlantic City, Oct. 7–19, 1935, 807–19.

26. John Brophy to William Green, Nov. 6, 1935, in Philip Taft, op. cit., II, 443, and Herbert Hill, op. cit., 4–5.

27. T. C. Carroll to William Green, Nov. 21, 1935, quoted in Philip Taft, op. cit., II, 443–44.

28. Ibid., 444. Jerry Hanks to William Green, Dec. 4, 1935.

29. Ibid., 445. D. H. Robertson to William Green, Feb. 25, 1938.

30. Report of the Proceedings of the Sixty-first Annual Convention of the American Federation of Labor, Seattle, Oct. 5–16, 1941. Randolph's speech is on 475–81, the debate on the issue on 481–92.

31. Report of the Proceedings of the Sixty-third Annual Convention of the American Federation of Labor, Boston, Oct. 4–14, 1943. Discussion on the issue is on 416–45.

32. Herbert R. Northrup, "Organized Labor and Negro Workers," *Journal of Political Economy*, no. 206 (June 1943).

33. Report of the Proceedings of the Sixty-fourth Annual Convention of the American Federation of Labor, New Orleans, Nov. 20–30, 1944, 491–94, 494–507.

34. Herbert Hill, op. cit., 2.

CHAPTER V

1. CIO publication no. 45, 1939.

2. Robert C. Weaver, *Negro Labor—A National Problem* (New York, Harcourt, Brace), 219–23.

3. "Unions and the Negro Community," *Industrial and Labor Relations Review*, Jan. 1964, 188.

4. Wilson Record, *The Negro and the Communist Party* (Chapel Hill, 1951), 144–45.

5. David A. Shannon, *The Decline of American Communism* (New York, 1959), 58–61; Herbert Hill, "The Communist Party—Enemy of Negro Equality," *Crisis*, June–July 1951.

6. Irving Howe and Lewis Coser, *The American Communist Party—A Critical History (1919–1957)* (Boston, 1957), 368–86; Charles A. Madison, *American Labor Leaders* (New York, 1950), 326–33; Max M. Kampelman, *The Communist Party vs. the CIO* (New York, 1957).

7. Herbert Hill, "Racial Practices of Organized Labor—In the Age of Gompers and After," *New Politics* IV, 2, 26–46; Ray Marshall, *The Negro and Organized Labor* (New York, 1965).

8. Irving Howe and B. J. Widick, *The UAW and Walter Reuther* (New York, 1949), 209.

9. Howe and Coser, 379–80.

10. "Is Japan the Champion of the Colored Races?," issued by the Negro Commission, National Committee, C.P., U.S.A., Aug. 1938, 44–45.

11. James W. Ford, "The War and the Negro People," Jan. 1942; William Z. Foster, "The Trade Unions and the War," June 1942.

12. Barbash, op. cit., 353–56.

13. Howe and Coser, op. cit., 414–18.

14. Quoted in Hill, "The Communist Party," loc. cit.

15. Op. cit., 215.

16. Record, op. cit., 272–73.

17. Nathan Glazer, *The Social Basis of American Communism* (New York, 1961), 181–82.

18. Record, op. cit., 273.

19. William Z. Foster, "Problems of Organized Labor Today" (New York, 1946), 28; Shannon, op. cit., 242–48.

20. Quoted in Howe and Widick, op. cit., 226.

21. Record, op. cit., 276–77; the details of this period are found in Shannon, op. cit., and Kampelman, op. cit.

22. Manpower Report of the President, March 1964, 275.

23. U. S. Department of Labor, "The Economic Situation of

Negroes in the United States," 1962, 7; "The Negroes in the United States—Their Economic and Social Situation," 1965.

24. Robert C. Weaver, *Negro Labor—A National Problem* (New York, 1946), 79.

25. Ibid., 86–87.

26. Ibid., 81.

27. Ibid., 105.

28. Ibid., 219–23.

29. Ibid., 85–86.

30. Herbert R. Northrup, *Organized Labor and the Negro* (New York, 1944), 120.

31. Op. cit., 63–77.

32. Ibid., 237.

33. Ibid., 219–20.

34. Marshall, op. cit., 45–46.

35. Ibid., 107.

36. John Hope II, *Equality of Opportunity—A Union Approach to Fair Employment* (Washington, D.C., 1956).

37. Marshall, op. cit., 181–83.

38. Ibid., 41.

39. John Brophy, *A Miner's Life*, John O. P. Hall, ed. Madison (1946), 245–46; Philip Taft, *Organized Labor in America*, 674–75.

40. Louis Ruchames, *Race, Jobs and Politics—The Story of FEPC* (New York, 1953), 13–21.

CHAPTER VI

1. Scott Nearing, *Income* (1915).

2. Ibid., 200.

3. Ibid., 175.

4. Ibid., 176.

5. See his regular editorial column "World Events" in the *Monthly Review*, an independent Socialist journal of opinion.

6. Cf. Herman Miller, *Rich Man, Poor Man* (1964).

7. Leon H. Keyserling, *Progress on Poverty*, Conference on Economic Progress (1964), 23.

8. *The New York Times* (Jan. 9, 1964). Recent collected works on the poverty question include:

Arthur B. Shostak and William Gomberg, eds., *New Perspectives on Poverty* (1965).

Robert E. Will and Harold G. Vatter, eds., *Poverty in Affluence* (1965).

Louis A. Ferman, Joyce L. Kornbluh, and Alan Haber, eds., *Poverty in America* (1965).

9. From the "Message on Poverty" (March 16, 1964), reproduced in Will and Vatter, eds., op. cit., 16.

10. Cf. C. Vann Woodward, *The Strange Career of Jim Crow* (1957).

11. See Robin Williams, "Social Change and Social Conflict: Race Relations in the United States, 1944–64" (unpublished paper, 1964), 4.

12. Michael Munk, "Revolution on the Farm," *Monthly Review* XIV (1963), 547.

13. Williams, op. cit., 4.

14. Tom Kahn, *The Economics of Equality*, League for Industrial Democracy (1964), 26.

15. L. Schnore and H. Sharp, "The Changing Color of Our Big Cities," *Trans-Action* (1963), 12–14. "It is no exaggeration to call the growth of non-white populations in our major cities one of the truly outstanding social trends of the twentieth century." Ibid., 14.

16. M. Grodzins, "The Metropolitan Area as a Racial Problem" in *American Race Relations Today*, Earl Raab, (1962), 98.

17. David Danzig, "The Meaning of Negro Strategy," ed. *Commentary*, Feb. 1964, 46.

18. M. A. Kessler, "Economic Status of Nonwhite Workers, 1955–62," *Special Labor Force Report* no. 33, U. S. Department of Labor, Bureau of Labor Statistics (1963), 3.

19. H. Rowen, *The Free Enterprisers* (1964), 264.

20. Ben Seligman, "Automation and the Union," *Dissent*, Winter 1965, 50–51.

21. Leon H. Keyserling, "Poverty and the Economy," *Nation*, June 7, 1965, 616; see also Robert H. Ferguson, "Unemployment: Its Scope, Measurement, and Effect on Poverty," New York State School of Industrial and Labor Relations, May 1965.

22. Quoted in Peter Irons, "The Cybernation Revolution," *Progressive*, Feb. 1965, 20.

23. Joseph Zeisel, "A Profile of Unemployment," in *Men Without Work*, S. Lebergott, ed., (1963), 124.

24. S. M. Miller, "Poverty, Race, and Politics," in *The New Sociology*, I. Horowitz, ed., (1964), 298–99.

25. Harold Baron, "Negro Unemployment," *New University Thought*, Oct. 1963, 44–45.

26. S. M. Willhelm and E. H. Powell, "Who Needs the Negro?" *Trans-Action*, Oct. 1964, 3.

27. M. Harrington, *The Other America* (1963), 71, 79.

28. Rowen, op. cit., 268–69.

29. O. R. Gursslin and J. L. Roach, "Some Issues in Training the Unemployed," *Social Problems*, Summer 1964, 95.

30. Kenneth B. Clark, *Dark Ghetto* (1965), 36.

31. Williams, op. cit., 19.

Notes for Chapter VI

32. Quoted in Kahn, op. cit., 17.

33. Williams, op. cit.

34. Danzig, op. cit., 45.

35. Paul Siegel, "On the Cost of Being Negro," unpublished paper, National Opinion Research Center (1964), 15–17.

36. Willhelm and Powell, op. cit., 3.

37. Clark, op. cit., 47.

38. These data have been compiled in an excellent report by L. E. Schaller and C. W. Rawlings, *Race and Poverty*, Office of Race and Religion (May 1964).

39. *The Negro in Cleveland*, 1950–1963, Research Department, Cleveland Urban League (1964), 18.

40. Ibid.

41. Batchelder, op. cit., 6.

42. David Caplovitz, *The Poor Pay More* (1963), 12–20.

43. Batchelder, op. cit., 13–14.

44. W. H. Ferry, "Further Reflections on the Triple Revolution," Center for the Study of Democratic Institutions reprint (Spring 1965), 11.

45. Willhelm and Powell, op. cit., 4.

46. J. C. Leggett, "Economic Insecurity and Working-Class Consciousness," *American Sociological Review*, April 1964, 234.

47. Shaller and Rawlings, op. cit., 27.

48. Gabriel Kolko, *Wealth and Power in America* (1962) 93–94.

49. Herbert Gans, "Some Proposals for Government Policy in an Automating Society," in Shostak and Gomberg, op. cit., 142–57.

50. *The New York Times*, April 27, 1964, 1.

51. Kahn, op. cit., 52–55.

52. These comparative costs were brought together by Martin Oppenheimer, "Disarmament and the War on Poverty," American Friends Service Publication (1964), 7.

53. Charles Silberman, *Crisis in Black and White* (1964), 308–55.

54. For a presentation of labor responses, see E. M. Kassalow, "Labor Relations and Employment Aspects After Ten Years," in Morris Phillipson, ed., *Automation* (1962), 316–33.

55. See the interesting account of the rank-and-file dispute with the leadership of unionist Harry Bridges in Stanley Weir, "The ILWU: A Case Study in Bureaucracy," *New Politics*, Winter 1964, 23–28.

56. Cf. James Matles (interview), "Against the Mainstream," *Studies on the Left*, Winter 1964, 43–54.

57. Seligman, op. cit., 44.

58. S. M. Lipset and R. Bendix, *Social Mobility in Industrial Society* (1959), 106.

59. Bert Cochran, "American Labor in Midpassage," in B. Cochran, ed., *American Labor in Midpassage* (1959), 39.

60. S. M. Miller, op. cit., 305.

61. D. Danzig, op. cit., 46.

62. Cf. Sidney M. Peck, *The Rank-and-File Leader* (1963), 166–72.

63. Ibid., 350.

CHAPTER VII

1. Harold Baron, "Negro Unemployment—A Case Study," *New University Thought* III (1963), 45.

2. U. S. Department of Labor, *Manpower Report of the President*, 1965, Table A-4.

3. Lester C. Thurow, "The Changing Structure of Unemployment: An Econometric Study," *Review of Economic and Statistics* XLVII, (May 1965), 142–43.

4. Illinois Department of Labor, *Illinois Job Seeker Survey* (1962), 44.

5. Susan S. Holland and J. Ross Wetzel, "Labor Force and Employment in 1964," U. S. Department of Labor, "Special Labor Force Report," No. 52, A-40.

6. Denis F. Johnston, "Educational Attainment of Workers, March, 1964," *Monthly Labor Review*, May 1965, 520–21.

7. This generalization is verifiable for the United States in 1964. See Holland and Wetzel, op. cit., A-37, and for urban Illinois in 1959, see *U. S. Census of Population*, 1960, Vol. 15C, Tables 58 and 60.

8. Alan B. Batchelder, *Quarterly Journal of Economics* LXXVIII (Nov. 1964), 529.

9. Ibid.

10. Chicago Urban League, "Notes on Problems of Negro Employment" (mimeo., Aug. 20, 1964), 2.

11. President's Committee on Equal Employment Opportunity, *Report to the President* (1963), 50. Figures are for 1963; Chicago Civil Service Region comprises Illinois and neighboring states.

12. Dale Hiestand, *Economic Growth and Employment Opportunities for Minorities* (New York, 1964), 87.

13. Joseph W. Garbarino, "Income Policy and Income Behavior," and Murray Edleman and R. W. Fleming, "Unemployment and Wage—Price Policies" in Ross, op. cit., 56–112.

14. Greenleight Associates, *Facts, Fallacies and Future: A Study of the Aid to Dependent Children Program of Cook County, Illinois* (New York, 1960), 9.

15. James M. Morgan, et al., *Income and Welfare in the United States* (New York, 1963), 56.

16. Karl E. and Alma F. Taeuber, *Negroes in Cities* (Chicago, 1965).

17. James Q. Wilson, *Negro Politics* (Glencoe, Ill., 1960).

18. "Chief Executives View Negro Employment," *The Conference Board Record*, (May 1965), 32.

CHAPTER VIII

1. Gompers to R. T. Coles, April 28, 1891. Quoted in Taft, *The AF of L in the Time of Gompers* (Harper, New York, 1957), 308.

2. Gompers, *American Federationist*, XII, 9 (Sept. 1905), 636. For a study of the racial practices of the AFL during this early period, see Herbert Hill, "The Racial Practices of Organized Labor—The Age of Gompers and After," in *Employment, Race and Poverty*, Ross and Hill, eds. (Harcourt, Brace & World, New York, 1967), 365–402.

3. AFL-CIO Third Constitutional Convention, *Proceedings*, Fifth Day. (The word "hell" is omitted from the official transcript.)

4. *Report on Employment*, U. S. Commission on Civil Rights (Washington, D.C., 1961), 161. See also *Negroes and the Building Trades Unions*, National Urban League (New York, 1957), and *The 50 States Report*, U. S. Commission on Civil Rights, (Washington, D.C., 1961). In these reports there are frequent references to specific discriminatory practices by labor unions.

5. See Herbert Hill, "Racism Within Organized Labor: A Report of Five Years of the AFL-CIO," *Journal of Negro Education* XXX (Spring 1961), 109–18.

6. Ibid., 109–18. For a study of the legal attacks on the discriminatory practices of the Railroad Brotherhoods and other unions, see Herbert Hill, "The Role of Law in Securing Equal Employment Opportunity: Legal Powers and Social Change," *Boston College Law Review*, Spring 1966, 625–53. For a historical discussion of the anti-Negro practices of the Railroad Brotherhoods, see Charles H. Houston, "Foul Employment Practice on the Rails," *The Crisis*, Oct. 1949, also "The Elimination of Negro Firemen on American Railways—A Study of the Evidence Adduced at the Hearing Before the President's Committee on Fair Employment Practices," *Lawyers Guild Review* XXXII (1944) and Clayton and Mitchell, *Black Workers and the New Unions* (University of North Carolina Press, Chapel Hill, 1939), 439–45.

7. Arthur M. Ross, "The Negro In the American Economy," in

Ross and Hill, eds., *Employment, Race and Poverty*, (Harcourt, Brace & World, New York, 1967), 8.

8. See Herbert Hill, "Racial Inequality in Employment: The Patterns of Discrimination," *The Annals of the American Academy of Political and Social Science*, Philadelphia, Vol. 357 (Jan. 1965), 30–47. Also Hill, "The Negro Wage-Earner and Apprenticeship Training Programs," New York, NAACP publication, 1960, and Hill, "Has Organized Labor Failed the Negro Worker?," *Negro Digest*, May 1962.

9. "Union Move—Racial Accord at S.F. Hotels Is Ruled Void," San Francisco *Chronicle*, Nov. 24, 1966, 1; "Negro Anger at the New Hotel Ruling," San Francisco *Chronicle*, Nov. 29, 1966, 1; also lead editorial in San Francisco *Chronicle*, Nov. 30, 1966, "The Breakdown of Job Equality," see "Union Role in Killing Rights Pact Criticized," East Bay *Labor Journal*, Dec. 2, 1966, 1.

10. In virtually every city in the United States craft jobs controlled by the construction unions of the AFL-CIO pay among the highest wage rates; see "Employment and Earning Statistics for States and Areas, 1939–65," issued June 1966, Bulletin No. 1370–3, Bureau of Labor Statistics, U. S. Department of Labor, Washington, D.C.

11. Harry Bernstein, "Unions Balk on Job Help for Watts Men," *Los Angeles Times*, Sept. 10, 1965.

12. Gunnar Myrdal, *An American Dilemma* (Harper, New York, 1944), 1102. Myrdal also observed that "the fact that the American Federation of Labor as such is officially against racial discrimination does not mean much. The Federation has never done anything to check racial discrimination exercised by its member organizations" (402).

13. *Report on Employment*, United States Commission on Civil Rights, 1961, Washington, D.C., 130.

14. Ibid., 130.

15. Ibid., 128–38.

16. New York City Commission on Human Rights, "Bias in the Building Industry—An Interim Report to the Mayor," Dec. 1963, 10.

17. Hearing Before the United States Commission On Civil Rights, Cleveland, April 1–7, 1966, 443–44, U. S. Government Printing Office, Washington, D.C.

18. *The New York Times*, "Cleveland Union Protest," Aug. 8, 1963.

19. The Cleveland *Press*, "24 Pickets Arrested at Federal Building," April 26, 1965. Photographs of pickets carrying signs reading "Mall '63—A Broken Promise—Integrate Now" appear on the first page as they are being arrested.

20. Hearing Before the United States Commission on Civil Rights, Cleveland, April 1–7, 1966, 443–44.

21. Roy Wilkins, Introduction to Herbert Hill, *The Negro Wage Earner and Apprenticeship Training Programs*, 1960, NAACP publication, iii.

22. See Herbert Hill, "Racism Within Organized Labor: A Report of Five Years of the AFL-CIO, 1955–1960," *The Journal of Negro Education* III, 2 (Spring 1961), 109–18.

23. Donald Shaughnessy, "A Survey of Discrimination in the Building Trades Industry, Report of New York State Advisory Committee to the U. S. Commission on Civil Rights, mimeo. (New York, 1963), 16–17.

24. *Lefkowitz v. Farrell*, C-9287-63 (N. Y. State Commission for Human Rights, 1964).

25. Text of this landmark decision of the New York State Supreme Court appears in *New York Law Journal*, Aug. 26, 1964, together with summary of the case.

26. Op. cit., 132.

27. Ibid., 131.

28. Ibid., 130.

29. *Mitchell v. R. & S. Plumbers and Mechanical Systems, Inc.* C-9092-62, N. Y. State Commission for Human Rights. See Herbert Hill, "Twenty Years of State Fair Employment Practice Laws; A Critical Analysis," *University of Buffalo Law Review* XIV, 1 (Fall 1964), 22–29.

30. Op. cit., 131.

31. Shaughnessy, op. cit., 21. Shaughnessy's study was the basis for the Report of the New York Advisory Committee to the U. S. Commission on Civil Rights, Aug. 1963.

32. See "Union Wages and Hours: Building Trades—July 1, 1965," Bulletin No. 1487, Bureau of Labor Statistics, June 1966, U. S. Department of Labor, Washington, D.C.; also "Area Wage Survey, The New York Metropolitan Area—April 1966," Bulletin No. 1465-82, Bureau of Labor Statistics, Aug. 1966, U. S. Department of Labor, Washington, D.C.

33. See Herbert Hill, Testimony Before New York City Commission on Human Rights, Construction Trades Hearing, New York, Sept. 26, 1966.

34. *The New York Times*, July 24, 1963.

35. *Congressional Record*—House, Sept. 26, 1967, 12495–96.

36. Peter T. Schoemann, "Racial Equality? Yes! Federal Control? No!" *United Association Journal*, Nov. 1963. Also Fed. Reg. 207 (1963).

37. *The New York Times*, May 2, 1964. See also editorial, "The White Supremacy Plumbers," New York *Post*, May 3, 1964.

38. New York *Post*, May 15, 3.

39. See Herbert Hill, Testimony Before Ohio Civil Rights Commission, City Council Chambers, Cincinnati, Aug. 31, 1965.

40. "Apprentices, Skilled Craftsmen and the Negro," New York State Commission Against Discrimination, 1960. See Harry Kursh, "Apprenticeships in America," rev. ed. (Norton, New York, 1965), 97–105. Also "Bias in Apprenticeship," editorial, *The New York Times*, March 12, 1960, and for California data see Harry Bernstein, "Areas of Low Negro Apprenticeship Told—At Least 23 Counties, 5 Trades Have No Trainees, Confidential Study Shows," *Los Angeles Times*, March 28, 1966, Dick Meister, "Bias Charge in Union Training," San Francisco *Chronicle*, Feb. 4, 1967.

41. Merrill Folsom, "6 Civil Rights Pickets Arrested in New Rochelle Hiring Dispute," *The New York Times*, Jan. 26, 1967. See also New Rochelle Human Rights Commission *Report on Integration of Work Force—Macy Site*, Jan. 16, 1967, which concludes, "That Negroes had been, and were continuing to be excluded by various means, from journeymen membership in certain building trades unions," and also, "That Negroes were systematically excluded from the apprenticeship training program of the building trades unions."

42. See speech of Sam Zagoria, member of NLRB, to the Twelfth Annual Institute on Labor Law, The Southwestern Legal Foundation, Dallas, Oct. 28, 1965, NLRB, Washington, D.C.

43. *Spanish Speaking Workers and the Labor Movement*, A Report of the Association of Catholic Trade Unionists (New York, 1957), 2.

44. P. 52, Article 8, Section 16 of the ILGWU Constitution (1959 ed.).

45. P. 14, Article 13, Section 6 of the ILGWU Constitution. For an analysis of union constitutions, see "Union Constitutions and the Election of Local Union Officers," Labor Management Services Administration, U. S. Department of Labor, April 1965, Washington, D.C.; also "Union Constitution Provisions: Election and Tenure of National and International Union Officers," Bulletin No. 1239, U. S. Department of Labor, 1958.

46. Kenneth B. Clark, *Dark Ghetto: Dilemmas of Social Power* (Harper & Row, New York, 1965), 43.

47. Ibid., 43.

48. Damon Stetson, "Stulberg Doubts a Garment Strike," *The New York Times*, Jan. 26, 1967.

49. Murray Kempton, "The Wage Fight," New York *Post*, Aug. 21, 1962.

50. Murray Seeger, "Governor Vetoes $1.50 Minimum Pay: New Bill Is Likely," *The New York Times*, April 17, 1965.

51. Peter Braestrup, New York *Herald Tribune*, Oct. 8, 1958.

52. Ibid., Oct. 7, 1958.

53. For a documentation of the status of nonwhite workers in the ladies garment industry in New York City and in the ILGWU, see Congressional Record—House (Testimony of Herbert Hill on Racial Practices of ILGWU), Jan. 31, 1963, 1596–1599. See also Herbert Hill, "The ILGWU—Fact and Fiction," *New Politics*, 1962, No. 2, 7–27.

54. U. S. Department of Labor, Bureau of Labor Statistics, "Occupational Earnings—Women's and Misses' Dresses," Aug. 1966, 1 (No. 66–176).

55. A. H. Raskin, "DD and the American Dream," *The New Leader*, April 11, 1966.

56. Gus Tyler, "The Truth About the ILGWU," *New Politics* II, 1, 12.

57. *The New York Times*, March 2, 1966.

58. See Herbert Hill, "Sewing Machines and Union Machines," *The Nation*, July 3, 1967.

59. Holmes v. Falikman, C-7580-61 (N. Y. State Commission for Human Rights, 1963); see Herbert Hill, "Twenty Years of State Fair Employment Practice Laws: A Critical Analysis," *Buffalo Law Review*, XIII (Autumn 1964), 34–35.

60. *The New York Times*, Aug. 14, 1962, "Garment Union Is Found Guilty of Coercion by NLRB Aide." The news report stated that "A National Labor Relations Board trial examiner found the International Ladies Garment Workers Union guilty of unfair labor practices today" and noted that the trial examiner urged, ". . . that the garment union leaders be ordered to stop 'interfering with . . . restraining and coercing' staff employees who are also members of the Federation of Union Representatives. The Associated Press report appearing in the New York *Post*, Aug. 13, 1962, stated, "The International Ladies Garment Workers Union was judged guilty today of unfair labor practices in trying to prevent its employees from forming their own labor organization." See Murray Kempton, "The Bitter Joke," New York *Post*, March 10, 1961, and "A Primer For Bosses," New York *Post*, May 9, 1961; also Peter Braestrup, "Union Within Union Set For ILGWU," *The New York Times*, April 15, 1961.

61. *Decision and Order*, April 29, 1965. Case No. 2-CA-8849. National Labor Relations Board, International Ladies Garment Workers Union, and Federation of Union Representatives.

62. Report of the General Executive Board to the Thirty-third Convention, ILGWU, Miami Beach, May 12, 1965, 57.

63. Ibid., 58.

64. Ibid.

65. See *Congressional Record*—House, Jan. 31, 1963, 1496–99

(Testimony of Herbert Hill on the Racial Practices of the ILGWU). See also Hill, "The ILGWU Today—The Decay of a Labor Union," *New Politics,* Summer 1962, and Hill, "The ILGWU—Fact and Fiction," *New Politics,* Winter 1963.

66. *Holmes v. Falikman* C-7580-61 (N. Y. State Commission for Human Rights, 1963).

67. *Hunter v. Sullivan Dress Shop,* C-1439-46 (N. Y. State Commission Against Discrimination, 1947).

68. AFL-CIO News, "80,000 Win 15% Hike in Dress Pact," Feb. 4, 1967, 1.

69. CORE, Press Release, April 16, 1967.

70. Ibid. See also *The New York Times,* May 3, 1967, "CORE to Organize within ILGWU."

71. Many articles, letters, and memoranda were involved in this debate. Among the most important are the following: Herbert Hill, "The ILGWU Today: The Decay of a Labor Union," *New Politics,* Summer 1962; Gus Tyler, "The Truth about the ILGWU," *New Politics,* Fall 1962, Herbert Hill, "The ILGWU—Fact and Fiction," *New Politics,* Winter 1963, (reply to Tyler); American Jewish Committee, National Labor Service, "Is the ILGWU Biassed?," document dated Nov. 5, 1962; Jewish Labor Committee, Memorandum dated Nov. 16, 1962 by Emanuel Muravchik, National Field Director (covering much the same material as the AJC document); Paul Jacobs, "David Dubinsky: Why his Throne is Wobbling," *Harper's,* Dec. 1962; J. Fogel, article in the *Jewish Daily Forward* (in Yiddish), Dec. 10, 1962, (reply to Jacobs); Henry Lee Moon, Director of Public Relations, NAACP, "NAACP And Labor" Letter, 31, *New Leader,* Jan. 7, 1963; Daniel Bell, "Reflections on the Negro and Labor," *New Leader,* Jan. 21, 1963.

CHAPTER IX

1. U. S. Dept. of Labor, Manpower Report of the President and a Report on Manpower Requirements, Resources, Utilization and Training 95, 106 (1964).

2. Hearings on S.773, S.1210, S.1211, and S.1937 before the Subcommittee on Employment and Manpower of the Senate Committee on Labor and Public Welfare, 88th Congress, 1st Session, 379, 380 (1963).

3. Northrup, Organized Labor and the Negro, 5 (1944).

4. United States Commission on Civil Rights, Book 3, Report on Employment, 95, 109 (1961).

5. Ibid., 138.

6. Ibid., 154.

7. The City of New York Commission on Human Rights, "Bias

in the Building Industry," An Interim Report to the Mayor, Dec.
1963.

8. Summers, "The Right to Join a Union," 47 *Columbia Law
Review* 33, 67, Note 198 (1947).

9. United States Commission on Civil Rights Report on Employment, 141.

10. National Labor Relations Act, Section 1(b).

11. Ibid., Section 8(a)(5).

12. Ibid., Section 8(a)(1).

13. Ibid., Section 8(a)(3).

14. Ibid., Section 9(c)(3).

15. See Fleischman, "Equality and the Unions," *Religion and
Labor*, Feb. 1961, 6.

LIST OF CONTRIBUTORS

HAROLD M. BARON, Director of the Research Department, Chicago Urban League, has been with that organization for six years. He was originally trained as an economic historian and holds a Ph.D. degree from the University of Chicago. In recent years he has engaged in studies of all aspects of urban racism.

ROBERT L. CARTER is General Counsel for the National Association for the Advancement of Colored People. His trial and appellate experience in the federal courts is extensive, and he has won twenty-three of twenty-four cases before the United States Supreme Court. He is a member of the Board of Directors of Northside Center for Child Developments, the New York Civil Liberties Union, the Advisory Committee for Law and Social Action of the American Jewish Congress, and the Workers Defense League, and the Board of Directors of the National Committee Against Discrimination. He has also written for law reviews and other publications.

HERBERT G. GUTMAN has been Professor of American History at the University of Rochester since 1966 and Associate Editor of *Labor History* since 1963. His articles have appeared in the *American Historical Review*, *Political Science Quarterly*, *Trans-action*, and other publications. He is now completing two works: *The Shock of American Industrialization* and *The Mind of the American Worker in the Gilded Age*.

HERBERT HILL is Labor Director of the National Association for the Advancement of Colored People and a member of the faculty of the New School for Social Research. He is editor of *Anger and Beyond: The Negro Writer in the United States* and co-editor with Arthur Ross of *Employment, Race and Poverty*. His articles have appeared in *Commentary, Buffalo Law Review, Annals of the American Academy of Political and Social Science, Phylon, New Politics, The Nation,* and other publications.

BENNETT HYMER has been a member of the Chicago Urban League Research Department since 1964. He is a graduate of McGill University (B.A., 1959), Northwestern University (M.A., 1962), and is currently a doctoral candidate at the latter institution.

MARC KARSON is a Professor of Political Science at North Central College, Naperville, Illinois. He is the author of *American Labor Unions and Politics, 1900–1918* and former National Education Director of the Amalgamated Clothing Workers of America.

MARIA L. MARCUS is an Assistant Attorney General of the State of New York. She was formerly the Associate Counsel of the National Association for the Advancement of Colored People and assisted in developing the cases of *Hughes Tool Company and Independent Metal Workers Union* and *United Rubber Workers, Local 12,* which have reinterpreted the National Labor Relations Act's application to Negro industrial employees.

RAY MARSHALL is Alumni Professor of Economics and Chairman of the Department of Economics at the University of Kentucky. He was the Director of Research Projects on Negro Participation in Apprenticeship Programs for the Office of Manpower, Automation and Training, U. S. Department of Labor 1965–66, and is the author of a number of books, including *The Negro and Organized Labor, Labor in the South,* and *The Negro Worker*.

AUGUST MEIER taught at Tougaloo College, Mississippi, and at Fisk University, and he is now Professor of History at Kent State University. He is the author of *Negro Thought*

List of Contributors

in America, 1880–1915; *Negro Protest Thought in the 20th Century* (co-edited with Francis Broderick); and *From Plantation to Ghetto: An Interpretive History of American Negroes* (with Elliott Rudwick). His latest book, co-edited with Elliott Rudwick, *The Making of Black America: Studies in Negro Life and History*, will appear this year.

SIDNEY M. PECK is an Associate Professor of Sociology at Case Western Reserve University and specializes in the field of industrial and political sociology. He is the author of a study on the social and political ideology of industrial unionists, *The Rank and File Leader*, and has written for professional and activist journals.

RONALD RADOSH, Assistant Professor of History at Queensborough Community College of the City University of New York, is co-editor with Louis Menashe of *Teach-Ins U.S.A., Reports, Opinions, Documents*. His articles, reviews, and essays have appeared in *The Nation, Science and Society, The Journal of American History* and he was an Associate Editor of *Studies on the Left*.

SUMNER M. ROSEN has taught at Northeastern University, Brandeis University, and Simmons College. He was a research associate with the Industrial Union Department of the AFL-CIO and held a research appointment at Harvard University. In 1965 he became Director of Education for District Council 37, American Federation of State, County and Municipal Employees, AFL-CIO. His articles and reviews have appeared in *The Correspondent, New Politics, Liberation, War/Peace Report*, and other publications.

ELLIOTT RUDWICK taught at Florida State University and is presently a Professor of Sociology at Southern Illinois University. He is the author of *W. E. B. Du Bois: A Study in Minority Group Leadership; Race Riot in East St. Louis, July 2, 1917*; and with August Meier co-edited *From Plantation to Ghetto: An Interpretive History of American Negroes* and *The Making of Black America: Studies in Negro Life*, which will appear this year.

List of Contributors

GUS TYLER is the Assistant-President of the International Ladies Garment Workers Union. He has been both an activist and a theoretician in America's labor, radical, and reform movements since the 1930s. He was editor of *The Socialist Call* and is the author of *Organized Crime in America* and *The Labor Revolution,* and his articles have appeared in *New Republic, Dissent, The New Leader, New Politics,* and other publications. His *Great American Riots* was published this spring.

THE FIRST AMENDMENT: The History of Religious Freedom in America—William H. Marnell, A472

THE FIRST NEW NATION—The United States in Historical and Comparative Perspective—Seymour Martin Lipset, A597

IDEOLOGY AND POWER IN THE AGE OF JACKSON—Edwin C. Rozwenc, ed., AD1

THE IMMEDIATE EXPERIENCE—Robert Warshaw, A410

THE INDIAN AND THE WHITE MAN—Wilcomb E. Washburn, ed., AD2

KILLERS OF THE DREAM—Lillian Smith, A339

LITERATURE AND THE AMERICAN TRADITION—Leon Howard, A329

MAN-MADE MORALS: Four Philosophies That Shaped America—William H. Marnell, A613

MARGARET FULLER: AMERICAN ROMANTIC, A Selection from Her Writings and Correspondence—Perry Miller, ed., A356

THE NATURE OF PREJUDICE—Gordon Allport, A149

THE NEGRO AND THE AMERICAN LABOR MOVEMENT—Julius Jacobson, ed., A495

ON NATIVE GROUNDS—Alfred Kazin, A69

THE ORGANIZATION MAN—William H. Whyte, Jr., A117

POLITICS IN AMERICA—D. W. Brogan, A198

POPULAR CULTURE AND INDUSTRIALISM, 1865-1890—ed. by Henry Nash Smith, AD5

THE POSITIVE THINKERS: A Study of the American Quest for Health, Wealth and Personal Power from Mary Baker Eddy to Norman Vincent Peale—Donald Meyer, A525

PROTESTANT, CATHOLIC, JEW—Will Herberg, A195

PURITAN VILLAGE: The Formation of a New England Town—Summer Chilton Powell, A441

QUEST FOR AMERICA—Charles Sanford, ed., AD3

RACE AND NATIONALITY IN AMERICAN LIFE—Oscar Handlin, A110

RELIGIOUS CONFLICT IN AMERICA—Earl Raab, ed., A392

TEACHER IN AMERICA—Jacques Barzun, A25

THE THEOLOGY OF JONATHAN EDWARDS—Conrad Cherry, Introduction by Will Herberg, A542

WHITE MAN, LISTEN!—Richard Wright, A414

WHO DESIGNS AMERICA?—ed. by Laurence B. Holland, A523

ANCHOR BOOKS

AMERICAN HISTORY AND STUDIES

AMERICAN HUMOR—Constance Rourke, A12

AMERICAN LIFE IN THE 1840s—Carl Bode, ed., AD4

THE AMERICAN LITERARY REVOLUTION 1783–1837—Robert E. Spiller, ed., AD6

THE AMERICAN NOVEL AND ITS TRADITION—Richard Chase, A116

AMERICAN POETRY AND POETICS—Daniel Hoffman, ed., A304

THE AMERICAN PURITANS: THEIR PROSE AND POETRY—Perry Miller, ed., A80

AMERICAN RACE RELATIONS TODAY—Earl Raab, ed., A318

AMERICAN SOCIAL PATTERNS—William Petersen, A86

AMERICAN STRATEGY: A New Perspective—The Growth of Politico-Military Thinking in the United States—Urs Schwarz, A587

THE AMERICAN TRANSCENDENTALISTS: THEIR PROSE AND POETRY—Perry Miller, ed., A119

CAN AMERICAN DEMOCRACY SURVIVE COLD WAR?—Harry Howe Ransom, A402

CASTE AND CLASS IN A SOUTHERN TOWN—John Dollard, A95

CAVALIER AND YANKEE: The Old South and American National Character—William R. Taylor, A351

CHRISTIAN SCIENCE: Its Encounter with American Culture—Robert Peel, A446

THE CIVIL WAR IN AMERICA—Alan Barker, A274

THE COMPLETE POEMS AND SELECTED LETTERS AND PROSE OF HART CRANE—edited with an Introduction and Notes by Brom Weber, A537

THE CONGRESSMAN—Charles L. Clapp, A426

CONSTRAINT AND VARIETY IN AMERICAN EDUCATION—David Riesman, A135

THE DEATH PENALTY IN AMERICA, Revised Edition—Hugo Adam Bedau, ed., A387

THE EMANCIPATION PROCLAMATION—John Hope Franklin, A459

THE EXPLODING METROPOLIS—the Editors of Fortune, A146

THE FEDERALIST PAPERS, Second Edition—Roy P. Fairfield, ed., A239